The New **C** SOURCEBOOK

The New **OPL** SOURCEBOOK

A Guide for Solo and Small Libraries

Judith A. Siess

 **Information Today, Inc.**
Medford, New Jersey

First Printing, 2006

The New OPL Sourcebook: A Guide for Solo and Small Libraries

Copyright © 2006 by Judith A. Siess

Publisher's Note: The author and publisher have taken care in preparation of this book but make no expressed or implied warranty of any kind and assume no responsibility for errors or omissions. No liability is assumed for incidental or consequential damages in connection with or arising out of the use of the information or programs contained herein.

Many of the designations used by manufacturers and sellers to distinguish their products are claimed as trademarks. Where those designations appear in this book and Information Today, Inc. was aware of a trademark claim, the designations have been printed with initial capital letters.

Library of Congress Cataloging-in-Publication Data

Siess, Judith A.
   The New OPL sourcebook : a guide for solo and small libraries / Judith A. Siess.
     p. cm.
   Rev. ed. of: The OPL sourcebook. 2001.
   Includes bibliographical references and index.
   ISBN 1-57387-241-5
     1. Small libraries--Administration. 2. Special libraries--Administration. I. Siess,
Judith A. OPL sourcebook. II. Title.

Z675.S57 S54 2005
025.1'97--dc22

                                                                    2005033112

Printed and bound in the United States of America

President and CEO: Thomas H. Hogan, Sr.
Editor-in-Chief and Publisher: John B. Bryans
Managing Editor: Amy M. Reeve
VP Graphics and Production: M. Heide Dengler
Cover Designer: Michele Quinn
Book Designer: Kara Mia Jalkowski
Copyeditor: Dorothy Pike
Proofreader: Pat Hadley-Miller
Indexer: Sharon Hughes

Table of Contents

PART 2 Resources—Edited by John Welford

Acknowledgments

I want to thank those people without whom I could not have written this book. I also owe a debt to John Bryans of Information Today, Inc. for his encouragement, to Tom Hogan, Sr. for getting me started in the book-writing business, and to managing editor, Amy Reeve.

Chapters 1–8 are my own work. The second part of the book, Chapters 9–20, was largely done by John Welford of Welford Writes, Leicestershire, U.K. John was the proofreader for *The One-Person Library Newsletter* and is an expert editor and indexer as well. He checked nearly every Web site and address in the book for accuracy — a huge task. He also arranged the resources that make *The New OPL Sourcebook* more than just another library management book.

Finally, I have to thank all the OPLs who contributed to this book by talking or writing to me or to one of the electronics lists that I monitor (currently numbering over 15 lists). I also appreciate the patience of my little family. Our two cats, Harry Potter and Hermione Grainger, found my lap to be taken by a laptop more often than they would have liked, but the piles of paper they could play in and knock to the floor helped make up for my unavailability for petting and playing. My wonderful husband showed his usual patience with a slightly distracted wife who worked into the night rather than coming to bed at a reasonable hour. Thank you, Steve.

Introduction

It is hard to believe that this is the third edition of the book that started as *The SOLO Librarian's Sourcebook* in 1997. As with the second edition (*The OPL Sourcebook*), there have been many changes in the library and OPL worlds. I have traveled to some new countries and met many new OPLs. I have written three more books, *Time Management, Planning, and Prioritization for Librarians*, *The Visible Librarian*, and *The Essential OPL: The Best of Seven Years of the One-Person Library,* and developed three successful workshops. Also, the newsletter, *The One-Person Library: A Newsletter for Librarians and Management*, which I edited and published since 1998, has evolved into a blog, OPL Plus (Not Just for OPLs Anymore). This blog is for librarians in smaller libraries—all kinds of libraries, anywhere in the world—not just for one-person or solo librarians. It provides management information links and marketing tips that you can use right now. Read it at http://opls.blogspot.com.

There have been a few changes in this edition. Instead of arranging the lists of resources (books, articles, Web sites, organizations, etc.) by type of resource, they have been arranged by subject. However, please do not just look at the resources in your own subject area. At least look over the other chapters—you never know when you'll need the information and you should at least know what's there. I have made no attempt to include every resource on these subjects , just all the ones that 1) I can find and 2) seem reliable and useful. Whenever possible, I have included the creator or owner of each Web site. If the information is not included, I could not find it, even after extensive searching.

Another change is that I no longer call the users of the library "patrons"; I use "customers," "users," or "clients" instead. The following quote from *The Visible Librarian* explains why.

xvii

Most librarians, especially those in public libraries, are unaccustomed to calling the people they serve customers. For years we have used the term patron or sometimes user. Perhaps we have avoided the term customer because it implies "an exchange [of money] occurring between the library and the people using the service." Yet the relationship with the customer has become so important that the Malcolm Baldridge National Quality Award "values customer and market knowledge, customer satisfaction, and customer-focused results, as a combination, higher than any other single measure for the award."

The time has come to change both our terminology and our thinking. As Koontz notes, library users are now also customers who demand, choose, and select among information products. Customers have expectations, including the expectation of being appreciated. They expect to get what they ordered and are not interested in why the library cannot deliver. They expect the information we deliver to be accurate, timely, and of value. They expect friendly employees, an attractive and easy-to-use facility, a wide and well-reasoned selection of resources, and a host of other wide-ranging and ever-changing services and products.

I have yielded to political correctness and no longer use "he" or "him" exclusively, changing most of these occurrences to "he or she" and "him or her." I still think it is cumbersome construction. However, I am not completely compliant. I persist in calling the places OPLs work "libraries" and where they are educated "library schools."

All the statistics in this book have been updated; as of early 2006, Web sites mentioned were active and books noted were in print. If you find a Web site is no longer available, you are sure to be able to find a site with similar information by using one of the many Web browsers (my favorite is still Google).

As with the previous editions, if there is anything you think should be added to the next edition of this book (Web sites, electronic lists, organizations, vendors, experiences, or facts), please send them to me at the address below.

Judith Siess

477 Harris Road

Cleveland, Ohio 44143-2537, U.S.A.

phone: 1-216-486-7443, fax: 1-216-486-8810

e-mail: jsiess@ibi-opl.com, Web site: www.ibi-opl.com

FROM THE INTRODUCTION TO THE SECOND EDITION

On the off chance that you have not heard of me, I will give you a little of my background. This may help you understand this book and my somewhat idiosyncratic way of looking at things. (Once, Guy St. Clair—the father of one-person librarianship—referred to me as a provocateur. I asked him if that meant "rabble-rouser." When he responded "yes," I considered it a high compliment. You may not agree with everything I say, but if it makes you think, I have done my job.)

I think I was destined to become a librarian. I started reading at 2-1/2 years of age and got my first library card at age four. Before I was 10, I had read all the children's books in the Urbana Free Library (Illinois, U.S.A.) and was sneaking upstairs to read the books for teenagers and adults (with the permission of the librarians I hasten to add). After college and graduate school (resulting in interesting but relatively useless degrees in anthropology), I finally went to library school. I had worked in libraries in grade school and junior high and had done term papers in high school and college using the great collection of the University of Illinois. I had even run a couple of small corporate libraries (and didn't do a bad job at all, looking back on it). Now I had a chance to get a formal library education.

I thoroughly enjoyed library school at the University of Illinois. I did a thesis, which wasn't required (or even encouraged). I did an internship at the U.S. Army Corps of Engineers Construction Engineering Research Laboratory under the late Martha Blake. (The internship was not required either, but it was here that I learned much of what I know about customer service and relationship building from my mentor, Martha Blake.) While in school, I worked for the Department of Agricultural Economics, first as a secretary, then as a statistical assistant, and finally running the Agricultural Economics Reference Room. The last was like having my own private laboratory. As I learned to do things in class, I put them into practice. We had online searching, a primitive online catalog (remember, this was 1980–1982), and even e-mail.

My first professional position involved starting a library for a small biotechnology research and development (R&D) firm in Ashland, Ohio. I got this job through the placement service at the annual conference of the American Society for Information Science (ASIS). I didn't know anything about enzymes (the area in which the company was doing research), but I knew enough to ask questions. Before I left for my final interview, I asked the librarian at the chemistry and biology libraries at the University of Illinois for a list of books and journals that they considered essential. These suggestions were invaluable. When I started the job, there was nothing in my "library" except a desk, chair, and telephone. Because I couldn't do much with these, I got my boss to send me to the mid-year meeting of ASIS. There, I met a professor from the College of Wooster (20 miles from my new job) who was teaching chemistry undergraduates to search chemical abstracts online. I figured that if he could teach chemists who knew nothing about searching, he could teach a searcher who knew nothing about chemistry. I wound up taking lessons from him for 10 weeks and became proficient enough to be effective in my job. This is an example of the creative solutions that OPLs often must use.

As happens, the company did not last. I was neither the first employee hired nor the last let go. About that time, my husband's job led us to Cleveland, Ohio. I worked a while for a friend who had started his own biotechnology company, serving as librarian (organizing his extensive reprint collection), secretary, administrative assistant, book-keeper, and payroll officer. I finally found a job subbing for a librarian on maternity leave at a contract chemical research facility. The work was interesting and I had a chance to familiarize myself with their large reference collection, but working in a library run by chemists was not what I had in mind either. Next was another maternity leave situation, this time at the National Aeronautics and Space Administration (NASA). I got to use their even larger reference collection and to learn from the large staff of librarians, but it, too, was not right.

Finally, I got a call from the chapter placement officer at my local Special Libraries Association (SLA) about a job at Bailey Controls Company (now a part of ABB Automation). I had seen the advertise-ment in the newspaper but thought I was overqualified because the position did not call for a library degree. The placement officer assured me that it was just what I was looking for—and she was right! I got the job and stayed nearly eight years. The job was interesting, challenging, frustrating, and rewarding. I was the only information provider for over 16,000 employees in what became a USD2 billion global firm. The job was reclassified as professional (at my insistence), and the library changed from the Engineering Library to the Corporate Information and Research Center. However, I eventually tired of trying to make sense of an increasingly bureaucratic organization and of try-ing to implement current information practices (especially knowledge management) in a company historically unwilling to share information between departments.

As I approached my 50th birthday and its attendant mid-life crisis, I decided this was not what I wanted to be doing. My first book, *The SOLO Librarian's Sourcebook*, had just been published. I left Bailey to start my own business, Information Bridges International, Inc. (IBI), with the intention to facilitate visits and exchanges among librarians around the world. Shortly thereafter, Guy St. Clair called and asked if I was interested in purchasing his newsletter *The One-Person Library:*

A Newsletter for Librarians and Management. I said "Yes!" and we made it happen. The exchange part of IBI was set aside while I learned the newsletter editing and publishing business. I have turned this part of the business over to Mel Westerman, retired business librarian from Pennsylvania State University, because I find writing *OPL* and teaching workshops consumes all of my time.

I have always been active in our professional associations, dating back to library school and the excellent example set by Linda C. Smith. My proudest accomplishment is helping to birth the Solo Librarians Division of SLA. Barbara Borrelli and I took it from caucus to division in six months—ignoring "everyone" who said it couldn't be done. (Hey, we OPLs do the impossible every day!) The division celebrates its 10th birthday in 2001 as the fourth or fifth largest division in SLA (out of 28 divisions) with about 1,000 members. I have served on local, division, and national committees and boards. I also make it a point to go back to my alma mater about once a year (and anywhere else that invites me) to tell library school students what life is like in the "real world." The library profession has been good to me, and I feel it is vital to give back to it.

Librarianship has changed since 1996. Knowledge management has not emerged as a trend, but a new way of thinking about and organizing information. The Internet and the World Wide Web have not gone away, nor has the unfortunate management perception that "it's all on the Internet and it's free," but as more and more companies are realizing that librarians have much to add. Library education has moved somewhat more to the information technology side of the profession. Yes, librarians are still being downsized out of existence as organizations merge, scale down, cut expenses, or even go out of existence, but new positions are being created in technology, research, and smaller enterprises.

This last trend has had great implications for OPLs. More OPLs are being created both by downsizing and the creation of new libraries. We are being recognized more and more as a unique type of librarian. Articles on one-person librarianship have appeared in

Spectrum (published by the American Association of Law Libraries) and *American Libraries* (from the American Library Association). *Library Journal* featured an OPL, Olga Wise of Compaq Computers, on its cover. Dan Trefethen, an OPL at Boeing in Seattle, Washington (U.S.A.), has been named a Fellow of the Special Libraries Association—the second OPL honored. (Guy St. Clair was the first so honored. *Note*: Since this was written, a third OPL has been named a Fellow of SLA—Officer Tom Rink of the Tulsa, Oklahoma Police Department.) The Library Association (U.K.) has created a new focus on special libraries, many of which are OPLs. This OPL renaissance has been repeated all over the world.

This book also benefits from my four years of publishing *The One-Person Library*. I have learned so much from my readers and contributors; from the various electronic lists (14 at last count) that I monitor to keep updated; from my travels to Australia, New Zealand, Germany, Canada, and the U.K. to give workshops; and from the extensive reading I have done on librarianship, management, time management, and technology. I have added a large number of Web sites to reflect the increasing amount of information on the Web and librarians' increasing reliance on gateways and lists of links. I have also become a member of library associations around the world (SLA, MLA, AALL, CSLA, ALIA, CLA, LIASA, CLA LA, and ASLIB at present). Reading their publications and attending their conferences has increased my awareness of not only the diversity of OPLs but also of how much we have in common. Therefore, I hope that all types of OPLs worldwide will benefit from this book. I enjoyed writing it. I hope you enjoy and benefit from it.

Part 1
The Basics

1

What Is an OPL?

An OPL is a one-person librarian. Yes, all librarians are just one person, but an OPL is someone who works in a one-person library, who is the only librarian (or only professional librarian) in a library or information center. The OPL does everything: acquisitions; cataloging; circulation; reference; even dusting the shelves and vacuuming the library, if necessary. An OPL is in a situation where there are no professional peers with whom to share problems, share ideas, or commiserate when things get tough. It is a challenging position but also a rewarding one. The OPL often does not have to go through layers of administration to get approval for purchases or new programs. The OPL knows exactly what is going on in his or her library: what is being checked out, the questions being asked, who is using the library, and such. The OPL is often perceived as the "information guru" in the organization—the one to whom everyone comes for answers. Finally, any and all successes (and, of course, failures) of the library are also those of the OPL. He or she can make of it whatever is in their vision and power.

Other names for an OPL are solo (in the U.S.A., the U.K., and Israel), sole-charge librarian (in Australia and New Zealand), or one-man band (used by ASLIB in the U.K.). I will use OPL in this book, if for no better reason than that the newsletter that I published until 2006 was called *The One-Person Library* (it has been succeeded by a blog called OPL Plus, found at http://opls.blogspot.com). In 1996, Guy St. Clair wrote,

"Until about 25 years ago, one-person librarianship as a recognized branch of specialized librarianship and information services did not exist" (St. Clair 1996c). The movement and even the term OPL can be attributed to St. Clair, formerly librarian at the University Club in New York, founder of *The One-Person Library: A Newsletter for Librarians and Management*, and principal in SMR International.

A BRIEF HISTORY OF THE OPL MOVEMENT

- 1972: Guy St. Clair was invited to lead a discussion at the 1972 Special Libraries Association (SLA) Annual Conference in Boston, Massachusetts, on "The One-Man Library." He said he would do so only if the title was changed to "The One-Person Library." This is the first instance of the term OPL being used. Hundreds of OPLs attended the session, overflowing the room.

- 1976: St. Clair's first article on the OPL was published, followed by several workshops and seminars.

- 1984: St. Clair founded *The One-Person Library* newsletter with Andrew Berner, also of the University Club of New York.

- 1986: The OPL Support Group is formed in Toronto, Ontario, Canada by solos in the local chapter of SLA. This is the first known organization of OPLs.

- 1986: *Managing the One-Person Library* was published, the first book on OPLs, by St. Clair and Joan Williamson.

- 1987: The first two-day, continuing education course on one-person librarianship was taught at the SLA Annual Conference in Anaheim, California, U.S.A.

- 1988: At the SLA Annual Conference in Denver, Martha Rose (Marty) Rhine led two roundtables on OPLs. She distributed a list to get participants' names and addresses so they could keep in touch; 99 people signed the list. Using the list as a base, Marty formed the Solo Librarians Caucus of the SLA with an initial membership of about 100.

• Late 1980s: The formation of the One-Man Band group of ASLIB (U.K.).

• 1991: The Solo Librarians Caucus became a full-fledged division of SLA, with Judith Siess as the first chairperson.

• 1991: Guy St. Clair was inaugurated as president of SLA. OPLs are recognized as leaders.

• 1991: *The Best of OPL,* by Guy St. Clair and Andrew Berner, was published, consisting of selections from the first five years of the newsletter.

• 1995: One-Person Australian Librarians (OPAL) was formed as a special-interest group of the Australian Library and Information Association (ALIA) after the Health, Law and Specials Conference in Sydney. Georgina Dale, Toni Silson (now Kennedy), and Therese Bendeich were its first leaders.

• 1996: The first German OPL roundtable was held, organized by Evelin Morgenstern of the Deutsches Bibliotheksinstitut (German Library Institute), Berlin, Germany.

• 1997: AspB (Arbeitsgemeinschaft der Spezialbibliotheken, the German Special Libraries Working Group) devoted its biennial conference to small special (OPL) libraries.

• 1997: VdDB (Verein der Diplom-Bibliothekare—one of the professional librarian associations in Germany) established the OPL Kommission, with Regina Peeters as chair. This special working group offers continuing professional education programs for OPLs at least twice a year.

- 1997: *Das Robinsoon-Crusoe Syndrom und was man dagegen tun kann* (The Robinson Crusoe Syndrome and What You Can Do About It) was published with reports from 24 OPLs describing their work.

- 1997: *The SOLO Librarian's Sourcebook*, by Judith Siess, was published.

- 1997: First meeting of SLIM, Special Librarians (many of them OPLs), in the Midlands, was held in Birmingham, England; Chris Crabtree and Margaret Brittin were the founders.

- 1997: One-Person Library Group formed as part of the Private Law Libraries Special Interest Group of the American Association of Law Libraries (U.S.A.).

- 1997: One-Person Library Recognition Award instituted by the Mid-Atlantic Chapter of the Medical Libraries Association (U.S.A.).

- 1998: *A Most Delicate Monster: The One-Professional Special Library*, by Jean Dartnall, was published in Australia.

- 1998: Information Bridges International, Inc., purchased *The One-Person Library* newsletter, with Judith Siess as the new editor and publisher.

- 1999: First meeting of Special Librarians in London (SLIL) was held; Bert Washington of Sports Marketing Surveys was the founder.

- 1999: Workplace Libraries discussion list was launched in April 1999 by the Library Association (LA) in the U.K.

- 1999: An electronic discussion list just for OPLs was established by the Library Association (LA) (U.K.).

- 1999: Workplace '99 Initiative was started by the LA (U.K.) to increase awareness of commerce, industry, government, and voluntary institutional libraries by Lyndsay Rees-Jones and Mark Field, professional advisors from the LA.

• 1999: The Solo Professional Network was set up by Steve Witowski of the East Midlands Branch of the LA—now CILIP—in the U.K.

• 2000: First meeting of Special Librarians was held in Cambridge, England (SLIC); Lis Riley was the founder.

• 2000: OPAL published its first book, *Evaluating Websites*.

• 2001: Initiative Fortbildung für wissenschaftlichSpezialbibliotheken und verwandte Einrichtungen (Initiative for Special Libraries and Similar Institutions) formed in Germany as Deutsches Bibliotheksinstitut (DBI) was dissolved.

• 2001: Chicago Area Solo Librarians group formed in Chicago, Illinois, U.S.A.

• 2001: Commission for OPLs and Special Libraries formed in Austria. Sonja Reisner was the first chair, followed by Heinrich Zukal.

• 2006: *The One Person Library: A Newsletter for Librarians and Management* evolved into a blog, OPL Plus (Not Just for OPLs Anymore).

WHERE OPLS WORK

OPLs can be found in all types of libraries, but most OPLs work in special libraries. A special library is one serving a specialized or limited clientele, with specialized or limited materials and services. The collection is often small. The OPL nearly always reports to a nonlibrarian, and the library is part of but not considered critical to the parent organization's main mission. The information that follows describes the situation in libraries in the U.S.A. For a look at OPLs elsewhere, see "An International View," later in this chapter.

Hospital Libraries

Until 1994, hospitals in the U.S.A. were required to employ professional librarians in order to maintain their accreditation. Unfortunately, the agency that accredits hospitals decided to delete all definitions of qualified practitioners, including librarians. Hospitals still must provide access to appropriate medical information and to hire "qualified" people. Even so, many hospitals still have libraries and librarians. Except in the large medical schools and hospitals, the librarian is usually an OPL. The needs of physicians are rapid delivery of current and accurate information having practical application, with cost usually being irrelevant. Many hospital librarians are also involved in patient services, archives, consumer health information, and administration of physician continuing medical education. Some librarians are even a part of the treatment team. This last practice is increasing with the advent of higher training levels for librarians and the computerization of medical information. Hospital libraries frequently have a staff of volunteers, possessing varying degrees of training and commitment, with which to work; having volunteers may or may not help the OPL's workload. The Medical Library Association offers a certification program in medical librarianship—the Academy of Health Information Professionals. Although certification is not required, for many medical librarian positions it is strongly encouraged.

Law Libraries

Librarians serving private practices, small law practices, and bar associations are often OPLs as are law librarians in government institutions, such as courts or agencies, and some public law libraries, but these make up only about 15 percent of law librarians. Most law librarians in academia and law schools, where a library is required for accreditation, are not

OPLs. Only 29 percent of law librarians have law degrees, but almost all (80 percent) have library degrees. Most employers use their law librarians to save lawyers' billable hours, to save attorneys' time looking for information, and to add to revenues by librarians doing billable information searches for clients. Sometimes OPLs perform other functions, such as archiving, managing records, managing dockets, conflicts checking, research for client and practice development, coordination of continuing legal education programs, Web page design, Web content management, and supervising paralegals. The future probably will see an expansion of the law librarian into many other areas: skill-based resource management; client current awareness services; support for speaking opportunities, such as seminars; research, reference, and technology training for clients; support for internal and client newsletters, management of paralegals, and formal legal research training for new staff.

The issues facing OPLs in law libraries are the need for rapid delivery of information, often with price insensitivity; the currency and accuracy of the information; the high degree of confidentiality expected; decisions regarding the fine line between legal research and interpretation; and employment of summer interns or law clerks. These temporary employees have high expectations of librarians and can add substantially to the librarian's workload. Academic law librarians are becoming increasingly responsible for teaching legal research techniques to students and get more involved in research, history, and comparative law. Law librarians must also deal with issues common to all librarians, such as timeliness, currency, accuracy, thoroughness, detail, rising costs and burnout, and emphasis on the practical uses of information. In a summary of several studies of how lawyers find information, researchers found that 50 percent to 60 percent of lawyers do not go to librarians for help, even if they have trouble finding the information themselves. They do not use the librarian to learn how to search, only to provide the documents they identify from their own search. (I would wager that similar results would be found in surveying any constituency—engineers, doctors, and even the public.)

Public Libraries

Surprisingly, a large number of OPLs work in public libraries. Nearly 80 percent of public libraries in the U.S.A. serve populations of under 25,000 and are staffed by only one professional (Vavrek 1987). Times are changing in small public libraries. The library director is the heart of the library, representing the library to the community, library board, and staff. Public librarians face the same issues as other types of OPLs: overwork, trying to do it all, and dealing with nonlibrarians as supervisors (the library board). They also face some unique challenges such as responsibility for building maintenance, raising money for new buildings, and coordinating bond issue campaigns. Although the pay for small public library directors is often abysmal, there are long hours and, as with all OPLs, you "run the show," there seems to be no shortage of applicants for directory positions.

Public or Private School Libraries

School librarians and media specialists are very often OPLs; in fact, some may serve two or more school libraries, with volunteers (often students) staffing the library when the librarian is not there. In the U.S.A., professional school librarians must also have a teaching certification. They are seen as an extension of the classroom and often assist teachers with special projects as well as run the library and teach library skills to the students. Some even have additional duties, such as holding story hours, teaching reading or English, providing computer instruction, advising student groups, running the bookstore, and supervising the lunchroom.

Prison or Jail Libraries

Most prison libraries remain one-person positions, despite recommendations for higher staffing levels. Some of their problems include motivating their inmate assistants, who may lack a strong work ethic, concern with confidentiality, and the dividing line between legal reference and legal advice. Another hot current issue is the computerization of prison libraries. Prisons are reluctant to replace books with computers because of the potential for online crime or other abuses.

Jail libraries are usually smaller and less likely to hire a professional. Their emphasis is on accessing legal materials and providing recreational reading to help with behavior control and encourage self-improvement. Lack of funds and censorship are major issues. Prison or jail librarians need to understand the political climate of the institution, possess patience and a sense of humor, be comfortable following the many rules, and have a professional demeanor.

Predictably, most of the information I found on prison libraries was on those in the U.S.A., so I will describe that situation first, in some detail. I will then present snapshots of various other countries. This information is not necessarily complete or representative, but gives an idea of the current (2005) situation.

U.S.A.

The Prison System

In 2004, there were 2.2 million prisoners in more than 1,100 prisons in the U.S.A. Most prisons are state institutions; there are only about 100 federal facilities, with a total of 173,000 inmates (Harrison and Beck 2004, 1). Local jails held only about 73,000 prisoners, or 5 percent of the total (Harrison and Beck 2004, 6). According to Singer, approximately 25 percent of prisoners are serving life sentences, 40 percent have sentences of more than 10 years, 75 percent have been convicted of violent crimes, and 30 percent are functionally illiterate. The prison population does not reflect the country's population as a whole. The inmates are overwhelmingly male (1.3 million vs. just over 100,000 women); minorities are over-represented (65 percent of the inmates are nonwhite: 44 percent black, 19 percent Hispanic, and 2 percent other); and the population is aging (33 percent over 45, an increase of about 70 percent since 1995). This profile presents a problem for prison libraries. Although "the prison community is a microcosm of the wider society with an increasingly diverse population, ...

the library staff remains predominantly European American" (Shirley 2003, 70) and, most likely, young, and female.

The Prison Library

In 1996 there were more than 1,000 prison libraries in the U.S.A. Part of the reason for so many libraries is that "an inmate on a recreation field or on a bed reading a book is not likely posing a threat" (Allen Overstreet, director of library services, Florida Department of Corrections, in Callea 2004). But the main reason is that the laws or courts of most states require the provision of access to legal materials to inmates. For example, in Pennsylvania, since 1978 the courts have mandated law library collections in prisons, but felt that "twelve to fifteen hours a week is constitutionally adequate for research" (Lemon 1997). A Florida television report complained that the state spent $1.5 million on books for prisoners. That worked out to $20 per inmate, compared to only $6 per school child. Why was this the case? Because state law required prison libraries be kept up-to-date (and law books cost much more than children's books). Some states have decided to close all their prison libraries in an attempt to cut down on frivolous lawsuits by inmates. A Texas study estimated that $25.5 million was spent by the state on lawsuits prisoners researched in the prison libraries ("Local School Libraries ..." 2005). Even the librarians complain about this cost. Callea wrote, "last year, the state [Florida] spent $1.7 million on law books for its 69 prison law libraries. Meanwhile, the general collection at Tomoka [Correctional Institution, Daytona Beach, Florida] consists mainly of worn paperbacks, and is dependent mostly on donations." It is possible that this expense may not even be necessary. Collins wrote, "historically, most agencies have attempted to meet their affirmative duty [to protected right of access to the courts] through the provision of law libraries, although the Supreme Court indicated ... that 'persons trained in the law' could suffice." He cites one case in 1996, *Lewis v. Casey*, that "encourages agencies to experiment with methods other than law libraries," because "law libraries alone cannot provide meaningful access to the courts for an inmate who cannot read." He suggested various alternatives: a law library, a law library "of considerably reduced size," paralegals or lawyers or library or combination thereof, noting that lawyers can only assist in negotiating with the prison and in drafting and filing of complaints, and cannot represent the inmate after a complaint is filed.

Singer (2000, 9) wrote that although the institution as a whole's nature is negative, the library's mission is a positive one—"improving the daily life of inmates and providing them with long-term skills, training and treatment." But the library is not a major concern of prison administrators. Some of them are staffed under a contract with a public or academic library, some are operated by the prison authority, or governance may be a combination of both (Lehmann 2003). No matter how the library is governed it operates in "a rigidly contained, imploded universe" (Singer, 8). Most likely the library is located in a limited, out-of-the-way space, is quite spartan (either deliberately or because of lack of money), and is very security conscious (Singer). Censorship is common, citing concerns with security or prisoner well-being. In one case the librarian operated with a 44-page list of restricted publications. "The library that I saw was sorely lacking. It was a small book closet consisting of a limited law library, some recreational reading material—paperbacks, magazines, and newspapers—and two typewriters. Inmates did not come to the library for information, they came because they were bored or they came looking for mischief" (Lemon).

Shirley sent a questionnaire to 110 librarians chosen from *Directory of State Prison Librarians* and received 35 responses. She found that the top 10 subjects represented in the prison libraries were: self-help, career guidance, science fiction, true crime, horror, biographies, romance, fantasy, mystery, and music. For the most part, the library staff chose the material, but 23 percent of the libraries said that inmates assist in collection planning. There was a high demand for fiction by black authors and material on African heritage, and these are the books most likely to be checked out and most stolen. However, the donors relied on by most libraries are predominantly white and most donations are of classic literature or textbooks. Lemon found that some of the most popular books were love poems—for writing to loved ones—and that "the library will generally have three funding sources: state money, inmate generated money, and gift/grant money." Most of institutional money—if any—will go for legal materials (Lemon).

"Of course many inmates who enter prison have never used a library. Yet by the time they leave, 80 percent of them have used ours. Many times what gets them in the door is the recreational material." But by the time they leave, "the prison library has become their information hub, as it assists with legal issues, education, computer skills, career information, resumes, and treatment" (Lemon). However, the range of services varies widely from state to state. In Pennsylvania, prison librarians can use interlibrary loan, but most public libraries are reluctant to loan materials to prisoners (Lemon).

The library at the Oshkosh, Wisconsin prison, as described by Purifoy (an inmate), is certainly at the high end. It is available about 18 hours per week, spread over six days, and inmates can visit up to three times a day for one hour each time (or two hours to use the law library). It is equipped with two electric typewriters, eight computer word processors, four video players, and three music CD players. There is even a computerized catalog, CD-ROMs with educational programs (spelling, math, astronomy, foreign languages), and a law library, staffed by an inmate, with everything from statutes to court reporters. This library is one of 11 libraries, one for each housing unit, with about 300 books per library, which are rotated among the units. For those in segregation (solitary confinement) there is an abridged law library and there is even a children's library in the visiting room, part of an inmate/child reading program (Purifoy 2000). Not surprisingly, in Wisconsin, 70 percent of inmates use the library (Lehmann in Schneider 2003). Singer wrote that in his maximum-security prison (also in Wisconsin), inmates must choose between going to the recreation area (gym) or library. In 1999 visits per inmate averaged 36 and books checked out were about 33 per inmate. The library also provided an outreach program to those confined or restricted and a photocopying and notary service that provided nearly 130,000 photocopies and nearly 800 notary transactions. The library was often noisy, an area for socializing, and there was the expected "rampant collection erosion" (a great way to say theft of materials), damage, and defacing of books. Often he had to "concentrate on resurrecting rather than building" (Singer, 13). According to Singer, in Wisconsin, at least, libraries are no longer an afterthought, their importance realized, long-range plans developed, with progress toward standardization of resources and services, some automation, and employment of more professionals. However, Singer wrote that prison libraries still need to be adequate, livable, attractive spaces, with adequate staffing (more than an OPL). In addition libraries need better funding, so that they can invest in automation and access to online services.

I seriously doubt that the description of the Oshkosh prison is typical of most prison libraries. However, the librarian at a well-equipped library is far more likely to write about his or her experiences than the poor librarian buried somewhere in a back corner of the prison with a small, out-of-date, and unused collection. Such is the nature of publishing.

The Prison Librarian

Although nearly all prisons have libraries, not all have a degreed or professional librarian operating them. "Only 31 of the state's prison libraries have professional librarians," wrote the director of library services, Department of Corrections, State of Florida. He also states that budget cuts make it hard "to recruit people 'trained as information specialists' to work in libraries that are several decades behind the times when it comes to technology" (Overstreet in Callea). "Prison is an inhospitable environment that challenges all you have learned at library school." Burnout is common, partly because librarians are not prepared for what they find behind bars. "Safety and security are given a higher priority than intellectual freedom. [There is a] them vs. us mentality" (Lehmann in Schneider). Curry (also in Schneider) calls it "subsistence librarianship," accompanied by a high level of frustration. Some of the problems that the prison librarian faces are non-English speakers (mostly Spanish), claims of race bias (usually not supportable), and problems that African-American males have with female authority figures. "The prison librarian must become very flexible in his or her approach to librarianship and be continually cognizant of the fact that the greater good sometimes must be purchased at the cost of principle." (Singer, 9). The librarian may not be "viewed not as a specialized professional, but as a useful and exploitable unit within the corrections' hierarchy" (Singer, 9).

A prison librarian needs a broad academic background, knowledge of prison dynamics, ability to work with ambiguity, adaptability, sincerity, and sense of humor (Lehmann in Schneider). LeDonne wrote, "the key to quality correctional library service is the turn of mind, the energy and the sense of dedication which the librarian brings to the job" (Lehmann, 69). Lehmann (7) continued, "new prison librarians have a better chance for success, if they have additional education or work experience in other areas like psychology, criminology, teaching, social work, or counseling." Also desirable are a few years of work experience, involvement in professional associations, flexibility, patience, emotional stability, a high tolerance for stress, commitment to follow through on promises, being comfortable working with people from other cultures or races or social strata, good communications skills and ability to listen, empathy, problem-solving skills, common sense, rational thinking, teaching skills, PR and marketing, ability to plan and set priorities (Lehmann). Some states may require you to be a certified prison guard as well as a librarian.

There is very little training offered for the prospective prison librarian. Of 88 library schools surveyed by the International Federation of Library Associations and Institutions (IFLA) in 1995–1996, only 24 had prison library service in their curriculum "and it is still not widely recognized as a viable career option" (Lehmann, 7). Singer lamented that "library school graduates are routinely placed in the correctional and institutional setting, *yet there are few academic programs or individual courses which train librarians for the unique challenges of such employment*" (8). The University of Wisconsin has a jail library volunteer program (see their Web site at http://slisweb.lis.wisc.edu/ ~jail). In 1992, Rhea Joyce Rubin developed a library planning model for prison libraries, which has been used in Massachusetts and Wisconsin. It includes roles for prison libraries: popular reading, independent learning, formal education support, recreation, legal information, treatment support, information on outside community, retreat, staff support, and school curriculum support for young inmates.

What is the reward for the prison librarian? What motivates them? The answer is personal and professional satisfaction. "It is indeed gratifying to know that one has made a difference in somebody's life and is remembered with fondness" (Lehmann, 9). On LiveJournal, an anonymous librarian wrote, "I have been in jail for 9 years. I love saying that. I just work there, honest." Comments like these from inmates make it worthwhile. "I forget that I am in prison when I'm in the library" (Lemon). "I do not think I would have been able to handle stressful situations if the library was not readily accessible to me" (Knudsen 2000). "Books form an escape, the only possible escape, from an oppressive environment ..." (Lehmann in Schneider).

Australia

The Australian government standards for prisons state that the purpose of the prison library is "to meet the recreational, educational, and other information needs of inmates ... and to provide information which will help them subsequently to re-establish themselves in the community." The standards continue, "every prison or similar institution with an average inmate population of 25 or more shall have its own library for the exclusive use of inmates, similar to a local public library." Smaller institutions are to be guaranteed an alternative to an in-house library, such as access to a public library, a bookmobile, or a traveling collection.

Canada

Although most prisoners in the U.S.A. are in state institutions, in Canada, if the sentence is more than two years, it is served in the national system. In 2003, University of British Columbia library school professor Ann Curry published a very detailed survey of Canadian prison libraries. She sent surveys to 51 institutions. Thirty-seven were returned, 14 from medium security institutions. The sample covered 81 percent of the men's prisons. She found that, to a large degree, their issues are similar to those of other libraries: a limited budget, a user population that is multicultural, multilingual, of varying age, and educational backgrounds, and high expectations for library services. However, prison libraries suffered from minimal support from their parent organizations, a very limited recognition of their value, and the implications of the obvious limits on prisoners' rights. (To a large degree, it seems to me that many corporate libraries face similar problems.)

Canadian prisons do not reflect the population as a whole. First Nations people are over-represented (3 percent of the country's population, but 17 percent of prisoners). The incarceration rate is comparable to that of other developed countries. Curry found that 80 percent of the libraries had inmates as staff and 30 percent had a qualified librarian on staff, either with a Dipl. Librarianship or MLS/MLIS (Curry in Schneider, Table 2). All the libraries had books, but most had journals and newspapers as well. About half had CD-ROMs or legal statutes. A third of the collections included audio, but only about one-fifth had videos (mostly for training or job preparation). Virtually none had access to databases or the Web (Curry in Schneider, Table 3). The inmates preferred fiction, newspapers, and legal information, in that order. Mystery, horror, science fiction or fantasy, and westerns were the top types of fiction requested. In nonfiction, history, legal materials, biographies, and self-help were the most popular. Seventy-two percent of the libraries were required to prohibit pornography and 67 percent censored material with "derogatory racial statements or themes." Only 14 percent of respondents were aware of any prison library guidelines. The Canadian Library Association has not developed any such guidelines.

Italy

Prison librarians in Italy belong to the ABC, the Associazione Biblioteche Carcerarie (Italian Association of Prison Libraries), founded in 2000. The ABC is a unit of Associazione Italiano Biblioteche, the Italian Library Association. The ABC was founded to serve "as a forum for communication among library staff working with and in the prisons. An equally important role of the association would be that of advocating for full professional status of prison librarians ..." (Costanzo 2005). The association is quite active. It has held several conferences and discussions, created a prison library in four cities, "accomplished a complete integration between the Sardinian prison libraries and the local library systems ... [through] development of a joint catalogue," provides interlibrary loan services, and provides training for prisoners who work in the library (Costanzo).

In most cases, the prison library is run by an "educator," "a well educated [person] who organizes and operates it at the best of his ability," and is not even located in the library (Costanzo). Prison standards state, "the direction of the [prison] must guarantee to all prisoners the easy access to the documents of the prison library ..." (Costanzo). A survey was sent to 205 prisons in Italy in 1992. Of the 79 responding, fewer than 10 had a working library, although some prisons had a contract with the city library to provide service to prisoners (Costanzo). Costanzo laments, "the general public do not understand that it takes real professionals to provide the broad range of library services needed ... We are considered 'invisible.'"

U.K.

"The fact that so little is known about prison libraries is one of the 'special problems' they face. ..." In fact, a survey commissioned by the Prison Libraries Group [of the Chartered Institute of Library and Information Professionals, U.K.] was banned from publication because of 'security concerns' " ("Reprieve for prison ..." 2003). "For similar reasons, prison governors severely limit (or ban) internet access and even physical visits [to the library] (20 minutes a week is typical). Stock, staffing budgets and the reading skills of many inmates are all poor" ("Reprieve for prison ...").

"The most pressing need is to convince prison governors of the value of libraries and prisons." An anonymous post on LiveJournal said that the inmates came into the library "for brief, but very intense periods. There was *no* time for in depth reference interviews!" The librarian continued, that he or she had ordered "more fiction than I have ever ordered in a long life as a college librarian." Personal security was also an issue. "You have to be careful what you say in front of the prisoners ... like to inadvertently give away anything about your habits. ... After all, you don't *really* want them trying to be buddies once they get out, now do you?!"

Zoo or Museum Libraries

The American Zoo and Aquarium Association/Librarians Special Interest Group (AZA/LSIG) consists of zoo and aquarium librarians as well as other persons working in zoos and aquariums who are responsible for the institution's library and operations. The group was formed in 1978, and as of 2004 had 90 members from zoos and aquariums on four continents. *The Directory of Zoo and Aquarium Libraries,* 9th edition (2003), compiled and edited by Jill Gordon, librarian at the Saint Louis Zoo, and updated by Stacy Rice of the National Agricultural Library, lists 41 U.S.A zoos along with 12 in other countries (Australia, Brazil, Canada, Germany, the U.K., the Netherlands, and Spain). A number of zoos use volunteers to staff their libraries, while many other zoos combine the job of librarian with another position. These libraries have historically been underfunded, understaffed, and underused. Facilities range from a small collection of books and magazines for staff use to a full-fledged library. The library may also have a relatively large number of volunteers. Most zoo libraries provide reference service to staff, and some do so for zoo members and the general public. Few of these libraries circulate items beyond the staff, provide online searching, or provide document delivery.

Church or Synagogue Libraries

Most larger churches and synagogues have libraries. They may be staffed by volunteers (often a retired librarian or schoolteacher), but some hire professional librarians. Nearly all of these are one-person positions. The church or synagogue library functions as a centralized place for materials for the organization's programs (a sort of learning and resource center), with the specific aim of promoting the spiritual development of its users. There are no specific educational requirements for the church or synagogue librarian, but dedication, friendliness, an enjoyment for working with details, neatness, patience, and a sense of humor are suggested. Funding and pay usually are minimal, but it is a rewarding field for the dedicated.

OPLs Not in Libraries

Infopreneurs

An *infopreneur* is just a fancy word for an information entrepreneur. Their work falls into two main categories: information retrieval and delivery, and information organization, or "information consulting." The infopreneur may design and produce databases, perform primary and secondary research, obtain documents, do abstracting and indexing, evaluate libraries, manage libraries, perform outreach and public relations, arrange for having materials translated, act as a records manager, train librarians, write or edit books and articles or newsletters— and almost anything else you can imagine. What does it take to be a successful infopreneur? It takes a combination of many different things: good speaking, writing, and telephone skills; good organizational skills; the ability to prioritize; the ability to solve problems; a broad base of knowledge; good computer skills; patience; a sense of humor; perseverance; dedication and hard work; enjoyment in working alone; enjoyment in decision-making; self-motivation; energy; creativity; confidence; optimism; intelligence; the ability to integrate disparate concepts; and the ability to sell yourself and your services. In other words, it takes the same skills as needed to be a good solo librarian. The newest buzzword is *intrapreneur*, a library-based information entrepreneur.

Competitive Intelligence and Market Research

An increasing number of librarians work in the competitive intelligence (CI) field, gathering information that will assist a company in maintaining its competitive edge. (It is not, as some think, only gathering information about one's competitors. It also means gathering information about a company's customers, keeping up with technology, and anything else that makes the company better able to compete.) Librarians are exceptionally well qualified to do CI. They are trained to search for, analyze, organize, and disseminate information, are experienced in working in an interdisciplinary environment, and usually have already built their own networks. Other traditional library competencies that transfer well to CI include online searching, the reference interview, current awareness, knowledge of bibliographic tools, computer skills, written presentation skills, and time management.

Other Nontraditional Positions

The nontraditional sector is probably the fastest-growing area of librarianship. A librarian's skills can be applied in many fields: a representative for a vendor of library supplies, databases, or other information sources; a writer, publisher, or consultant; working for a nonprofit organization, a government agency, an association library, in Web site development, or for a library consortium or network. The job opportunities are limited only by your imagination, creativity, interest, and persistence.

CHARACTERISTICS OF AN OPL

OPLs have more in common with other OPLs than they do with librarians in larger libraries in the same subject field. Guy St. Clair (1997) observed four common traits of OPLs: OPLs love their work; OPLs communicate; OPLs are sophisticated; and OPLs are confident. I have found that about 80 percent are OPLs by chance, only 20 percent by choice. However, many who started by chance now like it so much they wouldn't go back to a large library.

According to St. Clair and Williamson (1992), a library with an OPL may be the organization's first library, newly established and unsure of how many staff persons it needs and destined to grow to include a larger staff. It also can be a downsized library that formerly had several librarians but because of less demand, less money, or less management support, now is reduced to one professional. It can also be a library that is just the right size, one that needs only one well-trained, efficient professional to serve the organization's information needs. This is probably the most common situation.

Herb White, former dean of the library school at Indiana University, said that "perhaps we need to postulate that 'one-person library' is an oxymoron ... they are clerical centers for buying, lending, and recalling" (1988, 56). But the fact remains that there *are* OPLs, a lot of them, and library educators, researchers, management consultants, and even the rest of the library profession have ignored them.

How many OPLs are there? There is no accurate count, but in January 2005, SLA estimated that about one-half of their more than 11,000 members are OPLs, which means there are about 5,500 OPLs in North American special libraries alone. Since the Solo Librarians Division of SLA was formed in 1996, it grew from 350 to nearly 1,000 members, but declined to about 750 in 2005, as SLA's membership as a whole declined. However, it was still the fifth largest division (out of 28 divisions) in the organization. U.S. Department of Education figures show that most U.S. public libraries have no more than one professional librarian. One can see that the majority of libraries in the U.S.A. and Canada are OPLs.

Why would anyone want to be an OPL? The three most commonly heard reasons are independence, variety, and personal satisfaction. OPLs enjoy the ability to "run their own show," that is, set their own schedules and plan their own priorities with a minimum of supervision and interference. "Doing what I want to do, when I want to do it" has great appeal. OPLs make their own successes—and mistakes. They know exactly what's going on and the level of quality going out to customers. They value the close relationship developed with their customers, and the wide variety of tasks that must be done keeps them busy and not bored. OPLs have the freedom to be creative in their solutions. They gain the respect of their colleagues by being the sole information authority in the organization. They are the recipients of all the appreciation for library services (and all the complaints, too). As U.S. President Harry Truman said, "The buck stops here." OPLs also have the opportunity to shine and show others what trained information professionals can do. As one OPL wrote, "Librarianship, especially solo librarianship, is a terrific career for liberal arts graduates with a passion for learning, a knack for problem-solving, a touch of creativity, and a sense of humor."

The life of an OPL has its drawbacks, as well. The most commonly mentioned problems include professional isolation, lack of clerical support, reporting to a nonlibrarian, and low pay. Other negatives about being an OPL include a lack of preparation for the job (in library school, on the job, and elsewhere); lack of management support; lack of job security; poor physical working conditions; lack of time; frustration at not being able to "do it all"; lack of status; and lack of control concerning policy, personnel, or budget (or all three). There never seems to be enough time to get everything done. Filing, reading, public relations, and professional development fall victim to too little time. The lack of feedback and interaction with other professionals takes its toll; there is no one with whom to brainstorm. OPLs often feel that they are not appreciated by their organizations. "Mindless" clerical work seems to get in the way of doing "real" work. (Perhaps this requires an attitude transplant; clerical work isn't mindless. It can be a welcome respite from high-pressure decision making and planning. Since it *must* be done, who can do it better, faster, and more efficiently than an OPL?) Often OPLs tire under the strain of constantly having to explain themselves and their work to managers who do not understand them. The lack of feedback, status, and often credit for their efforts has its negative effects. If you are a person who needs constant reinforcement, this is not the job for you.

Because many OPLs are OPLs by choice, obviously the pros must outweigh (or at least equal) the cons. Most of OPLs are very happy, as shown by these quotes:

• "I love doing what I do. I cannot imagine not being involved with all aspects of running a library. It keeps me learning and constantly on the go."

• "It is a bonus being able to see interrelations of library functions. It makes you accountable."

• "I'm overworked and underpaid, but I love what I do partly because it has so many facets. The frustration is in not being able to juggle everything in the available time. I prefer being solo to being someone lost in a big library."

• "I like being a solo librarian so much that I can't imagine ever being interested in working in a big library."

• "This is an immensely satisfying business career."

The key is in fitting the right person to the job. What kind of person should an OPL be? Most agree that the main requirements include being flexible and creative; having a bias toward service, sharing, coalition-building, and idealism; being resourceful; finding enjoyment in working alone; being able to manage time, think analytically, and see the big picture; being naturally curious; and having good recall. Also required are good written and oral communication skills, good organizational skills, self-confidence, a sense of humor, patience, and a high tolerance for frustration. Members of the SOLOLIB-L electronic discussion list felt that an OPL must have confidence in making good decisions, an entrepreneurial attitude, comfort with networking, proficiency in gathering supporters, a lot of flexibility, good time-management skills, the ability to balance priorities, a love for the profession, the ability to cope with many bosses and patrons who think they are the OPL's only client, a readiness to take risks and learn something new every day, passion and enthusiasm, and a willingness to dive into any task. Can all these things be taught? No, they probably cannot. However, specific tools and techniques that help OPLs cope *can* be learned—in library school, on the job, or through continuing education. In general, OPLs wish they had known more about financial matters, management, corporate culture, networking, computer skills, assertiveness, time management, and public relations.

A WEEK IN THE LIFE OF AN OPL

One way to illustrate exactly what an OPL librarian does is to review a week in the life of an actual OPL. What follows is a summary of my activities for one week, in one job, at one corporation. It may or may not be typical of the work of an OPL, but it will give you a taste of what it could be like.

Monday

I got to the office at 7:30 A.M. I read my e-mail, read the postings on the electronic lists to which I subscribe, and listened to about five phone messages. E-mail includes several requests from my boss and users. Usually the phone messages ask me to follow-up on an order I've placed or to fill a request for a particular document.

About 8:30 A.M., I went to the mailroom for the morning mail. Monday is the heaviest mail day, so it takes a long time for the mailroom crew to get it sorted and into the mailboxes. I usually go back at about 11 A.M. for the rest (and to deliver what I've already taken care of), and then return after 1 P.M. for the packages. On a busy day, I will go back once again at 3 P.M. for any other mail. In my mail were ads for new services (most of which I recycled without opening), bills to be approved, magazines to be checked in (some of which I read), and internal requests for information or documents.

As usual, I ate lunch at my desk. Most days, I was only interrupted a couple of times. I didn't mind the interruptions since lunchtime is the only time some people can get to the library. I deliberately left my door open to be available to help. Remember, their questions do not interrupt my job, they *are* my job.

On Mondays, I usually checked with my boss to see if he had any special projects for the upcoming week. Because he is an engineer and not a librarian, this could be anything from creating a new database or cleaning up an existing one to locating an overhead projector for him to take on a trip. The rest of the day consisted of odds and ends.

On this particular Monday, I needed to prepare for my annual Open House, which was the next day. I spent about an hour getting my computer set up outside the library. Needless to say, it didn't work right away, which is normal—nothing is ever as simple as it seems. I left for home about 5:30 P.M.

Tuesday

Today was the annual Library Open House. At 8:30 A.M. the coffee was delivered, at 9:00 A.M. the cakes arrived (one for morning, one for afternoon—if I put both out at the same time they would disappear so quickly that I wouldn't have any left for later—food is a big drawing card around here). I also had lollipops, bookmarks (which read "When you absolutely, positively have to know ... ask a librarian."), stickers ("I visited my library today."), and notepads ("Have you tried the library?"). I placed announcements regarding this event in the company's weekly newsletter, in the library's monthly letter, and on bulletin boards on each floor. I also reminded everyone (upper management, in particular) via e-mail. By the end of the day, 110 people signed in (actually there were probably more since 200 pieces of cake disappeared). I answered many questions about the library and even managed to do some demos of library services. It was a very successful event.

Near the end of the Open House, the secretary to the chief executive officer of the company called. She needed me to find a press release on a new joint venture but, of course, I couldn't answer right away since the modem was in my office and my computer was in use for the Open House. As soon as the Open House ended (3 P.M.), I returned to my office and found the press release and sent it to the secretary via e-mail. I went home at about 5:15 P.M.

Wednesday

Since yesterday was the Open House, I didn't get many of my regular tasks done. Therefore, I had to do two days' worth of work in one day. This was the situation whenever I was out for a meeting, training session, SLA conference, illness, or vacation.

I wrote three purchase orders today, one of which was for five articles that were needed as soon as possible for a manager's presentation to a potential customer. I sent this order to an information broker. The articles came the next day, making the patron very happy. It was also a big interlibrary loan day. My boss wanted 12 articles on measuring research and development productivity. Using OCLC, I found that they were available from several area libraries. The location process took about an hour, including looking up the ISSNs and checking the local union serials list. (Note: One week later, five articles had been received, one was not available, and the rest had been shipped.) I typically processed about 30 ILLs a month, but once did 60 in one day. (I loaned only one or two articles a year, since my collection was very small and narrowly focused.) I actually went home on time (more or less) at 4:30 P.M.

NOTE: This week was way back in 1996 and times have certainly changed. Now, most likely I would be able to find the articles full-text on the Web or would have the other libraries fax them to me. But even that is time-consuming and I would still send large orders to a document delivery service.

Thursday

I continued working with a vendor's technical representative on a hardware problem that had been going on for more than six months. My users and I were a bit aggravated. The system worked, but not as it should. I tried to get the vendor to make some monetary concession as well as fix the problem. My job involved a significant amount of time dealing with vendors who may or may not provide the level of service

I expected and needed; this vendor was not the only one with which I had problems.

The vice president of engineering called to ask for information on software licensing. I did a quick search on a CD-ROM database, found 30 full-text articles and sent them to him via e-mail. The next day I got a nice note thanking me for my good work. It was little things like that note that sustained me on bad days.

I only wrote one purchase order, a rush order for four copies of a computer book. I faxed it to my book vendor, requesting next day delivery. The books arrived the next afternoon, and the patron was happy. My day ended at 4:45 P.M.

Friday

This Friday came at the end of the month—time for my monthly report. I put together the statistics, which include the number of items circulated; the number of books, patents, standards, or ILLs ordered; and the number of questions that I answered. Then I wrote a narrative describing what I did during the month, divided into direct patron service (e.g., tours of the library, special research projects), new services added, and continuing efforts. I also included my activities with SLA and my local multitype library consortium. For SLA I worked on the local chapter directory, attended one meeting, counted ballots for the Sci-Tech Division, and served on the nominating committee for the Engineering Division. I also attended one consortium meeting for special library directors. We each told of new resources and services in our respective libraries. These meetings were invaluable for maintaining a network of local contacts from whom I could borrow items and ask questions. The monthly report went to my boss, who abridged it to his boss, who summarized it for his boss, and so forth. I compiled a list of overdue books, but wound up putting in the "hold" file for now. It was time-consuming to send out notices, the return rate was less than 50 percent, and it antagonized my customers.

The highlight of my day was a phone call from Barbara Quint, editor of *Searcher* magazine. I had sent her an e-mail praising the timeliness and pertinence of the latest issue, and she asked if she could print my letter. We talked about library education, vendors, and the general difficulties of our profession today. I left for home at about 4:45 P.M.

AN INTERNATIONAL VIEW

There are OPLs all over the world. In the past 10 years I have traveled to South Africa, Germany, Spain, the U.K., Mexico, Canada, Australia, and New Zealand and have made it a point to talk with OPLs in each country. Through the miracle of e-mail I have been able to "talk" with OPLs in many other countries. Combined with 20 years of talking with librarians in the U.S.A., I have found that, fundamentally, we are all the same.

There are some differences, however. In some countries, library resources and organizations are less plentiful. Problems with currency fluctuations and the resultant high cost of online services and journals can cause major problems for many OPLs. Outside the U.S.A., more libraries are likely to be OPLs and the OPL is more likely to be a nonprofessional. Educational systems outside the U.S.A. are structured quite differently.

U.K.

"These are exciting times for solo librarians in the U.K.," wrote Sue Lacey Bryant, a library consultant and author, for *The One-Person Library* in November 1999. "New networks are emerging in the East Midlands and in London. The development of active, self-confident groupings of OPLs willing to learn from each other can only be of benefit to the profession as a whole." The Library Association (now CILIP) has helped greatly by the appointment of a liaison to the special library community, Lyndsay Rees-Jones, and by starting a solo electronic list and the workplace library list.

Bryant continued: "It has been clear for some time that an accurate assessment of the number of solo information professionals is vital. Without identifying the significance of OPLs within the profession and establishing a reliable picture of the sectors in which they are deployed the various professional bodies cannot possibly serve the interests of solo librarians. For example, the need for access to affordable Continuing Professional Education, structured in such a way that solo librarians can participate, is crucial."

The first year the LA gave members an opportunity to check a box marking them as a SOLO librarian or an OPL, 1,506 of the 24,506 personal members identified themselves as OPLs. Deleting those not actively working in libraries left 1,381 OPLs working in the U.K. who are members of the LA. Most OPLs worked in school libraries, industry, or commerce.

In 1999, the Library and Information Statistics Unit of the Department of Information and Library Studies, Loughborough University, surveyed 897 organizations. Of the 435 responses, 128 had no library and 22 had a very small library and thus were not included in the analysis; all national, public, and academic libraries and those firms with overlapping sectors were included. No survey has been done since this one.

OPLs in the U.K. have many networking resources. These include CILIP and several of its special interest groups (especially the Education Librarians, Health Libraries, Industrial & Commercial Libraries, Prison Libraries, School Libraries, U.K. eInformation—formerly the U.K. Online Users Group, University College and Research, and Youth Libraries Groups), the British (and European) Business School Librarians Group, Construction Industry Information Group, National Health Service Regional Librarians Group, and Information Officers in the Pharmaceutical Industry. One of the first OPL organizations outside the U.S.A. was the One-Man Band Section of ASLIB in the U.K., but it has not been active recently and ASLIB has gone from a public to private organization. In June 1997, Chris Crabtree and Margaret Brittin organized Special Libraries in the Midlands (SLIM) in Birmingham, England. SLIM members meet about three times a year. A similar group, SLIL (Special Librarians in London), meets monthly, thanks to the hard work of Bert Washington. Lis Riley formed Special Libraries in Cambridge (SLIC). CILIP launched its Workplace Libraries (British for corporate or company libraries, most of which are OPLs) discussion list in April 1999 and the East Midlands Branch of the LA established the Solo Professional network, set up by Steve Witowski. The Industrial and Commercial Libraries Group of the LA is made up primarily of OPLs and is quite active, often having joint meetings with SLIL.

Germany

The success of the OPL movement in Germany has been a direct result of the efforts of Evelin Morgenstern. While she worked at the now closed Deutsches Bibliothekinstitut (DBI), her responsibility was to identify issues that affect the Special Libraries branch of the profession and to organize activities for addressing these issues. In 2000, Morgenstern reported on the history of the German OPL movement.

> The story of OPLs in Germany can be told in two parts — before and after May 1995. What happened in May 1995? The first German OPL Roundtable was held, organized by Evelin Morgenstern, the Special Libraries' advisor of the Deutches Bibliotheksinstitut, and led by Guy St. Clair. Morgenstern had a strong desire to help her colleagues in eastern Germany who were making it clear to her that they were finding it difficult to cope with the changing conditions in their work situation. They had been accustomed to very generous staffing levels and were not prepared to accept their downsizing as "rightsizing" — something to which those in western Germany painfully had become accustomed.

What were OPLs like before May 1995? The leaders of the profession found the following:

- The role and relative importance of the OPL in the organization varies greatly, depending in part on the librarian's own perception of her or his role. A library with frequent and satisfied users provides the librarian with a chance to prove his or her merit and capabilities to the organization. In some organizations, however, the library is viewed as more of a service center than a library, providing copying, bookkeeping, telephone, and messenger services.

- If the library is not found in a central location, it is most likely to be located in the department where it is most needed, such as R&D. Most libraries seem to have fewer than 10,000 volumes, but 10 percent have over 40,000 volumes. Most OPLs do not have professional librarian status and many have no permanently assigned staff. In a great many of the OPLs there is no automation and what there is may have been selected by the organization and not the librarian.

- The topic of professional isolation among OPLs is a serious one. If the librarian feels, or truly is, isolated from other colleagues, he or she will not be able to judge the quality of work he or she performs. Networking is strongly urged.

- Both planning and financial responsibility in OPLs seemed to come under the well-known rubric: "Go ahead and do what you want, unless it costs money. Then prove to me it is really necessary to the organization." A supportive organization can give the librarian a great deal of autonomy. Selection of software, books, journals, and so on, should be made with the participation of the librarian in all cases. Note that they didn't go so far as to say "by the librarian."

- There is a great need for networking. Much of the current exchange of ideas and making of new contacts comes from attending meetings of librarians from OPLs. Groups such as the APBB (Arbeits-gemeinschaft der Parlaments-unde Behordenbiblio-theke) offer support, but it is up to the individual librarian to seek them out. It is also extremely important, and this cannot be stressed enough, that the organization allow and *encourage* librarians to attend meetings such as the annual librarians' day (Bibliothekartage), congresses, and workshops—not only for their continuing education, but also to cultivate professional contacts. Continuing education must be supported *financially* by the organization. If librarians are not permitted and encouraged in this area, they will lose interest in improving themselves, to the detriment of the organization.

- In many OPLs, services are restricted to providing books and periodicals as requested. In others, excellent and comprehensive provision of services is available. Librarians could use more information on specific marketing ideas *and more time and support for putting them into action*. If a librarian finds out which customers' needs are unfulfilled and conquers these new areas, it would be an excellent way to justify his or her existence.

The Roundtable could not limit itself to just time management, image, and lack of specialization, but had to work to raise awareness—on both sides. To force leaders of the profession and practitioners to look at the OPL differently, acknowledging its unique role and accepting that it could even become an example for the academic library. The OPL can offer better and more relevant information services because of its closeness to the customer, the organization, and the collection. This was a lesson everyone needed to learn.

After the Roundtable DBI saw how the meeting helped the research and support organization meet its basic goals to be a seismograph and interpreter of trends and to implement them in German and then pass the torch to others, all the specialized working groups (in medicine, the arts and museums, government and parliament, and church libraries) immediately started to offer continuing professional education courses or workshops for OPLs. In 1996, the first OPL workshop was organized by the APBB at Erlangen on Librarians' Day. The same year APBB also sponsored the first "Diplomarbeit" written at Fachhochschule Hannover on OPLs in the Hannover area. In 1997, the biennial conference of the Arbeitsgemeinschaft der Spezialbibliotheken (AspB), the Special Libraries Working Group, devoted a large part of its program to OPLs with Sue Lacey Bryant of the U.K. and Guy St. Clair of the U.S.A. presenting papers. The same year saw the birth of the OPL Kommission in the Verein der Diplom-Bibliothekare (VdDV), the association for academic or special libraries. They have been very active. They have compiled a database of OPLs with over 1,000 listings, set up an electronic list (to which nearly 100 librarians subscribed in the first week), and created a Web site.

For those not able to attend conferences, an impressive list of literature is now available. Two of Guy St. Clair's works were translated into German by DBI (and one is being translated into Japanese now!). Regina Peeters of the OPL Kommission edited *The Robinson Crusoe Syndrome and What You Can Do About It* with 24 detailed descriptions of OPLs in Germany with a strong emphasis on pragmatic approaches to problem-solving. The library schools (Fachhochscholen) have begun to introduce OPL-related issues in their curricula, although distinct training for one-person librarianship has not yet been established.

In 2000, those who attended the 1995 Roundtable were surveyed about the "after" existence of OPLs. It was their unanimous view that professional isolation no longer exists. If it does, it is the choice of the individual OPL; with all the networks, lists, OPL Kommission, databases, and so on, there is no reason to feel alone. Most of the other goals have been met to some degree—mostly depending on the attitude and personality of the individual OPL. In fact, personal competencies have begun to play a crucial role in Germany due to influences from the U.S.A. More continuing education courses are being organized to cover this area. OPLs themselves agree that they feel less isolated and are more aware of their own value. This self-confidence has improved the quality of professional service they deliver because they can measure their own performance against that of others. Both the leaders and the OPLs mentioned the problems of decreasing finances, which are now universal. This has sometimes led to quite a quality dilemma. OPLs have to take over other tasks involving as much as half their working time (especially at museum libraries). They feel doing so imposes quite a burden on their provision of high-quality service, but the smart ones have turned their non-librarian duties into a publicity campaign for the library.

Looking back on what has been achieved, it feels like a fairy tale—but it is not. The changes have been brought about by cooperation and investment of time and effort in the target group. Nevertheless, there is still much to be done and many questions remain unanswered:

- We [I include *all* OPLs] still need to bring about a certain mental change in our colleagues to make them understand that continued professional education is essential, even if not provided by the employers. It is a question of taking responsibility for one's own career. We also need to be concerned about the quality of the providers of such education. Volunteers are nice, but are they qualified? Are the courses still thought of as being "too American," especially since the German librarian often finds it difficult to see himself or herself as an entrepreneur?

- It seems to be fashionable for the leaders of the profession [in Germany, at least] to write one-person librarianship on their banner, but there are no visible consequences. The salary structure has not been reformed. Are OPLs in danger of becoming complacent and not seeking contact with fellow professionals in other fields? Is there an unrealistic expectation that any CE [continuing education] course should be customized for OPLs? [Such as preservation of historical library materials for OPLs—what's different for OPLs than others?]

All these problems are familiar and will probably go on forever, but we can hope it [they] will be approached with a positive attitude. As one OPL put it: "We must improve the information services, take them in a proactive way to management, and find at least one powerful advocate. That is my recipe for success and, indeed, survival."

Since the early days of Germany's reunification there has been a major change in German society at all levels. Government, educational institutions, and, of course, professional organizations have been required to organize and manage the shift from what were two separate and distinctly opposite points of view to a "unified" one. With the fall of

the [Berlin] Wall and the subsequent demands for reunification, challenges of a different sort had to be dealt with, since
two different cultures and two different ways of thinking
about work and the workplace (to say nothing about quality
service delivery and similarly sensitive issues) had to be
combined into one. The situation in Germany has been
complicated by the transition from the practice of "traditional librarianship" to the development of an information
delivery infrastructure for the 21st century, requiring major
shifts in thinking for information workers. A new perception about their professional status has come into play. Until
1995, OPLs were not even aware that they were in a position to raise awareness and "educate" these several societal
entities about the role (and the *value*) of one-person librarianship. Now they are starting to do it!

With this raised awareness has come new responsibilities, new methodologies, and, perhaps as important as anything else, recognition. OPLs are no longer thought of as
being (and the OPLs no longer think of themselves as
being) modest, humble, or shy. They have identified their
place in the library and information services workplace in
Germany and they enthusiastically accept their role as
change agents in the information management community.

In June 2000, after DBI went out of business, Morgenstern and
some of her colleagues founded a new group, "Initiative Fortbildung
für wissenschaftliche Spezialbibliotheken und verwandte
Einrichtungen" (Initiative for Continuing Education in Libraries,
Museums, and Archives). The association is continuing and expanding
work that Morgenstern started at DBI: consulting; organizational evaluation of special libraries; special projects; publication of professional
literature; and, especially, the offering, planning, and carrying through
of high-quality customized continuing education programs. The
Initiative " ... will make use of the innovative potential that is inherent

in every situation of change: we will attempt a much broader concep-
tion of continuing education and thus be able to embark upon new
ways not yet familiar to us. At the same time we will enlarge our spectrum of our target groups. The amazing thing is that *librarians* are taking
the initiative for founding this sort of association. [The] Initiative will
concentrate on specific topics and problems relevant to is [its] members.
Some of these may be strategic planning, management skills, the Internet,
and technology in general" (Morgenstern communication 2000).

Australia

Australia is another hotbed of one-person librarianship thanks to
pioneering work by Guy St. Clair and Meg Paul and the continuing
work of a dedicated group of One-Person Australian Librarians
(OPALs). Australia has one of the largest Internet user bases in the
world, enabling Australian librarians to embrace it and other new technologies at a rapid pace. The country has good special librarians, ones
who are well educated, professionally well-read, and able to network
well. However, they have had problems with downsizing, too, partly
due to the lack of information to back up the need for library services.

A survey conducted by the Australian Library and Information
Association (ALIA) in 1997 showed that only 47 of 83 top 100 companies responding had a library or information service (Walsh 1998).
ALIA didn't expect this to change because 92 percent of the companies
without a library said there was "no chance" of allocating funds for one
in the next 12 months. The information competency most valued by
management was "the ability to interpret requests for information and
respond quickly." Surprisingly, nearly one-quarter of the respondents
felt that their library resources did not meet the needs of their users.
The Australian library work force was characterized as

• Aging—because 72 percent were over 40 years of age;

• Poorly paid—because they receive pay increases of only 3.4 percent compared with a national average of 4.5 percent;

- Highly unionized—because 57 percent were unionized vs. a national rate of only 31 percent;

- Insecure—because 17 percent were in "permanent part-time" positions vs. the national average of 7 percent, more than 50 percent were concerned about job security in the future, and one-third felt threatened by new technologies; and

- Dissatisfied—because more than 40 percent said they had less say in decisions affecting their jobs than they had a year before, and more than 60 percent experienced more stress at work.

Australia is the home of the One-Person Australian Libraries (OPAL) special interest group of ALIA. At the ALIA Health, Law and Specials Conference in Sydney in 1995, five members of the Health Section's program committee (Georgina Dale, Frances Bluhdorn, Claire Pillar, Marion Steele, Toni Silson [now Kennedy]) decided there was a need to meet with other OPLs at the conference. This meeting drew large numbers of OPLs; therefore, Dale and Silson presented the case for a special-interest group to ALIA, which approved the idea in 1996. The first to convene was Georgina Dale, and the executive committee was made up of the five persons listed above plus Therese Bendeich. OPAL started a newsletter (*OPALessence*) in October 1996, an electronic list in December 1997, a Web page in 1998, a membership directory in 1999, and their first publication (*Evaluating Websites*) in 2000. The National OPALs group has changed a great deal over the years. While they once had chapters in most of the states, in 2005 there was only the national group and an informal one in Queensland, led by Denise Cadman. Their membership is large compared to other ALIA groups, with more than 250 members. Most of OPAL's activities involve informal meetings, but they still maintain an electronic discussion list. *OPALessence* is now available only in electronic format.

Frances Bludorn described Australian OPLs in 1996 by way of some wonderful analogies:

- "OPAL is an amorphous form of hydrated silica in the gel state. The amorphous nature is illustrated by its cross-sectional membership drawn from special libraries, health libraries, law libraries, public libraries ..."

- "OPALs are precious stones which have been used as gems."

- "Being the only gem of our kind in our organizations ..."

- "OPALs have existed underground since the beginning of time, their solid particles remaining suspended indefinitely, unaffected by bureaucracy. The formation of OPALs affords these suspended particles as [sic] sense of organisation in a loose but definite arrangement and [a] network while giving some rigidity and elasticity to ALIA's mixture."

- "The finest OPALs are found chiefly in Australia."

In 1996, Meg Paul at FLIS Pty Ltd., Melbourne, started *The Australasian One-Person Library*, a wraparound for *The One-Person Library* with local content. This publication was bought by Information Bridges International, Inc., in 1998, just prior to Paul's retirement.

South Africa

In 1996, I had the privilege of visiting the Republic of South Africa and finding out about the solo scene first hand. I was one of 10 librarians who made up the first People-to-People Citizen Ambassador Delegation in Special Librarianship and Information Services Management to the Republic of South Africa. The trip was arranged and led by Guy St. Clair.

Although none of the group's official visits was to an OPL, I had three opportunities to meet with OPLs in a less formal setting. The first was at a meeting of the South Africa Institute for Librarianship and Information Science (SALIS) Special Libraries Interest Section at the

University of Witswatersrand in Johannesburg. SALIS is an organization similar to the American Library Association (ALA). I also met with OPLs at a cocktail reception sponsored by the Special Libraries Interest Group of SALIS, Western Cape Division, and at a meeting with special library leaders at Ernst & Young in Capetown.

Most librarians (70 percent) attend one of the universities. There are three programs available at the universities: a four-year bachelor's degree, a fifth-year honors program, and a master's degree by research. Most graduates go to work at academic or national libraries. Librarians in corporate libraries are a mix of qualified and nonqualified employees. Compared with the Teknikon, the university program is more prestigious and the schools have more money to spend. The education is almost totally theoretical, although the University of South Africa (UNISA) requires two management courses. The internship is only three to four weeks long. One librarian said she didn't even know how to stamp a book when she graduated. She had been at university and her internship had been just cataloging a collection, involving almost no interaction with the librarian.

Overall, the OPL situation in South Africa is much the same as that in the rest of the world. All the OPLs I spoke with agreed that networking is very important and very helpful and also agree that library school does not prepare one to be an OPL. South African OPLs are somewhat smaller, with smaller staffs, in smaller companies, and having a little less automation than their counterparts in Europe and the U.S.A.

Louise Flynn (personal communication 2000) described South African OPLs as follows:

> Although there are several library associations and groups in South Africa that cater to both public and private sector libraries, there is no distinct support group or branch devoted solely to the area of one-person librarians. Many OPLs belong to more than one group—generally having a membership in one, or even two, of the main library organizations, as well as regular liaison with informal library

groups aimed specifically at the sector in which they oper-
ate. This makes it difficult to establish the exact number of
OPLs operating in South Africa, as the figures overlap.
Another factor that adds to the inaccuracy of current solo
status in this country is the fact that not all one-person
libraries have any association with a library body. However,
with the recent formation of the Library and Information
Association of South Africa (LIASA) as a merger of three
of the major library organizations, there is hope of more and
easier networking among OPLs.

In spite of the diverse range of one-person libraries in
South Africa, they [the OPLs] appear to share many of the
same issues in their daily work and in the long term. The
most common problems and concerns [were time management, budgetary constraints, and lack of computer equipment and support].

The full potential of electronic lists has still to be realized. The main hindrance is the fact that some of the smaller
libraries do not have a network, but need to dial up in order
to use their e-mail and only get the chance to do this once
or twice a day. So often, the responses only come days later.
Some libraries, OPLs included, belong to informal support
groups such as libraries using the same library management
software (e.g., Inmagic, ILIS, and so on) or working in a
similar field (e.g., financial services, engineering, law, and
museums). As an example of a user group, the museum
libraries have an exchange publication system in place
between museums and art galleries in South Africa and
internationally. Requests for materials are sent via e-mail,
and the libraries have a mutual agreement to send one
another brochures and other interesting items without
charges. In addition to making use of other libraries in the
specific fields, OPLs make extensive use of the larger

libraries in South Africa for support, including municipal libraries and major academic institutions.

NOTE: Louise is now married and living and working in England.

There are no organizations in South Africa especially for OPLs, but there are at least two organizations for special librarians, many of which are probably solos. The Library and Information Association of South Africa (LIASA) formed a Special Libraries Interest Group in 2004. That same year the group sponsored two programs at the LIASA annual conference. In 2005 there were about 200 special librarians in the organization, or less than 10 percent of the membership. The Sub Saharan Africa Chapter of SLA was established in 2001. All of its officers, and most of its members, are from South Africa (mostly in the Cape Town area), which is not surprising. The LIASA and SLA groups often work together on programming.

Latin America

In early 2000 I put a message on the biblio-progresistas electronic list looking for OPLs. I heard from more than 30 OPLs in Argentina, Cuba, Guatemala, Mexico, Peru, Uruguay, and Venezuela. The first thing I found was that many of the librarians had not heard of the terms solo or OPL. Once I explained what each meant, they expressed the same concerns as do OPLs in other parts of the world:

• Managers and even library directors are not library professionals.

• Library work is not valued.

• Salaries are low.

• Job responsibilities are often limited to technical processing.

• OPLs are responsible for arranging their own continuing education.

• Dedication to customer service is not always a priority.

• Lack of preparation for the information revolution exists.

• Concern exists over whether to drop the name "librarian" in favor of "information analyst."

• Lack of funding exists, with institutional cost-cutting hitting the library first.

• Concerns exist over assignment of unqualified or problem personnel to the library.

• Lack of adequate equipment exists, especially computers.

• School librarians are asked to "babysit" classes when teachers are absent.

• Public librarians are also asked to organize cultural activities.

• For some librarians the only work available is as consultants, organizing personal collections, or working on temporary contracts.

Canada

Canada has been a leader in one-person librarianship. In 1986, the first formal OPL organization was established by a group of OPLs in Toronto, with Penny Lipman as chair. The Toronto Solos group is now part of the Toronto SLA Chapter. The group is still active, meeting for lunch several times a year and in early 2005 it had 36 members. The issues facing Canadian librarians are similar to those of other OPLs, but seem focused on the following:

• Copyright protection in Canada is biased in favor of authors, to the detriment of users. Canada looks to the U.S.A. to take the lead on this issue.

- The consolidation of information sources, especially in the area of directories, has led to higher prices and a concern for the completeness of information.

- The twin issues of electronic storage of information and the replacement of print by electronic sources have major implications for permanence (archiving) of information.

- With the decrease in value of the Canadian dollar, currency exchange issues and costs of non-Canadian sources become more troublesome.

- Because Canadian employers must allow up to 12 months of maternity leave, with 17 weeks of that paid by the government, there is both the problem of providing a replacement for an OPL and the opportunity of temporary employment for those not wanting or unable to find a permanent position. (This is also an issue in Australia and some European countries. It is not a major issue in the U.S.A. because maternity or family leave is not as generous.)

Austria

The Austrian OPL Commission was established in January 2001. Sonja Reisner was the first chair, with Dr. Constantin Cazan as deputy. Heinrich Zukal took over as president of the Commission in September 2001 when Reisner was no longer able to serve. It is still a small group. This group focuses on four areas:

1.   Networking: regular meetings, Web page, electronic discussion list.

2.   Continuing education: time management, marketing, resource management, conflict management.

3. Public relations: "consciousness-shaping," improving the image of solos.

4. Support: for individual OPLs, model contracts, job descriptions.

OPL issues are being brought into training curricula. Dr. Cazan presents a half-day lecture on OPL issues as part of a six-month training course for the ADS and another colleague lectures on OPLs at the University of Krems in lower Austria. In addition, Zukal made a presentation on OPLs to the Associazione Italiana Biblioteche (Italian Library Association) in 2002. Dr. Cazan started another group in 2005 under the Austrian Documentation Society.

Elsewhere in the World

The concept of one-person librarianship in the rest of the world is somewhere between unknown and invisible. Although there undoubtedly are very many OPLs around the world—in fact they account for the majority of librarians—at present there is no good way of reaching them. OPLs are most likely working in developing nations, in very small libraries in very small communities or charitable institutions, and are unlikely to be degreed librarians (or to have even had any library training at all). In addition, they may not have access to the Internet, World Wide Web, or even e-mail. The challenge of locating these OPLs and helping them network and become more efficient and effective information providers is a great one, but one with the promise of great rewards.

Profiles of OPLs Around the World

In South Africa I met an OPL who is retired from an aircraft plant where she was downsized to an OPL situation. She did have a professional assistant and clerical help, but each successive manager cut more. However, the company was very generous with funding and she said she nearly always "got what I wanted." She was able to get out and network a lot. She feels it is even more important for solo librarians to network than it is for others to do so.

An OPL in a public library in South Africa found that patrons need more than just information and the librarian also serves a social function. She likes being an OPL because she has control and can often start her own programs without going through the bureaucracy. She is able to get a relief person so she can be active professionally, go to meetings, and present papers. She is very active in the Library and Information Workers Organization, a left-wing, nearly radical, quasi-trade union organization.

A part-time (14 hours per week) OPL at the South African Center for Health Policy—a government agency—doesn't feel too alone because she has lots of contacts, made before she retired from the Medical Library at the University of Witswatersrand. The Center is a very democratic organization, with no bureaucracy, but there is not good communication so she doesn't always know what's expected of her. She would like more time to get more done.

A new graduate of the Teknikon in Capetown, South Africa, described her library program. It was more like a U.S. junior or community college, providing a very practical education. The program was three years long, with an eight-month internship. Unlike in university education, theory, professionalism, management, public relations and marketing, customer service, and subject specialization were not taught. Fortunately, she developed a professional and customer-oriented attitude on her own and further developed it during her internship at Ernst & Young, an accounting and consulting firm. She said most students choose librarianship because they like books. One OPL worked in various types of libraries, especially in the rural areas of Guatemala where she worked on a project to distribute books to the most remote areas. She did this for three years, establishing six libraries for the GTZ of Germany. This has been the most satisfying job of her professional career.

A library student at the University of San Marcos, Peru, was an information analyst for a press agency in Lima and was working on its Web page. In his organization, there were no fixed working hours, very short deadlines, and a great deal of pressure. In addition, user needs were constantly changing. He was involved in a local networking group that was trying to make changes for the future of the profession.

A Canadian OPL worked for a think tank, providing support for five in-house analysts. Since her job was only four days a week, she worked one day a week at a pharmaceutical company doing retrospective conversion of the collection and checking and routing journals. She wrote, "The title librarian or library technician brings with it preconceived ideas. I'm sure there are people who think those in the library field read books all day and that it isn't a job that requires a lot of knowledge."

Another Canadian was hired as a summer student to help an MLS set up a hospital library. She worked in this position for five summers. Despite dropping out of the MLS program for personal reasons, the hospital she had worked for asked her to again work part time in the library. "I accepted and have never looked back." She managed libraries in several different hospitals in one community system.

> For the first year of the alliance, I rotated among the city sites. I had collections at each. This proved to be very frustrating for me as well as the staff. Staff had trouble finding me; it seemed that whatever they wanted was at the other site. I was constantly running back and forth. [Now] I stay in the main library where I can be a phone call away from the other two hospitals. With inter-hospital mail several times a day and the use of fax machines, I can get information to users when they need it. At my satellite site, a volunteer checks the library for me and we speak frequently. I'm sure that users at the other sites do not think the services are equitable and I need to do more marketing to inform users of how to reach me.
>
> The best thing about being an OPL is the diversity of the job. No two days are the same. I am allowed to expand my knowledge every day.

It is difficult to convince some older staff that you can contribute directly to good patient care. However, with the focus on evidence-based practice, key staff now seems to be very supportive of the library.

Being a solo also translates to being a jack of all trades and a master of none. In one day I can teach a Pubmed class, catalog a few books, update our hospital Intranet, find information on a disease I've never heard of, process ILLs and work on my budget or statistics. The key to survival has been a network of fellow librarians.

When an Israeli nonlibrarian decided to become an Information Professional (IP), she received help and tutoring from two experienced IPs who worked in two different industrial companies in Haifa. In addition, she took a course in online searching. She said she is self-taught, having learned the profession by reading, attending conferences, and interacting with other IPs. She had a wide range of clients, mainly industrial companies, but also a few consulting firms. She provided information services to companies mainly in northern and central Israel. The main difficulty that she encountered as she embarked on her new, independent course was getting the first clients, an effort that involved selling herself, including developing a sales pitch, making many cold calls, and overcoming her natural shyness. In addition, she had to manage with a very small initial income. She joined the Association of Independent Information Professionals and the Israel Society of Libraries and Information Centers, through which she had received great support from other IPs in Israel and abroad. She also gave back to the profession by teaching a course in Information Science at the Technion. She viewed teaching as a very important activity. Many of her students have found good positions as IPs.

Andrea Joosten lives in Germany in the west, near the border to the Netherlands, in a small city called Kleve. She works in a very romantic location—the Castle Moyland—"the beautiful land." The full name of her employer is the Foundation Museum Castle Moyland—

Collection van der Grinten Joseph Beuys Archive of the country of Northrhine-Westfalia. Since May 1997, the castle has been a museum of modern art, with more than 60,000 works of art collected by Hans and Franz Joseph van der Grinten and about 4,000 works by Joseph Beuys, who grew up in the area. The library includes 40,000 books in subjects related to the collection, more than 40,000 articles, 3,000 books, 20,000 letters, many leaflets, invitation cards, and printed matter from Beuys. She works with the art historians to help prepare exhibitions and to publish the catalogs, and helps the volunteers prepare their conducted tours through the collection of the museum, the topical exhibitions, the old castle and the lovely sculpture garden around it, and the herb garden. She also organizes four events during the year at which authors, critics, actors or musicians present literature—all in less than 20 hours per week. She manages with the help of more than 25 volunteers, who do all the technical work and carry out the events. Her work in the archive involves working with everyone from children with homework questions to dedicated and highly educated researchers. She is always surprised at how similar their questions are. Only the degree of specialization of the expected answer is different. What she dislikes most about her job is, "There is no one who speaks 'my language.' The next special librarian is an hour away which is a far distance in Germany. So I do not know how I could live without e-mail and without my work in the associations."

Toni Kennedy, Library/IT Manager at Lady Davidson Private Hospital, Bobbin Head Road, North Turramurra, New South Wales, Australia, was one of the organizers of OPAL, One-Person Australian Librarians. "The main reason I became a librarian was because I always spent so much time in the local library that I thought I should make some money out of it." She also juggled the management of 20 libraries in Sydney, southern New South Wales, Australian Capital Territory, four in Victoria and three in Tasmania. She visited the hospitals to meet the staff and show them her face and do a bit of marketing. "Many of these hospitals have never had a library service and are unsure exactly what they need it for." She had an assistant who comes in afternoons and did the photocopying and book processing. Most of the interesting questions came from the psych hospital in Victoria, about things like rave parties—what are they, what drugs are used and why. When asked for her advice to other librarians, she encouraged them to "join groups of similar like-minded people, and be willing to share what you know—it's a great feeling to be able to help people: not just your own users, but also your colleagues." Kennedy left her hospital job in 2005 for a position at the Corrective Services Academy.

2

Management:
General Concepts

O PLs are in the business of managing information and all its
associated services. They are "not just librarians. ... The tasks
that one-person librarians perform are not limited to information delivery any more. And it's those management tasks that really
separate the serious one-person librarians from the others. ..." (St.
Clair 1996a, 4). In a one-person library, you do all the management.
What you do (and don't do) is the difference between whether or not
the library succeeds. The success of your library is almost entirely up
to you. There are always factors beyond your control, such as your
prime-users being laid off or the company going under. Because you
can't control these things, forget about them and concentrate on what
you *can* control.

You must ensure that the library is seen as a critical part of the
organization and that it is involved in mission-critical issues. You need
to write a mission statement and tie it closely to the mission of your
organization. If you don't do this, you run the risk of being seen as
peripheral to the organization. When it comes time to make cuts in the
budget, space, or personnel, the library that is not seen as critical to the
fulfillment of the organization's mission will be one of the first to feel
the ax. You must make sure that the library is relevant to the lives of
your users. Management must know that you know more than anyone
else in the organization about its business; the users and their needs;

53

and the collection, organization, and dissemination of information. To cut you or the library would compromise the organization's competitive advantage.

Early in my musings on one-person librarianship I came to realize what I now call the "Four Hard Truths":

1. We must make ourselves the information experts. No one will give us our place in the information society. We can make ourselves the experts by virtue of our education and our customer orientation.

2. We cannot demand respect, we must earn it. We can do so by keeping up in our field, participating in continuing education, and developing professionally.

3. We probably never will be paid what we are worth.

4. We are all in the marketing business. We market our institutions, our services, and ourselves, and we do so all the time.

THE USER IS JOB ONE—CUSTOMER SERVICE

It cannot be stressed enough that customer service—putting the user first—is the most important factor in library success. You can have the best collection, largest staff, biggest budget, nicest furniture, and most up-to-date computers, but you will not last if your users don't feel the library helps them. It would be great if all librarians graduated from library school knowing this, but it isn't always so. If you are an OPL you probably already know this, but, please, don't skip this section. A reminder of these basic issues is important.

In the past, librarians called the people who use the library patrons. But times have changed and it is time to change both our terminology and our thinking. We could call them "users," because people choose to use the library, but there is a better term—"customers." Some object to using "customers" as it implies that they pay for our products and services. But our customers do pay, if not with money then with their time (and time is even more valuable than money—see Chapter 3). Even the services of the "free" public library are paid; they are paid in advance, through tax monies.

Who are your customers? Management, other professionals, secretaries and other clerical staff, manufacturing workers, the mailroom staff, and even the cleaning staff are all potential customers of the library. Ideally, all should be treated equally, but it would be foolish not to recognize that you will be much faster to respond to an inquiry from the president or managing director of your organization than from a worker on the assembly line. Just be sure that you are responding according to the importance of the answer to the continued existence of the organization, not to the position of the customer on the organizational chart.

What do your customers want? They want to get what they ordered—and are not interested in why the library cannot deliver. They want the information delivered to be accurate, timely, and of value. They want friendly employees, an attractive and easy-to-use facility, a wide and well-reasoned selection of resources, and a host of other wide-ranging and ever-changing services and products. But what do they *really* want? What is the *real* product of a library? It is not a book or article; it is not an online search; it is not even information. What your customers want are *answers*—they want their problems solved.

Your clients also expect the library to help lower their costs of doing business—by saving them time and, therefore, money. Another desire is for you to make getting information convenient for them. This can mean anything from taking requests over the Internet to putting databases and research services on their desktop computers.

"Anyone who has worked a reference desk has seen users pleased with a quick and mediocre answer when, with a bit more time and effort, they could get a better one." This is called "satisficing" or being only good enough (Tennant 2001, 39). Customers may also accept less than outstanding service because they feel that they have no alternative. They may be "required" to use the in-house library or they simply may not have explored other options. However, most of our customers do have options. Corporations like Disney, Amazon.com, and FedEx have raised the service bar for everyone, including libraries. "More people every day have experienced extraordinary service. They have seen world-class service, and now every service has to accept it. A service that does not jump to meet these rising expectations will have a small revolution and a customer exodus on its hands" (Beckwith 1997, 9). What may have been perceived as excellent service a few years ago is not acceptable today. Beckwith goes on to say that you should let your clients, not your industry or your ego, set your service standards. "Customer service is in the eye of the beholder." If they don't think it's good, it isn't (Talley and Axelroth 2001, 10). Look at your library, your products and services, and yourself—are they all as good as they should be. If the answer is no, what can you do to make them better?

One important thing to remember is that you can't be all things to all people. You will have to be selective, that is, about which services to offer and to whom they are offered. Choose what you can do best and what will be of greatest benefit to your parent organization, and then promote your services to those who can benefit most from them (for more on promotion, see Chapter 5). It is also necessary, sometimes, to say no. Some requests made may be out of the scope of your position, out of your range of talents, or just impossible to fit in. It often helps to have written policies to support you at such times.

You are likely to face some special challenges that will tax your customer-service dedication and try your patience. Every organization has prima donnas, clients that think the library and the librarian exist only to serve them. They will monopolize your time and resources—if you let them. That last phrase is the key. You are in charge of your own time. You have the right (and perhaps obligation) to say no. All members of the organization have an equal right to your services. You may have to remind a prima donna (gently) of this fact. Trying to teach these prima donnas how to find their own answers or do their own research also may work. A related challenge is reporting to more than one boss. The key here is communication—from you to each boss and between the bosses themselves. They may not realize that you are getting assignments from two (or more) people. Ask them to prioritize their requests. If you have serious conflicts you should ask them to meet and decide how to handle this situation. And if all else fails, go to the human resources department or your bosses' boss for guidance. Finally, there are some people who will never be satisfied, no matter how hard you try. Accept this fact and get on with life. You cannot please everyone. Just as in Olympic scoring, ignore the few who hate everything you do and the few who love everything you do and concentrate on those in the middle. Although you should try to personalize your services and products for your customers, you don't have time to do this perfectly for every customer. You need to let them know this. Explain that you have many customers and limited time and that you will do the best you can for them, but they need to be somewhat flexible.

You must be client-centered, not library-centered. By this I mean that you need to understand your clients' work and vocabulary by reading their journals, talking to them, and listening to them. Remember to be accessible, approachable, and friendly. Make sure your clients get what they came for—do more than point to the resource and forget them. Many clients are reluctant to ask the librarian for help. They try to find the information on their own, and they give up when they can't find it. Your desk should be situated where you can see your clients as they leave the library. If they do not appear to have found anything, gently ask, "Did you find what you needed?" If they say no, then offer to help them find the information. Some librarians offer to help clients when they enter the library. I prefer to ask clients as they are leaving, "Did you find what you needed?" Often they say, "no," even though they would not have asked for help. Also, before they go out of the door simply smile and say, "Thank you for visiting the library—come back again anytime." What other department in your organization says that? You will stand out in your customers' minds and they will be more likely to come to you next time they need information.

Always think and communicate in terms of how your services will benefit clients. Make things as easy as possible for your clients, even if it makes things a bit more difficult for you. Speak their language, that is, no library jargon (e.g., say "updating the collection" rather than "weeding," "buying books" rather than "acquisitions" or "collection development"). When entering items into the online catalog, be sure the subject headings are meaningful to your users. For example, at one time the Library of Congress subject term for computers was "data processing." How many users would search for a computer book under that term? You should substitute the subject term "computers" for "data processing." Although your goal may be to centralize information in the library, making it a one-stop shop for all information needs, it is sometimes appropriate to house parts of the collection elsewhere. For instance, you might want to have a satellite library for staff at an off-site facility or house the marketing reports in the marketing department. Doing so will raise additional problems regarding security and cataloging, but you can find ways to solve them. *All* materials, wherever they are housed, should appear in your library catalog, with a clear notation as to their location.

Presentation is very important. Instead of giving customers a printout of articles or list of Web sites, present them with a summary report with the answer to the original question. Remember, your real product is *answers*. Each customer and problem is different, so you must customize your product to the needs of each user. Know how each customer prefers to receive information—summarized, citations only, or with full text included. Note these and other preferences in a database or on cards in your Rolodex or in a computer file. (For example, Mr. Jones wants citations only, in date order. He is fluent in German and knows some French, so include cites in these languages.) Now, this is *very* important: Make sure that your name or the name of your library appears on every page of everything that goes out of your library. That way the user can't take the information you've provided to his or her boss and say, "Look what *I* found." Instead, it is obvious that *the librarian* found the information.

An OPL must be proactive. You must anticipate what your patrons will need and be prepared to provide it to them. Doing so involves planning, thinking, anticipating, and taking the initiative. As Stephen Covey pointed out, you must see every "threat" as an "opportunity" and be able to turn "complaints" into new service ideas (Paul and Crabtree 1995). St. Clair remarks that this proactivity is important because "the traditional library model, even the corporate library model, doesn't work in business anymore" (1995c, 1). How do you find out what your customers will find useful? Observe, listen, read both the library and industry literature, use your intuition, or do an information audit. (There is a wealth of information out there on information audits. Start with the Information Resources Center of the Special Libraries Association or the excellent book by Sue Henczel.) Make sure that when you start a new service you can meet the demand it will generate. Nothing turns off users more than unfulfilled promises. (Remember the old sales motto: A satisfied customer will tell one friend; a disgruntled one tells 10.)

Traditionally, people (and too many librarians) think that the library, especially a "captive" institutional library, has no competition. But there is always competition. When asked what the main competitor to the library is, most librarians will say, "the Internet." But the Internet isn't our main competition; neither are colleagues, vendors, other libraries, or information brokers. Our most dangerous competitor is simply "doing without." Herbert White put it this way, "Librarians must bear in mind that a report due on Monday morning will be delivered Monday morning with or without library input; the user will simply proceed as if all available information has indeed been located" (White 1984, 147–148). We are not necessary to the completion of the report. The customer has the ultimate power—to ignore us completely.

KNOW THY ORGANIZATION: ORGANIZATIONAL BEHAVIOR AND CORPORATE CULTURE

"Power is one of the last dirty words." But it makes organizations run (Kanter 1997). Perhaps the most important thing you can do to survive

and thrive in an organization is to know the organization you are working in. Every organization has a corporate culture, whether it is a business, community hospital, law firm, or other entity. Corporate culture
is made up of a system of shared beliefs, values, and assumptions.
Whether or not you agree with these values, you must accept them as
part of the organization. You need to know how the organization is formally structured and how it actually works, who is in power and who
is not. You need to understand what information the organization
needs, who needs it, how it is communicated, how it flows within the
organization, and how to market your information products. You also
need to know how team dynamics work, how to provide leadership and
vision, and how to be customer-driven.

What do you need to know?

- To whom do you report? Higher is usually better, but if you report
  to a too-busy top executive you may not get the attention you need.

- Are you classified as a professional and treated and paid
  accordingly? If you aren't, find out why not and what you can do
  about it, then start working to change this.

- How does your budget compare with similar departments, and
  does it include money for travel, professional development, and
  continuing education? Is your equipment as up-to-date as that of
  others in the organization? Librarians are notorious for being too
  complacent about under-funding. You can't be expected to do a
  competent, let alone outstanding, job if you don't have the
  appropriate resources. Make sure you know where you stand. If
  you aren't getting your fair share, then complain, make a plan, and
  get something done about it.

- What do people think of the library? Do all the members of the
  organization know where the library is (or even that there is a
  library)? Do they know the services the library offers and what it
  can do for them?

- What are the critical issues facing the organization and its industry, that is, the "hot buttons?" Where is the organization going in the future—the next year, five years, 10 years? How does it plan to get there? Who are the movers and shakers in the industry and the organization's competitors and partners? What are the key trade organizations, journals, and analysts?

- Every organization has written and unwritten behavioral rules: work hours, work ethic, dress code, writing style, and communication style. You must find these out. Although you don't have to follow the party line exactly, you do need to fit in. Remember that the corporate culture operates on both the organization and department level and that it may not be the same at both (St. Clair 1994). Who eats lunch with whom? It's probably not a great idea to always eat lunch with the secretary of your department. Invite a library user, nonuser, your boss, or even your boss's boss to lunch once in a while. Where you lunch may even be important. If all the managers go out to lunch all the time, what message do you send by eating in the cafeteria or at your desk?

How do you find out all this? Talk to people, ask questions, listen to the answers and even to the talk around the water cooler. Read mission statements, annual reports, long-range plans, organizational charts, catalogs, policies and procedures, budgets, and any other corporate documents you can get your hands on. Arrange for site visits to remote locations; I have found them to be extremely useful. People who are not located at the same site as the library tend to assume that it serves only that location. Visiting users in other places assures them that you really are there to help them, gives you a chance to see what their work is like, and puts faces to names. Don't forget to tour your own facility, including production and maintenance areas. Knowing what goes on in every nook and cranny of the organization is vital information you need to do your job well.

Part of being a successful OPL is the ability to communicate with management. You need to learn what information management needs and in what form it is needed. Then provide it—preferably *before* it is asked for. The format in which you provide information is very important regarding how it is received. Usually, the higher up an executive is, the less information she wants. What management really wants is an answer, not information. If that is beyond your scope, try to give whatever information you have in as concise a manner as possible. Provide the most important information first. Another key in dealing with upper management is to talk in their language. Management neither understands nor cares about library jargon. (For example, it took a lot of convincing for my boss to accept the word "weeding" as a real library term.) Read about management, and learn to use their jargon. Understanding and using terms such as return on investment (ROI), turnover, and mission-critical will enhance your professional status in the eyes of management. Don't confine communication with management to when they make a request. Feed them a steady stream of useful information.

You may find yourself with an impromptu opportunity to market your library, such as finding yourself in the elevator with someone you want to impress. Have a prepared "elevator speech" that has a beginning (the introduction), a middle (the pitch), and an end (a request for action, a meeting, or a visit). Although your time is limited, don't speak too fast. Finally, practice, practice, practice.

The "30-second commercial" is similar to the "elevator speech" but is designed to tell a stranger who you are and what value you can bring him or her. For instance, "I am Judith Siess of Information Bridges International. I specialize in management information for small and solo libraries. I write a blog, OPL Plus, and present workshops around the world. I just finished writing my fourth book." The use of the phrases "solo libraries" and "fourth book" usually generates questions or comments and gives me a chance to tell them more about me and my company.

3

Time Management, Planning, and Prioritization

If I had a nickel for every time an OPL said to me, "How do I find the time to do it all?" I could retire. Let's look at the question more closely.

1. How do *I* (the OPL, who has little or no help in the library)

2. find the *time* (which is finite and cannot be managed)

3. to do it *all*. (You cannot and should not do it all; do only the most important tasks)

Andrew Berner, library director and curator of collections at the University Club in New York and co-founder of *The One-Person Library: A Newsletter for Librarians and Management*, wrote that the "Three Ps" of effective time management are planning, prioritization, and procrastination:

> If ever there was a group for whom time management is an important concept, it's solo librarians. With so much to do and, generally, no one to whom work can be delegated, it becomes essential that the solo librarian be aware of the basic principles of good time management. Too often, however, the librarian seeks time management "tricks," things

63

that will enable a job to be done more quickly. In other words, they seek efficiency, where in fact they should be seeking effectiveness. Time management is not just looking for ways to cut down on the time it takes to do specific tasks (though that certainly can be a part of it). To be sure, there is much more to time management than simply being aware of the importance of planning, priorities and procrastination. Much can—and has—been written on each of them, as well as on the many other aspects of good time management. Still, these are three powerful tools (two to use and one to avoid) in any solo librarian's arsenal of time-management weapons. A knowledge of them can be used to help the librarian function not only in a more efficient manner, but— even more important—in a more effective manner as well. And after all, that's what being a one-person librarian is all about. (Berner in Siess 1997)

TEN MYTHS ABOUT TIME

1. *Myth*: Time can be managed. *Truth*: Activities are managed, not time itself.

2. *Myth*: The longer and harder you work, the more you accomplish. *Truth*: It is better to work effectively.

3. *Myth*: If you want something done right, do it yourself. *Truth*: Delegating is good if done properly, and for an OPL delegating is necessary.

4. *Myth*: You are not supposed to enjoy work. *Truth*: If you do not enjoy what you are doing, you will just become frustrated and feel as if you are always behind.

5.   *Myth*: We should take pride in working hard. *Truth*: Librarians should take pride in working smart.

6.   *Myth*: You should try to do the most in the least amount of time. *Truth*: It is better to do it right.

7.   *Myth*: Technology will help you do it better and faster. *Truth*: Technology can speed up routine stuff but not creative work.

8.   *Myth*: Do one thing at a time. *Truth*: Use your multilevel, multitasking abilities (or lose them).

9.   *Myth*: Handle paper only once. *Truth*: This is an impossible and unnecessary rule. (What planet do they live on?)

10. *Myth*: Get more done, and you will be happier. *Truth*: No, you will just get more done.

STOP WASTING TIME

We all waste time. This is inevitable. What is important is that we learn how we waste it and work toward eliminating as many of the time-wasting behaviors as possible from our work lives. Here are some of the most common ones.

- Attempting too much. This happens if you haven't established priorities and planned, are prone to making unrealistic time estimates, haven't let go of perfectionism, or are a victim of understaffing.

- Being confused about responsibility or authority. Perhaps you lack a job description, have been given responsibility without authority, or work with other employees who are unwilling to accept responsibility for certain projects.

- Being unable or unwilling to say no. This is the most common time-wasting behavior for librarians.

- Having incomplete information. Often, you must go to someone else for the information and a decision, because you don't know what information is needed, the information you need is not provided, or you lack the authority to make a decision.

- Managing by crisis. Many organizations function this way normally. Don't let the lack of contingency plans, overreaction to nonurgent issues, constant putting out of fires, procrastination of action until the last minute, and unrealistic time estimates invade your management style.

- Being disorganized. You have control over your own space and time. Do not allow fear to immobilize you by letting go of your fears of indispensability, loss of control, and forgetting. Don't allow a disorganized workspace, interruptions (including the telephone), and indecision undermine your plans.

One step toward effective time management is to analyze your workday to determine how much time you spend on various activities. There are several ways to do this. The easiest way is to do a time study. First, write down how you think you use your time. Make a list of the tasks that comprise your workday. Include everything, even time at the water cooler or coffee or tea bar, chatting with a colleague, talking on the phone, and opening the mail. Then make up a sheet or grid with all these tasks listed (Figures 3.1 and 3.2). (Don't forget to leave some space for "other," which are those tasks you forgot to include.) You'll need one grid for each day of the study. For at least a week (and even better, two weeks), mark the time you spend on each task. Do this as you do the task. Don't wait until the end of the day and try to recall how you spent your day. Write the time down, even if it is only one or two minutes. You can do this by simply making a note every time you change activities. For example, when the phone rings or someone interrupts you, write down the time and what you were doing. When the study is over, tally the totals for each task. (Don't do this every day because the results likely will influence how you use your time the next day.) Now you can see how you really use your time. Compare it to your prestudy estimate. I can almost guarantee that there will be some surprises.

There are a number of ways to manage your time more effectively. First, decide that you don't have to please everyone. You don't need everyone to like you; in fact, it is impossible.

Second, don't complain, just fix the problem. Your boss does not want problems, only solutions. Don't waste time worrying about problems; worry accomplishes nothing. Don't pursue a lost cause. Yes, it may be an important issue, but if it's going nowhere because of managerial resistance, lack of money, or lack of interest, you can't afford to waste your time on it.

Third, let go; don't be a perfectionist. "Done okay" is better than "perfect but not finished." Most of the time good enough *is* good enough. Resist the temptation to do small, insignificant tasks too well (such as making the monthly report a literary masterpiece). Make a handout or a sign for questions that come up frequently, or create a library frequently asked questions (FAQ) list on your organization's Web page. Don't do what you can buy; outsource what you can, such as cataloging, handling journal subscriptions, and document delivery. Choose the best providers, and let them do the work. If you look over the provider's shoulder constantly, you won't be saving your time.

Day: _____

Time	Quick Reference	Phone	Circ'n	Online & Web	House-keeping	In-house meeting	Outside meeting	Prof'l activities	Personal	Other
Day's total										

Figure 3.1 Sample Time Recording Form

Day: <u>Tuesday, September 15</u>

Time	Quick Reference	Phone	Circ'n	Online & Web	House-keeping	In-house meeting	Outside meeting	Prof'l activities	Personal	Other
8:00–8:15										
8:15–8:30										
8:30–9:00								Read j's		
9:00–10:30						Intranet task force				
10:30–11:30				E-mail						
11:30–11:45	John Smith									
11:45–12:00		Boss								
12:00–1:00									Lunch	
1:00–1:10									Husband	
1:10–1:15										
		Re: OL								
1:15–1:45										
Day's total										

Figure 3.2 Sample Time Recording Form— Partially Completed

Avoid Procrastination

The last of Berner's "Three Ps" is procrastination:

> ... not something that you should work towards, but something that you should avoid, and that is procrastination. Accept the fact that everyone procrastinates sometimes, and understand that guilt will not help to solve the problem. It is very important, however, to keep in mind that you should not assume that because everyone procrastinates it cannot be a serious problem. It can, in fact, rob you of your effectiveness on the job. No matter what you may think and no matter what you may have convinced yourself over the years, no one works best under pressure. Procrastination only insures that you will have to rush to complete a project, and that you will have insufficient time

to check your work and to create a superior product. Procrastination leaves no time for that great despoiler of work: Murphy's Law. If you leave yourself ample time for a project and something goes wrong, you'll be able to correct it and still meet your deadline. Without that sufficient time, however, your work will suffer, and no doubt your reputation will suffer along with it. (Berner in Siess 1997)

Why do you procrastinate? There are many reasons: the task may seem too hard, you may be afraid that you will fail, you may not have enough information, or you may be hoping someone else will do the task. If you don't know where to start, divide the task into smaller parts and start somewhere. What is important is that you start. Take care of unpleasant tasks the first thing in the day so you don't waste time dreading them. Fear of failure can be paralyzing; remember that failure is not a bad thing, assuming you learn from your mistakes. I have never heard of an organization going under because of a librarian's mistake, nor are many librarians fired because of one error. An occasional failure means that you are challenging yourself and not stagnating or becoming complacent.

If you don't have the information you need to do a task, find the information and get on with it. Putting off an unpleasant task, hoping that someone else will do it, seldom works. Other common excuses for procrastination (note that I used the term excuses instead of reasons, because procrastination is never acceptable) are an over-commitment to other projects (you haven't said no enough) or lack of motivation because you believe the task won't make a difference anyway (if you think that, you have an entirely different problem). List the things you have been avoiding. Prioritize them. Try to do at least one of them each day until you catch up. Also, you do *not* work best under pressure; almost no one does. This is just a rationalization for procrastination.

Interruptions can be a form of passive procrastination—a way to avoid working on something. You must learn to control interruptions. If you have a project that requires your complete and uninterrupted attention, hide; go somewhere no one expects you to be and work there.

Timing is important in knowing when to work and when not to. Look at your workday routine. Is it efficient? Does it fit your personal clock? If not, change it. Work on difficult projects when you're at your best. If you are a morning person, as most people are, this is the first two hours of the day. Save an easy task for the end of the day so that you accomplish something and go home satisfied, not frustrated. Stay focused on high-priority activities and limit the time you spend on low-priority tasks, no matter how easy or how much fun they are.

The Art of Saying No

A very important time-management tool is the word "no." As good librarians, obsessed with high-quality customer service, our first inclination is to say yes to every request that comes along—whether it's from a patron or the boss. But OPLs just cannot do everything for everyone. Sometimes the answer must be no. When is it appropriate—or even advisable—to say no?

- When the request is clearly out of your scope. (You do have a written mission statement, don't you?) Don't be afraid to tell a patron, "You should try the public library" when you don't have the resources to answer the question or recognize the question as being for an employee's child's homework.

- When someone else can answer the question better, or cheaper. This could be another library, another department in the organization, an information broker, and so on.

- When you've been asked to do something illegal or unethical. This could be copying an entire book, ordering something on the company account for personal use, or industrial espionage. You must simply tell the patron (or boss) that the request is illegal or unethical and your personal and professional code of ethics will not permit you to fill it.

- When you really don't want to do the job. This is a delicate decision, especially when it comes to your boss, but you should never do something you really don't want to do—you just won't do your best on it.

Why are you afraid to say no? You may want the approval of others, feel a false sense of obligation, haven't the time to think of a better answer, or just don't know how to say no. Perhaps you feel you just can't say no to your boss.

How do you say no? Remember that people take advantage of you only with your permission. Never say yes without thinking about it first. Don't just say no; offer a counter proposal, an alternative. Keep your goals and priorities in mind; if this project does not advance them, say no. When faced with a decision, focus on the business implications of your answer. It is your library and your responsibility; you have the right to set policy. Be firm; don't apologize—it weakens your no. Once you've said no, don't let yourself be badgered into changing your mind.

Other Ways to Make the Most of Your Valuable Time

Time is more valuable than money. After all, you can always get more money, but once time is gone it is gone forever. If it costs more to do it yourself than to hire someone to do it, hire someone. For instance, I found that it was "cheaper" to outsource document delivery to a service rather than spending time locating the documents on OCLC—and it was faster too. An added bonus was the money we saved by dropping our OCLC membership, but the real reason was the time it took away from more important tasks. If you don't value your time, no one else will.

Meetings

Meetings can also waste time. Some meetings, especially those involving planning or with your professional (library) colleagues, can be very worthwhile. However, many are not useful, and you should minimize the number of these you attend. If there is no reason to meet, don't meet. Mackenzie (1990, 137) lists various reasons for holding a meeting. I have added alternatives for achieving the same results without a meeting.

1.   To coordinate action. *Use e-mail.*

2.   To exchange information. *Use e-mail.*

3.   To motivate a team. *You really need to meet.*

4.   To discuss problems on a regular basis. *A meeting is necessary.*

5.   To make a decision. *You can either meet or use e-mail.*

If you do not have time to go to the entire meeting, attend only the part that requires your presence or gives you something of value. Ask if you can send a written report or send another person instead. Say that your boss said you should not go (but make sure he or she knows you are using this excuse). Do not be afraid to leave a meeting if all that you needed, or were needed for, is over. Say that you have another appointment, rather than staying to be polite. Never attend a meeting unless there is a set working agenda and a set ending time.

Before calling a meeting yourself, ask if the problem can be solved or decision reached without a meeting. "Hold a meeting [only] because it is needed, not because it is Tuesday" (Pollar 1996, 90). Phrase the call for a meeting in terms of the action to be taken—to plan, to decide, to evaluate, to solve—and state the problem (Ferner 1995, 177). Put the most important items on the agenda first to make sure they are covered.

Distribute a detailed agenda to all participants before the meeting. Set time limits for each item on the agenda. Keep track of the time and remind participants of the amount of time left—and do not extend the ending time. Do not plan too much for one meeting. Guide the group decision process, keeping people on track, limiting discussion, and trying for consensus rather than a vote. After the meeting, evaluate how it went, what decisions were made, and what action needs to be taken. Was the meeting worthwhile? Did the benefits exceed the costs, that is, the time spent of those who attended? Send out a post-meeting memo with action items for each participant. The length of a meeting is usually closely correlated with the number of people attending; have as few people as possible at a meeting. Avoid food at meetings; it will only slow them down. (If you must have food, save it for after the meeting—that will speed things up.)

Filing

Almost everyone dislikes filing. Here are some suggestions to save time. Never file envelopes unless the postmark is significant; put the address in your card file instead. Write a keyword on the item when you read it, before you put it in your filing tray. File according to how you'll use it, not where it came from. Follow Judy's first law of filing: If you have trouble finding something in the files, put it back where you first looked for it.

You can do only five things with any piece of information: Toss it, refer it (to someone else), act on it, file it, or read it. The following "logic-based disposal" rules make deciding what to do with a piece of paper easy:

- Does it require action on my part? If not, toss it or file it.

- Does it exist elsewhere? If so (and it is easy to get to), toss it.

- Is it outdated? If so, toss it.

- Will I really use it again? If not, toss it. Don't use "just in case" logic.

- Are there tax or legal implications? If so, file it.

• What's the worst thing that could happen if I don't have this info? If you can live with the answer, toss it.

• Does anyone else need this info? If so, file it or give it to them.

Your Reading List

Accept the fact that you probably will never be able to read everything you would like to (or think you ought to). Read with a pen in your hand. A quick scan is better than a complete reading that is never done. Split your reading list with a colleague. Tear out or photocopy articles you want to read, and put them in a folder; then take the folder with you everywhere. Take advantage of waiting time to whittle away your reading file.

E-Mail

E-mail helps us keep in touch with customers and colleagues. However, you can waste a lot of time on e-mail. Limit the number of times a day you check your e-mail; two or three times a day probably will be enough. Delete e-mail you've already read and acted upon, but if you think you might use an address again, file it somewhere; addresses are too hard to track down again. I have a separate folder labeled "addresses to save" and purge it regularly for ones no longer of use.

Telephone Calls

Control the telephone rather than letting it control you and your time. You do *not* have to answer it every time it rings. Use an answering machine or voice mail when you are working on a rush project, when a project requires all your attention, or when helping a customer. The message you record should clearly identify your library, you, or both. If you are out of the office for a day or more, the message should say when you will return and what to do or whom to call in the meantime. If you are just busy or on the phone, the message should say something such as: "I'm sorry that I can't help you right now, but I am now giving my full attention to another client. Please leave a detailed message with your information need, and I will get back to you as soon as I can." This says that you care about the client's question, are working with someone else, and will return the call. Listen to your greeting occasionally and make sure it is still appropriate. Check your machine frequently, and return calls as soon as possible. You want to become known for answering messages promptly so that customers will not be reluctant to leave messages for you.

Answer the phone with your name and the name of your institution. Be prepared to repeat it because most people do not listen to the initial greeting. "Keep a 'hot list' of important but not often called numbers by each telephone so you can find them in a hurry if needed" (Tomlin 2000, 8). An idea I got from the beauty shop is to put the telephone number by the person's name in your appointment book (or on your calendar) so you can call if a delay occurs or if you need directions.

Even More Time-Management Hints

Use multitasking to get more done. Always have something to read or do while you wait; while on hold on the telephone, check e-mail or open mail. Ask yourself, "Can someone else do this task?" Use the cataloging of others rather than doing your own. Outsource whenever possible (internally and externally). Carry a pen or pencil and paper with you at all times to write down thoughts as they occur to you. Keep a set of boilerplate files on the computer with common answers to common questions, headers, references, order forms, interlibrary loan requests, and so on. Store all documents you might use again on your computer. Arrange your office and desk to increase efficiency; put what you use most often close at hand. Allow time for unexpected problems; this will allow you to meet your deadlines without undue stress. If possible, group appointments so all the interruptions are together and you have more blocks of time to work. At the end of the day, check e-mail, check voice mail, go through the mail and to-do files, and review what you want to do the next day. You will feel better when you leave, and can leave the office at the office.

Manage Your Absences

As an OPL, it is mandatory that you get out of the office occasionally. You need to visit other libraries, make contacts, take continuing education courses, and attend professional conferences. You need to do so even more than librarians who work with large staffs, yet you may think you can't leave. You can; you are not indispensable. The organization can do without you; your career or family cannot. Take your vacation. Attend at least one professional conference per year.

Plan for each type of absence: temporary, short-term, and long-term. Temporary absences are those that take a few minutes, such as delivering a document, getting the mail, buying a cup of coffee, and going to the bathroom. Put a sign on your door or desk that says: "The librarian will be right back. Please wait, or leave a message." (Make sure you leave notepaper and pencils nearby.) You may be away for a day or two during a short-term absence because of an illness, a vacation, off-site training, or jury duty. If you know about the absence in advance, let people know with a sign or by e-mail. (It doesn't necessarily mean they will plan ahead, but at least they were warned.) Arrange to have your mail taken care of, and be sure to leave an appropriate message on your answering machine or voice mail (or have the phone calls sent to someone else to answer). It's a good idea to have a place for people to leave books and journals, requests for materials, and other things for you outside your door. Make sure it is a secured box so people can't take items out of it as well.

If you plan well for long-term absences, your clients will manage (not so well that they don't still need you, but enough to keep the organization running). Make sure you have a written manual of policies and procedures. Leave a list of sources to consult for reference, document delivery, help, and the name of a reputable information broker or consultant with whom you have set up an account. (There is an additional benefit to this. Your clients will find out the real cost of obtaining information and then will better appreciate the services you provide.) Your Web site or intranet page should have prominently posted "how-to" instructions and other Web sites that they may be helpful. Notify vendors to expect delays in processing invoices if they send them during your absence. You may want to suggest they send invoices early. Secure sensitive files and other paper and electronic data, such as circulation records, computer passwords or access codes, and original copies of software or videos. Don't forget to set your e-mail to "nomail" for the duration.

PLANNING

Why Plan?

Time management is important, but it will not be effective unless you first do Berner's two other Ps: planning and prioritization. What will the future bring for your library? What do you *want* it to bring? If there is going to be any chance for the future to turn out the way you want, you must plan. If you don't plan the future of your library, someone else will—and it's not likely to be the future you envision. Berner says of planning:

> Without a sense of where you want to go, how can you ever know if you are going in the right direction? Without planning you merely struggle through the day-to-day operations of the library—relieved no doubt, to get through each day—but you never bring your library any closer to realizing its ultimate goals. How can you if you have no idea what those goals are? Yet isn't that movement toward specified goals—for our libraries, for our parent organizations, and for ourselves—one of the things that marks us as professionals? Without it we are really nothing more than clerks. The most often-heard cry is, "but I don't have time for planning!" I can only respond by saying you'd better find the time. Doing long-range planning will give you the direction you need for intermediate planning and for short-term planning. Before you know it, you'll have a sense of direction, which may have been lacking in your work before, and suddenly you'll find that you can be making decisions about the work you

do (e.g., do I really need to do this?) rather than simply fill-
ing your day with tasks that seem to have no purpose.
Unfortunately, libraries rarely plan. Instead they react to
what others have already decided in such areas as budgets
and staffing and then "plan" to make the best of the situation. Proper planning, by contrast, is a proactive process. ...
(Berner in Siess 1997)

What Is Strategic Planning?

"Strategies are policies (written or unwritten) that guide organizational decisions, and they are tied inextricably to the nature, direction,
and basic purpose of an organization" (Penniman 1999, 52). "Strategic
planning is essentially a process of relating an organisation and its people to their changing environment and the opportunities and threats in
the marketplace; it is a process in which purposes, objectives and action
programmes are developed, implemented, monitored, evaluated and
reviewed. ... [It is] particularly concerned with anticipating and
responding to environmental factors, taking responsibility for change,
and providing unity and direction to a firm's activities. It is a tool for
ordering one's perceptions about future environments in which one's
decisions might be played out (Corrall 1995).

Planning also allows you to focus your thinking on the future. People
(and especially OPLs) often get so caught up in the moment, fighting fires
and keeping their heads above water, that they forget about the future—
where they are heading. Planning also saves time, fights uncertainty, helps
you focus on your objectives, and is critical for efficiency. In other words,
planning equals control. "The greatest value of the plan is the process, the
thinking that went into it" (Beckwith 1997, 61).

How Do You Plan?

First, decide what you want (or must) accomplish this year. Then, talk
to your boss. What does he or she expect for next year? What are his or

her priorities? Next, talk to your users. Get an idea of both their concrete needs and their dreams. Consider a user survey. Follow-up on complaints or requests that you weren't able to fill. Finally, talk to nonusers. Why don't they use the library? What could you do to draw them in? Now, take a look at your current services. Do all of them need to be continued? Can you justify continuing them? Which new services do you want to add? Why? How will the organization benefit from them? This is a good time for blue-sky thinking. Think not only of the possible but the impossible, and see if you can make it happen. Include some items from your wish list. Not only does doing so show that you are a forward thinker, but it also gives the powers-that-be something to cut (so they feel they've fulfilled their fiscal responsibilities).

You should now be able to make a list of goals for next year. "It is important to have a clear goal. However, this goal should be a stretch goal (one that seems at first glance to be impossible) and must relate directly to what your company is doing or is planning. It will be a moving target in that as you close in on it, it will change or you will be ready to upgrade it to something even more challenging, depending on the situation" (Wilson and Mount 1997, 21).

Vision and Mission Statements

You also need a vision statement and a mission statement. "A vision ... is a clearly articulated statement of what you wish your institution to become, i.e., a future-oriented statement" (Penniman, 51). A mission statement says "1) what the institution does, 2) for whom it does it, 3) how it does it, and 4) why." Put goals in writing so you can review them. Goals must be concrete, measurable, and achievable. Goals also must have deadlines and must be put in writing. Remember that you should have a reasonable expectation of meeting these goals, given the budget you are seeking. It also is important that you and your boss have a way of measuring or knowing when you have met them. List the key tasks required to achieve the goal, the order in which the tasks need to be done, and the resources needed to carry out each task. Set deadlines for your goals to keep you moving forward and minimize procrastination. Keep your eye on your goals. It is easier to determine what is important in the short run when you know what you want in the long run.

Then set priorities. Priorities are ranked goals. Then relate daily activities to goals and priorities. Finally, list the resources you need to meet these goals. Resources include money; resources, staff, equipment, technology, space, coordination, and authority. Your strategic plan should cover one year in detail and three to five years in a brief form.

The written plan should include the following:

• Your vision and mission statement.

• A summary of environmental forces and market trends.

• The key objectives and priorities of your plan, with annual, measurable librarywide goals and objectives. Describe where you are now and where you want to go.

• The human resource strategy and financial projections. Include resources needed, such as staff, money, and technology, along with where they will come from. Don't plan for a specific technology; rather, plan for a specific mission and a specific vision, and then use the available technology to fulfill your mission and vision.

• A timeline for the implementation of the plan.

• Ways in which you will allow for feedback, evaluation, and adjustments to the plan.

Don't forget that writing the plan, although an important process, is of no value unless you actually implement the plan.

You can find samples of other libraries' plans on the Web. Most will be from larger libraries, but you can get ideas from them. Your plan should follow the same format as that of your parent organization and have similar goals.

Do you say, "I don't have time for this"? Well, you'd better make the time. Strategic planning is a valuable management tool. It is also about management of change. Strategic planning strengthens the role of the library in the organization. It can demonstrate the librarian's competence and improves the image and visibility of the library. Planning provides a framework for policy formulation and decision making. Planning can help support your case for funding. Planning identifies critical issues and constraints. Planning can keep you on course.

PRIORITIZATION

Berner wrote,

> Not everything you do is of equal importance and you should be able to differentiate among your various tasks and duties to set your priorities. You should also be aware of the fact that priorities are not constant. While it is helpful to list tasks and goals in writing and to assign them a priority, you cannot make the mistake of thinking that they are carved in stone. Priorities are constantly shifting as new tasks and new developments come into play. Whatever you may be working on, for example, it is likely that if your boss calls or comes in with a request, that request is going to become your number one priority (unless, of course, your boss's boss calls with a request, and then you may have to reevaluate). The important thing is to recognize that whatever criteria you may use for determining priority—and there are many— you should always be working on your highest priority items at any given time. (Berner in Siess 1997)

Work efficiently. Eighty percent of your time is taken up by 20 percent of your tasks. Prioritizing and planning ensure that you are doing the right 20 percent. Here are five rules for decision-making using the 80/20 or Pareto principle:

1. Twenty percent of decisions are important, the other 80 percent are not. The trick is to figure out the most important 20 percent. Don't agonize over the unimportant decisions, and don't overanalyze your decisions.

2. The most important decisions often are those made only by default. The critical decision point may come and go before you recognize it. Make sure you are asking the right questions. The right answer to the wrong question is meaningless.

3. Always make a decision. Act as if you are 100 percent confident that the decision is right. Once you have made the decision, don't let yourself be pushed into changing your mind.

4. If it isn't working, cut your losses early and abandon the project or task.

5. If it is working, stay with it—even redoubling your efforts.

Question Things

Just because you *can* do something doesn't mean you *should*. You must question things:

• What is the objective? Will doing the task help me achieve my business or personal goals?

• WIIFM, that is, What's in it for me? What's the payoff going to be? How will I know if I'm successful? How will I be rewarded?

• Is this task something I want to do? Will doing it make me bored, unhappy, or even miserable?

- Is it something I have to do? Or, is it something someone else can do? Can I add value to the task? Or, is it something anybody could do?

- Do I have the time to do it? Am I willing to pay the price (in giving up my precious time) to accomplish the task?

- Is this trip necessary? Is there a better way to do it? Should it even be done at all?

- What if I don't do this? Will the world come to an end? Am I willing to accept the consequences that not doing the task may incur?

- WHIGTL, that is, What have I got to lose?

- Will it go away if I ignore it? If no one misses it, maybe it didn't need doing in the first place?

You don't have to do everything everybody tells you to do. You also don't have to do everything the way other people tell you to do it. Nor do you have to do everything according to someone else's time frame. Finally, you don't always have to do everything yourself.

You must be both efficient and effective. Efficiency is completing a task with the least possible amount of wasted labor, cost, or time. Effectiveness refers to the quality of the work, doing things right. Too many businesses spend lots of time making sure they are doing things right and not enough determining if they are doing the right things. Doing the wrong things right is the epitome of wasted time; doing the right things well is the epitome of efficiency and effectiveness.

4

Financial Matters

Budgeting, bill processing, and other financial matters are among the tasks most dreaded by librarians. Because, as one-person librarians we have no one to whom we can delegate, we must learn to dispel our fears and master some financial skills.

BUDGETING

The budget is a management tool that is often underestimated. As the librarian, you must have input into your budget. You should justify each item in terms of how it will save the time and money of your customers, but be realistic, remembering the financial situation of your parent organization.

There are many types of budgets, but none is best for all libraries. What is best is what management requires. A line-item budget lists items along with their proposed costs. A functional budget groups related activities and most often includes only expenses, not revenues. A capital budget accounts for long-term resources, such as buildings and equipment.

To begin the budget process, think about where you will be at the end of the current budget year. Factor in known internal or external cost changes and inflation. If you are adding new services, you may need to cut current costs. Perhaps you can consolidate operations, eliminate little-used services, or reduce expensive resources. If you charge for your services, consider increasing your prices. Also consider moving your costs to someone else's budget.

You need to be familiar with the budget or planning cycle of your organization. Budgeting can be a one-year process or may go on all year long. Make sure you understand your budget, how the numbers are derived, whether they are actual or estimated, and who has responsibility for what. If possible, find out the level of funding of other similarly placed departments. Try to locate all pockets of money for information in other parts of the organization and get all that money under your control. Get to know the finance people assigned to the library accounts. Talk to them throughout the year, not just at budget time or when there is a problem.

If your boss does not ask for your input on the library budget, prepare one and give it to your boss anyway—for the record—even if he or she does not use it. Preparing a budget is a good exercise and identifies you as a forward-thinking, responsible professional. Make sure that your boss knows that you won't ask for something unless you think it will help your customers (and *always* couch requests in those terms). He or she should also be convinced that you research your purchases and always make the most economical choices.

Point out to your boss that if the organization wants a library it must be willing to fund the library appropriately. An organization with one librarian who is interested in and able to manage all information expenditures can effect tremendous economies of scale and cost savings. Make it clear to management that an appropriate budget is something you, as a professional, expect.

Question everything when budgeting. Use the technique of zero-based budgeting (i.e., justify every expense, every year). Be realistic—include some pie-in-the-sky items, but understand that they are likely to be cut. However, don't be limited by available money; if a service is important enough (and you present it in the right way), the money will be found.

Prioritize your requests; put the most important items first. Know the difference between purchases that can be capitalized and those that cannot. Separate recurring and fixed expenses. Budgets are often based on office politics, so be sure to show how a service will make the organization and upper management look good, produce more, or save time. Be ready to negotiate, because a negative response is not always a final one.

Some categories that you should include in your budget are the following:

- Periodical subscriptions

- Book purchasing

- Online database services

- Document delivery

- Library-specific supplies

- Your training and continuing professional education

- Computer hardware and software

BOOKKEEPING

In order to create a budget you need data. Bookkeeping needn't be complicated. Use whatever method works for you. Some OPLs use Excel or Quattro Pro spreadsheets to keep track of expenditures. You can make each cost center or category a separate spreadsheet and link the spreadsheets to a summary sheet for monthly or annual reports. You can keep a running total of expenditures and subtract it from available funds. Other OPLs use an accounting program, such as Quicken, or a database, such as Access. You don't even need to use the computer. You can make folders for each category and put all the information relating to that category into the appropriate folder. But you must track every expense that goes through the library, including items ordered for others. Ask your accounting department for monthly reports and check them against your records.

I highly recommend charging back, at least for out-of-pocket items. Yes, it takes some time and can be a hassle (although less so if you do it right), but your customers will value your services more because they will see how much information you provide for so little money. My clients were almost always surprised at how little online searches cost. If everything is provided for free, two things will result: The customers will tend to over-use your services and undervalue them. Often people think of things as being worth just what they cost; a high-cost service must be better than a free one. Charging back puts the cost of information services into the budgets of those who use them, so that they are considered part of the cost of doing business. However, many organizations prefer that all information costs be covered by the library.

Here is one way to charge back without pain. Create a request form that includes the account number to be charged and a place for the signature of someone authorized to charge on the account. Include the copyright and ILL statements on this form. When the bill for the service or item comes in, you already have the approval. Just add the charge number, sign the form, and send it to accounts payable. You avoid sending the invoice to the requestor for approval, waiting for it to be returned, following up on it, requesting a second invoice when the requestor loses the original, and so on.

DECLINING BUDGETS

It is highly likely that sometime during your career you will be asked to cut your budget or spending. There are some ways you can minimize the impact on your library. The most important thing to remember is to anticipate the worst. Have a plan so you don't panic and make a wrong move. Go back to basics. Ask yourself what the library is supposed to be doing? Are you fulfilling its mission or have you gotten off the track with new projects that are peripheral to your central mission—taking care of your customers?

A cutback will not come as a surprise to you if you are plugged into what is going on. As the information guru in the organization, you should be in a position to hear all the news about promotions, lay-offs, new projects, and newly won contracts. Your connections to upper management will pay off big in times of crisis.

Library legend Herb White once said that if they tell you your budget has been cut by 50 percent, just ask "What 50 percent of my services do you want me to cut?" *Never, never* say, "I'll manage." By doing so you, a) do the profession and yourself a disservice, and b) make it more likely that your budget will be cut further in the future. After all, you've already shown that you can "do more with less." Resist the temptation to cut back-office expenses such as your continuing professional education or travel budget; in challenging times you have a greater need to learn new and more cost-effective ways to serve your users.

R. Lee Hadden (employed by the U.S. Government in Virginia) gives you the best way to deal with a budget cut.

> Cut library services and hours. Then let patrons complain directly to the administration. The administration will turn instead to a less assertive office to cut budgets. The absolute worst thing you can do is absorb the cuts with no change in patron services. If you accept the cuts meekly, you will train the administration that you are a free service that can be cut at will and without cost. You must show that any cut in library staff and services will cut the services to the library patrons first. If they say you should cut back on buying books, smile and ask sweetly which departments should be cut first and by how much, and would they please put that in writing.

I would even put a sign by the product or service that was cut saying, "(name of product) is no longer available due to budget cuts.

Direct complaints to (name of person who cut the budget)." Your customers' voices speak much louder than yours.

Former hospital librarian Anne Tomlin (2000) wrote, "Even in the worst of times, someone turns a profit. [In financial hard times] look for ways to (a) cut costs reasonably—in dollars or staff time, and (b) bring in departmental revenue by charging back costs to other departments, establishing fee-based services, or mining for grant monies. Even if the actual amounts [saved by the above measures] are small, it demonstrates your commitment to being a part of the cost-containment game." Or, as Herb White (1997b, 1) said, "*In the absence of money, there is always money. If it is worth doing, someone will find money to do it*" (emphasize mine).

You also need to position your library as a low-cost, high-value service. As far back as 1979, White (1995) observed, "The library cannot spend enough, no matter how extravagant we get, to affect earnings by even one cent per share. ..." This is still true. In fact, it is far better, and most likely cheaper, to have information and research services in-house rather than relying on outside sources, although any number of outsourcing services will tell your management the opposite. A budget crisis is also the time to call in any favors you have done for your customers. As Tomlin (2000) says: "Gratitude can bring on generosity. Going the extra mile creates a strong customer base of people who will be the library's more ardent advocates in good time[s] and, more importantly, hard times." You should have built up a network of advocates within the organization (especially at high levels) that will fight for you. However, if all of your efforts fail to get the message across, polish up your resume. A company that does not value your contribution is not where you want to work.

MONEY-SAVING TIPS

There are many easy ways to save money. Instead of purchasing expensive journals, you can retrieve articles from the Web, from document delivery services, by reciprocal lending arrangements set up formally through library networks and consortia, and through informal networks of colleagues. You also can save on book orders by buying on the Web or from a local discount bookseller, becoming a reviewer for library journals, or purchasing overstocked books directly from the government or publisher. Take advantage of group purchases through consortia, vendor discounts, prepayment deals that save shipping charges, and multiyear renewals that cost less than annual renewals. You can nearly always negotiate costs, fees, and even payment terms with vendors. One library allows coffee in the library only if people use lids sold by the library. I held annual book sales, offering the books removed from the collection to employees at a nominal cost. (Fundraisers also can serve as a chance to promote the library and remind users of its place in their lives.) Revenue can be generated by doing research or purchasing documents for outside customers (if your organization's policy allows). This is most commonly done by law or hospital libraries. When the library brings in "new" money (that is, from sources outside of the organization), it becomes more valuable to management and improves the possibility of avoiding major budget cuts.

CONCLUSION

Budgeting and finances need not be complicated or time-consuming. Just use your common sense, and streamline the process. Keep in communication with those who control your money. Make sure you understand what is going on in the organization, and make sure the organization understands what is going on in the library. Be sure your customers appreciate the value of information and of your services. Be prepared for the worst, and aim for the best.

5

Communication, Marketing, and Advocacy

O
PLs may be alone in the library, but they certainly are not alone in their organizations or profession. Therefore, knowing how to work well with others is especially vital for them. In this chapter you will find out about better communication, library promotion and publicity, networking, and professionalism.

COMMUNICATION

Almost nothing is more important to an OPL than communication. No one will know what you can do if you don't tell them. You cannot serve your users unless you know what they need or want. Doing so involves communication—not just public relations, conversation, or the reference interview, but *communication*.

Real communication is an interactive process. One person sends a message, and another receives it. When you are the sender, the key is to make sure that the message received is the same as the one you meant to send. When you are the recipient, make sure you are receiving the right message.

What Do You Need to Communicate and to Whom?

You communicate with your boss and your boss's boss (upper management). Former dean of the Indiana University library school, Herb White (1995, 213), said that "The purpose of management communication ... is to get something accomplished." Therefore, it is important to communicate with your boss and upper management in the same way as they do with each other. Use your elevator speech when you encounter the chief executive officer (or another top management person) in the elevator or hall. Your speech can be about your mission, capabilities, current money needs, hot news about a customer or competitor, or a recent accomplishment. Start with something to get his or her attention, then introduce yourself, make your pitch, and—most importantly—close the sale (that is, request action such as a meeting to discuss his or her information needs).

Users and management need to be reminded that you are a professional. If you have an advanced degree (library or otherwise), hang your diploma on the wall of your office (or library) and consider putting your degrees on your business card. Do not be intimidated by the degrees of your users. Remember that you, too, are an expert in your own field.

You need to communicate your value to others. Whenever a user says, "I couldn't have done this without you," or "Gee, now I have the information to cinch the contract," or "The information you gave me saved the company money," have him or her document how you helped and send the documentation to your boss. Put testimonials in your newsletter or frame them and hang them on the wall.

You communicate with your users. Make sure that they know about all the resources you have available—those in the library and the others that you have access to, such as subscription-only databases or other libraries via interlibrary loan. They should come to think of you and your library as a one-stop, full-service, low-cost supplier of high-quality information for your organization. Last, but definitely not least, your users need to know that *you* are the most important resource in your library. O'Leary (2000) wrote:

> Even the most information-literate end-user/customer is behind [the information tools learning] curve. Bob Schwarzwalder of the Ford Motor Company defines marketing as customer enlightenment, and describes his role as "Huckster-in-Chief," whose job is to sell and to really educate people on the power of information and the potential of what information technologies can do for them. Our customers understand their information needs, but they don't understand the tools that can satisfy them.

You communicate with your colleagues. It is especially vital for the OPL to stay in contact with other librarians since, as a rule, our collections usually are small and narrowly focused. We often receive questions for which we do not have ready answers. Therefore, it is good to know other librarians and the contents of their collections. I often called another library when I knew they had what I needed. I always got what I wanted because I had made the effort to visit other libraries and, thus, became more than a disembodied voice on the other end of the phone. I also had made it clear that I would reciprocate by providing information from my own collection whenever I could. You can find out whom you should visit by going to local, regional, and national conferences and meetings and talking with people.

You should also communicate with the public. When was the last time you read about an OPL in the newspaper or the nonlibrary press? If the rest of the world doesn't know what we do, maybe it's because we haven't told them. Why not write for the popular, business, medical, or legal press? Most publications, including the scholarly press, are hungry for articles, especially from a new angle, such as from the viewpoint of an OPL. To get published in a nonlibrary professional publication (such as a medical journal), offer to co-write an article with a member of that profession, such as a doctor, nurse, or lawyer, who uses and values your library. You may do most of the writing, but it is the MD, RN, or Esq. that will get the article published.

You are also on the receiving end of communication. Listen to your users to find out what information they need. A lot has been written about user information needs. Before I go further, I will get up on my soapbox and say a bit about them. Most user studies are not about user *needs*, but about user demands and sometimes about user wants. *Demands* are what the user asks for. *Wants* are what the user says he or she wants. *Needs* are what the user really wants but probably can't articulate without probing by the librarian. Here is an example from my own experience. A man came into the library and asked for an atlas (the demand). I asked him what he wanted it for so I could give him the right one. He said he was going to look up the mileage from Cleveland to Columbus (the want). After further questioning, I found out he wanted this number for his expense account (the need). I provided him with the official mileage that the organization authorized for Cleveland to Columbus, an entirely different number. If I had just filled his information demand, I would have done him a disservice by not meeting his information need. (Off my soapbox.)

The best way to find out what your users want and need is to ask them. Here are some questions to get you started.

- What tools do you use in your everyday information seeking?

- Where do you go for information other than the library? Why? Why not the library?

- How many times have you not looked for information because you didn't think you could find it, it would take too long, or cost too much?

- If money were no object, what would you like the library to do? (Caution: Be sure to tell them that you cannot guarantee that you will be able to do it, but you will try.)

Ask management what they expect from you and your library. Do they expect you to maintain the status quo or to be on the leading edge of technology and librarianship? Are you supposed to serve the entire organization or just one area? If you do not get an answer the first time you ask, keep asking (in different ways, if necessary) until you are satisfied that you understand exactly what is expected of you. After all, how can you meet the expectations of management if you don't know what they are?

How to Communicate Better

Words are not the only way you communicate. Words (or content) make up only a small part of the message you send. The sound of your voice accounts for a large part, but the major part of your message involves your appearance, look, and style.

1. Look the part of a professional. Act and dress professionally. Clothing details depend on the dress code in your organization. (All organizations have a dress code, whether written or informal.) If managers wear suits, then wear a suit. If the majority of your users dress casually, then dress like your users.

2. Say what you mean and mean what you say. In oral communications, your tone and inflection are very important. To see what I mean, say the following sentence seven times, each time emphasizing a different word: "I didn't say you took the money." People like to hear their names, so use them frequently. Make eye contact. Use hand gestures only when appropriate. When writing, make sure you read over what you write, especially with e-mail because it is very tempting to send a hasty and perhaps imprudent reply. Avoid slang and profanity in both speech and writing.

People have widely varying styles of communication. You must find out how the person you are communicating with wants to receive information. Some people want all the details; others want only an executive summary. If you send a long and detailed report to the executive summary–type person, he or she probably will ignore it. Should you report in writing, or will a report in person be better (such as when there may be questions you will need to answer)? Because today most workplaces are multicultural, be aware of the ways different cultures interpret words, gestures, and personal space. If your customer is not fluent in English, provide a translation or at least communicate in writing.

Sometimes you must deal with difficult people. We have all encountered someone who just isn't responding to us, who may even be obstructionist or downright hostile. Sometimes you can just ignore the person, but what if this difficult person is your boss or an important customer? Brinkman and Kirschner (1994) identify "The 10 Most Unwanted List" of difficult people. Here are a few I have met personally and my ideas for dealing with them.

1.   The know-it-all who doesn't like to be corrected or contradicted and blames you when something goes wrong. A common type, keep him or her well informed of your activities and the consequences of any action.

2.   The think-they-know-it-all who knows some stuff but likes being the center of attention. Sometimes you may just have to ignore his or her boasts.

3.   The yes person who, to avoid confrontation, says yes to everything and winds up overcommitted. To keep from becoming one of these, learn to say no.

4.   The maybe person who will do anything to avoid making a decision. Make it easy for him or her to make a decision, preferably in your favor, by giving several clear options and adding a box so he or she can just check off an answer.

5. The no person who always knows why something will not work. Use the same technique as for number 4, while reminding him or her that your other ideas have worked out well.

6. The whiner who is overwhelmed and brings his or her problems to you, but really does not want a solution. This person is just looking for a sounding board. Listen, but not long enough to interfere with your own work.

We all have to negotiate something from time to time whether it's a salary, a contract with a vendor, a deadline, or job responsibilities. Be realistic, be flexible, and present your side in terms of the benefits to the other side. As Guy St. Clair (1995d) put it, "Always stress the money angle." Show how you have progressed, and be patient. He also said (1993), "If you don't need a permanent record of the interaction, use the phone. If there is room for misunderstanding, write a memo. If you need a written response, write. If you need to 'talk' to more than one person, write rather than call."

THE ANNUAL REPORT

St. Clair and Williamson (1992, 138) said that the annual report might be "the single most important document the one-person librarians will produce during the year." You should definitely write one and send it to your boss and your boss's boss and, in summary form, to your users. Use the report to inform management of the problems and strengths of the library.

Make writing the annual report easier with advance planning and some organization. Keep statistics and notes during the year. If you use a diary or calendar, note what you accomplished each day or special things you want to include in your report. If you file a monthly or quarterly report, use this as the basis for the annual report, including just the highlights. Be brief, avoid library jargon (business jargon is fine), and assume the reader is interested and educated. Do not be afraid to toot your own horn because that's what the report is for. Keep the report simple.

Include a short history of the library, just enough to put the report in context and explain the role of the library in the organization. If you have a formal mission statement, include it. Mention any significant events held or special visitors, as well as significant purchases or gifts that have added to the collection. Show how they support your users and the parent organization. Concentrate on results and benefits to the organization, not statistics. List current services offered to your clientele and describe new and enhanced products and services introduced during the year. Were they successful? Will they be continued? Did any fail? A very important part of the annual report is a recounting of your professional activities (conferences or continuing education courses attended, offices held, papers written, and so on). Doing so reinforces your professional status and attitude. Be sure to show the benefits that your organization realized from these activities. If you received an award or received a thank you letter for something you did, include it.

There should be a section of the report that contains hard numbers. Include a financial statement (including fund surpluses and deficits), usage statistics, figures on acquisitions and technical services, and any measures of customer satisfaction that you have collected.

End the annual report with your plans and vision for the future. Which new services do you plan to implement or continue? Which might you eliminate? How will your plans and vision affect the users, and the budget? If written and used properly, the library annual report can be a record of what you have accomplished and what you hope to accomplish and is an effective marketing tool. Finally, make it look good. Get help from your organization's graphics department if you can.

ORAL PRESENTATIONS

At some point in your career you will have to make an oral presentation. It may be to your colleagues or upper management, or you may give a workshop. You will be nervous—every time. (If you are not nervous, it means you aren't taking the presentation seriously enough.) Know your audience. Make sure you are telling them what they want to know. The best way to calm your nerves is to be prepared. Know your material inside and out. Be flexible and prepared to skip sections in which the audience does not seem to be interested. Arrive early to check out the room and equipment. It is a good idea to have a backup (old-fashioned paper or transparencies) for audiovisual presentations.

Your presentation should state your purpose, support it with strong arguments and stories, give the audience a specific action to take, explain the benefits of that action, and then sum it all up. People remember best what they hear last. Speak simply; avoid jargon, acronyms, and idioms. When speaking to a multinational audience, avoid U.S.-centric examples. Make sure your gestures are appropriate; some common gestures used by Americans are considered obscene in other cultures. Present numbers graphically. If you are using handouts, try providing only an outline during the presentation, followed by a more complete set or copies of visual presentations after the session. (Doing so will allow your audience to concentrate on you and not your handouts.) Take a deep breath, then relax. You know your material and the audience is ready to learn what you have to say. They are yours.

WORKING WITH YOUR BOSS

Perhaps the most important relationship you have as an OPL is the one with your boss. It is even more important than the librarian-user relationship. Your boss probably does not and probably will never really understand and appreciate the library as much as you do, but he or she can be a powerful advocate for you and your library. It is important to make your boss look good. You will then look good, and he or she will support you when you really need it. Go to your boss with "solutions, not problems" (Merry 1994, 68) and remember that managers do *not* like surprises. Keep him or her informed of any potential problems. Try not to go over your boss's head—except when it is absolutely necessary. This is sometimes necessary when a problem arises that will affect the library and your boss isn't willing or able to help. You should keep your supervisor informed about what you are doing and what you plan to do so that he or she can respond to any suggested changes from upper management in the way that you would like. You can be the best librarian the organization has ever had and your users can love you, but if your boss is not convinced of your worth you will not last long. Most likely you report to a nonlibrarian; your boss is probably not the top official in the company. In fact, your boss can be someone entirely outside of the organization (such as a mayor or a board of trustees). Your boss has many other people to supervise. Your boss is not interested in the library's day-to-day operations or problems, but only that the library functions well. The library's budget is usually a small part of the organization's overall financial plan. Finally, your boss may or may not be a library user.

What can you do to improve your relationship with your boss? You probably will have to educate your boss, especially if you are establishing a new library for the organization. Even if there has been a library at your institution forever, you have to let the boss know who you are, your work style, and what you plan to do. You also have to learn the same about your boss. What are his or her priorities for the library? Is the budget expandable? To whom does your boss report? And what are the priorities of your boss's boss? How does he or she want to communicate? How often? Should you report in person, by written report, or by e-mail? Does your boss want all the details (probably not) or just a summary of your activities? Perhaps your boss wants only a report of major accomplishments or problems. (If you report a problem, be sure to include how you plan to address it.)

Does your boss really have power, or is he or she just a supervisor with the real decision-making authority resting at a higher level? If your boss is just a supervisor, resist the temptation to go over his or her head and right to the decision maker. Organizations want you to follow the rules and lines of communication. Of course, you can always copy your boss's boss on memos that you think your boss will be tempted to ignore or not act on. That way you can have your cake and eat it too. If you have a boss that is really blocking your ability to run the library, consider finding a new boss.

Kevin Kearns (1997) advised that you do not have to use psychological tricks to deal with your boss, nor do you have to become friends with your boss. You don't have to change your style completely to get along with your boss, although you may have to make some modifications. Most importantly, you do not have to give in to your boss. Learn to disagree respectfully and constructively. If you have tried all these strategies and still cannot get along with your boss, you have only two choices: put up with it or start polishing that resume to look for a new job.

What about library committees? Many OPLs swear by them; some probably swear *at* them. Library committees can be quite effective, but they must be advisory and not decision-making committees. All must know that you, the trained librarian, are the one responsible for the library. A library committee should not include your boss but should be composed of library users who are knowledgeable about the needs of the organization and how to get things done. If there is to be a committee, three members are ideal, with a maximum of five.

THE CARE AND FEEDING OF NERDS, OR HOW TO WORK WITH YOUR COMPUTER PEOPLE

Many OPLs complain about a lack of cooperation from the organization's computer people. Do you get quick and friendly service for your library hardware and software when you need it, or are the computer people unresponsive? Do you work together to bring new information services to your common users, or are you always in conflict over who is responsible for what? Your answers may make the difference between seamless service and chaos and frustration.

Martin writes (2000, 8): "Far from viewing nerds as superheroes who will save us from technology, many librarians often end up feeling frustrated, confused, or stupid after an encounter with a nerd. I think this is partly because we don't understand the language they speak and partly because we look at the world a bit differently than they do." I doubt if *they* feel the same way after talking to us, so why should we feel this way?

The roles of librarians and information technology (IT) people are inherently different.

- IT provides the pipeline, technology, expertise, project planning, and management—and usually has the money.

- IT gets the glory but must also deal with organization-wide, conflicting demands. All administrative departments are dependent on IT, creating conflicts and competition for resources.

- The goals of IT are a robust infrastructure and system availability and reliability.

- "Computer nerds don't necessarily want to share their knowledge with others .... [They] enjoy the mystique that surrounds them and they like knowing they're the only ones who can fix computer problems. Nerds also worry that if they give users too much information it might end up as more of a mess for the nerd to clean up later" (Martin 2000, 8).

- "Nerds have difficulty admitting they don't know everything about technology." [An OPL might say] "I don't know but I'll find out, but nerds may feel ashamed or uncomfortable about what they see as their lack of knowledge" (Martin 2000, 8, 10). Nerds may say that something can't be done when they really mean they don't know how to do it. You must state your requirements and expectations explicitly.

- The library has a strong orientation toward service, and the librarian has expertise in researching. The library provides a systematic, centralized, and coordinated method of retrieving, filtering, and storing information.

- The library has niche software products that are out of the IT mainstream, with relatively few primary users. Library vendors may be small companies. It is not feasible for IT to train many help-line staff about library applications. Programs may not be as well debugged and require lots of IT staff time for a small number of users. It also may be better for some vendors to work with IT, not through the librarian. The library handles print, CD-ROM, and Internet services; IT provides stable platform.

- Goals common to both the library and IT include providing excellent service to the firm and clients, intuitive access at the desktop, and systems to increase communication and collaboration.

Technology and librarians are two sides of the information coin. Too often, however, those that work in IT—not the librarians—get all the glory, money, and impressive titles. Librarians are thought to be involved only with acquiring and storing information in books. Librarians are increasingly dependent on IT because they are involved in organization-wide systems, rather than just a few terminals in the library. It is possible, and necessary, for IT and the library to work together. The first step is to make sure both groups understand each other's goals, jargon, and issues. It is critical to communicate frequently and electronically. Librarians should ask the advice of IT before purchasing new applications.

Since librarians usually need IT more than IT needs them, they need to make the major effort to improve the relationship. The library often is one of the first groups to adopt and benefit from new technologies; librarians must move from dependency to collaboration. Help IT by providing instructions and cheat sheets for after-hours IT support for library services and by acting as liaison between users and

IT for troubleshooting. Provide IT with library plans for budget, staff, and products that will involve IT.

INTERPERSONAL NETWORKING

It is safe to say that all librarians network in some manner. Formal networking involves the use of established organizations and much of it, especially in special libraries and OPLs, arises out of necessity. Networking is a major factor not only in reducing the OPL's feeling of professional isolation, but also in providing reference, document delivery, interlibrary loan, acquisitions, and continuing education services.

Your informal network includes your friends, co-workers, current and former colleagues, teachers and fellow students from library school. Although often ignored in this age of electronic communication, informal or interpersonal networking is arguably more important than its formal counterpart. We rely on contacts with other professionals (at meetings, on electronic discussion lists, through professional reading, and on the telephone) to make decisions on which books to buy, which vendors to use, and which meetings to attend. We call other librarians when we have a reference question that is out of our scope or need information from a reference book we do not own. Do not abuse nonlibrarian sources, thank your sources, and share information. I have found that informal networking, that is, calling a colleague, is often faster and less expensive than an online search. Quint said (1996a, 4), "Libraries do not cooperate, librarians do." OPLs share their knowledge, experience, and resources.

Our professional organizations (such as the American Library Association or the Special Libraries Association) are a wonderful source for meeting people and making contacts. Attend not only national meetings, but also the more frequent local or regional meetings. Go for the networking even if the topic is not of immediate interest to you.

LIBRARY PROMOTION: SELF-SERVING OR JUST GOOD SENSE?

To succeed or even stay alive, the OPL must constantly emphasize the value of the library. This continual justification is necessary for all types of libraries, even in those once thought immune to budget cuts, downsizing, and even closing, such as public and academic libraries. You must be visible and indispensable, add value, and take risks (St. Clair 1994). You need to make sure that everyone, especially those in a position to make decisions that affect the library, knows how important the OPL and the information you provide are to the organization. You must know and be able to show the economic impact of the library.

As I wrote in *The Visible Librarian*,

> Our customers see us handling books, chatting with a customer, and enforcing rules. No one sees us reading reviews of newly published books so we can decide which to buy. No one sees us reading manuals for new software or following electronic discussions of which databases or search engines are the best for which questions. No one sees the catalogers struggling with a difficult book or CD that doesn't seem to fit into any one category. No one sees the interlibrary loan people searching for a hard-to-find article. No one sees the reference librarian searching five different databases to find that elusive fact. And no one sees the librarians in budget meetings or buttonholing politicians or management to try to get a few more dollars for the library. Muir wrote, 'A physicist may take eight years to formulate, and a biochemist one day to replicate, but a librarian can do ten years of research in an hour—that's powerful! But does anyone out there *know*?' (1993, 41). That's the problem in a nutshell. *We* know what we can do, but everyone else does not. We have been invisible far too long. It is time to take off our cloak of invisibility, timidity, complacency, and

modesty and reveal ourselves to the world as we really are
and can be—The *Visible* Librarian!

All librarians, but especially OPLs, must promote, or market, the
library and yourself all the time. Every contact with someone outside
the library is a marketing opportunity. Another name for this is public
relations (PR), or promotion. Here are some of the common excuses
for *not* doing marketing—and my counterarguments.

- *PR takes too much time.* Many of the best PR techniques take
  little or no time.

- *PR takes too much money.* It costs almost nothing to create an
  interesting bulletin board, write an article for your organization's
  in-house publication, or create a poster.

- *It is unprofessional to advertise.* On the contrary, it is
  unprofessional to hide your light under a bushel, let others take the
  credit for what you do, let your library be downsized or closed
  because no one knew what you could do.

- *I already have too much to do. Promotion would just bring me
  more work for which I do not have the time or resources.* When
  was the last time you looked at your priorities? Are you spending too much time on low-priority tasks and not enough on the
  high-profile, high-impact, very professional tasks only you can
  do?

- *Other departments in the organization don't do it, so why should
  the library have to?* If everyone else buries his or her head in the
  sand, should you do the same? Maybe those other departments
  have already done their marketing, and so everyone already
  knows how valuable they are? (Of course, they should continue
  marketing to ensure that people don't forget about them, as
  should you.)

• *Advertising sounds so self-serving. No one will believe it if it comes from the librarian.* There's a big difference between tooting one's own horn and reminding others of services that can help them. Ideally, you will be able to quote satisfied users (the higher-up in the organization the better) in your publicity. But if you don't tell people how good, useful, helpful, and knowledgeable you are, who will? Better you than no one.

• *I don't know what to do. PR wasn't covered in library school.* Lots of things we need to know weren't covered in library school. So, learn how to market. Take a class, read a book, subscribe to a journal, or ask a colleague.

How to Promote Your Library

Every time you meet someone, send an e-mail, or write a letter you have an opportunity to explain how you and your library can help your clients do their jobs "better, faster, cheaper" (the librarian's mantra). No one will do it for you. No one knows more about your library and its users than you do. No one has more to gain—or lose—than you do. Therefore, *you* have to be the one to promote your library and yourself.

Make everyone in your organization aware of you and your library. Every single piece of paper (or e-mail) that goes out of your library should have your name or your library's name on it. A logo, mascot, or slogan can help get this message noticed. (Avoid using a book, computer, or cat as your symbol.) Ask your organization's graphics department to help you design a professional-looking logo. If possible, your logo, slogan, or mascot should appear on every page of search printouts, routing slips, notepads, etc.

Keep your publicity low-key and friendly, but businesslike. Avoid all library jargon. (For instance, "We can get information from almost any library in the state" is clearer than "We participate in the State ILL system.") Use bulleted text rather than straight text. And a sense of humor never hurts.

You have to develop a library newsletter; it is not hard to do. Create a simple newsletter using any word-processing software, or get really fancy with a desktop publishing program. There are a lot of good graphics available on the Web or ask your organization's graphics department to work with you on a total package. Use the same logo and color theme as in your brochures, other handouts, Web site, and intranet pages.

What should you include in your newsletter? New services; information on products or services you feel are underutilized; new books, journals, or even standards or photographs (but don't make it only a list of new acquisitions); conferences you've attended recently, papers you have given or articles you've had published; testimonials from satisfied customers; sample reference questions to stimulate users' thinking about what you can do; jokes; and quizzes. You also can get promotional materials from your professional association. In short, your newsletter can include anything that will help show users and potential users how you can help *them*. Your newsletter should be published often enough to remind users that you are there, but not so often that it gets repetitive or stale or intrudes on your other work. Once a month is usually enough, but it should at least appear once per quarter. Distribute it by e-mail, post it on the bulletin boards, offer it as a handout in the library, or whatever method works in your organization.

The best advertising is word of mouth from satisfied customers. Whenever a user thanks you or raves about you, ask him or her to put it in writing or write down what is said and ask, "May I quote you on that?" Keep a copy of all testimonials and send one to your boss for the file kept on you. You may also want to send a copy to your boss's boss or use it (with the user's permission, of course) in your library newsletter, brochure, or Web site.

Before you start promoting your library, look at your products and services to determine which services you will promote. Don't promote any service or product you cannot support. Concentrate on high-value services (such as online searching and competitive intelligence). Next, define your target markets. Is the target audience for this publicity effort everyone in organization, just one or two departments or only the movers and shakers? Then, define the competition. Even if you are the only library or librarian in the organization (or community), you have competition. Where do nonusers currently get their information? Can you compete with them? Do you *want* to compete with them? What makes you and your library better than the competition? What are your advantages? What can you do better than anyone else? Finally, follow-up is critically important. One-shot promotion isn't enough; experts say that you need tell people about a new service *at least* three times before they really pay attention. Check back with your users after introducing a new service to see if they like it. One way of following up is RBWA (Reference By Walking Around). Get out of the library and visit your customers, stopping to talk to people if they are not too busy. Ask what they are working on, and offer to help. Just the act of walking around—being seen—reminds people that you exist and that you might be able to help them. I can't count the number of times I have talked to someone at their desk, in the cafeteria, or in the hall and had them say, "Oh, yes, that reminds me. Can you get ...?" Take a few of your brochures with you on these walks.

More Promotion Ideas

- Get a list of new employees and follow up with a personal call or visit.

- Write a column for your organization's internal magazine or newsletter. Public librarians can do the same for the local newspaper as a PR vehicle; even the free neighborhood newspaper is good for an article now and then.

- Create a bulletin board to catch the eye of users and invite them into the library. Highlight new or important services on a bulletin board. Take advantage of the expertise of the publishing industry and post the book jackets of new books on the bulletin board. Be creative—use pictures, jokes, puns, puzzles, and cartoons. Change the board at least every two weeks.

• Have an open house. Food is critical—"Feed them and they will come." If you are providing free coffee or tea, advertise it at every coffee and tea station in the organization. Announce it in all in-house publications. Provide something with the library's name on it for users to take back with them, such as pencils, Post-It pads, or buttons. Ask customers to sign a register so you have a record of how many attended and for follow-up. Invite vendors (e.g., Dialog, LexisNexis, West, or other database producers) to demonstrate their wares (and provide the food).

• Celebrate a special day. You can celebrate National Library Week (which focuses on public libraries) or International Special Libraries Day, but I think it is better to celebrate something that focuses on your users, such as Engineers' Week, Doctors' Day, Law Day, or Nurses' Week. Materials for Library Week are available from your national library association, ISDL artwork from SLA's Web site, or you can make your own.

• Honor a library user of the year—a supporter or one who has checked out the most books or requested the most searches. Interview your winner, post his or her picture in the library, and perhaps give him or her an inexpensive gift.

• Celebrate one of the patron saints of libraries. St. Lawrence the Librarian was one of the seven famous deacons of the early church. August 10 is his feast day. St. Jerome, also known as Hieronymus, Eusbius, or Sophronius, helped establish the papal library. His feast day is September 30 (Hadden 1991).

One Last Word on Public Relations

I would like to end with some wisdom from a seemingly unlikely source. Harry Beckwith is a super-salesperson and motivational speaker. His book, *Selling the Invisible,* should be required reading for all librarians—the invisible is service.

- "The core of service marketing is the service itself" (Beckwith 1997, 3). Make sure it is the best it can be.

- "You cannot be all things to all people; you must focus on one thing" (103). Find out the hardest thing your customers need to do, and "position yourself as the expert at that task" (107).

- "Your first competitor is indifference" (171). I have always preached that a library's biggest competitor is doing without. We learned in library school that if it is too difficult (or too expensive) the users will not use the library.

- "Attack your first weakness; the stereotype the prospect has about you" (176). Be approachable and technologically savvy. Never, ever, say "Shhh."

- "Talk about him [your customer], not about you" (209). Be customer- and answer-centric, not library-centric.

- "Services are human. Their successes depend on the relationships of people. The more you can see the patterns and the better you understand people, the more you will succeed" (245).

ADVOCACY

As professionals, we must be concerned about our image and guard our professional demeanor and ethics. We also have an obligation to continue to grow as professionals. "Our profession suffers from an identity crisis, caused in part by supervisors (and users) who do not share our professional identity (Drake 1990, 152)." In 2004 the first library action figure came out. While it is wonderful that there is such a figure, I was horrified that it depicts a woman in a severe suit with a long skirt and sensible shoes whose "action" consists of bringing one finger to her lips as if saying "shhh." This is not what we need; we need an action figure that resembles a punk rocker, a beautiful, curvaceous woman, or a very macho man. Most people assume that anyone who works in a library is a librarian. Thus, when a member of the clerical staff cannot answer their question, is rude, or gives misinformation, they form a negative image of librarians. This situation is especially bad in public libraries but also holds true for other types of libraries. As OPLs we are especially vulnerable to this misconception even if we have clerical assistance.

White (1984, 95) wrote, "Librarians are often taken for granted, and they are often patronized; it is assumed that many of their requests are well-meaning and idealistic, but not practical." One problem is that we have not been taught how to measure and express the library's contributions to the organization's bottom line. What is even more damaging to the profession is that we accept our poor image and lack of status. We do not do our profession any good by failing to set up explicit standards for librarians. At present, there is no consistency in the degree of preparation offered by the ALA-accredited library schools, no competency requirements, and no requirements for continuing professional development (except in medical libraries, the U.K., and now in Australia, with their certification or chartering programs). Librarians need to be more proactive and decisive. We have to promote and defend the library and get managers to see the library and the librarian as strategic resources. We must defend our turf against those who would deny our information collection, analysis, and dissemination expertise. Our title and place in the organizational structure need to be appropriate. Even if we do not manage a staff, we manage information. Therefore, the title of manager should be ours.

What does it mean to be a professional? Herb White (1995, 53) writes, "The smaller the professional staff, the more important it becomes to select truly excellent professionals." Because an OPL is as small a professional staff as one can find, professionalism is especially important for us. As St. Clair (1996a, 3) puts it, "If you stop to worry whether you *should* be doing this or that part of the task, whether it is *appropriate* or not, you'll never get around to doing what you're supposed to be doing." Clerical tasks are just as much a part of the job as are the professional tasks, and St. Clair (1976, 234) says it is very important to "Always think of yourself as a professional, even when performing nonprofessional tasks." Often this may mean working longer hours, whatever it takes to get the job done. However, you can overdo a good thing. Herb White (1995, 210) reminds us that there is life outside of work, saying, "Burnout for librarians seems to me both foolish and unnecessary. Work hard, work well, work effectively. Work until quitting time. Then go home and enjoy the rest of your life. Let the people with the proportionately higher salaries do the higher proportion of the worrying."

Professionalism also requires a continuing commitment to maintain your skills, which includes spending time and money on continuing education. You must assume responsibility for your own continuing education to reinforce your standing as a professional dedicated to keeping current and to continue to provide users with the best possible service. However, it is definitely worthwhile to go to meetings or training sessions; I have to keep up with this ever-changing profession. Besides, if I never left, my customers would take me for granted; I would become "a piece of the woodwork." When I am not here (and no one is doing my work), they realize what I do for them and are somewhat more appreciative.

6

Along the Information Superhighway: The OPL and Technology

Technology. Just the word conjures up mixed feelings: excitement, anxiety, and stress. How are we going to keep up with something that, by the time we get a handle on it, has already changed into something else? Technology is one of the biggest aids to the one-person librarian (OPL), but you must become the master (or mistress) of technology, not let it become your master.

WHAT THE INTERNET IS AND IS NOT

I wrote this in 1996 (Siess 1997), but it is still true today.

What It Is

- A great communications tool

- A great leveler (if made available to all, in public libraries or other locations)

- A giant "mail-order" catalog

- A great information dissemination tool for business (technical manuals, product literature, catalogs, technical support, software)

- A great information dissemination tool for government (bills, position papers, feedback from people to government)—but not a substitute for print

- An ephemeral storage medium

- Cheap

What It Is Not

- A good reference tool (except for posting questions on listservs among professionals)

- Secure

- The answer to all information needs (you still need verified sources)

- A substitute for libraries (books are more user-friendly and better for most reference)

- A substitute for librarians (we need them as information guides and consultants and evaluators and indexers)

- An archival medium

- Fast (if you're looking for an *answer*, not just hits)

The downside to the Internet includes information overload, time wasted surfing the Net or reading a large number of e-mail messages— many of them spam—hardware crashes, software glitches, viruses, user-hostile interfaces, disappearance of well-loved print resources, lack of time to keep up with all the new sites and services, and poorly thought-out ventures by new dot-com companies.

Some people think that the Web threatens our profession. There is some truth in this fear. Is there a librarian who hasn't heard, "It's all on the Internet, and it's all free?" More and more information available to end-users at their desktops leads some in upper management to wonder why or if they really need a librarian. It's time to educate our bosses and our customers, to emphasize that end-users cannot do as thorough a search as can a librarian. Management needs to learn that end-user searching simply is not cost-effective. Do they really want a highly trained and highly paid doctor, lawyer, or engineer spending billable time searching for information, when a highly trained and (unfortunately) lower paid librarian can find higher quality information faster and less expensively? Information overload is not our only concern; we also need to worry about *mis*information. Our customers certainly know their subject matter, but they do not know which sources to consult or how to search effectively, and may not be able to determine if the information found is reliable. That is *our* expertise. Perhaps we should promise that we won't practice medicine, law, engineering, or whatever, if those in other professions don't practice librarianship. Fletcher (1996, 44) sees great opportunities for information intermediaries: "Knowing how to get information economically, how to synthesize material, how to distill facts to answer questions, and how to extract the right question from the client" are our core competencies and, at present, no online search engines exist that can do what we do. Fortunately for us, this is still true. Unfortunately, we haven't been able to convince all of our customers.

DEFINING THE LIBRARIAN'S ROLE IN THE INFORMATION SOCIETY

What part we are going to play in the newly defined information society? We are increasingly called on to provide instant access, 24/7/365 (24 hours a day, 7 days a week, 365 days a year) to all the information our users want, at the user's desktop, with an interface that requires no learning curve. We must go back to basics, our core functions: our ability to manage knowledge resources, in all forms; our ability to focus on the users, which differentiates us from Internet service professionals; and our facility for using tools and technologies. I have divided our potential roles into four categories: searcher and navigator, teacher, evaluator, and policymaker.

Searcher and Navigator

Most people do not know how to find information efficiently. Too sweeping a statement you say? Most people have trouble locating sites and need help they are not getting from automatic search engines. Leibovich (2000) found that students would rather do research on the Web than in the library, even if they can't find the answers. They don't understand the importance of choosing the right key words, synonyms, and getting information from multiple sources. Students also are more likely to choose the first hits they find, rather than the best ones. They assume what they find is true, without checking for accuracy or bias. Librarians must intervene. Remember, libraries provide access, and librarians provide assistance.

Although more and more people will find the easy answers for themselves using the Internet (and, occasionally print sources), we will still be needed to do the difficult searches. We also will be needed by those who do not want to do their own searching for whatever reason. In fact, there have been several anecdotal studies showing that the Internet and other electronic resources actually add to librarians' workload, because users do the easy searches themselves, leaving the more difficult and more time-consuming ones for us, the experts.

Teacher

We must teach our customers how to formulate searches, modify them, search multiple sites, and evaluate sources. The most significant way we can help our customers to use the Web effectively is the same way we help them with print sources, that is, by teaching them how to ask the right question.

We also need to teach users when to search for themselves and when they need to come to us. This teaching role is never-ending. Just when we get comfortable with one set of tools, technologies, or users, a new set will come along.

Evaluator

Picasso said: "Computers are useless. They can only give you answers." A major role for the librarian will be to choose the appropriate resources, tools, systems, and interfaces. The tools we use may change, but the mediator role will not. We must use both the new and old tools. Although it will become less important to build physical collections, the selection, evaluation, and reevaluation of books, journals, and electronic sources will always be critical in an organization's ability to compete and thrive. If we don't do this, who will? Will it be end-users, computer people, administrators, finance people? Imagine the chaos that would ensue if any of the above were to be put in charge of recommending information resources.

R.A. Schneiderman (1996), a computer consultant and not a librarian, wrote:

> Librarians have been managing complex information for over two hundred years. If we were smart, we'd let librarians rule the Net. Computers aren't very good at cataloging information even when the information ... is already quite specialized. If we're going to catalog the web, people will have to do the bulk of the work. [Other professions have done some of this work,] but if librarians [were] in charge, they would have insisted that every web author have access to simple programs that helped them briefly catalog any document or collection of documents they put up on the web. If someone moves their web, there is no easy way to find it. ... As a result, extremely valuable information sometimes disappears off the web without a trace. Librarians have spent years handing these ... problems ... and their experience would have been invaluable if computer scientists had been smart enough to use it.

Policymaker

Griffiths (1996) also warns, "Technology can be a black hole for money." We can serve as the central point for the ordering of resources to ensure minimal duplication and maximal use of scarce monies. Many OPLs already serve this function for books and journals, but we should also be responsible for the electronic resources. Librarians also know how to obtain the materials found by searching. Tenopir (2000) writes, "Libraries must employ a variety of strategies for document access, including full-text databases, electronic-only journals, commercial document delivery services, automated interlibrary loan, and cooperative collection development." How much money and time would be wasted if our customers had their own ILLs (and books, and subscriptions)? How many invoices and how much chaos would be created? Instead, the librarian can centralize purchases, plan acquisitions, negotiate terms, track their progress, and even make sure copyright regulations are followed.

It is inevitable that the computer people will be making the buying decisions for the hardware and even the software. However, we need to communicate with the computer people to ensure the technology will run the resources our mutual customers need. We must work together to keep the focus on the problems technology can solve and not on the technology itself. Crawford (2000, 49) recently wrote, "Your job is to recognize that technology offers tools, that those tools interact in complex ways, and that tools aren't ends in themselves. ... Most tools should be nearly invisible. They should do their work without intruding on the task at hand. [Finally,] the only thing we really have to look forward to is more change." We must get comfortable with the constant change in technology; learn to take risks, identify opportunities, take action; and realize and accept that anything new will be obsolete within a couple of years.

COLLECTION DEVELOPMENT IN AN ELECTRONIC WORLD: CHOOSING FORMATS AND EVALUATING RESOURCES

I sometimes find myself thinking, "Gee, wasn't life easy when we just bought a book or subscribed to a print journal?" I must be getting old, longing for the good old days. But think of how little information we were able to provide then and how long it took. We now have the possibility of providing far more information, faster, in a more usable form, and to more users. Instead of looking back, we should be looking forward to the "good new days."

First, look at your institution and your users. Where are the users located? Are they mostly in the same building or all over the world? Does the institution perceive itself as being on the cutting edge of technology and expect you to be the same? How technologically savvy are the users? Do the users *want* a virtual library? Do the users need 24/7 desktop access to information? If so, do the users need this access for all the information or just certain sources? Are the users willing to pay for this information, either directly or by giving the library (you) more resources? How often do the users need historical information, the kind that is neither in electronic form nor likely to be so for the near future?

Then look at your library. Is there information there that is "never" or seldom used? Have you been acquiring "just-in-case," and are you ready to move to "just-in-time" acquisitions? Do you have backfiles of journals that are covered by one of the major electronic services? How is your relationship with the information technology (computer) people? It had better be a good one if you are going to go electronic (or you'd better be a techie yourself). What is your collection development policy? (You don't have one? It's in your head? Don't feel guilty. Most OPLs do not have a written collection development policy, but maybe this is a good time to write down those intuitive guidelines you've been operating under.)

Now, look at the available resources. What is available in electronic form? At what cost? Here are some items to look at when evaluating resources in print vs. electronic formats:

- Reliability and continuity (Will it be here tomorrow?)

- Content (coverage and arrangement)

- Appearance (easy to navigate?)

• Search and retrieval (options and ease of use)

• Access (a book can be used by one person at a time, CD-ROMs can be networked but have practical limits, Web access is available to all at the same time)

• Technology requirements (What is the cost? Who will update it?)

• Ownership (often you only lease electronic information)

• Archival properties (How long will the medium last?)

• Training requirements for staff and users (How much? By whom?)

• Cost (unfortunately, often the determining factor)

• Space requirements (electronic is a clear winner here)

Will the new medium replace the old? Of course not. Crawford (49) wrote, " 'Media' is a plural noun, implying that there will continue to be more than one medium of communications and entertainment. Librarians must decide which media work for their libraries and their users. The more media, the more complex that decision." There always have been and always will be multiple formats. When CD-ROM first came along it was predicted that it would revolutionize home entertainment (it has), eliminate low-density media (it has supplanted but not replaced floppies and now has been somewhat replaced by other, faster media), and revolutionize publishing (there has been some change, but definitely not a revolution). Why wasn't CD-ROM more successful? Networking CD-ROMs wasn't as easy as we thought it would be. Storage capacity, while better than for floppies, is being exceeded by the demands of new software and data. Although transfer and access speeds are increasing, CD-ROM is still slower than the Internet. Now the Web is supposedly the be-all and end-all, and CD-ROM is out of favor. In the future something new will come along and then the Web will be passé; however, print, disc, CD-ROM, and the

Web will all continue to coexist. After all, we all still have some microfilm or microfiche, don't we?

We've always had to choose formats; now we just have more choices and user and librarian training is a bigger concern. We have many more products available. Some are just repackaging of old services in new formats, but some are really novel and exciting. Even for old products, there are multiple delivery options (dial-up, CD-ROM, print, the Web). When print was our only option, selection tools were easy to find; user training was almost unnecessary. There were many providers of information, most of which had been in business for a long time, and could be expected to stay in business in the future. Pricing was simple and straightforward. Ownership of the item was clear and permanent. Sharing (ILL) methods were already established and open to all. Our users knew what to expect and how information would be delivered (in print, on paper). Virtual libraries and 24/7 access to information outside our own libraries were unheard of.

If all this isn't enough to boggle your mind, there are some additional issues you should think about. This move to electronic information is going to change the thinking of the whole library world about collections. The number of volumes and journal titles a library has will become meaningless. Libraries will be judged by the breadth of sources they make available to their users. If large academic and public libraries no longer keep large backfiles of journals (or even current issues), what will small libraries do for document delivery, especially if electronic publishers restrict licenses to institutional users? Membership in multitype library consortia may become more attractive than ever. What happens when a publisher goes out of business or discontinues a title? We had better hope that some library somewhere has decided to keep that journal in its collection in the old-fashioned but reliable print form. Another issue is that the licensing agreements for these electronic offerings usually are quite complex. Your legal department will get involved, adding another layer to the bureaucracy and another delay in providing access to that information.

PURCHASING ONLINE

It is becoming increasingly advantageous to purchase even print materials via the Web. Amazon.com and the other online booksellers often can offer lower prices and fast delivery. Make sure that you are ordering online for the right reasons, not because your purchasing department says you have to, or because it is easy. Compare the total price to other suppliers. Don't forget about the cost of processing a separate invoice. Using a company credit card is almost always required to purchase online. (Do not, I repeat, do not, get coerced into using your own personal credit card. If your organization wants you to pay by credit card, management should authorize one for you.)

THE FUTURE: WHERE ARE WE GOING?

Smock (1995, B1) said, "We have been spoiled by the computer on *Star Trek* which instantly answers Captain Kirk's requests." Your customers have come to expect instant service from you, but it is not quite possible yet. In 1995, *InfoWorld* writer Bob Metcalfe (1995) predicted the imminent collapse of the Internet due to lack of money and support. Users would get bored with the Internet and its hype and lose interest. The security, privacy, and censorship issues and capacity problems would overwhelm the system. The impending collapse would be good, dispelling the myth of the Internet that Metcalfe (1995, 61) describes as a "wonderfully chaotic and brilliantly biological and homeopathically self-healing" system and leading to the realization that "it needs to managed, engineered and financed as a network of computers ..." Metcalfe was wrong. The Internet and the Web have thrived and prospered. Users are probably more hooked on the Web than ever. Serious problems such as security, privacy, censorship, unwanted e-mail (spam), and system crashes due to undercapacity or viruses persist. However, there has not been, and does not appear that there will be, a collapse.

I have other concerns. Electronic myopia is the name I give to the increasing tendency of people, primarily the young, to discount any information that does not appear in electronic form—if it isn't in electronic form, it doesn't exist. Some teachers even require students to use the Web to answer questions that could be answered faster and easier using so-called old-fashioned print resources. If this trend continues, what are the implications for all data that are not in the form of bits and bytes? Will this data continue to be produced and find a market? What will or will not be digitized? Gillies (2000) expected that materials not in English, in non-Western alphabets, humanities and social science information, historical documents, and nonword items and artifacts (such as art, noncontemporary music) will not be digitized, or at least will be far down in priority. Will we, in effect, throw away all learning before the early 1980s just because it isn't available or even indexed online?

If electronic-only publication had been the mode in the past, who would know of the Magna Carta, the writings of the ancient Greeks and Romans, or the U.S. Declaration of Independence and Constitution? How would our history have been changed? Finally, electronic publishing has serious implications for the rights and interests of authors. First, who will pay for the publications of research? Second, what provisions will be made for copyright and royalty payments? The law in this area seriously lags behind the technology. Third, and most important (to me at last), is the issue of content integrity. What guarantees will there be that the work one accesses online is the same as the one originally written? It is all too easy to download material, change a few words—just enough to change the meaning—and upload the altered document to the Web again. We've all seen doctored photographs; will we be seeing doctored research in the future? And how will we recognize it?

Efforts are being made to archive the Web and digitize existing printed materials. Some of these projects have been done by major universities, but private firms such as Google are getting involved. Will information formerly available for free someday be available only from a for-profit company?

Finally, despite manufacturers' claims, we do not really know the life expectancy of electronic media. It just hasn't been around long enough. What's more, even if the media and the data survive for eons and eons, will the software and hardware to access the media and data survive? Vendors of these systems go out of business frequently, leaving orphan, unsupported programs and hardware. What good is a storage medium that will last for 100 years if the data on it cannot be accessed? Is it economically feasible to convert data for each new system? Who will take responsibility for the conversion and who will pay for it?

WHAT ABOUT A VIRTUAL LIBRARY?

Some librarians have been asked by their managers to convert their physical library into a virtual library, a library-without-walls, or a cybrary. One of the first such efforts was by Michel Bauwens (1993), who coined the term *cybrarian* to describe his role in the virtual library. He recognized declining financial and personnel support by his company. He determined that senior management needed current, accurate, selective information on competitors, markets, and regulations in an attractive, readable, and usable form—and they needed it fast (Matarazzo and Drake 1994). He dismantled his print library, freeing up the time and money it had taken to manage it. Many other firms have done the same thing. These virtual libraries provide desktop access to newswires, databases, market research, library catalogs, electronic newspapers, internal business documents, and many other services. Document requests are handled electronically, and often there is an electronic mailbox for questions. Librarians may not even be located on-site, instead working at home. In-house collections are small or even nonexistent. Collection development consists of evaluating information services, negotiating license agreements and contracts, training, and user support. Reference interviews are conducted by telephone or e-mail, not face-to-face. In fact, some librarians may never even meet their users.

If it seems likely that you will be asked to go virtual, first ask yourself if that is the way you want to go. If not, you may want to look for another position. If you want to accept the challenge, develop a plan—before management comes to you with *their* plan. Create a timeline for canceling print subscriptions, disposing of printed materials in your library (can you sell them to your customers or a used book dealer, or send some to another library—perhaps in a developing country) and very importantly, notifying your customers of the upcoming changes. Be sure that you include your job and yourself in the plan.

I leave you with some words of wisdom.

"The information highway is paved with rhetoric, metaphors, and the scar tissue of misinformed executives." Cisco Systems advertisement, 1996

"Take a book, remove the cover, remove the title page, remove the table of contents, remove the index, cut the binding from the spine, fling the loose pages that remain so they scatter about the room. Now find the information you needed from that book. This is the Internet." Michael Gorman, 1995

"The roads are built by the communications companies. The vehicles are built by the computer manufacturers. The services are built by the content providers. What is the role of the information professional? We provide the signage, the travel guides, the maps and most importantly—the drivers' ed." Jose-Marie Griffiths, Dean, School of Information, University of Michigan, U.S.A., 1996

"In the long run, the only way the Net will rise to its true potential is if librarians become an integral part of the discussion of the Net's future." R.A. Schneiderman, computer consultant (not a librarian), 1996

7

Other Issues:
Education, Downsizing and
Outsourcing, and Knowledge
Management

EDUCATION FOR
ONE-PERSON LIBRARIANSHIP

I am, for the most part, disappointed in education for librarianship. I know it is improving; some schools are doing a great job in preparing students for the real world. However, most could do a much better job. Too many librarians are graduating unprepared for the cold cruel world of work. Graduates have not had enough exposure to the different types of libraries in which they might work. Special and one-person libraries are barely mentioned at some schools. How many students know about the opportunities in zoo or prison libraries? How aware are students of the realities of budgets, corporate culture, conflicting demands on time and resources, library boards and committees, the realities of planning and prioritization, the importance of networking and continuing professional education, and the rest of the things they don't teach you in library school? How many have worked in a library, other than as a graduate assistant? How many have done an

131

internship or, better yet, several internships in different kinds of libraries? Have students taken courses in business communications and presentation skills? Do they know how to write an effective memo? Have students had substantial experience in conducting reference interviews, a critical skill?

As I became active in SLA and the Solo Librarians Division, I began asking other OPLs if they had learned these skills in library school. Most agreed that their education had not adequately prepared them for life in the real world of one-person librarianship. When I speak with OPLs around the world, I always ask, "What do you wish you had learned in library school?" The most common responses are time management and more on management, corporate culture and office politics, finances and budgeting, and negotiation. There's nothing new about this; complaints about library education can be traced as far back as 1906 (Rothstein 1985). The nature of the complaints has been amazingly consistent: too little practical training, no education for leadership, educators being out of touch with the needs of the profession, instructors needing to be practitioners and not just teachers, the work not really being at graduate level, and courses being too geared toward public libraries. Most people realize that a mix of the theoretical and the practical is necessary, but disagree on the mix; educators emphasize or concentrate on the theoretical background of the profession while employers want graduates who have the skills to be effective workers as soon as they start their jobs.

Graduates, especially OPLs, need to have knowledge not only of theory and skills but also must be prepared for what they do not yet know. They need to know the questions to ask and how to find the answers to situations that develop once they are on the job.

Tees (1986, 191) noted that most studies of special library needs have been made of large libraries and are not necessarily relevant for the more common small libraries. Because special librarianship is not emphasized in most library schools, it is more probable that the special librarian did not anticipate being in this situation and may not have chosen to take courses emphasizing skills needed in a special library.

In addition, many management courses assume that you will be managing people. OPLs assume a managerial role early in or even at the beginning of their careers. OPLs are much more likely to need entrepreneurial and business skills, because they are running their own little businesses.

We all must take the problem of library education seriously. In life, when we want things to improve, we take the responsibility of envisioning that future and then doing something about it. The same is true for library education. What have *you* done recently to improve things at your alma mater or local library school? Have you gone back to your library school and sat in on some classes to see what is being taught? (If your school is too far away or closed, go to the one nearest to where you work.) Have you volunteered to be a guest lecturer or even an adjunct faculty member? Have you spoken to the student chapter of your professional association? You say that it is too far, you are too busy, or whatever? Nonsense. Using the Internet, you can lecture from a distance, or you can visit on a weekend. Have you ever served as a mentor or hosted an intern? This is a great way to help students find out about one-person librarianship and doesn't take as much time as you may think. Someone already in the profession probably helped you when you were getting started. Repay them by helping someone else. Repaying the debt is personally rewarding and it is a professional responsibility. The future of librarianship lies in the hands of this generation, not the next. *You* can make a better future for all of us. I urge you to get started now.

Finally, receiving your library degree should be only the beginning of a librarian's education. Mickey (2000) wrote, "New hires straight out of library school frequently still need extensive training before they're truly up to speed. Keeping up in this field is a classic case of adult continuing education." Who will pay for this education? In some cases the employer will, but in many cases OPLs must pay for their own training. Instead of complaining or, worse, not participating in continuing professional education, consider it an investment in your future. I am concerned when I hear librarians say, "If my boss won't pay to send me to the conference, then I won't go." If you are a professional, then you do what is necessary to keep your skills up-to-date. If this means paying your way to a conference or course, then pay. Scholarships are available to many conferences (and most are not awarded because no one applies for them). Make the conference part of a family vacation. Remember that the information you receive will make you a better librarian; if being a better librarian does not help you on your current job, it will on the next. Cynthia Hill of Sun Microsystems (in O'Leary 2000) says, "People need to recognize that they have a professional portfolio. They take their competencies with them. They don't belong to the organization." Every conference and course I have attended has given me something. I always would come away more confident of my abilities or with new information that would come in handy down the road. Continuing education is an opportunity a professional librarian cannot afford to neglect.

Where can you find continuing education opportunities? Library schools offer some continuing education courses, but often they are only or primarily for their own graduates and take place on campus, often for a week at a time, which makes it difficult (if not impossible) for most OPLs to take advantage of them. Every library association provides continuing education opportunities at conventions and conferences, and many also offer computer- or Web-based courses and teleconferences. A survey done by SLA showed that 62 percent of solos did not attend the most recent annual conference and 70 percent did not attend SLA education courses. However, 63 percent said they had gone to non-SLA courses in the past year (Bender 1994). Although this survey is rather dated, I doubt if the numbers have changed much. One source of continuing education that is often forgotten is the library and computer software and hardware vendors. Courses are offered in locations around the world, cost little or nothing, usually take only one day, and are nearly always very practical. You can also keep up-to-date by reading professional journals and newsletters; taking in-house training courses (offered on management, technology, and your users' fields of work); participating in online user and discussion groups; and taking the many courses offered by regional library organizations, nonlibrary sources, such as Toastmasters, and at your local university or community college in the departments of computer science, business, or communications.

DOWNSIZING AND OUTSOURCING

Some people are confused about the difference between outsourcing and downsizing. *Downsizing* is to reduce the number of people working in the library. Many OPLs become OPLs by being downsized from a larger staff; an OPL also can be downsized by losing clerical support. Of course, the ultimate downsizing is cutting all staff and closing the library. In contrast, *outsourcing* is to contract out some services, while keeping the library open.

Downsizing

Downsizing is now a business reality. As librarians, we know that the *real* way to save money is to have more well-trained information intermediaries and fewer expensive end-users doing their own searching for information, but all managers do not understand this. Libraries are not alone in being downsized. Many companies are doing away with lower-paid secretaries and having higher-paid professionals doing word processing and photocopying, which makes no more sense to me as having engineers and doctors search for information. While the existence of a library used to be a given in many organizations, it is no longer seen as absolutely necessary. For instance, in the past, a medical library with a degreed librarian was required in the U.S.A. for accreditation; however, today, JCAHO (the Joint Commission on Accreditation of Hospital Organizations) requires only that medical professionals have access to appropriate medical resources, which is often interpreted to mean the provision of access to the Web and a few medical databases, not having a library with a professional librarian. Although a librarian is now a member of the JCAHO standards committee, it is doubtful that the requirement for a library or librarian will be reinstated. Public libraries are not immune to downsizing, either.

Branches are closed, hours are cut, and librarians are replaced with clerks. Only academic libraries seem to be immune; a library is required for accreditation, but its budget can still be cut and librarian positions eliminated. Could the future hold the same fate for some academic libraries as befell hospital libraries, that is, replacement by Web access?

Reasons for Downsizing

What makes our profession so vulnerable to downsizing? Bryant (1995, 7) says, "solo librarians are perpetually vulnerable to 'downsizing,' and ignore ... reports of the dissatisfaction of employers at their peril." OPLs are especially vulnerable because they are smaller and often less visible.

Cram (1995, 107) wrote:

> Two issues play a critical role in contributing to the vulnerability of libraries to closure or gradual withdrawal of support: the tendency of librarians to market their libraries and library services as a product class rather than as a unique service delivering specific and quantifiable benefits; the view of the library as a cost centre, a vulnerability exacerbated by the tendency of librarians not to take the needs of the accountants and lawyers who manage our organisation seriously.

An organization's attitude toward information is of vital importance to a library's success. If your management does not value information, then find a way to change the attitude; if management does value information, then nurture this attitude. Most organizations and librarians do not have good ways to evaluate and value the library, so libraries are often viewed as an expendable overhead expense. There are also other departments in some organizations that claim to be able to do the work of the library. The library must advance the stated (and unstated) missions of the organization, align itself with revenue-producing departments, and become known as *mission-critical*. You must be known for supplying information in whatever form is necessary, not just in print. It is probable that the organization's decision makers are not direct users of the library (even if much of their information comes from the library indirectly through their subordinates). Because these decision makers don't use the library, they don't think it is of value to the organization. If this is your situation, act to change this perception; convince upper management "that even though information may not be their core business, information is at the core of their business and their competitive advantage in the marketplace" (DiMattia 1995).

How to Avoid Downsizing

There is no way to guarantee your library will not be outsourced or downsized, but here are some suggestions that you can use to make you less vulnerable. You should be doing these things anyway; if you aren't, start now.

- Provide information directly to the chief executive officer. Do you know his or her information needs? Have you made a presentation to the board recently? Find new roles for the library to replace ones that are obsolete, little used, or that can be outsourced. "Are you performing duties simply because you've always done them?" (Wilson and Mount 1997).

- Think like a chief financial officer. What are the financial drivers of the organization? Which departments are growing and which are contracting? Which departments are critical to the mission of the organization? Which are profit centers? Answers to these questions may tell where the money is, and where it will be in the future. Identify the person in upper management who controls the library's money and make sure he understands the library and its advantages (Bates 1997).

- Librarians often make the mistake of marketing only to users. You must market to the ultimate decision makers. Present "meaningful" statistics to top management, that is, sales closed, lives saved, lawsuits won, new association members recruited or contracts received because of information from the library. Also make sure they know about any money you've brought into the organization by selling library products and services to outside customers and the time and money you've saved them by centralizing the ordering of information products, efficient online searching, etc. Management does not care about circulation, the size of the collection, number of interlibrary loans, and so on. Tell them about the unique services you provide that outsourcing can't (rapid response, confidentiality, knowledge of the organization, and having a vested interest in the organization's success).

• Keep your library, technical, and business skills current. Make sure the library looks up-to-date, modern, neat, and uncluttered. Is your publicity as good as it could be? Does it adequately convey all the facets of your services? Be a team player; serving on organization-wide committees or task forces shows that you are a valuable and contributing member of the organization.

• Find (or create) library champions. These advocates should be as highly placed as possible (vice presidents speak louder than secretaries). Ask users how the information received from the library contributes to their achieving departmental or organizational goals, especially if they are in line (revenue-stream, as opposed to staff or supporting) positions, whether or not they actually use the library themselves.

• Understand the corporate culture of your organization. Mark Estes (in Quint 1996b, 16) says: "If you, the librarian, don't know your world, you're a fool. It's the responsibility of any professional librarian to pay attention to their work environment."

• Beat them to the punch. Take information to the desktop—before you are asked to. Develop a virtual library—before you are required to. Benchmark library services—before you have to.

Financial crises and downsizing gives you the opportunity to a reassess your goals, objectives, and strategies. Determine new priorities and how to reach them with the new levels of resources. Let your customers know of the changes and their implications and that the library will continue to help them, although maybe differently. Concentrate on the essentials, delegate what you can, and use partnerships and alliances. Ask, "Why are *we* doing this task? Could someone do it better? What would be the consequences of letting someone else do it? Is this task integral (critical or strategic) to the mission of the organization? To the mission of the library? What are the costs associated with doing this task? What would be the cost of outsourcing this task?"

Perhaps you can downsize your space. Do you really need it all? Can you weed some books or journals? Can you share resources with another institution? Can you become more of a "virtual" library? St. Clair points out (1996b, 7) that "the delivery of information is not constrained by space."

Not all closings are the librarian's fault. Some are political, some have ulterior motives, and some are just budgetary. But in some cases it is the librarian's fault. The library and information services were not promoted to the right people, the decision makers, or did not keep up with what was needed. Professional skills were not updated in terms of computer literacy, technical orientation, or business techniques. Our jargon or services did not keep up with needs. Here are four case studies that show various ways to cope with downsizing, some successful and some not. Perhaps they will give you some ideas.

Four Case Studies in Downsizing

Case Study 1: From six to two in easy stages. An OPL at a large branch of one of the top 10 law firms says that at first there were three librarians (a manager, an assistant librarian, and cataloger) and three clerical people. First one clerical position was eliminated, then the cataloger. Then the library manager left. The OPL became the manager-librarian-cataloger, and they outsourced the filing. He was down to one clerical person, a filer. He said, "I don't know what these extra people did! Yes, sometimes I'm stretched but eventually I catch up and the attorneys are super!"

Case Study 2: They did it right, but got downsized anyway. They did everything right. They publicized the library with a logo, a brochure, well-attended open houses, visits to off-site facilities and department staff meetings, new employee orientations, user surveys, and even a special reception for management. Their statistics demonstrated growing usage across all business areas. So, how did they go from a staff of 11 (five professionals and six support staff members) in 10,000 square feet to a staff of two in 2,500 square feet? The fact is you can do everything recommended by library management books and gurus and still not be able to save your library. A library, like the other units in a company, is subject to all the management tools (or fads) of the moment. Downsizing is a way of life in the corporate world and can hit anywhere. The library is neither exempt nor singled out.

Although automation and more efficient procedures led to substantial savings, management was insistent on complete cost recovery (including space at premium rent charges; the cost of all support services provided, such as accounts payable and mail; and even a percentage of administrative costs above the actual costs of the library). The library instituted cuts even without management pressure. When staff members left they were not replaced. The collections were weeded, and library space needs were reduced. Now there were eight (four librarians and four support staff members) in 5,000 square feet. Then came the corporate mandate to all units to "decentralize." They presented a report to top management documenting negative cost and service implications, but it didn't matter. Decentralization was to happen, regardless of cost, service, or anything else. The corporate library was reduced to three librarians providing reference and research services and document delivery through an outside vendor. They moved into a suite of office cubicles. The business groups made other provisions for meeting their information needs.

Two years later, the pendulum swung back. Cost savings were the key corporate objective. Where they had "decentralized," now they "consolidated." Two major collections that had not been part of the original library were added, but when the dust settled they were down to a staff of four (two librarians and two support staff members). A year later, a major business segment accounting for 40 percent of library use moved to another site. The library dropped one librarian and one very capable support person. They manage to keep up with customer requests for information and documents; however, just about everything else falls behind, and outsourcing is still a threat.

Case Study 3: Being proactive and anticipating downsizing. Dan Trefethen (1996) then of TRA Associates in Seattle, Washington, was faced with losing his assistant, who was just finishing up a records management certificate program at the university. Trefethen developed a win-win situation—or at least one that he could live with—a phased-in layoff. He went to his boss, the financial-administrative manager of the firm. He was a bottom-line guy. Like most bosses, he knew nothing substantial about the library. The thing management hates most is for a librarian to dump a problem on them, especially one that costs money they weren't counting on spending. However, the thing management likes most is for their people to come to them and say, "We have an opportunity here to improve your bottom line, and the job situation here." Then they listen.

Trefethen told his boss they could cut his assistant, but he just wanted to do it in an orderly fashion. First: Set a target date. Second: Tell the assistant what he needed to accomplish by that time. Third: Decide what he was going to have to *not* do when he was a true OPL. This was the perfect chance to get rid of nonessential tasks. He worked with the departments to reassign some of them to other units that now had more staff. He even exchanged some clerical tasks for information tasks from the other units or for computer upgrades. You might even pick up some projects because of downsizing in other departments, so you will need additional resources to handle them. You offer to fall on your sword (as the Roman Centurions did), because it is not as bad as the alternative. Trefethen (1996) says, "One advantage: the librarian 'mystique.' If they don't really know how you do what you do, they're not in a good position to micromanage you or to critique your downsizing strategy. We always say that knowledge is power. The corollary is that lack of knowledge is lack of power. Use the knowledge to your advantage."

Case Study 4: A tale of two libraries—What's the moral? In the first
case, management hired a consulting firm to study the library. They
found only a small core of users. The librarian declined to be involved
in the study. The library was closed. No one was too upset, except the
librarian. In case two, the librarian heard rumors of a corporate reor-
ganization and went to his prime users with a questionnaire on library
services and satisfaction. He followed up on it, raising users' awareness of the library. The library was not downsized even though every
other department was. The moral? You have to be proactive. Don't
wait until they come to you. Assume there is going to be downsizing
and cutbacks and have a plan (St. Clair 1994).

Outsourcing

Outsourcing is a part of business life. Most major corporations now
outsource at least some services. Outsourcing—that is, paying someone
else to do a part of your job—can be a big time-saver for OPLs. You
can outsource work to another department within the organization or to
an outside organization.

When and What Should You Outsource?

Do you use a subscription such as Ebsco or Swets? Do you buy catalog cards from OCLC or another source? Do you purchase books
from a jobber or wholesaler? If so, you are already outsourcing some
of your work. Outsource when it is to your advantage, when you can
control it, when it can improve service levels at no extra cost, when a
contractor would more easily be able to stay current with technology,
and when you need expertise not available in-house. Caldwell (1996)
says, "What we outsource is not our organization's core business, but
it is that of the vendor, who is in a better position to deliver a quality
product." Outsourcing can allow you to increase services without
adding head count, something management is always trying to avoid.
It can also take care of a temporary overload. Outsourcing is also
appropriate when you will be absent from the library for a relatively long
period of time (for a vacation, illness, or professional development).

Finally, outsourcing can be a good way to offer a new service with minimal risk. If it doesn't go over well, you can just cancel the contract.

Contract out those tasks you do not do well so that you can concentrate on what you do best. If you are not a cataloger, contract out cataloging to give you more time to do the online searching or database building that you do outstandingly.

Outsource only nonstrategic work; you do not want to lose control of those activities essential to the institution's mission. Reevaluate outsourcing periodically. What made sense to outsource last year may not make sense today.

What about external outsourcing? An outsourcer may approach senior management directly, saying that the library is not their core competence or is not cost-effective and should be outsourced. If you haven't already sold management on the value of your information expertise, it may be too late; they may agree to outsource information services. You lose, your customers lose, your organization eventually loses (market share, ability to innovate, etc.). Only the outsourcer wins.

IBM information guru Laurence Prusak (1993) wrote, "When closing a library, management usually asks, 'What do we do with the books?' Instead, management should ask, 'What do we do without the service?' " When one company I worked for closed my library, someone asked what were the users going to do? I replied, "Without." It is up to us to make sure that management asks the right question and that our users do not have to "do without." By making ourselves indispensable to the organization, keeping plugged into what's going on, being proactive and prepared, and providing the best service possible, we will be doing all we can to avoid being downsized or outsourced.

KNOWLEDGE MANAGEMENT

The globalization of markets and the economy, the presence of increasingly rapid change, customers demanding more from organizations, a more mobile workforce, the change in employer/worker relationships, and the availability of technology to aid in knowledge management

(KM) have made knowledge management one of the most-often heard phrases in librarianship and management. Is it just the latest buzzword or a passing fad, or is it here to stay?

What is Knowledge Management?

In 1997, early KM experts Nigel Oxbrow and Angela Abell of TFPL Ltd. defined KM as:

> the art of making creative, effective and efficient use of ALL the knowledge and information available to an organization—for the benefit of clients. Its implementation requires a review of the organization's values, culture, infrastructure, and management of intellectual assets.
>
> Knowledge Management is a *new focus* on information and knowledge, creating a knowledge-valuing environment, where information is shared, managed and used.

The important features of KM can be summarized as:

1. KM is purposeful, not random or accidental.

2. There are specific funded processes in place to capture organizational knowledge.

3. Human, experiential, tacit information is captured that would otherwise be lost.

4. This information is used, not just collected.

5. The information used is to increase the organization's competitive advantage.

The core of the knowledge proposition is to create value. Specific objectives of KM are to increase competitiveness, respond quickly to change, improve decision making, leverage intangible assets, reduce risks, reduce costs, and reduce duplication of effort (Oxbrow and Abell 1997).

KM and Your Organization

What are the consequences of not having a KM system in your organization? The organization has no commonly held mode for, no process or systems to support, and no metrics or systems for evaluating and measuring knowledge creation and dissemination (Bonaventura 1997). A good KM system enables an institution to avoid excess costs, duplication of effort, mistakes and their repetition, wasted time, and missed opportunities (Oxbrow 1998). Another consequence is what R.M. Taylor calls *organizational amnesia*. Organizations fail to retain knowledge acquired and lessons learned in the past and the people who had the knowledge leave, with no retrievable record remaining. This results in suboptimal decision making, failure to capitalize on potential new initiatives, restriction of the growth and development of the organization, and the overuse of some knowledge resources. "The essence of Knowledge Management is connection and collection." Both connecting people with information and connecting people with people are important. The organization must encourage sharing and use of information and enable conversion of information into knowledge (Bonaventura, 153).

Constraints or barriers to implementing KM include:

- Time (pressure to get it done quickly, not necessarily collaboratively)

- "Knowledge is power" syndrome (no rewards for sharing, rewards for what you know, not what you accomplish)

- NIH ("not invented here") or a reluctance to consider nontraditional ideas

- Lack of coherent knowledge vision and leadership

If the corporate culture isn't suitable, no KM project can succeed. You don't need to change the entire corporation at once. If you start in one area and it succeeds there, other departments will *want* to adopt it. To succeed, make sure you have buy-in and commitment from all stakeholders. An important tactic is quick wins. Focus on KM's impact on the business and emphasize quick, visible results to make participants feel good.

Can an OPL Do Knowledge Management?

KM requires a creative or innovative information specialist who becomes known as the expert in internal as well as external data sources, the monitor of technical standards and who can make use of his ability and experience in training users on information systems (Field 1997). As Nicholson puts it, knowledge managers must know about information technology, industry or subject knowledge, information management, value-added skills (analysis/synthesis, of information) training and skills transfer, teamwork, communication and interpersonal skills, change management. Sounds like a description of an OPL, doesn't it?

Oxbrow has said that KM is *more* than *traditional* librarianship and that the instigator of a KM project is unlikely to be the librarian. Unfortunately, this has been and still tends to be the situation. However, *we* should be the ones to lead KM initiatives, or at least to be heavily involved in them. One KM vendor gets it. He wrote, "We don't want to make the Knowledge Management process *too* automatic. It still must involve human input and *thinking on* such issues as how to categorize knowledge, what each item means and why it is in the repository" (Bonaventura). Who better to provide that input than librarians? Knapp (1998) predicted, "as organisations sort out their technology and cultural issues they will then realise the true value of information skills — and information specialists are going to get rich very soon." It hasn't happened yet, but you can still make it a reality in your organization.

So, can you get involved with KM? Should you? Of course you can.

- Do you have the skills? If you are a successful OPL or solo, you probably already do; if you don't, you can learn them.

- Do you have the desire, are you ready to be an active participant in a KM project, do you have the commitment and confidence? Only *you* can decide.

- Do you have the time? You'll find the time if you really want to do it.

Is KM for everyone? No. There are some organizations in which a KM project will *not* work; for instance, an organization "that thrives on control and exists in a constant state of crisis" (Coccia 1998, 32). Broadbent adds that,

> some organizations act as though their major competitors are other parts of their own organization rather [than] external firms or agencies. This is often reinforced by reward systems that focus on individual performance only, despite the fact that the organization might espouse notions of 'empowerment' and 'team based work groups.' If the cultural soil isn't fertile for a knowledge project, no amount of technology, knowledge content, or good project management practices will make the effort successful. (34)

Law firms are traditionally late adopters of technology, and KM has been no exception. KM was discussed at SLA conferences beginning in the mid-1980s, but not until the early 2000s by the American Association of Law Libraries, and as of this writing, is still considered a leading-edge technology by most law firms. However, no matter what it is called or how much it is taken for granted, knowledge management is not going away. We need to know what it is and how we can contribute. Then we need to let others know what we can do and have the confidence to go out and do it.

8

The Future of One-Person Librarianship

What will be the future of one-person librarianship? Will there even *be* a future? And if there is one, what do we need to do to prepare for it? Wait a minute. Why are we even asking if we have a future? Do teachers, doctors, or lawyers wonder if *they* will be around in the future? Of course not. Then why do we ask? Is it because information is becoming more available or because librarians are insecure? Unfortunately, it is probably insecurity more than the ubiquity and commoditization of information. Our profession has always had and still continues to have a very poor self-image, which leads to more introspective questioning of the future than is probably either necessary or healthy. However, I will still answer the question as I see it.

TECHNOLOGY

The future of solo librarianship, like that of the profession as a whole, will be greatly affected by technology. In the previous edition I predicted, "the greatest impact may come from client-server technology providing information at the desktop, with graphics, sound, and video; in full text with copyrights taken care of; from databases of internal documents; and by way of personalized news updates—all available from anywhere in the world to anywhere else." That future is already here for most of us. If we aren't already providing information to our clients this way, we soon will be—or we won't be employed. It is just the way things are and we must adjust.

One certainty about technology is that the tools available to us today will change tomorrow—in fact, they are likely to be obsolete tomorrow. How should we deal with this? First, accept that, a) the system you have today could be bought tomorrow for less and with more power and, b) this situation will not change. Avoid techno-lust, the belief that new is always better than old and that the future will always be better than the present. Do not assume that any and all improvements are worthwhile. Technology by itself is worthless; its only value comes from the difference it makes in our service to our customers. Stear, a computer industry analyst wrote: "Librarians have two choices: Manage the change created by the Information Revolution. Move from the role of processor to become a process manager." Or "resist change if you believe that your skill as an intermediary searcher is invaluable. Stand your ground if you can be the lowest cost provider of this service. There are still some highly skilled craftsmen who can repair typewriters" (1997, 80). Only you can decide which road you will follow.

"What happened to the predictions of the paperless society?" Although information has been moving to electronic form for years, first to CD-ROM (still widely used), then via fee-based dial-up services (which still have a place), to full-text resources on the Web, and to who knows in the future, all forms of information—including paper—will continue to coexist; each improvement adds to, rather than replaces, the old.

At the National Online Meeting in May 1995, Vance Opperman, president of West Publishing, said:

> There is no doubt that some print publications should disappear. Those that are used primarily on a paragraph-by-paragraph basis (ready reference, dictionaries, and statistics), whose probable use is less than 10 percent of the whole over its life (back runs of little used serials, government documents,

and conference proceedings), and those for which delays in publication outdate the information (consumer and price guides and financial information) are probably best done electronically—but not everything.

Paper will persist for several reasons. The most important is that acid-free paper remains the best archival medium, accessible to all without added technology. E-books were expected to become *the* method of publishing, but this hasn't happened yet and some major publishers have gotten out of the e-book business. Even if e-books become inexpensive and user-friendly, some people will still prefer paper—for its disposability, smell, feel, or a myriad of other reasons. (I, for one, will not be impressed with e-books until I can take one into the bathtub without fear of destroying it if I drop it into the water.)

Despite the tendency of some people to view technology as some kind of a god, to be venerated and offered sacrifices, technology is still just another tool to help us solve our customers' problems. We must continue to ask whether the technology can pay its way and if the benefits are worth the cost (and remember that time is a very important cost). Crawford and Gorman (1995) also identify a potential problem with an all-electronic library, the danger of losing perspective. If we only look at preselected topics (the ones in our computerized profile, online newspaper, or custom alert), we may not get a well-rounded view of the world. The researcher runs the risk of only finding the material available online. If it hasn't been indexed, it becomes invisible. The researcher also may make document retrieval decisions based on what's available online in full text rather than what will present a well-balanced view of the issues. There is also the danger of "The Young Scholar's Peril." The Young Scholar will define a field so narrowly and search so restrictively that he will miss important research. The Young Scholar will spend so much time keeping up with new postings in this area that there will be no time to organize, analyze, and synthesize all that constitutes original research. I included this in the last edition of this book, four years ago, and the problem has not gone away. In fact, if anything, the problem is even worse. Google makes it too easy to find "a" source, when what we should be looking for is "the" (authoritative) source. Teaching this to our users is one of the best things we can do as librarians.

In 1988, Riggs and Sabine asked library leaders to predict what libraries would be like in 1998. I've included the response I gave in 2001, as well as my response as of this writing in 2005.

- School librarians will be more involved in teaching. *2001*: This has come true, as it has become true of public librarians and special librarians. *2005*: As far as bibliographic instruction, yes; other teaching, not so much.

- More in-house databases will exist. *2001*: True, but many are not physically in-house, but on the Web. *2005*: The databases are not on the Web, but on organizational intranets.

- More and more computers will be networked together. *2001*: True. *2005*: Even more true, with the advent of wireless networking.

- More full-text periodicals will be available electronically. *2001*: True, but there are probably not as many as they expected. *2005*: Even more is available online in full text; in fact, some journals exist only electronically, not on paper.

- More people will access the library from home. *2001*: This has come true, but even more access information on the Web rather than their local library. Many customers of special libraries access the services of their organization's library at the desktop, and the number is increasing every day. *2005*: Remote access is still increasing. Some librarians will never even see their customers face-to-face.

- Libraries will be connected by fax machines. *2001*: This is true, but more and more interlibrary communication is done by e-mail these days. *2005*: Fax is still used, but documents can now be transmitted via e-mail (as PDF files) or are accessed directly from the Web.

- More multimedia will be available. *2001*: Boy, is this true! *2005*: Records and tape have nearly disappeared, CDs and DVDs dominate. People are now creating their own multimedia with MP3 files and streaming audio and video.

- Basic reference questions will be answered by technology, making reference more of a reader's advisory function. *2001*: This hasn't happened yet and does not seem to be looming on the horizon. *2005*: Again, the future is not here yet—and that's a good thing for us.

- Public librarians will serve as advisors, more like special librarians. *2001*: Increasingly, this is being seen as an appropriate role for public librarians but is not universal yet. *2005*: This role is continuing to evolve for public librarians, but special librarians are already taking on the role of advisor rather than intermediary.

- Document delivery will be done online. *2001*: This is true in some cases but is not the rule and definitely is not happening as fast as our customers would like. *2005*: This is rapidly becoming the norm, but since not everything is available online we still need the old-fashioned methods. Our users continue not to understand why they can't have everything instantaneously and for free.

- More active research will be done by librarians for a fee. *2001*: More and more public and academic libraries are developing fee-based information services, and more and more special libraries are charging in-house customers for their services. *2005*: Public and academic library users resist paying fees, but more and more libraries are charging for almost everything.

One caveat: the above is true of the developed world. The developing countries lag behind, but some are catching up rapidly.

Riggs and Sabine (1988) also asked what library users would be like in 2001. Again, you'll find my responses from 2001 as well as 2005.

- The client will expect materials from anywhere in the world available instantly. *2001*: This is true, especially for users of special libraries. Unfortunately, this ideal service is not available yet. *2005*: Full-text online was supposed to solve this issue, but it is still neither instantaneous nor complete—yet.

- More library education will occur in public schools. *2001*: This varies widely, both in the schools and in other organizations. Librarians still need to make sure that their customers understand which services their library can provide and how to use them most effectively. *2005*: Although there is more emphasis on information literacy in the public schools, it is still not nearly enough. Students still do not understand the difference between information and reliable and accurate information.

- Users will have raised expectations. *2001*: This is most definitely true, thanks to the Web. *2005*: Expectations are higher than ever— higher than is realistically possible.

- Users will be more adept at using technology. *2001*: Younger and more affluent users are very techno-savvy, but older and less affluent users have not really had the opportunity or access to develop these skills. It remains our job to educate our users. *2005*: While the young are mostly expert with computers, the digital divide still exists between the technology haves and have-nots. Between the developed and developing world this is even truer.

- Users will be more visually oriented. *2001*: This is especially true of younger users. *2005*: Books often seem to be an endangered species; everything must be digital, visual, interactive, and flashy.

Finally, the question was posed as to what the impact of technology would be. They forecasted the following:

- Productivity will increase. *2001*: This is partly true. Technology helps us do things faster, but we are also asked to do more things. Overall, it is a draw. *2005*: We seem to spend even more time working with technology, trying to make machines work the way they are supposed to work. Productivity per individual may be up, but there are fewer individuals working. Still a draw.

- New job responsibilities and positions will be created for librarians. *2001*: This is increasingly true, especially in corporate libraries. *2005*: Very true—we must constantly reinvent ourselves just to stay employed. Unfortunately, many librarians feel that they must leave librarianship (or at least the title librarian) to make an impact.

- Technology will not result in reduced staff but in the creation of more positions. *2001*: This is not true for most of us who find downsizing a constant threat. *2005*: Downsizing is even more threatening. Many librarians have lost their jobs and there's no sign of a change in the near future.

- Too much emphasis will be placed on technology and not enough on results. *2001*: Unfortunately, this too has come true. *2005*: This is even worse than before. If a librarian doesn't use a computer to locate information, he or she is viewed as old-fashioned or obsolete.

- Finally, less physical contact with our users will occur. *2001*: This is increasingly the situation as we deliver more services to remote users by way of the Internet, intranets, and the Web. *2005*: Still true and still increasing.

What Clare Hart, CEO of Factiva, said in 2000 is still mostly true (169–170):

> Today's online librarian has shifted from being the sole source of knowledge to really managing the process by which people, user[s], gain and apply that knowledge. The

entire information culture has become much less controlling in nature and now resembles a more open-access, free-range environment. It is the librarian, acting in many important capacities, who plays the pivotal role in bringing these impressive knowledge networks to internal and external audiences. The librarian is seen, and respected, as the Knowledge Professional who steers their organizational efforts, exerting a great deal of influence on the creation, development and management of network content and delivery. It's not just how much you know, but the relevant value of what you know that is the truest measure of information quality. Once again it is the trusted librarian who will protect and define that quality standard, ideally before it ever becomes an issue for endusers.

However, too many of us, especially OPLs, are losing our roles to nonlibrarian analysts, the information technology (computer) people, or to end-users themselves.

At the end of 2004, Outsell, the information industry market research firm, made some predictions for 2005 (Healy and Curle 2004, 5) that I expect will be of importance for a longer period of time. At the same time, Paula Hane of the magazine *Information Today* also made some predictions, some of which coincide with those of Outsell. My comments follow each prediction.

Outsell: "The democratization of information and information access, shifting power from creators and distributors to users. IT will get more personal as a generation matures. Experimentation and variations on blogs and RSS feeds will proliferate, increasingly making publishers of us all (and cutting the traditional ones out of the loop). Better tools for personalized filtering of RSS feeds will emerge."

Hane: "New ways to personalize and aggregate content will expand. RSS, or something like it, will be an enabler. Corporate blogs will be increasingly important for communication and collaboration."

Siess: Many librarians perceive these trends as a threat to our jobs. However, they are and must be seen as opportunities. We must take the lead on bringing RSS, blogs, and other personalized information sources into our organizations. If we fail to lead our users we will be ignored and fall further out of the loop.

Outsell: "The liberation of content from its containers, which is taking power away from those who see themselves in the book, magazine, newspaper, database, or directory business rather than the information business. Information management roles will converge and be less defined by the content types the deal with."

Hane: "Open access is an ongoing story. The consensus seems to be that multiple publishing models will coexist while things settle down."

Siess: As both a user and producer of content, this trend both delights and worries me. As a user, it is wonderful to be able to find full text on the Web—no more interlibrary loan, no more expensive document delivery services to rely upon, just look in Google and download the article. How convenient! On the producer side, I have two concerns. As a publisher, I will lose my source of revenue if I put *The One-Person Library* newsletter up on the Web for free, but if everyone else does it, what options do I have? As an author, I am not as concerned about revenue (although most authors are), but about the integrity of the information. What is to prevent someone from downloading my work, rewriting some parts—and changing the meaning, and uploading it back to the Web. The work will appear to be mine, but will present a different meaning than I intended. I have no idea how these issues will be resolved, but they must be resolved (or publishers and authors will not participate in Open Access). However, I finally decided that getting the information out quickly was more important and have turned the newsletter into the blog, OPL Plus.

Outsell: "The power of technology all around us, with tools to find content, break it down, and build new kinds of content and new distribution streams."

Hane: "Content-analysis technologies will continue to develop. Access to massive amounts of content means that we desperately need tools that can extract meaning and trends from unstructured data sources."

Siess: These predictions are right on the mark. With the tremendous amount of information coming at us, how do we make meaning of it? While a bit leery of machine content-analysis, I think it is probably better than no analysis at all, which is what usually happens when one is confronted with too much information—we just ignore most of it.

Outsell: "Power shifts as the traditional publishing model evolves into a 'content supply-chain' model."

Hane: "Books and other print resources will continue to make their way to the digital world."

Siess: I think that this is the most important trend of all. Information will be information, whether it come via print, audio, video, or on the Web. Librarians need to become content indifferent. Library catalogs will need to index and provide access to all formats equally. More importantly, we need to convince our users that we deal with much more than books—we answer their questions using information in whatever format it is found. Our library walls are elastic; our library size is infinite.

THE LIBRARY OF THE FUTURE

In 1996, Michael Gorman focused on three aspects of the library of the future, that is, the madness—a network of human and electronic resources available in only one form, that is, electronic; the reality—the library as a place with or without walls, influenced by money or the lack of it, requiring us to do more with less; and the dream—a library freely available to all, staffed by skilled professionals, marked by local and national cooperation, intelligently using technologies old and new, with free access to remote resources. In 1995, Gorman and Walt Crawford questioned the vision of all data-information-knowledge being online and universally available; everyone being able to make effective use of this data and happy to pay; and copyright problems being solved as "irresponsible, illogical, and unworkable." Libraries as physical entities will not cease to exist, nor will print. These authors also pointed out the dangers of the "Enemies of the Library," which include enemies within, such as the suicidal librarian (those who call themselves information specialists and library managers without library educations), and doomsayers among library school faculty (predicting the death of print and removing the word "library" from the name of the school). "Librarianship will die if librarians and library educators kill it off" (1995, 107). Also on the enemies' list are those who deny or minimize the professionalism of reference librarianship; those who encourage users to develop the research skills needed to replace the librarian, that is, assuming that they even want to do so; and the new barbarians who believe that facts are all that are important, not knowledge, organization, or preservation.

In an article in *Library Journal*, Schement (1996, 35) saw the threat coming from another direction. "In the long run, the decline of community threatens librarians most severely. However, the information society is evolving away from the traditional notion of community." The library of the future must first teach *mediacy skills* (a term coined by Toni Carbo, who defined *mediacy skills* as literacy, plus knowing where to find information, plus knowing what to do with it). Next, the library should be put in every household (by way of television, the Internet, reference resources, and mediacy services). Finally, new communities of the 21st century should be built—that is, virtual communities. Thus the library turns from a territorial institution to a functional institution. Libraries must act decisively; talk with other libraries, museums, schools, and media; develop alliances because "not only do librarians have a great stake in the information society, but all of us as citizens have a great stake in the success of libraries" (Schement 1996, 36).

FUTURE ROLES OF THE LIBRARIAN

> I love librarianship and all it stands for, and I am quick to say to any young person who comes to me for career advice that librarianship is the best of all careers because it can engage you intellectually while you are being of service—truly of service—to others. But I also tell them that it is a career in which everything changes. It always has and it always will, and they must be willing to deal with change throughout their careers. That, in a nutshell, is what's exciting about librarianship. (Guy St. Clair in St. Clair and Berner 1996)

More and more of us will be working outside of libraries. Whether in an organization or on our own, the location of a librarian in a physical library may be unnecessary and, in some cases, undesirable. In the corporate sector, librarians are moving out of the library into the business units, working alongside other professionals to provide the information needed for informed decisions right at the point of the decision. This is also happening in the academic world. Subject specialists are no longer confined to the library. They may work in the building where the majority of their clientele works, whether or not the library materials are at the same site. Information commons are being created beside areas where students naturally gather (the cafeteria, for example), with computer terminals and librarians. Taking the library to the user is also a trend for public libraries. They establish mini-branches in shopping malls, downtown store fronts, schools without libraries, and even nursing homes and senior citizen centers in order to attract users and facilitate access to and help with finding information—the modern equivalent of the bookmobile (which still thrive in many areas, rural and urban).

D. Scott Brandt (in O'Leary 2000, 22) says that in the future, our new roles may not be "itemized in job descriptions and obtained through training regimens. Instead, 'new roles' must be understood as attitudes, aptitudes, and approaches, as a set of capabilities that can be quickly and effectively applied to whatever new need or opportunity arises. These new roles are harder to define, to acquire, and to apply, yet they are and will be more important to the survival and success of librarians than anything to which a position announcement can be attached." We will have to unlearn some old roles and rules and learn the new ones.

Partnering or team-building skills will become even more vital in the future. We thought that knowledge management or the building of institutional intranets and Web pages would create a partnership between librarians and computer departments. In some cases this has been true, but in others the computer sector took both their role and ours. We have to emphasize to management that *content* is what is important on these systems, not the systems themselves, and that we, librarians, are the ones best equipped to find, verify, organize, and deliver content to end-users. Librarians have great potential for contributing to healthcare as part of care and research teams, but the establishment is very slow in realizing this. Law librarians can aid in prospecting for new clients and creating and delivering continuing legal education programs, but again there is only slow recognition of this role.

We cannot aim low. Merry (1994) noted that in the organization of today the chief information officer (CIO) usually is an IS/MIS/IT (computer) person. This position should actually be called the CTO, or chief technology officer. The CIO should be a librarian or an information professional. Some librarians have already made it to the top. Librarians have become bank vice presidents (Carol Ginsburg at Deutsche Bank, New York, New York), partners in consulting firms (Trish Foy at PriceWaterhouseCoopers, Stamford, Connecticut), and confidants to chief executive officers (CEOs) (Lisa Guedea Carreno at Highsmith, Fort Atkinson, Wisconsin) (in Buchanan 1999), but there are so few of these high-level librarians that one can remember their names. That should not prevent us from aspiring to these positions, however.

THE FUTURE FOR SPECIFIC TYPES OF LIBRARIANS

The Fifth Information Innovator's Institute, held in 2000, focused on the role law librarians would play in law firms in the next five years. The participants found that the added value of being current has diminished—it has become a given—and the new added value is in linking information from diverse sources to save lawyers' time (Shaffer 1996, 5). For example, if an attorney enters the administrative code section dealing with a specific type of drug, the system should automatically generate links to medical journal articles about related research. Another finding of the institute was that we have moved from computer systems designed, implemented, and maintained in-house to ones purchased off the shelf or located on the Internet and accessed from around the world. Because we no longer have to spend time developing the products, we can now focus on content (information) instead of technology.

Medical librarians are already moving out of the library and into the future. One example is clinical librarianship, where the medical librarian receives special, accelerated medical training and then becomes a part of the patient team. The librarian accompanies physicians on rounds. Equipped with a laptop computer, a wireless modem, an Internet connection, and access to medical databases, the librarian can often provide instant answers to clinical questions. When the answer cannot be found immediately, the librarian returns to the library (or his or her desk or cubicle) and engages in a lengthy search, delivering the answer (not raw data or articles) to the physician within hours. More and more medical librarians participate in either clinical or grand rounds, but this is by no means a universal occurrence.

The small public library is also changing and will continue to do so. More emphasis is on nonprint collections (videos, CDs, and DVDs).

Access to the Internet is both a boon and a bane. The public library is probably the best institution to offer Internet access to the person who does not own a computer, but cost and content are big problems. Who will provide the technology? Who will train all the librarians? New services bring more customers into the library, but sometimes the money is not available to expand facilities and services to accommodate them. More and more users access the library from the comfort of their own homes, via the Web. However, many libraries, public and otherwise, have seen an increase in traffic in the library even as visits to and use of their Web site increase. It seems that availability of information at home can whet the appetite for more information, including that available only in the library. The academic library is probably the type of library most able to guarantee its existence in the future.

The physical appearance of future libraries may be very different from today's library. Many libraries now have a café or coffee bar. More areas for group collaboration are needed as more individual research is done off-site. Even the exterior and interior designs are changing. The library at George Mason University in Fairfax, Virginia, U.S.A., has neon on the outside and window displays similar to those in a retail establishment. In 2004 I participated in a tour of New Zealand public and academic libraries offered by John Stanley Associates, an Australian firm working with libraries worldwide to incorporate concepts from the retail sphere into library design (and services) in order to attract and satisfy customers. Many of the libraries looked nothing like the wood-paneled, rectilinear, dimly lit library of my youth. There were neon signs, bright lighting, ramps connecting many levels of shelving, interspersed with reading areas with comfortable seating upholstered in vibrant colors. Librarians were located throughout the buildings, not just at the usual reference and circulation desks. One library, located in the same complex as a museum, had artifacts displayed along with the books on the subject. Music was everywhere, and not just quiet background music, but live performers. Although these libraries seemed chaotic to me, they were wildly popular with their constituencies. All reported large increases in number of users and library visits. There is a lesson here for all of us—change, adapt, get "with it," or die.

THE FUTURE OF ONE-PERSON LIBRARIANSHIP

Back in 1986, Guy St. Clair was confident that one-person librarians (OPLs) would continue to exist and their numbers would increase. He predicted that in the future there would be more interaction among OPLs and more literature written about them. This has all come to pass. The Solo Librarians Division of SLA has grown and thrived. OPL or Solo groups have been formed in many countries, such as Australia, Austria, Canada, Germany, Israel, Switzerland, and the U.K. Books about OPLs have been written in the U.S.A. (by Berner, Williamson and Siess), in Germany (by Peeters), and in Australia (by Dartnall). Many articles about OPLs have appeared in the library literature around the world, and some have even been seen in the nonlibrary press (such as the profile of Highsmith's librarian and her CEO—"The smartest little company in the world"—in *Inc.*). OPLs even have their own journals: *Flaschenpost* (published by Juergen Plieninger of the University of Tuebingen, Germany for the German OPL Initiative—the name means letter in a bottle, a reference to the Peeters' book, *Das Robinson Crusoe Syndrom*), *Flying Solo* (for members of the SLA Solo Librarians Division), and *OPALessence* (published by the One Person Australian Librarians group of ALIA). There is even an OPL Archive at the Library of the University of Illinois at Urbana-Champaign (where both St. Clair and I went to library school).

Instead of OPLs being downsized out of existence, it is likely that more will be created. Some of these, unfortunately, will be from the downsizing of larger libraries. Many more, however, will come from the realization that information is absolutely necessary for an organization's success and that a trained information professional, that is to say a librarian and not a computer person, is the best one to handle this responsibility. To quote St. Clair (1987, 267), managers "will find that they get more value for their money by employing one highly skilled and effective librarian/information specialist instead of a team—however small—of generalists who are not as skilled" and "there is also recognition in the profession that one-person librarianship just might become a standard for library staffing in the future. [Often] one excellent, efficient, and enthusiastic librarian or information specialist is preferable to two or more who do not provide the same level of service for users." Although there have been drastic changes in the information climate since he wrote those words, the desire for good library service and good information delivery has not changed. The OPL more than ever is able to serve an organization's information needs with little or no assistance.

We will, of course, continue to have challenges. The idea that *"everything, for free"* is on the Internet is an obstacle we all have faced and it will continue to be a problem. We must show our patrons that they have only found the tip of the information iceberg and the rest can best be found by trained information professionals who know where to look (for instance, in fee-based databases or in other librarians' collections). The teaching of information literacy, the ability to locate, evaluate, and use information, will become increasingly important. A second major challenge is downsizing. "We need to show our management how invaluable we are so we will not be downsized right out the door." We have a responsibility to those who follow us—to help newcomers find out how great it is to be an OPL. "If we do our best, we can have a very rewarding future!" (Austin 1996).

In 1997, Mary Ellen Bates, a library consultant wrote, "the future of solo librarians is very positive. Solos are in the front line of the battle for the hearts and minds of information consumers—they can run lean and mean operations within their organizations to educate, consult with, and provide in-depth research for the professionals within their organizations." Their roles will be to teach consumers how to shop around and select the most appropriate information resources, train them in the most cost-effective search techniques, and support them when they need more complex research done that goes beyond the capabilities of the end-user's search tools. Sometimes it is difficult to give up some of the online searching—this is the part that many solos enjoy the most. But in handing over the basic tools to library patrons, OPLs can build their jobs into that of information consultant and guru instead of information gofer. And remember, our customers come back to us when they find that they're not finding what they want. When they realize that it isn't all at their fingertips on the Web, they begin to really appreciate our information gathering and analysis skills.

When asked, "What is your vision for the future of libraries staffed by one librarian?" Jill Hamrin Postma, co-founder of the Chicago Area Solo Librarians, replied, "I see all of us developing our networking skills more and more as staff is cut back. We have to network with each other to keep fresh and informed. If we can get funding, new technologies will be so exciting! We can have wireless, portable devices where people can pick up information out in the field. We will not be tied down to the desktop anymore. Librarians have jumped into technology more than other professions even though this has transformed their jobs. Reference librarians get fewer reference questions now" (Arist 2004).

MY VIEW OF THE FUTURE

I said in the first edition of this book (*The SOLO Librarian's Sourcebook,* 1997) that librarianship would increasingly depend on technology. This is still true. In fact, technology has become more important than we imagined at the time. Therefore, we must be sure we become the masters of technology. Because it is unlikely that our current or prospective employers will be willing to train us in the new technology, it remains our responsibility to find, obtain, and—all too often—pay for this training ourselves.

We must realize that we are the only ones who can make our own future. We are responsible for our destiny. The computer or the Internet will not be able to answer every question, will not replace the human touch, cannot greet the user with a smile, cannot provide the personalized information that our customers have come to expect.

It is clear that to remain part of the information mainstream, we must change. No longer will it be enough to be passive information providers; we will have to take a proactive role in promoting information services and the importance of our role in the process. Our educational system will have to change so that library schools produce graduates who meet the needs of their future workplaces, whether in a traditional library or not. We must change our image with the public. We must stop whining and demanding respect and begin earning it by our actions.

We need to have more contact and interchange among OPLs. Networking is now and will continue to be imperative for survival. Fortunately, networking is getting easier every day. There are multitudes of electronic discussion lists. Organizations serving OPLs are growing and beginning to cooperate. For those in developing countries, networking is even more important. Therefore, it is incumbent on experienced OPLs to establish and maintain mentoring relationships with OPLs elsewhere so that they will no longer feel unprepared and alone. We can also communicate to library students, prospective students, and those new to the profession the joy of working in a one-person library and increase the odds that they will find productive and enjoyable employment.

Note that I use "we" throughout these thoughts. None of us can sit back and wait for the future to happen—for "them" to make changes. We all have to take an active part in making the future happen the way we envision it. We need to have the right education, the right attitude, and the right image. We need to make sure that not only are we experts, but that we are experts in the right things. We need to have the breadth and depth of knowledge required by our employers, customers, and society; we also need to make sure that they know what we have to offer. We have to convince them that we are the best (maybe the only) ones to help them meet their goals. We must position ourselves to become an indispensable part of their business plan. Then, and only then, will we not have to worry about the future. Then, and only then, will we be paid what we are worth. Then, and only then, will we become full partners in the worldwide information process.

As the Hebrew sage Hillel said, "If I am not for myself, who will be for me?" No one is going to make our future for us. *We* have to do it.

"If I am for myself alone, what am I?" But we cannot be concerned only with ourselves. We must be for our customers—that is our mission—and we must give back to others, especially those coming into the profession after us.

"If not now, when?" Finally, we have to act now—before we are marginalized out of existence. There is no tomorrow—the future is now!

Part 2
Resources

Edited by John Welford

9

Business, Management, and Economics

ADVERTISING

AdCritic.com, http://www.adcritic.com

Includes new ads, news, opinion, their own top 20, print and design, music, and more. From *Advertising Age*.

Adflip, http://adflip.com

"The world's largest" searchable database of old print ads, especially automobiles. I'm not sure how you'd use it, but it is fascinating.

BUSINESS

Print Resources

Business Rankings Annual Lists of Companies, Products, Services, & Activities Compiled from a Variety of Published Sources, Thomson/Gale, 2003, ISBN 0-7876-6695-5, USD390

CBD Research Directories

Very complete directories on European industrial and trade associations, American companies, Asian and Australian companies, and European companies. Prices range from £125–£250. Some were not very current (editions in the early 1990s). Some available on CD-ROM, none available online. http://www.cbdresearch.com/listbooks.htm

Plunkett's Retail Industry Almanac, Plunkett Research, ISBN 1-891775-16-1, USD200, with CD-Rom

"Complete" guide to the U.S. retail industry, major firms, contacts, shopping centers, statistics, and business trends. Plunkett also publishes similar works for the InfoTech, Engineering, Internet/Telecommunications, Entertainment/Media, Health Care/Biotech, Finance/Investments, Engineering/Technology, and Energy industries. Plunkett Research, Ltd., PO Drawer 541737, Houston, TX 77254-1737, U.S.A., phone: 1-713-932-0000, fax: 1-713-932-7080, http://www.plunkettresearch.com

Sackers, Nicole, Michelle Nutting, and Sinead Williams. Free Australian and New Zealand Business Information Resources: A Report from the Melbourne Business Information Group. *Online* 28(5), September/October 2004, http://www.infotoday.com/online/sep04

Standard and Poor's Industry Surveys, http://sandp.ecnext.com/coms2/page_industry

Associations

The Food Institute, One Broadway, Elmwood Park, NJ 07407 U.S.A., phone: 1-201-791-5570, fax: 1-201-791-5222, e-mail: info@foodinstitute.com, http://www.foodinstitute.com

Grocery Manufacturers of America (GMA), 2401 Pennsylvania Ave., NW 2nd Floor, Washington DC 20037 U.S.A., phone: 1-202-337-9400, fax: 1-202-337-4508, e-mail: info@gmabrands.com, http://www.gmabrands. com

Web Sites

10K Wizard, http://www.10kwizard.com

Free real-time online access to public company filings to the U.S. Securities and Exchange Commission. From 10K Wizard Technology LLC, Dallas, Texas, U.S.A.

Bloomberg.com, http://www.bloomberg.com

"Your complete source for news moving the oil, gas, and electricity markets from one of the authoritative sources in the field. Includes markets, money, magazines and books, entrepreneur network, life, media, charts, tools.

Board Analyst, http://www.thecorporatelibrary.com/Products-andServices/board-analyst.html

A range of screening tools and access to comparative data across firms and individual directors previously impossible with any other tool, along with a unique, investment-oriented rating system that ties it all together. From the Corporate Library, The Corporate Library is an independent investment research firm in Portland, Maine, U.S.A.

Business & Company Resource Center, from Thomson/Gale, http://www.galegroup.com/BusinessRC

Also Business & Company Profiles ASAP and Business International & Company Profiles.

Business Daily Review, http://businessdailyreview.com

A daily roundup of the best feature stories and book reviews in online editions of business magazines.

Business History, http://www.let.leidenuniv.nl/history/res/bushis

From Leiden University, The Netherlands, this site has links to the corporate histories hidden in corporate Web sites. Also hints for finding such histories.

Business Publications Search, http://www.bpubs.com

I love their advertising line: "No homepages. No indexes. No surfing—just content. Because your time is worth something." You can search for an article from business publications by category or keyword, then download the article—free. From BPubs.com and professional librarians Steven Matthews, the Knowledge Services Director at Clark, Wilson in Vancouver, British Columbia, Canada.

Business Reference on the Net, http://marylaine.com/busref2.html

A presentation by Marylaine Block for the Prairie Area Library System on September 8, 2004. Includes indexes and search tools, directories, statistics, company information, personal finance, consumer information, small business, marketing, international business, management, and business law.

CEOExpress, http://www.ceoexpress.com

Business portal "designed by a busy executive for busy executives." Many, many links to news, markets, government, statistics, research, law, and marketing resources. Searchable by marketplace or resource. Started by an experienced executive.

Companies & Executives, from Factiva, http://www.factiva.com/products/fce/fce.asp?node=menuElem1822

Information on companies, industries, and executives from Reuters, Dun & Bradstreet, Factiva, Bureau van Dijk, Hoover's, Standard & Poor's, Mergent, Thomson, Freedonia, IBIS, Marquis Who's Who, and Forrester.

Companies House, http://www.companieshouse.gov.uk

U.K. "equivalent" of the U.S. Securities and Exchange Commission. Free searches limited to the following information, but can order full reports for a fee. Name and registered office, date of incorporation, SIC code, previous names, branches, and overseas details.

Company Dossier, from LexisNexis, http://www.lexisnexis.com/CompanyDossier/

Find U.S. and global company overview information, financials, competitive information, executives, subsidiaries, current news articles and press releases, docket listings, litigation trends and risks, trademarks, inside and outside counsel, auditor, bank information, and more.

Company Profiles and Business Information Center, http://www.datamonitor.com

From Datamonitor, covers seven industry sectors: Automotive, Consumer Markets, Energy, Financial Services, Pharmaceuticals and Healthcare, Technology, and Transport and Logistics.

The Corporate Library, http://thecorporatelibrary.com

Weekly news briefs, special reports, links, glossary of terms, best practices of corporate governance and databases of corporate officers and past articles. Searchable and free.

The Economist Marketing Guides, http://www.economist.com/encyclopedia/Articles.cfm?section=975278&type=action

Short, useful articles on everything from advertising to test marketing, in British and U.S.A. versions.

EntreWorld, http://www.entreworld.org

A portal just for the small office–home office entrepreneur from the Ewing Marion Kauffman Foundation, Kansas City, Missouri, U.S.A.

Executive PayWatch Database, http://www.aflcio.org/cgi-bin/aflcio.pl

CEO Compensation Index by Company, from a labor union, U.S.A. only.

Hoover's, http://www.hoovers.com

Free searching by company name, ticker symbol, IPO, keywords, executive names, or Duns number, or browse alphabetically, by industry, location, or stock symbol.

Kellysearch, http://www.kellysearch.com

More than 2 million U.K. and other companies and 10 million products, from the same publishers as Kompass, but with no contact details or financial information (but free instead of subscription).

Librarian's Toolbox for Business, http://www.sls.lib.il.us/reference/ workshop/business/toolbox.html

A list of print and online resources that can help you find business information. Part of Business Reference: A Cycle of Workshops from the Suburban Library System, Burr Ridge, Illinois, U.S.A.

Power Screener, http://www.investor.reuters.com/ReadHTML.aspx? target=%2fopinion%2ffind%2ftutorial

This free site (after registration) from Reuters lets you screen their database of nearly 10,000 companies on 84 different criteria, such as price, earnings, value, dividends, or growth rates. You can even create your own screens. Highly recommended by Find/SVP.

Securities and Exchange Commission (U.S.A.), http://www.sec.gov/ edgar/searchedgar/webusers.htm

Search their EDGAR database for free. Supports the following types of searches: public companies and filings, latest filings, historical records, mutual fund prospectuses. HTML and PDF versions of the actual forms available.

Thomas Global Register, http://www.tgrnet.com

Free global directory of companies by product or service. Registration required. Gives company name and address, telephone and fax, number of employees, year founded, lines of business. Also can request a quote or documentation online and can create one's own contact list.

Trade Association Forum, http://www.taforum.org/

Links to information on U.K. trade associations, the business sectors they represent, jobs, government, quality measurement, and suppliers. Free registration required. Produced by the Forum, a quasi-governmental group.

International Business

Cerved Business Information, http://www.cerved.com/xportal/
home-eng.jsp

Detailed data in English from Italian chambers of commerce, with
financial statements, director information, and benchmarking tools.
Searchable. Covers about 4 million companies. Fee-based, but you
can pay-as-you-go by credit card (or sign a prepaid contract). Prices
seem reasonable considering that this is data that would be hard to
find elsewhere.

Directory of International Electricity and Gas Utilities, http://www.
utilityconnection.com/page3x.html

Information on 438 International Electric & Gas, Municipal,
Cooperative, State, Federal, Water and Wastewater Utilities. Also,
propane resources, deregulation, customer choice, transmission services, conservation, user organizations, regulation, rates, conferences,
capital and equity markets, commodity prices, and other news and
information. From the Utility Connection, Atlanta, Georgia, U.S.A.

Europages: the European Business Directory, http://www.europages.net

Search more than 550,000 companies by product or service, activity, or company name—in one of 25 languages. From Eurédit SA,
France.

Greek Business Information, Evresi, http://www.evresi.gr

Search categories include apparel, electronics, insurance, government, food, construction, hardware, magazines, cultural organization,
antiques, bookstores, legal services, shipping and cruise lines, airlines,
automobiles, and travel agents. Links to other Greek portals, financial
sites, and career opportunities.

IBIC Global Gateway, http://globalgateway.t-bird.edu/GlobalGateway/

Lists of links, with ratings of quality, from Thunderbird, the
American Graduate School of International Management. Career
Planning, Case Studies, Countries and Regions, International Studies,

Modern Languages, News, Search Engines and Metasites, Statistics, Travel, and World Business.

International Energy Information, http://www.eia.doe.gov/emeu/ international/cy_index.html
Country by country information, from the U.S. Department of Energy.

International Monetary Fund, Bureau of Languages Terminology Database, http://jolis.worldbankimflib.org/BLS/term.htm
Multilingual directory of more than 4,500 terms, without definitions, designed for translators in the business field. Includes acronyms and currency units.

UDI's Electricity Bookmark, http://www.platts.com/Analytic%20 Solutions/UDI%20Data%20&%20Directories/Electricity%20Book marks/
Links to more than 1,000 power producers, power plants, and distributors around the world.

World Nuclear Power Plants, http://www.insc.anl.gov/plants
Using maps that plot all nuclear power plants, one can find the name, owner, type, output, status, suppliers, fuel details, core configuration, control system, and vessel and containment. From the International Nuclear Safety Center, Argonne National Laboratory, Illinois, U.S.A.

Free Australian Business Information Sources

Australian Bureau of Statistics, http://www.abs.gov.au

Australian Investor, http://www.australianinvestor.com.au
Special feature allows you to compare a company with up to three competitors, and other investment information, registration required.

Australian Productivity Commission, http://www.pc.gov.au
Industry reports.

Australian Stock Exchange, http://www.asx.com.au

Bourse Investor, http://www.bourseinvestor.com

Australian share prices back to the early 1990s, registration required.

Business Entry Point, http://www.business.gov.au

Extensive links to government and business organizations, searchable subset of the official Australian Business Register, links to federal, state, territory, and local government Web pages.

Equities Info, http://www.equitiesinfo.com

Direct links to more than 1,000 annual reports.

Free New Zealand Business Information Sources

ANZ Economic Publications, http://www.anz.com/nz/about/media/economic.asp

Full-text reports on the economy and industry and *Weekly Market Focus* reports.

Market New Zealand, http://www.marketnewzealand.com

News and industry reports, assistance with trade inquiries, large exporter database, registration required, but a free trial is available.

New Zealand Companies, http://www.companies.govt.nz

Some good information, but fee-based, only announcements are free.

New Zealand Stock Exchange, http://www.nzx.com

Announcements, price data, indices, trade summaries, and statistics.

Reserve Bank of New Zealand, http://www.rbnz.govt.nz

For monetary policy and statistics.

Statistics New Zealand, http://www.stats.govt.nz

Statistics on economy, industry, environment, people, and census data. Downloadable Excel file.

International Company Financials

Corporate Information, http://www.corporateinformation.com
Provided by Wright Investors' Service.

Sedar, http://www.sedar.com
For Canadian filings, a joint project between the Canadian Securities Administrators (CSA) and CDS INC, a subsidiary of the Canadian Depository for Securities Limited.

SkyMinder, http://www.skyminder.com
For international financial reports. Fee-based from Economy.com, West Chester, Pennsylvania, U.S.A., Sydney, and London.

MANAGEMENT AND ECONOMICS

Dismal Scientist, http://www.dismal.com
Economic and financial information. Free two-week trial available.

Econ Data & Links, http://zimmer.csufresno.edu/~johnsh/econ/econ_EDL.htm
From John Shaw, Emeritus Professor of Economics, California State University, Fresno, California, U.S.A.

Economic History Database, http://www.eh.net/databases
Provides an online location for researchers in economic history to make their data series available to other professionals and interested scholars. Ten such series were directly available when the site was accessed, with many more being listed as available via the named researcher. The data in question is quite disparate, so it will either be of great use to an individual scholar, or of no use at all! From Miami University, Ohio, U.S.A. and Wake Forest University, North Carolina, U.S.A.

Economic Policy Institute Issue Guides, http://www.epinet.org/content.cfm/issueguides_issueguide
The guides include facts at a glance (reference sheets), FAQs, key tables and charts, key EPI publications, and other resources. Currently

available guides are: living wage, minimum wage, offshoring, poverty and family budgets, retirement security, social security, unemployment insurance, and welfare. Also from the EPI are economic indicators and snapshots, online calculators, and editorial material.

Economics Departments, Institutes and Research Centers in the World, http://edirc.repec.org/

From Christian Zimmermann, Department of Economics, University of Connecticut, Storrs, U.S.A.

Encyclopedia of Economic and Business History, http://www.eh.net/encyclopedia

Provided by Miami University and Wake Forest University, the EH.net encyclopedia has "high-quality reference articles," which are "written by experts, screened by a group of authorities, and carefully edited. You can search or look by topic. The top 10 articles for 2003 are included. Not every subject is included, but the ones that are seem good. Some of the fascinating subjects included are Advertising Bans, Baseball, Fraternal Sickness Insurance, 16th–17th Century Netherlands, Protestant Ethic, Tractors, and Women Workers—British Industrial Revolution.

Free Management Library, http://www.mapnp.org/library

Complete, highly integrated library for nonprofits and for-profits, with 675 topics in 72 categories from advertising to volunteers. From the Management Assistance Program for Nonprofits, St. Paul, Minnesota, U.S.A.

Harvard Business School Working Knowledge, http://hbsworking-knowledge.hbs.edu

"Authoritative business and management insights," articles, interviews, and management issues of all kinds. Free.

How Much is That? http://www.eh.net/hmit

Find out the comparative value of a U.S. dollar or U.K. pound for any two years from 1789 (for the dollar) or 1830 (pound) to 2003. Uses various measures of purchasing power, so you can really "lie with statistics." Also provides inflation rates for the U.S.A. and U.K. (1600s to present), price of gold (from 1257!), real and nominal Gross Domestic Product for U.S.A. and U.K. (U.K. from 1086!!), exchange rate of the dollar and 40 other countries (1913+) and interest rates for the U.S.A. and U.K. from 1790. Fascinating site! From Miami University and Wake Forest University.

IDEAS, http://ideas.repec.org

Billed as "the largest bibliographic database dedicated to economics and available on the Internet," this site has more than 200,000 items, including articles, software, and working papers, all searchable. Many can also be downloaded (mostly the working papers). Coverage is international. From the University of Connecticut, Storrs, U.S.A., Dept of Economics.

Market Research.com, http://www.marketresearch.com

An easy-to-use tool for tracking down market research reports across a wide range of industries worldwide, plus country reports, etc. Abstracts and tables of contents are available for many of the reports, and the database also acts as a bookshop for obtaining print and online copies of reports. Covers *Market Share Reporter, Investext, Adweek,* and other trade magazines.

Research Papers in Economics, http://econpapers.repec.org/

"A collaborative effort of over 100 volunteers in 44 countries to enhance the dissemination of research in economics. The heart of the project is a decentralized database of working papers, journal articles and software components." More than 300,000 resources are listed, two-thirds of which are available online. Much of this material, but by no means all, is free to download from the organizations that hold it.

Statistics Resources, http://www.infoctr.edu/buslib/Statistics.htm

List of links from Stuart Graduate School of Business Library, Illinois Institute of Technology, Chicago, U.S.A.

Statistical Resources on the Web Comprehensive Economics, http://www.lib.umich.edu/govdocs/stecon.html

From the University of Michigan, Ann Arbor, U.S.A.

Statistical Sources and Other Resources Online for Economic Historians and Economists, http://www.economics.utoronto.ca/munro5/Stat Resources.htm

From Professor John H. Munro, Department of Economics, University of Toronto, Canada.

Statistical Sources for Economics Selected Resources, http://www. stthomas.edu/libraries/guides/econ/Econstats.htm

From the University of St. Thomas Library, Minneapolis, Minnesota, U.S.A.

Technical Reports and Working Papers in Business and Economics, http://www.loc.gov/rr/business/techreps/techrepshome.php

A portal, provided by the Library of Congress, to a huge amount of grey literature that can be downloaded in full-text format, free of charge.

U.S. Economic Research Data, http://fraser.stlouisfed.org

FRASER (The Federal Reserve Archival System for Economic Research) has links to scanned images of historical economic statistical publications, releases, and documents. It is designed to be used with FRED II (Federal Reserve Economic Data, http://research.stlouis fed.org/fred2/) to create uninterrupted data series. Includes such oldies but goodies as All Bank Statistics 1865–1955 and Banking and Monetary Statistics 1914–1980. Thank you to the St. Louis (Missouri, U.S.A.) Federal Reserve Bank for making this information available.

NONPROFIT ORGANIZATIONS

Development Resource Center, http://www.drcharity.com/links.html

Fundraising ideas, information and resources for nonprofits, volunteers, telemarketing, marketing, public relations, and start-up. From Diane Hodiak, a real estate agent in Seattle, Washington, U.S.A.

Nonprofit Good Practice Guide, http://www.npgoodpractice.org

This resource is a project of the Philanthropic and Nonprofit Knowledge Management Initiative at the Dorothy A. Johnson Center for Philanthropy & Nonprofit Leadership, Allendale, Michigan, U.S.A., and the W. K. Kellogg Foundation. Topics include accountability and evaluation, advocacy, communications and marketing, foundations and grant making, fundraising and financial sustainability, governance, management and leadership, staff development and organizational capacity, technology, and volunteer management.

STRATEGIC PLANNING

Business.com, http://www.business.com

Click on management, strategic planning, research and reference, then white papers for white papers on strategic planning, from all kinds of sources. From a Business.com, Inc., Santa Monica, California, U.S.A.

10

Computers and the Web

BOOKS AND ARTICLES

Buckley, Peter, Duncan Clark, and Angus J. Kennedy. *The Rough Guide to the Internet*, 10th ed. New York: Rough Guides, 2004, ISBN 1-84353338-3 (paper).

Spasser, Mark A. Science and Engineering Sources on the Internet: Selective Webliography for Health Sciences Authors. *Issues in Science and Technology Librarianship*, Summer 2004, http://www.istl.org/04-summer/internet.html

SEARCH ENGINES

Australian Search Engines, http://www.webwombat.com.au
Categories include careers and education, entertainment, finance, games, lifestyle, motoring, shopping, travel, and auctions. From Wombat Technology, Melbourne, Victoria, Australia.

Country-Based Search Engines, http://www.philb.com/countryse.htm
A total of more than 2,000 search engines and 210 countries, territories, and regions. Most are listed by country, but there are lists of regional and worldwide search engines as well. From Phil Bradley, Internet Consultant, London, U.K.

The Cybercafe Search Engine, http://www.cybercaptive.com

As of December 2004, the database contains listings for 5,763 verified cybercafés, public Internet access points, and kiosks in 161 countries. Searchable by location.

Is There a LISTSERV for …?, http://www.lsoft.com/lists/listref.html

This is the official list of LISTSERV-brand electronic lists. As of February 2005, there were 54,117 public lists out of 325,699 LISTSERV lists. You can search by subject, country, or number of subscribers.

NewPages Guide to Web Links, http://www.newpages.com/NPGuides/weblinks.htm

Portals and search engines, quick reference, metasearch sites, best of commercial Web guides, and useful library-created subject guides. From a group representing independent bookstores, publishers, literary periodicals, record labels, and newsweeklies.

New Zealand Search Engine, http://nzsearch.co.nz

Search under business services, community and the arts, computers and Internet, education and training, employment, entertaining and leisure, farming and agriculture, finance and law, government and reference, health and beauty, personal and family sites, shopping, sports and recreation, or travel and tourism. From New Zealand City Ltd, Auckland.

Search Engines Worldwide, http://home.inter.net/~takakuwa/search/search.html

As of February 2005, this site had 3,105 search engines in 211 countries. From Toyo Takakuwa, a mining engineer from Tokyo, Japan.

Search engines indexed by people, not machines:

First Gov, http://www.firstgov.gov
U.S. government portal.

Google, http://www.google.com

Open Directories indexed by people, not machines:

Open Directory Project, http://www.dmoz.org
Also available in Catalan, German, Spanish, French, Italian, Korean Dutch, Japanese, and Portuguese.

U.S. Government Printing Office, http://www.gpoaccess.gov

Wikipedia, the Free Encyclopedia, http://en.wikipedia.org/wiki/Main_Page
Articles available in many languages.

Yahoo, http://en.wikipedia.org/wiki/Main_Page

CREATING BETTER WEB PAGES

Convert .pdf to html, http://www.adobe.com/products/acrobat/access_simple_form.html
Free conversion of simple files, with a link to the advanced form.

Do Search Engines "See" Your Web Site?, http://www.marketleap.com/siteindex
Input the URL of your institution (or your own URL) and see how well it shows up on the major search engines. You can also input key words or phrases and see if your site comes up on the first three pages for each search engine. Easy, fast, and well worth checking. From MarketLeap, San Francisco, California, U.S.A.

User Interface Engineering, http://www.uie.com/articles
This group publishes some very good articles on Web-site usability. Subjects include (in descending order by number of articles): design strategies, usability testing, user behavior, writing for the Web, searching, brand strengthening, rich Internet applications, personas, user and task analysis, paper prototyping, designing with Web standards, and content management systems. Free e-mail newsletter available. From an Internet-training firm, Middleton, Massachusetts, U.S.A.

What Do People Read First on a Web Site?, http://www.poynterextra. org/eyetrack2004/main.htm

A research program called Eyetrack III observed 46 people for one hour as they read mock news Web sites. The readers' eyes most often looked first at the upper left of the page, then went to the right. Once they finished reading the top of the page they went on to the bottom. Contrary to what is usually thought, they don't necessarily look at photographs first. If you want people to read carefully what you have written, use smaller type; larger type may encourage scanning. Underlined headlines discouraged their test subjects from reading the information below them. The first few words of a headline must grab the reader's attention; this is even more important the farther down on the page you go. As expected, shorter paragraphs are more likely to be read than longer ones. If the introductory paragraph is in boldface, the article is much more likely to be read. For images, the larger the better. These are only preliminary findings, but they may help you in designing Web pages that will be read.

ACCESSIBILITY

Adaptive Technology for the Internet, http://www.ala.org/ala/ products/books/editions/adaptivetechnology.htm

Online version of the excellent book by Barbara Mates, from the American Library Association.

The Adaptive Technology Resource Centre, http://www.utoronto. ca/atrc

The Adaptive Technology Resource Centre advances information technology that is accessible to all; through research, development, education, proactive design consultation, and direct service. The ATRC is part of the Resource Centre for Academic Technology at the University of Toronto, Canada.

Alliance for Technology Access, http://www.ataaccess.org

Links to many resources, including grant money. Also offers advice on site design. ATA is a network of community-based Resource

Centers, Developers, Vendors and Associates dedicated to providing information and support services to children and adults with disabilities, located in Petaluma, California, U.S.A.

Bobby, http://www.cast.org/bobby

A free utility to check your Web pages for accessibility — very thorough and easy to use. From the Center for Applied Special Technology, Ottawa, Ontario, Canada and Lexington, Massachusetts, U.S.A.

DO-IT Program, http://www.washington.edu/doit/Resources/webdesign. html

Links to information about accessible Web design. DO-IT stands for Disabilities, Opportunities, Internetworking, and Technology and is a collaboration of Computing & Communications and the Colleges of Engineering and Education at the University of Washington, U.S.A.

IBM Accessibility Center, http://www-306.ibm.com/able

Advice on employment law and adaptive computer technologies. You can download a demo of their voice-recognition software to test your Web page's accessibility. Also has case studies, product accessibility information, developer guidelines, laws and standards, accessibility regulations, and other downloads.

Review of Free, Online Accessibility Tools, http://www.webaim.org/techniques/articles/freetools

A review of eight tools for checking Web pages for accessibility, which are available free online: Accessibility Valet Demonstrator, AccMonitor Online, Bobby, Cynthia Says, TAW, Torquemada, Wave 3.5, and WebXact. From Peter Blair of WebAIM, Web Accessibility in Mind, a nonprofit organization within the Center for Persons with Disabilities at Utah State University, U.S.A.

WebABLE, http://www.webable.com

Links to white papers, projects and plans, news articles, legal information, and guidelines and standards, tools and utilities on adaptive technology.

Web Accessibility Initiative, http://www.w3.org/WAI

Guidelines, checklists, techniques, technology, evaluation and repair, translations, alternative browsers, and links to events and policy from the World Wide Web Consortium (W3C), located in Cambridge, Massachusetts, U.S.A.

OTHER WEB SITES

AARP Computers & Technology, http://www.aarp.org/computers

Not just for senior citizens, this site has some great "how-to" guides on subjects such as "How to install Windows XP Service Pack 2" or "Using RSS Feeds." There are also sections on learning to use the Net and reviews of hardware, software, gadgets, Web sites, and books. A useful resource for anyone.

All About WiFi, http://www.wifilibrary.org

Have a question about the WiFi wireless protocol? You can learn about security, mobility, management, and interoperability in the WiFi concerns section. There are also links to WiFi resources and a hotspot locator (though only for U.S.A. libraries).

Care and Handling Guide for Preservation of CDs and DVDs, http://www.itl.nist.gov/div895/carefordisc/index.html

Best practices for storage and cleaning, information on the life span of discs, and a one-page quick reference guide. Available in HTML or PDF format, from the U.S. National Institute of Standards and Technology.

Comparison Charts for Electronic Equipment, http://www.pcworld. com/resource/allinfocenters.asp

Computer magazine *PC World* has created information centers with reviews, comparison charts, articles, downloads, and pricing on just about any electronic equipment you might be interested in buying. Included are desktop and laptop computers, digital cameras, DVD drives and recorders, e-mail/instant messaging/voice Internet protocol devices, monitors, office tools, printers, spyware, and security. There are also areas just for Windows users and an upgrade center, as well as lists of top-rated products. Not every product is discussed here, but it's worth checking out before making a purchase.

Computer Policy Law, http://www.educause.edu/icpl/

Links to many full-text articles on the subject and to policies that have been drawn up by various institutions. Produced by the EDU-CAUSE/Cornell Institute for Computer Policy and Law, Ithaca, New York, U.S.A.

Computer Security, http://www.istl.org/02-fall/internet.html

An article from *Issues in Science and Technology Librarianship*, fall 2002, by Jane Kinkus of Purdue University, U.S.A., with updated links.

Geek.com, http://www.geek.com

This very geeky site has everything a computer person could want, from product reviews to articles, technology news, buying guides, and tips and tricks. However, for the merely nerdy, there is a weekly cartoon about technology that, for my money, is the best part of the site.

Ghost Sites, http://www.disobey.com/ghostsites/

An online magazine by Steve Baldwin, New York City computer consultant, devoted to reporting the disappearance of Web sites. It includes an alphabetical list of "death notices" that can be checked for confirmation that a site has died. Will it report its own demise should this ever happen?

Google Hacks, http://www.oreilly.com/catalog/googlehks

Want to learn tricks and tips for the Google search engine? This is the site. Most of the content of the new book, *Google Hacks*, is available in summary at the Web site. For instance, "Getting Around the 10 Word Limit" for a query.

Have You Hugged Your Sysadmin Today?, http://www.sysadminday.com

Did you know that the last Friday of July is System Administrator Appreciation Day? This site tells you all about it and has a description of a sysadmin's duties, gift ideas, and links to sysadmin humor.

Helping Professionals Become Better Web Searchers, http://working faster.com/

Research tools and training for serious Web users. Most of the company's information costs, but there are some interesting tips on the Web site. From Rita Vine and Working Faster.

Hoaxbusters, http://hoaxbusters.ciac.org/

From the U.S. Department of Energy's Computer Incident Advisory Capability, mostly e-mail hoaxes and chain letters, with special attention to computer virus hoaxes.

Home Computer Security, http://www.cert.org/homeusers/Home ComputerSecurity/

A very detailed, step-by-step tutorial from the Software Engineering Institute at Carnegie Mellon University, Pittsburgh, Pennsylvania, U.S.A. Includes checklists, examples, and glossaries, available in both HTML and PDF formats.

HotSpotList, http://www.wi-fihotspotlist.com

If your customers are wireless users, here is list of WiFi 802.11b hotspots around the world so they can stay in touch on the road.

Information Security Dictionary, http://www.yourwindow.to/ information%2Dsecurity

Ever wanted to know what "beta" means in relation to software or what "extranet" is? This site has those definitions and many more. Some are even tongue-in-cheek (see "Finagle's Law," for instance). The dictionary is part of the site of Information Security Policies and Disaster Recovery Associates, Altricam, U.K. Also available are various policies and procedures, with some downloadable forms.

Innovative Internet Applications in Libraries, http://www.wiltonlibrary. org/innovate.html

A super-cool site for getting ideas for new Internet projects. Categories are: ages and stages, book and reading lists, e-journals, local databases, personalized interfaces, newsletters, evaluation, special collections and online exhibits, tutorials and guides, virtual reference desk, virtual tours, Web forms, and miscellaneous. A must see—and not just for public librarians. From the Wilton Public Library, Connecticut, U.S.A.

Internet News, http://www.websearchguide.ca/netblog/

I'm not a big fan of Weblogs (yet), but this one from Gwen Harris at the University of Toronto, Canada is neat. You can find "articles and news about Internet use, search tools, current awareness tools, and general use."

Internet Statistics and Demographics, http://www.clickz.com/stats/

"Trends & Statistics: The Web's Richest Source" from ClickZ Stats, formerly Cyberatlas.

Internet World Stats, http://www.internetworldstats.com

Internet usage statistics and population statistics for the world and regions, top Internet usage, penetration, and languages. Also country links and international directories by region and for the EU, and marketing pages for broadband, the Internet Divide, Internet growth, a coaching library, industry statistics, market reports and research, and search engines and directories.

J-Lab: Cool Stuff, http://www.j-lab.org/coolstuff.html

From the Institute for Interactive Journalism of the University of Maryland, U.S.A., this site has some really neat experimental interactive programs and games.

Old-Computers.com, http://www.old-computers.com

Need to find out about an obsolete computer? Perhaps to run old software? You can probably find information on the model you need on this site. There is also a museum, a magazine, a store (of course), and links to related sites. The most popular systems are Commodore 64, MIT Whirlwind, Amiga 500, and the Univac 1. Absolutely fascinating!

PalmSource, http:www.palmsource.com

"You know your Palm Powered device is a great calendar and address book. But if that's all you use, you're missing out on the best parts." Here are expert guides to many other uses. They are arranged by interest (genealogy, aviation, languages, time management), profession (dentistry, education for students and teachers, medicine, real estate), or task (browsers, budgeting, e-mail, project management, time tracking). And these are just a few of the categories. I looked at the one for medical students; there were 14 pages of programs available (free, cheap, and "not cheap, but worth it"), testimonials, and Web links. This is a fantastic resource if you have one of these devices. From PalmSource, Inc., Sunnyvale, California, U.S.A.

PDA Classroom, http://www.pdaclassroom.com

"The mission of PDAClassroom.com is to provide teachers with the skills, motivation, and confidence to incorporate handheld technology into the 21st century classroom in an effort to increase student success." Presentations, software, hardware, tips, and articles are available for free, but you can subscribe for USD40 to get a 10-day modular curriculum for handhelds, special activities, quizzes, and lesson plans.

SiteLines: Ideas about Web Searching, http://www.workingfaster.com/sitelines

If you want some good tips on information literacy, Web searching, search engines, and Internet filters, you can search this site or subscribe to get tips regularly. From a training group called Working Faster and Rita Vine, a professional librarian, Web search trainer, and lead site evaluator.

Top Ten DotCons, http://www.ftc.gov/bcp/conline/edcams/dotcom

"Con artists have gone high-tech, using new technology to peddle traditional scams. Scam artists can be just a click away." This site from the U.S. Federal Trade Commission covers Internet auctions, access services, credit card fraud, international modem dialing, Web cramming, multilevel marketing or pyramid schemes, travel and vacation, business opportunities, investments, healthcare products and services. Even includes a form to file a complaint.

Urban Legends and Folklore, http://urbanlegends.about.com
From About.com.

Urban Legends Reference Page, http://www.snopes2.com
Check out those rumors. There is an icon to tell you if it is true, false, or unconfirmed, with details. Searchable. Rated excellent in *Library Journal*.

Virus Information Library, http://vil.nai.com/vil
From McAfee and Network Associates, this has detailed information on viruses, where they come from, how they work, and how to remove them. You can also find out about virus hoaxes and the top corporate user threats.

To find domain name ownership:

Allwhois, http://www.allwhois.com
From Alldomains.com Boise, Idaho, U.S.A.

Whois Source, http://www.whois.sc

11

Government

INTERNATIONAL AND MULTINATIONAL

CIA World Factbook, http://www.cia.gov/cia/publications/factbook/
   Information on countries around the world, from an American viewpoint, of course.

Country Briefings, http://www.economist.com/countries
   Fact sheets, forecasts, political forces, political and economic structure, and economic data, from *The Economist*. Also available for cities at http://www.economist.com/cities/

FIRST: Facts on International Relations and Security Trends, http://first.sipri.org
   Free service from the Stockholm International Peace Institute. Statistics and facts on military expenditures, arms production and trade, memberships and agreements, events, conflicts and peace keeping activities, political system, and country indicators. Recommended by Gary Price of the George Washington University, Washington, DC, U.S.A.

Flags of the World, http://www.theodora.com/flags/flags.html
   Also includes some non-country flags (such as African-American, states and provinces, and Olympics) and information on geography, people, government, economy, transportation, communications, and

defense (from the CIA Factbook), and a flag identifier tool (really neat). From Information Technology Associates, Coconut Creek, Florida, U.S.A. and Glyfada, Greece.

Government Gazettes Online, http://www.lib.umich.edu/govdocs/gazettes/

Links plus a bibliography.

National Anthems of the World, http://www.national-anthems.net/

Includes brief facts and maps, lyrics of the anthems, downloadable vocal and/or instrumental versions (in MP3) and shows what the front cover of a passport from the country looks like.

Official Document System of the United Nations, http://documents.un.org/

"ODS covers all types of official United Nations documentation, beginning in 1993. Older UN documents are, however, added to the system on a daily basis. ODS also provides access to the resolutions of the General Assembly, Security Council, Economic and Social Council, and the Trusteeship Council from 1946 onwards. The system does not contain press releases, UN sales publications, the United Nations Treaty Series, or information brochures issued by the Department of Public Information." Access used to be subscription only, but is now free. There are about 800,000 documents available, with about 100,000 added per year. Training guides are available.

Statistical Resources on the Web Foreign Government Data Sources, http://www.lib.umich.edu/govdocs/stforeig.html

Both comprehensive and country-specific statistics. Foreign government data is also available from other U.S.A. and international sources on the Statistics page and the Foreign Statistics page. From the University of Michigan, Ann Arbor, U.S.A.

UNESCO library portal, http://www.unesco.org/webworld/portal_bib

Web sites of national libraries, government information services, and library associations, as well as online resources and news of interest to librarians.

Worldwide Comparative Statistics, http://www.nationmaster.com/

Nationmaster contains statistics from such sources as the CIA World Factbook, United Nations, World Health Organization, World Bank, World Resources Institute, UNESCO, UNICEF, and OECD for the following regions of their constituent countries: Africa, Asia, Europe, Middle East, North America, Oceania, South America, Central American and the Caribbean, and Southeast Asia. Many detailed statistics are available for the following subject categories: Agriculture, Background, Crime, Currency, Democracy, Disasters, Economy, Education, Energy, Environment, Food, Geography, Government, Health, Identification, Immigration, Industry, Internet, Labor, Language, Lifestyle, Media, Military, Mortality, People, Religion, Sports, Taxation, and Transportation. For example, under Internet, there are data on broadband access, communication technology patents, hosts, Internet charges, Internet service provides (and per capita), Linux Web servers (and per capita), live journal users, secure servers, uses (and per capita), and Web sites. Full service is available only to "supporters"; for individuals that means USD50.00 per year.

AFRICA

WoYaa! African Web Portal, http://www.woyaa.com/index.html

The arts, commerce, information, education, entertainment, government, health, news, music, regions, sciences, culture and history, sports, and tourism. Available in English and French. As of February 2005 there were more than 1,400,000 links.

ASIA

Bridge to Japan, http://pages.britishlibrary.net/bridgetojapan/

Excellent set of Japan-related links, originally created by Chris Dillon, Faculty of Arts and Humanities, University College London, with the support of the Diawa Anglo-Japanese Foundation in 1995, and maintained in the U.K. by the Japan Library Group.

International Research Center for Japanese Studies (Nichibunken), http://www.nichibun.ac.jp/welcome_e.htm

Links for Japanese Studies in Japan and around the world, to Web sites of their institutions, scholarly periodicals, scholarships and fellowships, and research projects.

National Diet Library, http://www.ndl.go.jp/en/index.html

Digital library, with images of materials in digital form, and full-text database of minutes of the Diet (parliament), parliamentary documents, official gazettes, statute books, publications of government offices of Japan and other countries and documents of international organizations with links to the digital versions, and selections from NDL's collection of Japanese books about politically important figures in modern Japanese history. Search can be done by their names. Publications from the Meiji era to the present are covered. Japanese only.

AUSTRALIA

AusInfo, http://www.australia.gov.au

Official government site for Australia. Includes resources for Australians (education, employment and workplace, health, benefits, culture, heritage, sport, economics, finance and tax, travel, communities and services), businesses (start-up, investment, employer responsibilities, grants and financial assistance), and nonresidents (immigration, study, customs, employment, visas). Information about the government (acts and legislation, government publications, the Constitution, Parliament, for employees) and about the country (facts and figures, weather, fact sheets, visiting, and "student homework help").

Commonwealth Publications Official List (Australia), http://www.
publications.gov.au/

Semi-weekly list of publications from the executive branch and
Parliament, government publications at the National Library, Parliamentary
resources, legislation, gazettes, statistics, and online bookstores.

New Zealand and Pacific Island Information, http://webdirectory.
natlib.govt.nz/index.htm

Includes arts and literature, history, business and economy, community and social studies, news, media and publishing, education, recreation, environment, regions, libraries, biographies, religion, government,
law and politics, science and technology, and health. Also a Maori subject list and Pacific Island Web sites. From the National Library of New
Zealand Te Puna Matauranga o Aotearoa.

BRITAIN AND EUROPE

European Governments Online, http://www.europa.eu.int/abc/govern
ments/index_en.htm

From EUROPA, this site has links to the main governmental sites for the
EU member states, new member states, applicant countries, and other
European countries. There are also sections on "Europe in 12 lessons," key
figures, history, maps, traveling, flags, anthems, Europe Day, Eurojargon, a
Glossary, and Treaties and the Law. It's nice to see this all on one page.

NORTH AMERICA

Abbreviations and Acronyms of the U.S. Government, http://www.
ulib.iupui.edu/subjectareas/gov/docs_abbrev.html

If you've ever needed to decode the abbreviation of U.S. government agency, here is the Web site for you. Plus, it has links to the
agency or program's Web site. From Indiana University–Purdue
University, Indianapolis, Indiana, U.S.A. Check out their Military
Acronyms and Glossaries page too at http://www.ulib.iupui.edu/
subjectareas/gov/military.html

The American Presidency, http://www.americanpresident.org

Two perspectives on the presidency: the Presidency in History (detailed biographies of each of the 43 past and present Presidents and First Ladies; biographies of Cabinet members, staff, and advisers; timelines detailing significant events during each administration; and multimedia galleries to explore) and the Presidency in Action (information on the function, responsibilities, and organization of the modern presidency, with detailed descriptions of the areas of presidential responsibility, updated organization charts, staff listings, and biographies of past and present staff and advisers).

CoolGov, http://coolgov.com

Features funny or interesting information on government Web sites in categories including cheap stuff, government education, health, history, international affairs, law enforcement, maps, money, nature, rules and regulations, science, space, spooks 'n spies, transportation, video, widgets and toys, and work. One example: "Curious, but true ... the White House maintains a list of slang terms used in the drug trade" (from the Government Education page).

FedStats (U.S. Home Page), http://www.fedstats.gov

Statistical profiles and maps of states, counties, cities, congressional districts, and federal judicial districts; statistics by geography (international comparisons, national, state, county, local); published collections of statistics available online (including the *Statistical Abstract of the United States*), Federal agencies with descriptions of the statistics they provide, links to their Web sites, contact information, and key statistics; press releases from individual agencies; kids' pages on agency Web sites, selected agency online databases, and Federal statistical policy (budget documents, working papers, and *Federal Register* notices).

Government Statistical Sources, http://www.law.northwestern.edu/law library/research/govt/statistical.htm

Links with descriptions, including census, criminal justices and crime reports, labor, policy, and indexes. From the Pritzker Legal

Research Center, Northwestern University, Evanston, Illinois, U.S.A. (A shorter URL for the above link: http://snipurl.com/css9).

Información Gubernamental en Español, http://library.nevada.edu/govpub/spanishgovlinks.html
From the University of Nevada-Las Vegas, U.S.A., comes this guide to Spanish-language government Web sites in the U.S.A.

MetroDynamics, http://proximityone.com/metros.htm
Statistical information and comparisons by Standard Metropolitan Statistical Areas in the U.S.A. From Proximity, Alexandria, Virginia, U.S.A.

New Documents Blog, http://www.resourceshelf.com/docuticker
Daily update of new reports from government agencies, nongovernmental organizations, think tanks, and other groups from Gary Price and the Resource Shelf.

NIOSHTIC-2: The NIOSH Resource Database, http://www.cdc.gov/niosh/nioshtic-2/
A bibliographic database of occupational safety and health publications, documents, grant reports, and other communication products supported in whole or in part by the National Institute for Occupational Safety and Health (NIOSH). More than 34,000 articles with abstracts and some full-text links. All are searchable by disease, injury, cause, or occupation.

Plogress, http://www.plogress.com
This blog lets you look up what bills have been sponsored by any U.S. congressperson. Roll calls from votes starting in 2005 will soon be added and updated daily, and other enhancements are planned. Very interesting and you can see that this requires a lot of work.

Product Recalls, http://www.recalls.gov
Here you can find recall official information for consumer products, cars, boats, food, medicines, cosmetics, and environmental products like pesticides. You can search by product, keyword, or company. Also available in Spanish.

Safety and Health Issues: Workplace Violence, http://www.osha-slc.gov/SLTC/workplaceviolence

Workplace violence, standards, hazard awareness, possible solutions, and links to additional information, from the U.S. Department of Labor, Occupational Safety & Health Administration.

SOMNIA: Spotlight on Military News and International Affairs, http://www.cfc.forces.gc.ca/spotnews_e.html

Produced by the Canadian Forces College, Toronto, this site features news and commentary on Canada and the international community, archives, a daily quotation, and events on this day in Canadian history, from the *New York Times*. Not updated on weekends or holidays.

State and County Quick Facts, http://quickfacts.census.gov/qfd/

Quick browsing for U.S.A. national, state, county, and city (more than 25,000 population) statistics on people, business, and geography.

Statistical Sites on the World Wide Web, http://stats.bls.gov/bls/other.htm

Official United States Bureau of Labor's links to statistics and information from more than 70 agencies in the U.S. Federal Government, state labor market information, international statistical agencies and many other nations.

Uncle Sam: Who's Who in U.S. Government, http://exlibris.memphis.edu/resource/unclesam/whos.html

Links to biographical information for the executive branch, cabinet, congressional committees, Congress itself, administrators of federal agencies, Joint Chiefs of Staff, Supreme Court, and Who Was Who, all from the Government Documents librarians at the University of Memphis.

United States Government Information Sources Statistical Sources, http://www.lib.uiowa.edu/govpubs/us/#statistical

Sources outside the government, documents on the Internet, and historical documents, compiled by the University of Iowa, Ames, U.S.A.

12

Journalism and News

JOURNALISM

The Atlantic Monthly Online, http://www.theatlantic.com

Free and with some features not available in print. The online archive is complete from November 1995 to present, and selected earlier articles (from 1857!) are also available.

Experts Database, http://www.collegenews.org/x2736.xml

Need someone to comment on a news story? This database provides a keyword searchable list of professors from "leading national independent liberal arts colleges" who will talk to the media. Provided by the Annapolis Group, this gives reporters access to experts they might otherwise not encounter—a breath of fresh air.

Internet Archives of 9/11, http://web.archive.org/collections/sep11.html

Files of print and television coverage of the attack on the World Trade Towers on September 11, 2001. See also http://www.poynter. org, which has a large section on the attacks, including PDF files of newspapers from 9/11 and subsequent days. From the Internet Archives Wayback Machine.

The State of the News Media 2004, http://www.stateofthemedia.org

This "annual report on American journalism" covers newspapers, online, network and cable and local television, magazines, radio, and ethnic media. It is a product of the Project for Excellence in Journalism of Columbia University. You can browse it online or print it out, but beware—the report is 7 megabytes or 350 pages long.

Willings Press Guide, http://www.willingspress.com

Subscription-based access to U.K. and worldwide details on newspapers, business magazines, ration and television stations and production companies, Web publications, and news and photography agencies. Publisher is located in Chesham, Buckinghamshire, U.K.

NEWS

BIOTN, The Best Information on the Net, http://library.sau.edu/bestinfo/

General news and news on specialized topics such as sports, weather, finance, health, science, and music. Chosen by librarians at O'Keefe Library, St. Ambrose University, Davenport, Iowa U.S.A. More information than you could possibly want.

Catholic News Service, http://www.catholicnews.com/

Daily news about and for Catholics worldwide. There is also a link to the electronic version of *Origins*, a print publication of official Catholic documents. Searchable.

Kidon Media-Link, http://www.kidon.com/media-link/index.shtml

Links to newspapers, television and radio stations, and magazines all over the world, organized by country.

NewsDirectory, http://newsdirectory.com

Links to newspapers, television and radio stations, and magazines all over the world, organized by type of resource.

News from the Caucasus, http://www.eurasianet.org

News and analysis on Central Asia, the Caucasus, Russia, and Southwest Asia. Daily news by country, newswires, features, current affairs, book reviews, and photo essays. From the Central Eurasia Project of the Open Society Institute, New York City, U.S.A.

NewsMax.com, http://www.newsmax.com

The most interesting section of this site is its collection of jokes told by David Letterman and Jay Leno on late-night television in the U.S.A., but there is also an archive of political cartoons and some international news links that could be useful.

Obituaries 101, http://www.big101.com/OBITUARIES101.htm

Links to the obituary section of newspapers online in every state. Don't count on archives; many don't have them. Interesting, but of limited usefulness.

OnlineNewspapers, http://onlinenewspapers.com

Links to newspapers around the world.

The Paper Boy, http://www.thepaperboy.com and http://www.thepaper boy.com/magazines

Newspaper (more than 3,000 from 135 countries) and magazine directories, by subject with short description and subscription information. From an entrepreneur in Perth, Australia.

Rocketnews, http://www.rocketnews.com

This "Breaking News & Weblog Search Engine" comes highly recommended by Web gurus Gary Price and Genie Tyburski. It searches more than 10,000 news sources, 45,000 Weblogs, books, market research, and white papers. You can search back only five days, however. Very recent results are presented on their home page first by subject, then by geographic area (worldwide coverage). They also produce Rocketinfo Desktop, which will allow you to save your search and archive it or e-mail the results. There is a free trial, but the cost is only USD30.00.

Topix.net, http://www.topix.net

More than 150,000 topically based, micro-news pages presenting stories from more than 10,000 sources. Each of these micro-news pages is focused on one particular subject or locality with separate pages devoted to each of the 30,000 cities and towns in the U.S.A., individual pages for every company, industry, health condition, sports team, university, celebrity, and thousands of others. You can set it to deliver links to local news by ZIP code. Some sites require registration, but all are free. Also available are links to local sports teams, maps, aerial photos, movie times, TV listings, restaurants, and census information. This site can't help but be useful.

World Press Review, http://www.worldpress.org

This database has a sampling of stories from newspapers around the world, country profiles, interviews, and maps. Divided by geographic region. It is easy to search. Good for seeing local news from an international viewpoint. Also has links to travel and dining, world newspapers, country maps and profiles, documents in the news, think tanks and nongovernmental organizations, and archives. You can set up an RSS newsfeed from this site.

13

Language, Literature, and the Arts

LANGUAGE AND LITERATURE

Translation

American-English/English-American Translation Guide, http://www. accomodata.co.uk/amlish.htm

From Accomodata World of Travel in the U.K. Look at their home page for links to the official British monarchy site and one on marmite, a uniquely British food.

AUSIT, http://www.ausit.org

Visit this site from the Australian Institute of Interpreters and Translators to get a list of accredited translators in Australia.

The Best of British: An American's Guide to Speaking British, http://www.effingpot.com/

Categories include slang, people, motoring, clothing, around the house, food and drink, and odds and sods. Cleverly written. You can also buy the book of the same name by Mike Etherington or participate in their discussion forum.

Do You Need a Translator? Or Can You Help Someone Else?, http://www.translatorplanet.com

Here you can post a translation job for bids or can bid on someone else's. I put a project up on the site and received six bids (all fairly reasonable) the same day. From Terry Forsyth of Pasadena, California, U.S.A.

National Accreditation Authority for Translators and Interpreters (NAATI) (Australia), http://www.naati.com.au

Lists the organization's members and contact details. Can be searched by state and language

Translate-Free.com, http://www.translate-free.com

Links to services that translate Web sites and other materials, language schools, and books.

Translating British to American and Vice Versa: The English-to-American Dictionary, http://www.english2american.com

As of February 2005 there were 587 words in the dictionary. Also on the site: information of Cockney-rhyming slang, links to similar sites, and a contributor list.

Web translators:

Babel Fish, http://babelfish.altavista.com

12 languages to and from English, six to and from French.

Free2Translation.com, http://www.free2translation.com

Seven languages to and from English, three more from English only.

Google Language Tools, http://www.google.com/language_tools?hl=en

Five languages to and from English, five to and from French. This is system used by many other translators.

Systran, http://www.systransoft.com/index.html

12 languages to and from English, five to and from French. This is system used by many other translators.

WorldLingo, http://www.worldlingo.com

To and from any of 13 languages.

Word Play

Bibliomania, http://www.bibliomania.com

The 2,000 full-text out-of-copyright literary works are a good reason for knowing this site, but there are also study guides, teacher's resources, and reference works that make it particularly valuable as a learning resource. Some of the reference sources are *Brewer's Phrase & Fable, Brewer's Readers Handbook,* the 1913 edition of *Webster's Dictionary, Soule's Synonyms, Grocott's Quotations, Roget's Thesaurus,* and *Simonds History of American Literature.*

BuzzWhack, http://www.buzzwhack.com

"Dedicated to de-mystifying buzzwords," with definitions, Buzzword of the Day, and an archive. A creation of John Walston, formerly an assistant managing editor with *USA Today,* with help from some of his friends.

ChichéSite, http://clichesite.com/index.asp

Definitions and explanations of clichés, sayings, phrases, and figures of speech, searchable, mostly from the U.S.A., but adding words from other countries. Categories include aging, business, help, lying, sex, agreement, children, hope, marriage, sports, anger, death, justice, money, time, beauty, easy, jealousy and envy, put-downs, and the weather.

Dictionary.com, http://dictionary.reference.com

Access to *The American Heritage Dictionary of the English Language, Webster's Revised Unabridged Dictionary* (1998), WordNet (from Princeton University), The Free On-line Dictionary of Computing, Jargon File, *CIA World Factbook,* Easton's 1897 Bible, Hitchcock's *Bible Names Dictionary,* and the *U.S. Gazeteer.* There are also links to puzzles, various language resources, dictionaries for other languages (French, German, Italian, Latin, Spanish), specialty dictionaries (crossword, legal, and medical), Thesaurus.com, a translator, and a word of the day. From Lexico Publishing Group.

How to Write, http://www.ccc.commnet.edu/grammar/

Collection of useful advice on how to write English prose, divided into levels (sentence, paragraph, and essay). Also sample business letters, application letters, etc., interactive quizzes, form for submitting questions, recommended grammar books, more than 200 quotations about writing, and grammar goofs. From the Capital Community College Foundation, Hartford, Connecticut, U.S.A.

The Maven's Word of the Day, http://www.randomhouse.com/wotd/index.pperl?date=19960613

From Random House, with etymology and word origin. With archives.

Merriam-Webster Online Dictionary, http://www.m-w.com/home.htm

OneLook, http://www.onelook.com, dictionary portal

As of February 2005, there were 6,168,428 words in 992 dictionaries indexed.

Word Detective, http://www.word-detective.com

This is the free online version of a newspaper column by Evan Morris that answers readers' questions about the meaning and derivations of English words and phrases. The latest issue is posted, and back issues are presented as an archive with the words listed alphabetically. The archive runs to more than 1,300 entries.

Word Origins Online, http://www.etymonline.com/

For the word geeks among us, the Online Etymology Dictionary is a treasure. You can browse the listings or use the search feature. Searches bring up the word you wanted, but also other irrelevant occurences of your search term. But it's still a wonderful resource.

Other Web Sites

Allyn & Bacon Public Speaking Web site, http://wps.ablongman.com/ab_public_speaking_2

Six modules help you to assess, analyze, research, organize, deliver, and discern.

Association of Proposal Management Professionals, http://www.apmp.org

Training, information, and resources.

Best-Selling Books Database—and More, http://asp.USAtoday.com/life/books/booksdatabase/default.aspx

From *USA Today*, this site has the week's 150 top best sellers (in the U.S.A. only, unfortunately). While there, be sure to investigate the other links on the site: movie box office report, DVD releases, top albums and singles, Nielsen TV ratings, Critic's Corner, Book excerpts, and other *USA Today* features. Fascinating!

Common Errors in English, http://www.wsu.edu/~brians/errors/

Literature for Children, http://palmm.fcla.edu/juv/

"Literature for Children is comprised of volumes from the Publication of Archival, Library & Museum Materials project of the State University System of Florida libraries. It is a growing collection of digitized titles published, predominantly in the United States and Great Britain, from the 17th through the 20th centuries." As of January 2003, there were 397 titles and more than 58,000 pages.

More Grammar Info than You'll Ever Need, http://homeschooling.gomilpitas.com/explore/grammar.htm

From A to Z's Cool Homeschooling, this site has all kinds of grammar games and exercises for students in kindergarten through high school. There are also ads for grammar drills and books—not as annoying as most ads since they are really relevant to the site. Check out the science experiments section if you have school age kids. From Ann Zeise, a homeschooler herself.

National Burns Collection, http://www.burnsscotland.com

This site provides a gateway to Scotland's national treasure, poet Robert Burns. A partnership of museums, galleries, and libraries all over Scotland. There are photographs, virtual tours of Burns sites, and of course the poetry and song.

National Poetry Almanac, http://www.poets.org/page.php/prmID/68

Read a daily article about poetry or a poet, past or present. Even better, search for your favorite poem or poet. You can even create your own poetry "notebook" from their selections. From the Academy of American Poets.

The New Dictionary of Cultural Literacy, http://www.bartleby.com/59/

Searchable, browsable, and free access to the third edition of this guide to what you need to know to be "cultured" (at least in the U.S). Links are provided to "read more about it." By E. D. Hirsch Jr., Joseph F. Kett, James Trefil (Third Edition: Completely Revised and Updated).

Online Directory of English as a Second Language Resources, http://www.cal.org/ericcll/nche/esldirectory

"Only the best resources," limited to sites as a whole, not individual Web pages. From the U.S. Center for Applied Linguistics, Washington, DC.

Presentation-Pointers.com, http://www.presentation-pointers.com/index.asp

Articles on Communicating Effectively, Building a Presentation, Planning a Presentation, and Communicating in Your Specialty. From a maker of projectors, but very helpful.

Presenters University, http://www.presentersuniversity.com/

Includes courses in Presentation Delivery, Content, and Visuals; a forum for asking questions of others; free software, PowerPoint templates. Corel masters, and art; and presentation-oriented books. You can also get Presentation Pointers delivered free via e-mail.

Read Print, http://www.readprint.com

Here you can find everything from a Shakespeare sonnet or story by O. Henry to an entire book by Emily Bronte or Leo Tolstoy—that is, literature in the public domain. Everything is very readable and, most importantly, free! They even take requests.

Readability Scores for Web Pages and Word Files, http://www.read ability.info

Is your writing readable? This site analyzes either a Web page or an MSWord file and gives you several measures of the readability, including grade level, complexity, and average sentence length. It is so easy.

Say How? http://www.loc.gov/nls/other/sayhow.html

Thank you to the Library of Congress for this long list of proper pronunciations of names of politicians, artists, and entertainers both current and historical. There are more names from the U.S.A., but coverage is worldwide.

Textalyser, http://textalyser.net

Ever wanted to know how readable your writing is? Or the writing of someone else? This site will give you detailed statistics on any text you put into it, including complexity factor, length of sentences, and two different measures of readability.

U.S. Copyright Renewal Records, http://www.scils.rutgers.edu/ ~lesk/copyrenew.html

Here you can check to see if the copyright on any book published from 1923 to 1963 has been renewed . (All books published after 1964 are still under copyright.) If not found here, the book is in the public domain. From Michael Lesk, a professor at Rutgers University, New Jersey, U.S.A.

THE ARTS

Art and Architecture Thesaurus, http://www.getty.edu/research/ conducting_research/vocabularies/aat/

Thank you, Getty Museum, for this vocabulary database, "a structured vocabulary of more than 133,000 terms, descriptions, bibliographic citations, and other information relating to fine art, architecture, decorative arts, archival materials, and material culture." Check out their other databases, the Union List of Artist Names and Thesaurus of Geographic Names.

ArtCyclopedia: the Fine Art Search Engine, http://www.artcyclopedia.com/

ArtsEdge: the National Arts and Education Information Network, http://artsedge.kennedy-center.org/

ARTstor, http://www.artstor.org

As of April 2004, the collection contained about 300,000 images, but is expected to grow to more than 500,000 by 2006. Images are organized into general and specialized collections and include: the Carnegie Arts of the U.S. Collection, Huntington Archive of Asian Art, Illustrated Bartsch, Mellon International Dunhuang Archive, and the MoMa (New York) Architecture and Design Collection. ARTstor is a project of the Andrew Mellon Foundation. The images are only available to authorized institutional users who pay a license fee, and may only be used for educational and scholarly purposes.

Design Directory, http://www.dexigner.com/directory/

Links to design sites all over the world. The categories with the most links are graphic design, regional, Web design, industrial design, animation, architecure, logo and branding design, digital design, urban design, and advertising design.

Graphic Witness: Visual Arts and Social Commentary, http://graphicwitness.org/ineye/sitemap.htm

Find information and links about artists (divided into pre- and post-1950) and journals. Interesting, but I can't judge its usefulness since I haven't worked in this field.

The Image, http://www.theimage.com

This private site has information and images of minerals and gemstones, along with somewhat related sections on digital photography; how microscopes, video cameras and other instruments work; a bibliography; Web authoring; and GIFology (how the GIF format works and is used).

Images from the Victoria and Albert Museum, http://images.vam. ac.uk

More than 20,000 images from this British Museum are now available online. Reproduction for personal or nonprofit use is freely permitted; licenses are available to for-profit organizations. This site has a good search engine; I put in "candelabra" and got 45 images, "horse" got 327, and "horse 18th" got 14 images of horse related paraphernalia from the 18th century. You can click on the image and get all the details and a larger picture.

International Art Museum Directory: ArtSeek, http://www.artseek.com/institutions/museums/

National Image Library, U.S. Fish & Wildlife Service, http://images. fws.gov

A wonderful online collection of public domain still-photos. Some are of fish and other wildlife, but there also beautiful landscapes and pictures of people—some from the early days of the Service. There are 455 just from Alaska. The search engine produces strange results sometimes.

Pathe Stills, http://www.britishpathe.com

More than 12 million historic photographs dating from the beginning of the 20th century.

PubHub: A Repository of Foundation-Sponsored Reports, http://www. fdncenter.org/research/pubhub

The Foundation Center collects "reports and issue briefs created by or with foundation resources." Most of them are on the arts community, but other subjects creep in. The actual report is available in PDF format.

The WWW Virtual Library for Theatre and Drama, http://v1-theatre. com/

Founded in 1996, this nonprofit site has links to theatre resources in over 50 countries. Categories include: academic training, book dealers, conferences, plays online, journals online, discussion lists, plays in print, theatre books in print, theatre companies, and Theatre on File (movies made from plays, as recommended by experts and scholars).

MUSIC

Care and Handling Guide for Preservation of CDs and DVDs, http://www.itl.nist.gov/div895/carefordisc/index.html

Best practices for storage and cleaning, information on the life span of discs, and a one-page quick reference guide. Available in HTML or PDF format, from the U.S. National Institute of Standards and Technology.

Music to Download—Free and Legal, http://www2.acc.af.mil/music/patriotic

If you like patriotic (American) music, or Christmas music, or John Phillip Sousa marches, you can download selections free from this site from the U.S. Air Force Heritage of America Band. (As a Sousa fanatic, I was thrilled to find this one.)

Pronouncing Dictionary of Music and Musicians, http://woi.org/dictionary/

This site has the pronunciation for almost every composer, conductor, soloist, opera, aria, or musical term you can think of. But read the guide to pronunciation first—the method is somewhat idiosyncratic.

SongFacts.com, http://www.songfacts.com/

The Top 100 Songs from Movies, http://www.afi.com/tvevents/100years/songs.aspx

Prepared for a television special, here are the American Film Institute's 100 greatest songs from movies and the other 300 that were nominated. There are links to other AFI lists, such as heroes and villains, thrills, and comedies. Hokey, but fun.

Wedding Song Library, http://www.ultimatewedding.com/music/

14

Law, Legal Libraries, and Copyright

BOOKS

Alexander, Miles J. *State Trademark and Unfair Competition Law*. New York: C. Boardman, 2003, ISBN 0-87632-556-8.

Ambrogi, Robert J. *The Essential Guide to the Best (and Worst) Legal Sites on the Web*, 2nd ed. New York: ALM Publishing, 2004, ISBN 1-58852-117-6.

Arden, Thomas P. *Trademark Law Guide*. Chicago: CCH Inc., 2003 (out of print).

Cornish, Graham. *Understanding Copyright in a Week*. London: Hodder and Stoughton, 2000, ISBN 0-340-78241-2. Cornish works at the British Library.

Crews, Kenneth. *Copyright Essentials for Librarians and Educators*. Chicago: American Library Association, 2000, ISBN 0-8389-0797-0.

Gilson, Jerome and Ann Gilson Lalonde. *Trademark Manual of Examining Procedure*, 3rd ed. Newark, NJ: LexisNexis Mathew Bender, 2003.

Hawes, James E. *Trademark Registration Practice*, 2nd ed. St. Paul, MN: Thomson West, 2003.

McCarthy, J. Thomas. *McCarthy on Trademarks and Unfair Competition*, 4th ed. St. Paul, MN: West Group, 1996.

Milgrim, Roger M. *Milgrim on Trade Secrets*. New York: Mathew Bender, 1997, ISBN: 0-82051738-0.

Parsons, Matthew. *Effective Knowledge Management for Law Firms*. Oxford, UK: Oxford University Press, 2004, ISBN 0-19516968-9. Has an accompanying workbook and a blog, Excited Utterances, http://excitedutterances.blogspot.com

Rusanow, Gretta. *Knowledge Management and the Smarter Lawyer*. New York: ALM Publications, 2003, ISBN 1-58852116-8.

Samuels, Jeffrey M., ed. *Patent, Trademark and Copyright Laws*. Washington DC: Bureau of National Affairs, 2004, ISBN 1-57018442-9.

Schneider, Deborah and Gary Belsky. *Should You Really Be a Lawyer? The Guide to Smart Career Choices Before, During & After Law School*. Seattle, WA: Decision Books, 2004, ISBN 0-94967557-9.

Trademarks Throughout the World, 4th ed. St. Paul, MN: Thomson West, 2003, ISBN 0-87632126-0.

Wall, Raymond. *Copyright Made Easy*, 3rd ed. London: Aslib, 2000, ISBN 0-85142-447-3.

Welkowitz, Davis S. *Trademark Dilution: Federal State and International Law*. Washington, DC: Bureau of National Affairs, 2002, ISBN 1-57018313-9.

ARTICLES

Ambrogi, Robert J. IP Blogs: Pocket Parts for a Digital Age. *PLL Perspectives* 16(2): 12–13, Winter 2005, or *Law Technology News* 11(10), October 2004.

Tjaden, Ted. Researching Canadian Law. *AALL Spectrum* 5(2): 14–15, October 2000. A great overview.

JOURNALS

There are far too many to list here. Check http://www.hg.org/journals.html for a good list. But here are a couple that are not on that list.

Internet for Lawyers, http://www.netforlawyers.com

Free monthly newsletter. Subscribe at the Web site. From Carole Levitt, JD, MLS and Mark Rosch, Culver City, California, U.S.A. The site also has information on training, online CLE (continuing legal education), books, seminars, articles, and marketing.

Internet Law Researcher, http://www.internetlawresearcher.com

11 issues/year, USD200. Glasser LegalWorks, 150 Clove Road, Little Falls, NJ 07424, U.S.A. phone: 1-800-308-1700 or 1-973-890-0008, fax: 1-973-890-0042, e-mail: orders@glasserlegalworks.com, http://www.glasserlegalworks.com. Chock-full of article and Web links.

DIRECTORIES

American Law Sources On-Line, http://www.lawsource.com/also/

Links to every state, plus territories and possessions. Includes Amicus Curiae briefs, interstate, multistate and boundary compacts, uniform laws, law schools, law reviews and periodicals, and legal monographs. From LawSource.com; site also has laws from Mexico and Canada.

Federal Judges Biographical Database, http://air.fjc.gov/history/judges_frm.html

From the Federal Judiciary Center, covers current and historical persons.

Finding and Using Electronic Lists for Law, http://www.lib.uchicago.edu/~llou/lawlists/intro.html

Lyonette Louis-Jacques, a law librarian and lecturer at the University of Chicago (Illinois, U.S.A.), provides lists of electronic lists in the law field and instructions for using them. There are also links to lists in Spanish and French.

Government Gazettes Online, http://www.lib.umich.edu/govdocs/gazettes/

Links, languages, frequency of publication, cost of access, dates online, format, and description of contents. A project of a student at the School of Information, University of Michigan, Ann Arbor, Michigan, U.S.A.

Legal Journals on the Web, http://library.osgoode.yorku.ca/mr/linksjournalyork.htm

From York University Law Library, Toronto, Canada.

Martindale-Hubbell Lawyer Locator, http://lawyers.martindale.com/xp/Martindale/home.xml

Search for lawyers by name, firm, location, or law school attended.

Online Directory of Law Reviews and Scholarly Legal Periodicals, http://www.lexisnexis.com/lawschool/prodev/lawreview/ (links to materials from here)

Includes general and special focus student-edited law reviews, non-student edited peer review and trade journals, and university presses. Compiled by Michael H. Hoffheimer, Professor of Law, University of Mississippi, U.S.A. Print version free to law professors, last updated December 15, 2004.

GENERAL PORTALS

FindLaw for the Public, http://www.findlaw.com

Sections for legal professionals, corporate counsel, the public, small business, and students. Law tools, software, books, legal news, find a lawyer, and subject-based sections, including legal news, U.S. federal law, U.S. state law, research, legal subjects, U.S. government resources, international resources, message boards, and newsletters. FindLaw is now part of Thomson.

LawIDEA Open Directory, http://www.lawidea.com

"An extensive legal links directory with over 17,000 legal related resources." From LawGuru, includes firms and attorneys, courts, directories, law libraries, organizations, reference, consultants, education, careers, law enforcement, products, publications, and databases.

LawKT.com, http://www.surfwax.com/products/lawkt.htm

This site allows you to search the full text of more than 50,000 publications and articles from 280-plus law firms. For example, when I searched for "fair use" (fair dealing in the U.K.), I retrieved 31 documents. You can even download them in PDF format for free. Formerly known as Legal Researcher, this database from SurfWax is available free.

SOSIG Law Gateway, http://www.sosig.ac.uk/law

Put together by the Institute of Advanced Legal Studies and University of Bristol Law Library, this site "provides guidance and access to global legal information resources on the Internet. The service aims to identify and evaluate legal resource sites offering primary and secondary materials and other items of legal interest. Descriptive records and links are created for legal service sites and specific documents." There are subsections on general law, U.K. law, EU law, other jurisdictions, international law, and law by subject areas.

The Virtual Chase, http://www.virtualchase.com/index.shtml

"Legal Research on the Internet," from Genie Tyburski of U.S.A. law firm Ballard Spahr Andrews & Ingersoll. Search engines, company information, people finder, government resources, information quality, and teaching Internet research skills.

INTERNATIONAL LAW

British and Irish Legal Information Institute, http://www.bailii.org

"Comprehensive access to freely available British and Irish public legal information." Also includes information from Australia, Canada, Hong Kong, and Pacific Islands.

Constitutional Court (South Africa), http://www.constitutionalcourt.org.za/site/home.htm

Full-text database of all Constitutional Court cases handed down since the first hearing in 1995, including full judgments, summaries of judgments highlighting the main questions of law decided in each case as well as heads of argument, pleadings, and documents. Also included is the Constitutional Court's library catalog of more than 50,000 volumes (including books, journals and law reports) in the fields of Constitutional, Public and International and Human Rights Law, with tables of contents of the textbook collection, and (in the near future) free online access to an extensive index to the South African legal periodical literature. Site also has links to legal Web sites with free online collections of legislation, case law of major jurisdictions and general legal Web sites. From the Faculty of Law, University of Witwatersrand, South Africa.

Electronic Information System for International Law, http://www.eisil.org

A free database of primary materials, authoritative Web sites, and research guides, divided into 13 categories: from air, space and water to human rights to criminal law. Developed by the American Society of International Law, Washington DC, U.S.A.

EUR-Lex: European Union Law, http://www.europa.eu.int/eur-lex/en/index.html

"The portal to European Union law," this site has the EU *Official Journal*, legislation, treaties, legislation in preparation, parliamentary questions, case law; and "documents of public interest." Available in many languages.

Foreign Filings: Perfect Information, http://www.perfectinfo.com

Filings at foreign exchanges. Offices in New York, London, and Hong Kong.

Freedom of Information Web Resources, http://www.cilip.org.uk/professionalguidance/foi/webresources

Links to U.K. sites: government departments and regulators; primary and secondary legislation and codes of practice and other official publications for England, Wales, and Northern Ireland; links for Scotland, Europe, and international resources; publications and information resources; and organizations and association with an interest in freedom of information; and news. From the Chartered Institute of Library and Information Professionals, London, U.K.

The Global Legal Information Network (GLIN), http://www.glin.gov

Searchable database of laws, regulations, judicial decisions, and other complementary legal sources contributed by governmental agencies and international organizations. These GLIN members contribute the official full texts of published documents to the database in their original language. Each document is accompanied by a summary in English and subject terms selected from the multilingual index to GLIN. From the U.S. Law Library of Congress.

GSI, http://www.gsionline.com

Some foreign filings. Offices in London, Washington DC, and New York.

Her Majesty's Stationery Office, http://www.hmso.gov.uk/

Search all U.K. legislation dating back to 1988 (new legislation—the most recent two weeks—on a separate page), full text of all Public and Local Acts of the U.K. Parliament, the Explanatory Notes to Public Acts, Statutory Instruments and Draft Statutory Instruments; and Measures of the General Synod of the Church of England. The Chronological Tables of Local and Private Acts; Government's Information Asset Register (IAR). The IAR lists information resources held by the U.K. Government, concentrating on unpublished resource;

Command Papers are Parliamentary Papers, which derive their name from the fact they are presented to the United Kingdom Parliament nominally by "Command of Her Majesty," but in practice generally by a Government Minister. A list of Command papers published since 2001; the London, Edinburgh and Belfast Gazettes are the Official Journals of the United Kingdom, Scotland and Northern Ireland; and the Civil Service Year Book. The name of the office will change to Office of Public Sector Information in 2005.

Hieros Gamos, http://www.hg.org

Legal guides for various states and countries, legal forms, books, and law review; in various languages. Headquartered in Houston, Texas, U.S.A.

International Calendar of Legal Events, http://www.iall.org/calendar/show.asp

This calendar is published in the *International Journal of Legal Information* from the International Association of Law Libraries. It includes worldwide events.

LawPORTAL: an Australian Legal Portal, http://www.lawportal.com.au

Daily court lists, links to legislation, regulations, cases, Hansard, Parliamentary Papers, tax information, accounting standards, business and domain names, Australian newspapers, and banking and investment information. From the Australasian Legal Information Institute, a joint facility of the University of Tasmania and the University of New South Wales Faculties of Law.

Legal Resources in the U.K. and Ireland, http://www.venables.co.uk

Includes information for individuals, information for companies (arbitration, mediation, buying legal advice online), information for lawyers (news, legal resources, publishers, jobs, software, Web services), and students (law schools, courses, careers, and special offers). From Delia Venables, Computer Consultant for Lawyers and Writer on Legal Internet Topics, Lewes, East Sussex, England.

Proceedings of the Old Bailey, London, 1674–1834, http://www.
oldbaileyonline.org

Talk about your specialized databases! If you are interested in crime, justice, punishment, history, and social culture of 17th-, 18th-, or 19th-century London, you've come to the right place. This "online edition of the largest body of texts detailing the lives of non-elite people ever published, containing accounts of over 100,000 criminal trials held at London's central criminal court" is searchable by keyword, name, crime, type of punishment, or date.

SOSIG Law Gateway, http://www.sosig.ac.uk/law

Put together by the Institute of Advanced Legal Studies and University of Bristol Law Library, this site "provides guidance and access to global legal information resources on the Internet. The service aims to identify and evaluate legal resource sites offering primary and secondary materials and other items of legal interest. Descriptive records and links are created for legal service sites and specific documents." There are subsections on general law, U.K. law, EU law, other jurisdictions, international law, and law by subject areas.

U.S.A. LAW

The Guide to Law Online, http://www.loc.gov/law/guide/us.html

Prepared by the U.S. Law Library of Congress Public Services Division, an annotated guide to sources of information on government and law available online. Links to International and Multinational, Nations of the World, U.S. Federal (including U.S. Code, Constitution, executive branch, legislative branch, legal guides, and general sources), and U.S. States and Territories.

Labor Research Portal, http://www.iir.berkeley.edu/library/labor
portal/

Find just about everything you need to know about U.S. labor laws and information at this site from the Institute Relations Library at the University of California, Berkeley, California, U.S.A.

Political Advocacy Groups, http://www.csuchico.edu/~kcfount

This directory of U.S. lobbyists contains short descriptions and contact information (including e-mail and Web sites) for registered political advocacy groups representing specific causes. They are arranged by subject and are searchable (full-text Boolean). In order to assess the influence of these groups, icons identify those most cited in newspapers and those rating the performance of members of Congress. There is even a bibliography of sources on advocacy and lobbying. From Kathi Carlisle Fountain, Reference Librarian, California State University at Chico, U.S.A.

SeniorLaw Resources, http://www.seniorlaw.com/resource.htm

SupportGuidelines.com, http://www.supportguidelines.com

Billed as "The Comprehensive Resource for the Interpretation and Application of Child Support Guidelines in the United States," this site from Laura Morgan, a Family Law counselor in Charlottesville, Virginia, U.S.A., has links to the guidelines for each state, child support calculators, court cases, news and articles. It's the kind of site you hope you don't need, but it's nice to know it exists.

INTELLECTUAL PROPERTY (COPYRIGHT AND TRADEMARK LAW), MOSTLY U.S.A.

Canadian, American, British and International Copyright, http://www. cla.ca/resources/copyright.htm

The latest information on revisions to Canada's Copyright Act and regulations; position statements by associations and governments on copyright reform; interpretations of Canadian copyright law; issues related to digital information and media copyright; international copyright law and the Multilateral Agreement on Investment (MAI); collective and performing rights societies; and some readings and writings on Canadian, U.S.A., and international copyright, from the Canadian Library Association.

Center for Intellectual Property and Copyright in the Digital Environment, http://www.umuc.edu/distance/odell/cip

Current issues and resources, workshops and conferences, research initiatives, and "ask the intellectual property specialist." From the University of Maryland University College, Adelphi, Maryland, U.S.A.

Copyright and Copyleft, http://www.edu-cyberpg.com/Internet/copy left.html

Copyleft is a sort-of-profit company that supports free and open source software by donating a large portion of each sale to various organizations that develop or support the development of free software.

Copyright Primer, http://www-apps.umuc.edu/primer/

Macromedia Flash Player–based tutorial produced by the Center for Intellectual Property and Copyright at the University of Maryland, U.S.A. Covers more than 20 topics, with case studies and additional links. There is also a Digital Copyright Primer at http://www-apps.umuc.edu/dcprimer/enter.php and a digital copyright electronic list (subscribe at beginning of Primer).

Current copyright readings, http://copyrightreadings.blogspot.com/

"Bibliography of current articles on the Digital Millennium Copyright Act, the TEACH act and other copyright issues. Maintained by M. Claire Stewart, Head, Digital Media Services, Northwestern University Library," Evanston, Illinois, U.S.A.

Deep Links: Intellectual Property, http://www.eff.org/deeplinks/archives/cat_intellectual_property.php

From the Electronic Frontier Foundation, about IP, privacy, and technology.

European Patent Organization database, http://ep.espacenet.com

Search all patent applications from member countries, plus English abstracts for more than 30 million patents, including those from Japan.

Intellectual Property, Copyright, and Fair Use Resources, http://www.albany.edu/~ls973/copy.html

Copyright law, organizations, Web sites, electronic lists, guides, readings, and university library Web pages on copyright. From Lorre Smith, State University of New York at Albany, U.S.A.

The Invent Blog, http://nip.blogs.com/

From Stephen M. Nipper, IP lawyer with Dykas, Shaver & Nipper, LLP, Boise, Idaho, U.S.A., this blog also has posts on unique and noteworthy inventions and inventors.

IP Australia, http://www.ipaustralia.gov.au/index.html

News from IP Australia, official notices, trademark hearings, patent hearings, forms and publications, IP professionals, links, information on international IP bodies, document sales and an online IP glossary. From the Australian government.

IP Blogs, http://www.ipjur.com

From Patent Attorney Axel H. Horns' blog on Intellectual Property Law, focused on German and European patents and trademarks.

IPKat, http://www.ipkat.com

Intellectual property news and issues, particularly from the U.K. and Europe. Produced by London-based intellectual property lawyers Jeremy Phillips and Ilanah Simon. Also has favorite links and reading lists for Phillips' courses.

IP Mall, http://www.ipmall.fplc.edu

Lots of information and links to the most valuable IP resources in the world (patents, copyrights, trademarks, trade secrets, licensing, technology transfer) from Franklin Pierce Law School, Concord, New Hampshire, U.S.A.

IP News Blog, http://www.ipnewsblog.com

From students and faculty of Franklin Pierce Law Center, Concord, New Hampshire, U.S.A.

The Itelprop.ca Blog, http://www.intelprop.ca/blog

About Canadian IP law, from Peter Eliopoulos of Eliopoulos Intellectual Property, Mississauga, Ontario, Canada.

LawSites, http://legaline.com/lawsites.html

"Tracking new and intriguing Web sites for the legal profession." From Robert J. Ambrogi, Rockport, Massachusetts, U.S.A., author of *The Essential Guide to the Best (and Worst) Legal Sites on the Web*.

Navigating the Patent Maze, http://lorac.typepad.com/patent_blog

Seattle, Washington, U.S.A., patent lawyer Carol Nottenburg focuses on finding and using online patent data and biotechnology patent law worldwide.

Nerd Law.org, http://www.nerdlaw.org

A somewhat irreverent look at patent law for "nerds at heart" from Kimberly Isbell, IP lawyer in Washington, DC, U.S.A.

PatentLawLinks, http://www.patentlawlinks.com

"Links for patent professionals and savvy investors," case law, search engines, worldwide patent office sites, law firms, statutes, journals, associations, search firms, and forms.

Patent Lens, http://www.bios.net/daisy/bios/50

Here is a free patent database for the life sciences, developed by CAMBIA, a nonprofit research center affiliated with Charles Sturt University in Australia, and made available on the Web by BIOS (Biological Innovation for Open Society). Sponsored by the Rockefeller Foundation, IBM, and the government of the Australian Capital Territory. There is the capability to search on many criteria at one time and it is very fast. As of February 2005, the site had full text of over 1.5 million life science patents from the U.S.A., Australia, and Europe. In addition to patent information (including the patent family information from INPADOC), there are white papers on technology patent landscape and intellectual property tutorials. What a wonderful find!

Patently Obvious, http://patentlaw.typepad.com

From Dennis Crouch, Patent Attorney with McDonnell Boehnen Hulbert & Berghoff LLP, Chicago, Illinois, U.S.A. Very complete review of every appellate opinion directly related to patent law, most regulatory and legislative change, and some district court opinions.

The Trademark Blog, http://tools.schwimmerlegal.com/blog/

News and commentary on trademark and name domain issue, from New York City lawyer Martin Schwimmer, vice president of the IP constituency of ICANN (Internet Corporation For Assigned Names and Numbers).

U.S. Library of Congress, http://www.loc.gov

Link to Thomas, search engine for legislative histories.

U.S. Patent and Trademark Office, http://www.uspto.gov

Forms; a glossary; resources for inventors, business, musicians, artists, authors, technology developers, trademarks, logos, and brands, legislators, patent attorneys, trademark attorneys, and the media; global and international resources, kids' pages.

World Intellectual Property Organization, http://www.wipo.int

News and information, patents, international marks, industrial designs, copyright, enforcement of IP rights, IP law, international classifications, arbitration and mediation, and innovation and promotion. There is also the WIPO Worldwide Academy, with five core programs: professional training, distance learning, policy development, teaching and research. The tailor-made programs, including its distance learning, have had more than 30,000 participants since its inception in 1999.

OTHER WEB SITES

Agricultural Law, http://www.agriculturelaw.com

News, special reports, laws, and regulations on agricultural law; there's even a dictionary. From McLeod, Watkinson and Miller, Washington, DC, U.S.A.

Find Associations, http://www.findlaw.com/06associations/foreign.
html

Legal associations and organizations, both foreign and international,
from FindLaw.

Internet Case Digest, http://perkinscoie.com/casedigest/default.cfm

Important developments in Internet law, including cases that have
significant implications for Internet legal issues even if they are not
directly related to the Internet. From the law firm of Perkins Coie,
Seattle, Washington, U.S.A.

Journalists' Guide to the Geneva Convention, http://www.journalism.
org/resources/tools/ethics/wartime/geneva.asp

Everything you need to know about the POW guidelines from the
Project for Excellence in Journalism, Washington, DC, U.S.A.

Law Professor Blogs, http://www.lawprofessorblogs.com

"Blogs by law professors for law professors." Includes 25 blogs on
many fields of law including a fantastic law by law librarian blog,
complete with many useful links. Editor-in-Chief is Paul L. Caron,
University of Cincinnati (Ohio, U.S.A.) College of Law.

Legal Research Guide: Statistical Resources, http://www.virtualchase.
com/resources/statistics.html

From Genie Tyburski, Librarian at Ballard Spahr Andrews &
Ingersoll LLP, U.S.A.

Privacy Knowledge Base, http://www.privacyknowledgebase.com

Billed as "the world's most comprehensive privacy resource," this
fee-based site covers privacy and data protection issues in banking,
consumer reporting, credit, health, insurance, investments, pharmaceuticals, telecoms, direct marketing, Internet, human resources, higher
education, and travel and hospitality worldwide. The cost seems reasonable, only USD295 per year for single-user unlimited access and
USD795 for a five-user license, from the Privacy Council, Dallas,
Texas, U.S.A.

LAW LIBRARIAN RESOURCES

50 Recommended Links for Legal Researchers, http://www.llrx.com/extras/shorttakes7.htm

From law librarian Sabrina I. Pacifici, one of the founders of LLRX.

Annotated Guide to a Select Group of Reliable Free Web Sites for Legal Researchers, http://www.llrx.com/extras/va_cle.htm

A wonderful resource from Sabrina Pacifici, editor, publisher, and Web manager of LLRX.com. Includes portals, federal and state law and law reviews, court rules and dockets, corporate information, news and current awareness.

Law-Related Movies, http://www.law-lib.utoronto.ca/law-505/movies/movies.htm

From the Bora Laskin Law Library at the University of Toronto, here are recommendations for law-related movies for "students who want a break from their studies." (Good for others, too.) The movies are arranged alphabetically, by law subject, and in a top 10 list. There are also links to other law-related movie lists.

Lawyer Jokes, http://www.megalaw.com/clock/jokearchive.php

From MegaLaw.

LLRX (Law Library Resources Xchange), http://www.llrx.com

The wonderful newsletter and Web site from Cindy Chick. This is one site not to miss!

Other Law Libraries, http://www.lawidea.com/cgibin/odp/index.cgi?/Society/Law/Law_Libraries/

Lists associations and reference libraries for Australia, Canada, Japan, the U.K., and the U.S.A.

Public Library Collection Guidelines for a Legal Research Collection, http://www.aallnet.org/sis/lisp/collect.htm

Part of the Public Library Toolkit from the American Association of Law Libraries.

Sellier European Law Publishers, http://www. sellier.de

European Community private law and international commercial law. Geibelstrasse 8, 81679 München (Munich), Germany, phone: 49-89-47-60-47, fax: 49-89-470-43-27, e-mail: info@sellier.de

TMtopics: Trademark Email Discussion List, join at http://www.inta.org/legal/tmtopics.html

From the International Trademark Association, New York, U.S.A.

15

Libraryland Stuff

REFERENCE SOURCES

All That JAS: Journal Abbreviation Sources, http://www.public.
iastate.edu/~CYBERSTACKS/JAS.htm

Registry of Web sites that list or provide access to full titles of
abbreviated journal titles. From Gerry McKiernan, Science and
Technology Librarian and Bibliographer, Iowa State University
Library, Ames, U.S.A.

Answers.com, http://answers.com

Enter the topic on which you want information and presto!—you get
the answer. First there is a dictionary definition (from the *American
Heritage Dictionary*), another definition (from WordNet at Princeton
University, U.S.A.), an article from Wikipedia, and cross-references to
other Wikipedia and Answers.com entries. Sprinkled through the
entries are links to other definitions and articles.

Bartleby, http://www.bartleby.com/quotations

You can search more than 85,000 quotations or get the quotation of
the day (which are archived). Sources: *Bartlett's Familiar Quotations,
The Columbia World of Quotations, Simpson's Contemporary
Quotations*, and *Respectfully Quoted: A Dictionary of Quotations*.

Biography resources, http://www.ala.org/ala/acrl/acrlpubs/crlnews/backissues2002/january/biographyresources.htm

Information on the famous, infamous, and obscure, from Susan Schreiner and Michael Somers, *College & Research Libraries News*, January 2002.

Bookfinder.com, http://www.bookfinder.com

Here you can find the top 10 most requested out-of-print books, by category and searchable (new/used, audiovisual, title)—and many other neat resources. Produced by 13th Generation Media, based in Berkeley, California, U.S.A.

Bookpage, http://www.bookpage.com

General interest reviews of up to 100 new releases (fiction, nonfiction, business, children's, spoken word audio, and how-to books). Designed specifically to be distributed by booksellers and libraries to consumers. Reviews tend to be short, but some include author interviews. Searchable archives back to 1996. From ProMotion, Inc., Nashville, Tennessee, U.S.A.

CBD Research Directories, http://www.cbdresearch.com/listbooks.htm

Very complete directories on British research institutes, British government agencies, British and Irish associations, European industrial and trade associations, European professional and learned societies, Current British and European directories, pan-European associations, American companies, Asian and Australian companies, and European companies. Prices range from £74–£250. Some were not very current (editions in the early 1990s as of 2005). Some available on CD-ROM, none available online.

Electronic Journal Miner, http://ejournal.coalliance.org

From the Colorado Alliance of Research Libraries, this site allows you to search through hundreds of peer-reviewed electronic journals. However, it only looks at the titles, not the contents.

The Gumshoe Librarian: "Where in the World Is ...": A Bibliography of Recommended Web sites for Global Research Issues, http://www.llrx.com/features/gumshoe.htm

First presented at the 2004 American Association of Law Libraries conference, this is a list of 73 sites for business, places, and useful services around the world, banking resources, and data on terrorism and security issues.

H-Net Reviews, http://www.h-net.org/reviews/index.cgi

Scholarly reviews of books and multimedia, searchable by author, title, year of publication, publisher, ISBN, reviewer, date of review, Library of Congress call number or subject heading. From Humanities and Social Science Online, an international consortium of scholars and teachers.

Holidays on the Net, http://www.holidays.net

"Your Source for Holiday Celebration." Here you can find listings of holidays all over the world, as well as greeting cards, crafts, pictures, and recipes.

HowStuffWorks, http://www.howstuffworks.com

Divided into computer stuff, auto stuff, electronics stuff, science stuff, home stuff, health stuff, money stuff, and just stuff. From a company in Atlanta, Georgia, U.S.A. They also have a CD version and books through John Wiley.

Information Please Almanac, http://www.infoplease.com

Facts and factoids from one of the standard reference works.

International, Country-Based Search Engines, http://www.philb.com/countryse.htm

Need to find a search engine in Monaco or Eritrea of Samoa? This site is your best bet. Phil Bradley, a librarian—now a consultant—in the U.K. has links to 2,086 search engines in 216 countries. There are also a few regional or global search engines, too. This should be in your bookmarks if you ever search for international information.

Internet Movie Database, http://www.imdb.com

More than 400,000 titles and 1.6 million names of movies and stars. Also recommendations, top 250, and trailers. Searchable and free. If you need more detail, such as in-production charts, movie company directories, rankings of title and people, daily box office figures, entertainment news, calendars, and a message board, you can sign up for IMDbPro for only USD12.95 per month—with a free trial available.

Kirkus Reviews, http://www.kirkusreviews.com/kirkusreviews/index. jsp

Book reviews designed for librarians, from one of the most respected review journals. Categories include fiction, mystery, science fiction, foreign language, nonfiction, and children's. Very short summaries available free, subscription required for more—online only subscription is USD37.50 per month.

Librarians' Index to the Internet, http://www.lii.org

Links from librarians for librarians. Categories are arts and humanities, business, computers, education, government, health, home, law, media, people, ready reference and quick facts, recreation, regional (California emphasized), science, and society and social science. Also featured collections such as California and Washington Wine, holidays, humor, mysteries, and the Olympics. Free subscription to weekly list of new resources available (17,000 subscribers in 85 countries as of February 2005). Managed by librarian Karen Schneider and the Universities of California-Berkeley and Washington, U.S.A.

National Public Radio Audio Archives, http://www.npr.org/archives

I think we've all had a customer come in and say, "I heard something on NPR on the way in, can you find more on it?" Here's help in the form of audio archives of most NPR programs. You can search by keyword or program. There's even a natural language interface—fill in the blanks: "I'm looking for a story about ... that I hear ... while listening to ..." Then you can download the audio (for a price).

New York Review of Books, http://nybooks.com/archives

Very selective reviews of books. Archives back to 1963 searchable by author, author of review, title of review or book, or date or review. Abstracts available online for free; to get the entire review requires a subscription—for USD20.00 for individuals, from USD890 for libraries.

Project Gutenberg, http://www.gutenberg.org

Books in the public domain (pre-1932) collected by Michael Hart, Salt Lake City, Utah, U.S.A.

Quick Answers To Odd Questions: Ready Reference Sources, http://www.batesinfo.com/tip.html

Internet guru Mary Ellen Bates's Tip of the Month. (While you're there, read tips from prior tips months.)

Quotations Page, http://www.quotationspage.com

More than 21,000 quotations online from more than 2,500 authors as of February 2005. Browse by author or subject or search.

RefDesk, http://www.refdesk.com

"The single best source for facts on the Net," (Mary Ellen Bates) has a Reference Site-of-the-Day, Facts-of-the-Day, and many links to reference resources arranged by subject (beginner's guides, facts encyclopedia, indispensable sites, journalist's tools, essential reference tools, homework helper, quick research, newspapers, and search engines and many, many others). Created by Bob Drudge, father of author Matt Drudge.

ReferenceDesk.org, http://www.referencedesk.org

Sections on finding people, quotations, encyclopedias, government resources, magazines and newspapers, and English tools (dictionaries, grammar guides, thesauri).

Thousands of Place Names, http://www.lowchensaustralia.com/names/placenames.htm

Links to lists of place names all over the world. Included are many from Australia (where the list owner lives), such as cities, places in native languages, history of Western Australian town names, rivers, Sydney suburbs, and birds. Also includes names for Finnish farms, places in the Artic, Eskimo (Inuit) names, Florida Keys, London, house names, from antiquity (Greek, Roman, Phoenician), funny town names, lakes, rivers, and just a list of "interesting or unusual place names." Good for reference, trivia, ideas for names of children or pets, or for just browsing.

Urban Legends Reference Pages, http://www.snopes.com

Hear a rumor? Check it out at this site. Categories include everything from automobiles to wooden spoons, including Cokelore, Disney, food, holidays, legal, love, medicine, movies, music, religion, and science. For your trivia file: a snope is a measure of length used by students at the Massachusetts Institute of Technology. Derived from the use of a student named Snope to measure the length of a bridge, it equals 5 feet, 7 inches. Maintained by Barbara and David Mikkelson, California State University, Northridge, U.S.A.

The Virtual Reference Library, http://www.virtualreference library.ca/

The Toronto (Ontario, Canada) Public Library staff selects and indexes more than 10,000 Internet sites in more than 25 categories. Annotated and searchable by keyword. Highlights Canadian sites, but includes sites from all over the world.

COLLECTION DEVELOPMENT

Guidelines for a Collection Development Policy Using the Conspectus Model, IFLA, 2001, http://www.ifla.org/VII/s14/nd1/gcdp-e.pdf

Collection development policy guidelines for school library media programs by Montana State Library, Helena, Montana, U.S.A. Includes a section of weeding in school libraries. Conspectus means an overview or summary of collection strength and collecting intensities, arranged by subject, classification scheme, or a combination of both; a synopsis of a library's collection. First developed by Research Libraries Group and later adapted by the Western Library Network, http://msl.state.mt.us/slr/cmpolsch.html.

Links to Collection Development and Selection Policies, Multimedia Seeds: A Starting Point for Audio, Video, and Visual Resources, http://eduscapes.com/seeds/

From Annette Lamb and Larry Johnson, Indiana University–Purdue University, Indinanpolis, Indiana, U.S.A.

MANAGING E-RESOURCES

Liblicense, http://www.library.yale.edu/~llicense/index.shtml

Licensing Digital Information: A Resource for Librarians, from Yale University Library, U.S.A. Includes a model license, glossary, bibliography, national site license initiatives, software, licensing terms and descriptions, resource links, and developing nations initiatives. Link to the liblicense-l discussion list and archives.

Model Licenses (for all types of libraries), http://www.licensing models.com

Four standard licenses (for single academic institutions, academic consortia, public libraries, and corporate and other special libraries) sponsored by and developed in cooperation with subscription agents (EBSCO, Harrassowtiz, and Swets) by John Cox Associates, Towcester, Northhamptonshire, U.K.

New Edition of Subject Index to Literature on Electronic Sources of Information, http://library.usask.ca/~dworacze/SUBJIN_A.HTM

Includes over 2,000 indexed titles. continuously updated. Available is the bibliography (http://library.usask.ca/~dworacze/BIBLIO.HTM) and an Introduction explaining how to use the index (http://library. usask.ca/~dworacze/SUB_INT.HTM). Compiled by Marian Dworaczek,

Monograph Coordination, University of Saskatchewan (Canada) Library.

New Jour, http://gort.ucsd.edu/newjour/
Alphabetical and chronological list of new journals and newsletters available on the Internet. The list owners are Ann Shumelda Okerson (Yale University) and James J. O'Donnell (Georgetown University). Operations are managed from the Lauinger Library of Georgetown University and the archive is provided courtesy of the University of California at San Diego Libraries (U.S.A.).

Serialst, http://www.uvm.edu/~bmaclenn/serialst.html
An electronic discussion list, (Serials in Libraries Discussion Forum) based at the University of Vermont, U.S.A.

Watson, Paula D. E-journal Management: Acquisition and Control. *Library Technology Reports* 39(2), March/April 2003.

MANAGEMENT

Flanagan, Neil and Jarvis Finger. *Just About Everything a Manager Needs to Know.* Brisbane, Queensland, Australia: Plum Press, 1998, ISBN 1-57387-210-5. This book is like a compilation of every management book I've ever read. Each topic is presented on two pages, so you can get help or a quick answer in just a few minutes.

Gordon, Rachel Singer. *The Accidental Library Manager.* Medford, New Jersey: Information Today, 2005, ISBN 1-57387-210-5. An excellent book on library management for those who have not been trained as managers. There's even a short sidebar with me on being an OPL. Highly recommended.

Stanley, John. *Just About Everything a Retail Manager Needs to Know.* Kalamunda, Western Australia: lizardpublishing.biz, 2004, ISBN 0-97501180-4. Don't be fooled by the title; there's a lot in here for librarians. You will get many ideas for making the library a more attractive and inviting place, for publicizing the library, and for serving your customers better. Stanley is a consultant to libraries around the world.

Sutton, Dave. *So You're Going to Run a Library: A Library Management Primer.* Englewood, Colorado: Libraries Unlimited, 1995, ISBN 1-56308-306-X. Great for small libraries, especially public ones, but also relates to corporate or other nonpublic libraries. Written for the nonprofessional, especially the volunteer, so it is simple, very well organized and easy to understand—but comprehensive. One nice feature: a symbol for "ask a librarian" for complex issues.

GRANT WRITING

Books and Articles

Becker, Bill. Library Grant Money on the Web: A Resource Primer. *Searcher* 11(10), Nov/Dec. 2003, online at http://www.infotoday.com/searcher/nov03/becker.shtml

The Big Book of Library Grant Money. Chicago: American Library Association, 2002, ISBN 0-8389-3520-6.

Grants for Libraries and Information Services. From the Foundation Center, annual, ISBN 1-59542-029-0.

Kight, Dawn Ventress and Emma Bradford Perry. Grant Resources on the Web: Where to Look When You Need Funding. *C&RL News* 60(7) July/August 1999, http://www.ala.org/ala/acrl/acrlpubs/crlnews/backissues1999/julyaugust4/grantresources.htm

National Guide to Funding for Libraries and Information Services, 8th ed., 2005. From the Foundation Center, annual, ISBN 1-59542-039-8.

Web Sites

American Library Association Awards and Scholarships, Grants and Fellowships, http://www.ala.org/Template.cfm?Section=awards

CRISP (Computer Retrieval of Information on Scientific Projects), http://crisp.cit.nih.gov

A searchable database of federally funded biomedical research projects conducted at universities, hospitals, and other research institutions. The database, maintained by the Office of Extramural Research at the National Institutes of Health, includes projects funded by the National Institutes of Health (NIH), Substance Abuse and Mental Health Services (SAMHSA), Health Resources and Services Administration (HRSA), Food and Drug Administration (FDA), Centers for Disease Control and Prevention (CDCP), Agency for Health Care Research and Quality (AHRQ), and Office of Assistant Secretary of Health (OASH).

Finding Funding for Your Project, http://www.normicro.com/grantinfo. htm

Grants & Financial Support for your Digitization Project: Some Suggested Resources. From Northern Micrographics, La Crosse, Wisconsin, U.S.A.

The Foundation Center, http://www.fdncenter.org

Links to funders and philanthropists. One of their products in the Foundation Finder, a free, searchable, look-up tool providing contact information and basic fiscal profiles for U.S.A. private and community foundations. Offices in Atlanta, Cleveland, New York, San Francisco, and Washington, DC, U.S.A.

Funding and Grant Sources for Libraries, http://www.libraryhq.com/funding.html

From LibraryHQ, New York, New York, U.S.A.

Gates Foundation (public libraries only), http://www.gatesfoundation.org/Libraries/

The Bill & Melinda Gates Foundation awards the majority of its grants to U.S. 501 (c) (3) organizations and other tax exempt organizations identified by foundation staff according to the objectives of four program areas: Global Health, Education, Global Libraries, and Pacific Northwest. Gates is the founder of Microsoft, Seattle, Washington, U.S.A.

GrantsNet (U.S. Dept. of Health & Human Services), http://www.hhs. gov/grantsnet

GrantsNet is an Internet application tool created by the Department of Health and Human Services (DHHS) Office of Grants Management and Policy (OGMP) for finding and exchanging information about HHS and other Federal grant programs. GrantsNet serves the general public, the grantee community, and grant-makers (i.e., state and local governments, educational institutions, nonprofit organizations, and commercial businesses).

Guidestar: The National Database of Nonprofit Organizations (U.S.A.), http://www.guidestar.org

GuideStar (Williamsburg, Virginia, U.S.A.) generates and distributes extensive programmatic and financial information about more than 1 million American charitable nonprofit organizations. It operates www.guidestar.org, a free, public Internet service and the nation's leading source of information about nonprofit organizations.

Institute for Museum and Library Services (U.S.A.), http://www.imls. gov/grants/library/index.htm

The Institute of Museum and Library Services is an independent Federal grant-making agency dedicated to creating and sustaining a nation of learners by helping libraries and museums serve their communities. The Institute fosters leadership, innovation, and a lifetime of learning by supporting the nation's 15,000 museums and 122,000 libraries. Based in Washington, DC, U.S.A.

Internet Library for Librarians, http://www.itcompany.com/inforetriever/ grant.htm

Internet resources for applying library grants and funding, maintained by Internet Library and InfoWorks Technology, Cranberry, Pennsylvania, U.S.A. for Librarians Editorial Team.

Internet Nonprofit Center, http://www.nonprofits.org
Resources for online fundraising. From the Evergreen Society, Seattle, Washington, U.S.A.

Joint Research Grant General Information, http://www.aallnet.org/sis/obssis/research/researchinfo.htm
Information on applying for a grant from the American Association of Law Libraries Online Bibliographic Services and the Technical Services Special Interest Sections.

Proposal Writer.com, http://www.proposalwriter.com
Links to proposal development resources, government contracting and procurement, legal, and contractual and financial information related to government contracting. From Deborah Kluge, Consultant.

Proposal Writing: Online Resources, http://grants.library.wisc.edu/organizations/proposalwebsites.html
Links to proposal and grant writing resources from nongovernmental sources (including a grant writing school, how to write a mission statement and winning proposals), research (applying for NIH grants, federal sources, including a tutorial and government resources), and other sites. From the Grants Information Center, University of Wisconsin, Madison, U.S.A. There's also a list of print resources at http://grants.library.wisc.edu/organizations/proposalbooks.html

Sea Coast: Grant Writing Guide, http://www.npguides.org/index. html
Free grant writing tools for nonprofit organizations, including guidelines, tips, sample inquiry letter, what goes into a proposal, sample cover letter, budget, proposals. Links to grantmakers, resources, and glossaries. From SeaCoast Web Design, Portsmouth, New Hampshire, U.S.A.

RECORDS MANAGEMENT

ARMA International, 13725 W. 109th Street, Suite 101, Lenexa, Kansas 66215, U.S.A., phone: 1-913-341-3808 or 1-800-422-2762, fax: 1-913-341-3742, http://www.arma.org
The association for records managers.

Australian Records Manuals and Schedules, http://www.naa.gov.au/recordkeeping/dirks/dirksman/dirks.html

DIRKS: A Strategic Approach to Managing Business Information (also known as the DIRKS Manual) provides government agencies with practical guidance on managing business information and records. It complies with the eight-step methodology recommended in the Australian Standard for Records Management and is primarily for use by Australian Government agency information and records management project teams and consultants

Inventory Forms and Other Information, http://www.archives.gov/records_management/initiatives/targeted_assistance_brochure.html

From the U.S. National Archives and Records Administration. Includes records management basics, policy and guidance, federal laws relating to records management, records schedules, and publications.

PRISON LIBRARIES

Articles and Books

AALL Files Brief in Prisoners' Rights Case, From the Desk of Susan E. Fox—AALL Executive Director, 11 September 2003, http://www.aallnet.org/press/ftdo_091103.asp#3 (5 January 2005)

American Association of Law Libraries, Contemporary Social Problems Special Interest Section. Recommended Collections for Prison Law Libraries. In Arturo A. Flores, *Werner's Manual for Prison Law Libraries, 2nd ed*. Littleton, CO: F.B. Rothman, 1990.

American Association of Law Libraries, Standing Committee on Law Library Service to Institution Residents. Contemporary Social Problems Special Section. *Correctional Facility Law Libraries: An A to Z Resource Guide*. Laurel, MD: American Correctional Association, 1991.

American Association of Law Libraries, Social Responsibilities Special Interest Section. Standing Committee on Law Library Service to Institution Residents. *Recommended Collections for Prison and Other Institution Law Libraries*. Chicago: AALL, 1996.

American Library Association, Association of Specialized and Cooperative Library Agencies, with American Correctional Association. *Library Standards for Adult Correctional Institutions, 1992*. Chicago: ALA, 1992, ISBN 0-8389-7583-6. Excerpts online at http://www.ala.org/ala/ascla/asclaissues/librarystandards.htm

American Library Association, Association of Specialized and Cooperative Library Agencies. *Library Standards for Juvenile Correctional Facilities*. Chicago: ALA, 1999, ISBN 0-8389-7988-2.

Arizona DOC Eliminates Prison Libraries, Targets Politically Active Prisoners, *Maoist International Movement* Web site, http://www.etext.org/Politics/MIM/agitation/prisons/censor/az/az.elim.libraries.html

Australian Institute of Criminology, Existence and Purpose of Prison Libraries, *Australian Prison Libraries: Minimum Standard Guidelines*, http://www.aic.gov.au/research/corrections/standards/PrisonLibraries/existence.html

Bowden, Teresa S. A Snapshot of State Prison Libraries with a Focus on Technology. *Behavioral and Social Sciences Librarian* 21(2): 1–12.

Callea, Donna. Romance Novels, Legal References Best Sellers Behind Bars. *Tallahasse.com* 16 May 2004, http://www.tallahassee.com/mld/Tallahassee/newes/local/8681506.html

CILIP Criticizes Report on Role of Prison Libraries. *CILIP Library and Information Update*. April 2003, http://www.literacytrust.org.uk/Database/prisonlibs.html

Collins, William. Inmate Rights and Privileges: Access to the Courts. *Association of State Correctional Administrators Contracting Manual*, pp. 61–62, http://www.asca.net/public/contract.pdf

Collis, Roy and Liz Borden, eds. *Guidelines for Prison Libraries*. London: LA Publishing, 1997.

Costanzo, Emauela. "ABC" and the Italian Prison Libraries. *World Library and Information Congress: 69th IFLA General Conference and Council, August 2003, Berlin, Germany*, http://wotan.liu.edu/dois/data/Papers/juljuljin5086.html

Curry, Ann. Canadian Federal Prison Libraries: A National Survey. *Journal of Librarianship and Information Science* 35(3): 141–152, 2003, http://www.slais.ubc.ca/RESEARCH/current-research/curry-JOLISMay29_03.pdf

De Carolis, Elena. The Right to Read: The Experience of Prison Libraries, *Bollettino Associazione Italiana Biblioteche* 2000(3):363, http://www.aib.it/aib/boll/2000/00-3-363.htm

Hartz, Fred R. Prison Libraries—The Realities. *Catholic Library World* 59:258–261, 1988.

Helo, Marty. Incarcerated Librarian. *The Unabashed Librarian* 76:20–21, 1990.

Hemp, Susan. Transparent Walls: Library Services to Prisoners. *Against the Grain* 8:46–47, 50, 52, 1996.

Kaiser, Frances E., ed. *IFLA Guidelines for Library Services to Prisoners*, 2nd rev. ed. The Hague: IFLA, 1995, IFLA Professional Reports No. 46, ISBN 90-70916-55-X. Includes personnel, collections, physical facilities and equipment, funding and budget, services, communication and public relations, glossary, and bibliography.

Knudsen, Mark. How My Library Affect My Life in Prison. *Education Libraries* 24(1):20, 2000. By an inmate.

LeDonne, Marjorie. Survey of Library and Information Problems in Correctional Facilities: A Retrospective Review. *Library Trends* 26(1): 53–70, 1977.

Leech, Mark and Deborah Cheney. *The Prisons Handbook 2000*. Winchester, U.K: Waterside Press, 2000, ISBN 1-872-970-82-1, c. £44.00. Relevant law, list of all prisons of England, drugs and alcohol in prisons, religion and race relations, criminal justice resources on the Internet, penal case law, reports from government, statistics, and more.

Lehmann, Vibeke. Prison Librarians Needed: A Challenging Career for Those with the Right Professional and Human Skills. *65th IFLA Council and General Conference, Bangkok, Thailand, August 1999*, http://www.ifla.org/IV/ifla65/papers/046-132e.htm

Lehmann, Vibeke. The Prison Library: A Vital Link to Education, Rehabilitation, and Recreation. *Education Libraries* 24(10): 5–10, 2000.

Lehmann, Vibeke. Prisoners' Rights of Access to the Courts: Law Libraries in U.S. Prisons. 60th IFLA Meeting, August 1994, http://www.ifla.org/IV/ifla60/60-lehv.htm

Local School Libraries Struggle While Prison Libraries Get Millions, WFTV.com, http://www.wftv.com/print/3302191/detail.html

Prison Library. *LiveJournal* list, http://www.livejournal.com/community/libraries/360441.html

Purifoy, Randy. You Are Here: A Guided Tour of the Oshkosh Correctional Institution Prison Library. *Education Libraries* 24(1): 18–29, 2000. By an inmate.

Reese, Diana. Collection Development. In Rhea Joyce Rubin and Daniel Suvak, eds., *Libraries Inside: A Practical Guide for Prison Libraries*. Jefferson, NC: McFarland, 1995, ISBN 0-78640061-7.

Reprieve for Prison Libraries Following Protests by Librarians. *CILIP Library and Information Update,* December 2003, http://www.literacytrust.org.uk/Database/prisonlibs.html

Rubin, Rhea Joyce. *The Planning Process for Wisconsin Institution Libraries*. Oakland, California: Rubin Consulting, 1997.

Rubin, Rhea Joyce and Daniel Suvak, eds. *Libraries Inside: A Practical Guide for Prison Librarians*. Jefferson, NC: McFarland, 1995. Has video and audio series.

Schneider, Julia. Three Experts Describe "How to be a Successful Prison Librarian: Preparation for a Foreign Land." *Interface* 25(3), 2003. (Web Companion Newsletter of the Association for Specialized and Cooperative Agencies, a Division of the ALA) http://www.ala.org/ala/ascla/asclapubs/interface/archives/contentlistingby/volume25/successprisonlib/howsuccessful.htm

Shirley, Glennor L. Correctional Libraries, Library Standards, and Diversity. *Journal of Correctional Education* 54(2): 70-74, June 2003.

Shirley, Glennor L. Prison Libraries and the Internet, Column 2, June 2004. *Behind the Walls @ Your Library: Library Service in Prisons, ALA Office for Literacy and Outreach Services*, http://www.ala.org/ala/olos/ouotreachresource/prisoncolumn2.htm

Singer, Glen. Prison Libraries. *Bulletin of the Eastern Canada Chapter, SLA*, 66(1):8–14, Fall 2000, http://www.sla.org/chapter/cecn/Archive/bulletin/Nov_2000 (5 January 2005) (excellent article, good description), also in *Education Libraries* 24(1):11–16, 2000.

Trammell, Rebecca. *Werner's Manual for Prison Law Libraries*, 3rd ed. Buffalo, NY: William S. Hein & Co., 2004, ISBN 0-83770161-9. Part of AALL Publication Series.

Wade, Anne. Resources on the Net: Professional Development (Prison Librarianship and Inmate Literacy). *Education Libraries* 24(1): 34–36, 2000.

Organizations

American Correctional Association, http://www.aca.org

Correctional Education Association, http://www.ceanational.org

The Corrections Connection, http://www.corrections.com

Family and Corrections Network, http://www.fcnework.org

Federal Bureau of Prisons, http://www.bop.gov

National Institute of Corrections, U.S. Department of Justice, http://
nicic.org

Office of Correctional Education, U.S. Department of Education,
http://www.ed.gov/offices/OVAE/AdultEd/OCE/index.html

Other Resources

Correctional Library Issues Bulletin Board, http://database.corrections.
com/bulletins/results1.asp?SubjectID-35
   From Corrections.com "The Official Home of Corrections."

Corrections Related Sites, http://www.geocities.com/Heartland/4787/
prisons.html
   From Christopher M. Grimes of Bermuda.

Libraries for Incarcerated Youth, http://leep.lis.uiuc.edu/seworkspace/
jailbait/incyouth.htm
   What we're up against, the scope of the need, planning library services, the role of the librarian, services for staff, special considerations
for in-house libraries, collection development, Web sites for further
exploration, and bibliography. From Lee McLain and Kate McDowell,
master's students at the Graduate School of Library and Information
Science, at the University of Illinois at Urbana-Champaign, U.S.A.,
done for a class project for Professor Christine Jenkins's course LIS
406: Media, Programs, and Methods for Work with Children and
Young Adults in School and Public Library Settings

Prison Libraries Group of CILIP, http://www.cilip.org.uk/groups/prlg/
prislg.html
   Site includes a Survey of Automaton in Prison Libraries and Prison
Libraries Group Conference Report.

Prison Links, http://www.prisonlinks.com/
   As of February 2005, there were more than 400 links in the following categories. Activism, articles, books, legal publications, prison
publications, civil rights, crime statistics and rates, death penalty/

capital punishment, official and nonofficial sites relating to the Department of Corrections, officers and other U.S. Dept. of Corrections Web sites, drug war, ex-offender resources (disenfranchisement, drug and anger rehabilitation), healthcare, immigration, inmate locater, legal, Native American issues, news and information, online support communities, organizations, penal history, prison art, prison labor, prison privatization, prisoner life, rehabilitation, religion and spiritual, sentencing consultants, and sentencing reform.

Prison Zone, http://www.prisonzone.com

Prisons.org, http://www.prisons.org.uk

Publishers of *The Prisons Handbook, Prisoners' Pocket Directory, Converse Prison News,* Institute of Prison Law Accredited Legal Training, and *Prison Today.com* (daily prison news). From MLA Press Ltd, Manchester, U.K.

The Sentencing Project, http://www.sentencingproject.org

U.S. Dept. of Justice, Federal Bureau of Prisons Library, http://bop.library.net/

Search their online catalog.

DISASTER PLANNING

Alire, Camila. *Library Disaster Planning and Recovery Handbook.* New York: Neal-Schuman, 2003, ISBN 1-55570373-9.

Disaster Preparedness and Response, http://palimpsest.stanford.edu/bytopic/disasters

Prepared by Conservation Online, here is a list of disaster plans, case histories, bibliographic resources, and other documents on disaster preparedness. It is very comprehensive.

FLICC, Federal Library and Information Community Preservation and Binding Work Group (U.S.A.), http://www.loc.gov/flicc/

Sample disaster recovery contract, list of resources, etc.

Harvard Library Disaster Preparedness Information, http://preserve. harvard.edu/emergencies/
   Good bibliography.

Hoehl, Susan. An Ounce of Prevention: Integrated Disaster Planning for Archives, Libraries, and Record Centres. *Medical Reference Services Quarterly* 22(1):88–89, 2003.

MISCELLANEOUS BOOKS

Baldwin, Virginia and Julie Hallmark, eds. *Information and the Professional Scientist and Engineer*. Haworth Information Press, 2003, ISBN 0-78902163-3.

Green, Elisabeth. A Core Reference Collection for the Very Small Library, from Council on Foundations Annual Conference, Chicago, Illinois, 2002, http://www.foundationlibraries.org/cof2002/basics/cdrefsources.htm

MARKETING AND ADVOCACY

Books

Diamond, Wendy and Michael Oppenheim. *Marketing Information: A Strategic Guide for Business and Finance Libraries*. Binghamton, NY: Haworth Press, 2004, ISBN 0-7890-6006-X.

Owens, Irene. *Strategic Marketing in Library and Information Science*. Binghamton, NY: Haworth Press, 2003, ISBN 0-7890-2143-9.

Siess, Judith. *The Visible Librarian: Asserting Your Value with Marketing and Advocacy*. Chicago: ALA Editions, 2003. ISBN 0-8389-0848-9.

Walters, Suzanne. *Library Marketing That Works!* New York: Neal-Schuman, 2004, ISBN 1-55570473-5.

Web Sites

Compare Public Libraries, http://nces.ed.gov/surveys/libraries/publicpeer

Here you can compare one library to either similar libraries or specific libraries you have chosen. The amount of detail is mind-boggling, but printing it is somewhat problematic because it is too wide for most printers. But it's still interesting and potentially useful. From the U.S. National Center for Education Statistics.

DateDex, http://www.datedex.com

This site lists lots of special days and observations around the world. It isn't complete, but you can find all sorts of dates to commemorate.

Demonstrating the Impact of Your Services, http://webjunction.org/do/DisplayContent?id=1218

Here you'll find a tool kit of excellent resources to help you show how you add value to your organization. One article well worth reading is "Value Proposition for Libraries: How a tool borrowed from the business world can help you clarify your library's value and find points of intersection with your funders' concerns." From WebJunction, the work of five organizations, led by OCLC.

Dialog Quantum2, http://quantum.dialog.com/q2_resources/marketing

Staging an Open House or Promotional Event, 5 Tips for Getting Started (in marketing), 6 Simple Steps to Promoting your Intranet, 10-Step-Guide to Promoting the Information Center.

Examples of good library Web sites from Fiona Bradley, aliaNEWGRAD list. Her criteria: logical navigation, two clicks or less, consistent structure, accessible by those with special needs, short URLs that make sense, and good design (it looks good).

Jessie Street National Women's' Library, http://www.jessiestreet
womenslibrary.com

National Library of Australia, http://www.nla.gov.au

New York Public Library, http://www.nypl.org

Suburban Library System, http://www.sls.lib.il.us

University of Western Australia, http://www.library.uwa.edu.au

Friends of Canadian Libraries, http://www.friendsoflibraries.ca/market.html
Links to and information about library-related products and fundraising merchandise.

Friends of Libraries U.S.A., http://www.folusa.org
Fundraising ideas, programs, and projects.

Gale Group, http://www.gale.com/free_resources/marketing/index.htm
Free marketing resources for academic, public, school, hospital, law, and military/government libraries; also, support materials and marketing for public libraries in Spanish.

Hospital Library Advocacy Weblog, http://hosplib.blogspot.com
Jeannine Cyr Gluck, director of the medical library, Eastern Connecticut Health Network, started this log to help hospital librarians demonstrate their value to management. Many of the links would be of use to any librarian.

Internet Use in [Public] Libraries Fact Sheet, http://www.urbanlibraries.org/Internet%20Study%20Fact%20Sheet.html
Impacts of the Internet on public library use, details and information on the use and costs of filters. From the Urban Libraries Council, Evanston, Illinois, U.S.A.

Keeping it Simple, http://www.nsls.info/marketing/keepingsimple.html
From the North Suburban Library System (Illinois, U.S.A.), includes: Learn the Tools to Write a Marketing Plan, Using Print Materials to Promote and Enhance Your Library's Image, Communicating with the Media, and Developing Partnerships.

LexisNexis InfoPro, http://www.lexisnexis.com/infopro/training/toolkits
National Library Week (U.S.A.) toolkit and more.

Library Lovers Month, http://www.librarysupport.net/librarylovers/

Ideas for promoting libraries and some publicity materials. From the Friends of California Libraries.

LifeWorks, http://science.education.nih.gov/LifeWorks.nsf/Interviews/ Robin+Meckley

"Check Out a Success Story" features an interview with Robin Meckley, medical librarian at Scientific Library, National Cancer Institute at Frederick, Maryland, U.S.A.. There is also a link to "Learn more about Medical Librarian." This site has a lot of information, including a job description, education required, skills and abilities, and more. LifeWorks also has profiles of other medical professions. From the U.S. National Institutes of Health.

Marketing: The Power of Ten, http://www.lis.uiuc.edu/clips/2003 _09.html

Includes: 10 ways John Cotton Data promoted his libraries, 10 reasons for marketing library and information services, 10 barriers to marketing, 5 marketing strategies, 10 Web marketing resources, 10 marketing ideas for virtual reference, 10 recent books on library and information marketing, and tips from various types of libraries. From the Current LIS Clips: Library and Information Services Marketing, Graduate School of Library and Information Science and the Library and Information Science Library, at the University of Illinois-Urbana-Champaign.

Marketing: Sources for Marketing Information and Library Services, http://dis.shef.ac.uk/sheila/marketing/sources.htm

From Sheila Webber, Dept. of Information Studies, Sheffield University, U.K. Excellent collection of links for general texts and articles about marketing and information or library services, planning, market research, promotion and public relations, pricing, positioning, specific sectors, specific countries, Library Friends groups, and a separate list of links to sources about marketing in general.

Marketing and Public Relations Sources, http://www.library.on.ca/ Profinfo/MarketPR.html

Articles and links, including ideas from other libraries, images and graphics. From the Southern Ontario Library Service, Canada.

Marketing Information Available from Vendors: Factiva InfoPro Alliance, http://www.factiva.com:80/infopro

Marketing the Information Center: Stay Visible in a Virtual World (a short course).

Marketing Our Libraries: On and Off the Internet, http://www.library supportstaff.com/marketing.html

Lots and lots of great ideas and links for all types of libraries, though more for public libraries.

Marketing the Library, http://www.olc.org/marketing

Web-based training for public libraries, six self-paced library marketing training modules and links to marketing resources, examples, quizzes and exercises. From the Ohio (U.S.A.) Library Foundation.

Marketing Treasures, http://www.chrisolson.com/marketingtreasures/ indexmt.html

The fabulous Chris Olson is now offering her monthly newsletter *Marketing Treasures* via e-mail (to sign up go to http://www.chris olson.com/marketingtreasures/mtsignup.html). She also offers the archives at http://www.chrisolson.com/marketingtreasures/mtarchives. html as PDF files. These sites have loads of great marketing ideas.

Marketing Treasures Resources, http://www.chrisolson.com/marketing treasures/mtresources.html

From Chris Olson, marketing guru. Includes Web sites, vendor resources, advocacy, eCatalogs with library promotion information, the ALA @Your Library campaign, National Library Week, U.S.A. state library marketing campaigns, learning opportunities, etc. Back issues available as PDF files at http://www.ChrisOlson.com/marketing treasures/mtarchives.html

MLS: Marketing Library Services, monthly newsletter from Information Today, Inc. Excellent and worth the subscription price, but if you can't afford it, check their Web site for free articles, http://www.infotoday.com/mls/mlsl.htm

KM AND INFORMATION SCIENCE RESOURCES

Books

Nardi, Bonnie A. and Vicki L. O'Day. *Information Ecologies: Using Technology with Heart*. Cambridge, Massachusetts: MIT Press, 1999, ISBN 0026264042-2.

Parsons, Matthew. *Effective Knowledge Management for Law Firms*. Oxford: Oxford University Press, 2004, ISBN 0019516968-9.

Rusanow, Gretta. *Knowledge Management and the Smarter Lawyer*. New York: ALM Publications, 2003, ISBN 1-58852116-8.

Web Sites and Online Publications

"If only we knew what we already know," http://findability.org/topics/research.php#InformationSeekingBehavior
  Links to studies of information-seeking behavior, taxonomies and facets, information retrieval, and pervasive computing.

Journal of Information, Law and Technology, http://elj.warwick.ac.uk/jilt/

Knowledge Management, http://www.kmmag.com

KM White Papers, http://www.kmworld.com/publications/whitepapers/index.cfm
  Best Practices articles.

Law Practice Today: ABA Law Practice Management's Monthly Webzine, http://www.abanet.org/lpm/lpt

Law Technology News, http://www.lawtechnews.com

LLRX, http://www.llrx.com

Managing Knowledge in Health Services, http://www.shef.ac.uk/scharr/mkhs/

This book by Andrew Booth and Graham Walton is now out of print, but the publisher (Facet Publishing, part of CILIP) has put the entire text online for free. I wish more publishers would be this thoughtful.

LIBRARIES AND BOOKS

AllReaders.com, http://allreaders.com

Bibliomysteries, http://www.bibliomysteries.com

Books related to the library world or having a librarian as a major character. Also quotations, murder weapons, and a word game. Created by academic librarian Marsha McCurley.

Books by Boat?, http://www.bookboat.com/main.htm

Many of us are familiar with a bookmobile, but have you heard of a bookboat or books delivered by camel or donkey? The Prince Rupert Library (British Columbia, Canada) is building a new library and on its Web site, there's research on various kinds of libraries. It is a fascinating view into alternative delivery methods.

Canadian Libraries: How They Stack Up, http://www.oclc.org/ca/en/index/compare/default.htm

Their contributions as economic engines, logistics experts, valued destinations, information providers, and as a profession. Similar to the report for the U.S.A., found at http://www.oclc.org/reports/2003libsstackup.htm

Canadian Library Gateway, http://www.collectionscanada.ca/gateway/index-e.html

Search for library information and online catalogs, browse lists of library Web sites, link to national union catalogs, interlibrary loan information, the *Directory of Special Collections of Research Value in Canadian Libraries* and more. From the National Library of Canada.

Directory of Zoo and Aquarium Libraries, http://www.nal.usda/gov/
awic/zoo/ZooAquaLibDir.htm

9th ed., 2002, revised 2003. Originally compiled and edited by Jill
Gordon, St. Louis Zoo (Missouri, U.S.A.) and revised by Stacy Rice,
National Agricultural Library, Washington, DC, U.S.A.

The European Library, http://www.europeanlibrary.org

All documents, reports, presentations, etc. that were created after
the European Library Office started work in June 2004. The European
Library Office will translate the results from the TEL project into the
operational service TheEuropeanLibrary.org, launched in March 2005.
"The European Library, TEL, is a pioneering collaboration between a
number of European national libraries. Created under the auspices of
CENL, the Conference of European National Librarians, it will establish a professionally designed and maintained single access point to
their holdings spanning a range of collections in all the partner
National Libraries so that the informed citizen in any country can uti-
lize the resources not only of his or her own national library but also,
during the same search session, the resources of any other partner
national libraries which may hold material relevant to his or her interest. This discovery and access tool will be multilingual and it will support the various character sets in use in CENL libraries." There is also
a presentation, "The European Library: What Now? From project to
service," for use by librarians.

Eye on Books, http://www.eyeonbooks.com

All sort of things for book lovers: audio interviews with authors,
book summaries, quotations, and a section (Writers' Craft) with advice
on writing your own book (mostly for fiction, however). From Bill
Thompson, a radio personality who has done more than 9,000 author
interviews.

How To Find Out-of-Print Books, http://marylaine.com/bookbyte/
getbooks.html

LibDex, http://www.libdex.com

Directory that indexes more than 12,000 library home pages, browsable by country, online catalog vendor, or keyword. From Peter Scott, Internet Projects Manager in the University of Saskatchewan Library, Saskatoon, Canada.

Libraries-Online, http://www.libraries-online.com

Gateway to the British Library, universities in the U.S.A., universities worldwide, U.K. higher education and research libraries, U.K. National Grid for Learning, Cambridge and Oxford Universities' Libraries, Livings Words—a Web site for schools and colleges, school and public libraries on the Web.

Library Portal Germany, http://www.goethe.de/kug/prj/bib/bil/enindex. htm

An overview of German libraries, national and international cooperation, education, associations, other library projects of the Goethe Institut, libraries of national importance, regional libraries, and special, academic, public, school, and children's libraries. There's even a glossary. From the Goethe Institut, Munich, Germany.

Online Books, http://digital.library.upenn.edu/books/

A directory of 19,000+ books available free online.

¿Se Habla Espanol su Catálogo?, http://espanol.denverlibrary/org/dewey.html

A Spanish translation of the Dewey Decimal system.

Schweitzer, Marko, ed. *World Guide to Library, Archive and Information Science Associations*, 2nd ed. Munich: Saur, 2005, ISBN 3-598-21840-0, IFLA Publications 112–114. 633 international and national organizations from more than 130 countries, more than 170 new. Contains addresses, contact data, officers, membership, goals and activities, publications and other details, with a variety of indexes.

U.S. Libraries: How They Stack Up, http://www.oclc.org/reports/2003libsstackup.htm

World of Reading: Book Reviews for Kids, by Kids, http://www.worldreading.org/

From the Ann Arbor District Library, browse by subject, search by title or author, or browse by the country reviewers come from to find out what books are popular with kids in other countries.

PROFESSIONAL ISSUES

Hiring Preferences in Libraries, http://www.camden.lib.nj.us/survey/results.htm

Preliminary survey results show that 82 percent of respondents would hire someone with a degree earned online, but 32 percent felt that traditional study was better. From a survey designed and administered by Maureen Wynkoop as a project for the MLS degree at Southern Connecticut State University.

IT White Papers, http://www.itpapers.com

"The Web's largest library of technical white papers, Web casts, and case studies," on computer-related issues. From a commercial firm, free registration is necessary to download information (and they say that they will share your information with other companies).

Legal Issues for Libraries: A National Update, http://www.silo.lib.ia.us/for-ia-libraries/continuing-ed/LEGAL-ISSUES-FOR-LIBRARIES-6.3.pdf

Based primarily on information received at Lawyers for Libraries Training Seminar sponsored by the American Library Association Chicago Regional Training Institute held on May 12–13, 2003.

Library Q: Queer Internet Resources for Librarians and Library Users, http://carbon.cudenver.edu/public/library/libq/

The Library Worker's Guide to Lesbian, Gay, Bisexual, and Transgender Resources. (Not working as of November 2005, but site says will return.)

LibrarySpot, http://www.libraryspot.com

A librarian portal, divided into Reference Desk, Reading Room, Must See Sites, Lists, Feature Archive, Words of Wisdom, Sites of the Year, Library Site of the Month, and Reference Site of the Month. From StartSpot Mediaworks, Inc., Evanston, Illinois, U.S.A.

Library Stuff, http://www.librarystuff.net

A blog from Steve Cohen, librarian in Smithtown, New York, U.S.A., to help you keep up with evolving library technology.

LibraryWorld, http://members.lycos.co.uk/bluedolphinprint/library world/libworld.html

"To provide library professionals with links to virtually every aspect of librarianship." Includes technical services, technical support, acquisitions, periodicals, education, staff training and development, special collections, government publications, special libraries, legal issues, notice board, and reference desk. From the U.K.

List of Links to the Grey Literature, http://www.ala.org/ala/acrl/acrlpubs/ crlnews/backissues2004/march04/graylit.htm

An article by Brian Mathews in *C&RL News* 65(3), March 2004.

Online Insider, http://www.onlineinsider.net

A blog from Internet guru Marydee Ojala on new technology.

OPL Plus (Not Just for OPLs Anymore), http://opls.blogspot.com

A blog by Judith Siess for librarians in smaller libraries—all kinds of libraries, anywhere in the world—not just for one-person or solo librarians. Management information, links, and marketing tips that you can use right now.

Outline of Library of Congress Subject Headings, http://www.loc.gov/ catdir/cpso/lcco/lcco.html

The Researching Librarian, http://www.researchinglibrarian.com

"Web resources helpful for librarians doing research." Including databases, funding, journals, statistics, tools, current awareness, and proceedings. From Beth Ashmore, Samford University, Birmingham, Alabama, U.S.A.

Library Buildings

Building Libraries and Library Additions: A Selected Annotated Bibliography, ALA Library Fact Sheet Number 11, http://www.ala.org/library/fact11.html

Arranged by type of library.

Jones, David J. Is Your Building 'Future Proof'? *inCite*, October 2003, http://www.alia.org.au/publishing/incite/2003/10/future-proof.html

Library Building and Design Portal, http://www.slq.qld.gov.au/serv/publib/build

Architects and consultants, community spaces, fittings, furniture and shelving, landmark libraries, library spaces, planning tools, recent projects, seminars and papers, standards and guidelines, subsidy and funding, from the State Library of Queensland (Australia).

STARTING A LIBRARY

Malone, Samuel A. *How to Set Up and Manage a Corporate Learning Centre*. Hampshire, U.K.: Gower, 1997, ISBN 0-566-07818-X.

Pantry, Sheila and Peter Griffiths. *Creating a Successful E-Information Service*. London: Facet, 2002, ISBN 1-85604-442-4. Excellent lists of further reading, including Web sites.

KEEPING UP

Web Sites

Dynix Institute Archives, http://www.dynix.com/institute/

List of upcoming Webinars and archives of past ones. The Webinars are free and very good.

Gary Price's Resource Shelf, http://resourceshelf.freepint.com

News articles, professional reading, links to resources. Sign up to get a weekly reminder of new additions.

Guidelines for Medical, Legal, and Business Responses, http://www.
ala.org/ala/rusa/rusaprotocols/referenceguide/guidelinesmedical.htm

Developed by members of the American Library Association
designed to assist information services staff in meeting user needs and in
responding to users requesting medical, legal or business information.

It's All Good, http://scanblog.blogspot.com

A blog from three OCLC Online Computer Library Center staff
about "all things present and future that impact libraries and library
users."

Librarian's Toolbox for Business, http://www.sls.lib.il.us/reference/
workshop/business/toolbox.html

"A business librarian's tools of the trade: sources that don't contain
the information sought but that help you find and use sources that do."
Part of "Business Reference: A Cycle of Workshops" by Nell Ingalls,
Hinsdale Public Library and Laura Johnson, Suburban Library System
Reference Service, Hinsdale, Illinois, U.S.A.

LisNews, http://www.lisnews.com

News stories from around the world about library and information
science, mostly from the U.S.A. From Blake Carver, Buffalo, New
York, U.S.A.

Mary Ellen Bates's Tip of the Month, http://www.batesinfo.com/tip.
html

This is a free service in which supersearcher Mary Ellen Bates provides a useful tip on finding elusive information. You can sign up for
a free e-mail subscription.

Price's List of Lists, http://www.specialissues.com/lol

Links to the Fortune 500 and other top 10–type lists, organized by
subject headings based on the two-digit 1997 U.S. NAICS Codes. Free
registration required. From Gary Price of the Resource Shelf.

Progressive Librarians around the World, http://libr.org/international

A site for activist librarians, organized by country or region, from Rory Litwin, California Research Bureau, California State Library, U.S.A.

Search Engine Showdown, http://www.notess.com/search/ and Search Engine Watch, http://searchenginewatch.com

Showdown evaluates Internet search engines from the searcher's perspective. Watch has tips and information about searching the Web, analysis of the search engine industry and help to site owners trying to improve their ability to be found in search engines, with free newsletters available. Extra content with membership. Both are from Greg R. Notess, Montana State University, Bozeman, U.S.A.

Special Libraries Association, Washington DC Chapter Book Club, http://www.sla.org/chapter/cdc/bookclub.html

Find out what professional books are being read by chapter members, some with reviews.

Journals

American Libraries, American Library Association, http://www.ala.org/alonline/

Also from ALA, many journals and newsletters of their constituent groups, such as *Reference & User Services Quarterly.*

ASIS&T Bulletin, American Society for Information Science and Technology, http://www.asis.org/Bulletin/

Australian Library Journal, Australian Library and Information Association, http://alia.org.au/publishing/alj/

Also from ALIA: *Australian Academic and Research Libraries,* http://alia.org.au/publishing/incite, http://alia.org.au/publishing/Orana (not online).

Information Outlook, Special Libraries Association, http://www.sla.org/content/Shop/Information/index.cfm

Information Today, Information Today, Inc., http://www.infotoday.com/periodicals.shtml

Also from Information Today, Inc., *Computers in Libraries, EContent, KM World, Online, Searcher, CyberSkeptic's Guide to Internet Research, The Information Advisor,* and *MLS: Marketing Library Services*.

The Informed Librarian, http://www.informedlibrarian.com

Links to the tables of contents of more than 275 library-related journals, many of them full text. Editor's picks noteworthy articles, guest editorials, featured books, archives back to 2003. Free registration or an enhanced option for a small fee (USD29 for an individual).

Journal of AHIMA (American Mental Health Information Management Association), 10 issues per year, free to members, non-members: USD80 in U.S.A., USD90 in Canada, USD100 in other countries.

Library Journal, Reed Business Information, http://www.libraryjournal.com/

Also from Reed, *Publishers Weekly*, http://www.publishersweekly.com (selected articles only for nonsubscribers), *School Library Journal*, http://www.schoollibraryjournals.com, and *Corporate Library Update* (not online).

Library Quarterly, University of Chicago Press, http://www.journals.uchicago.edu/LQ/journal/home.html

Library Trends, University of Illinois at Urbana-Champaign, U.S.A., http://www.lis.uiuc.edu/puboff/catalog/trends/issues.html

Online Periodicals and Newsletters for Librarians, http://nnlm.gov/libinfo/mgmt/onoline.html

From the U.S. National Library of Medicine. Also from National Library of Medicine: health information, librarian and health educator resources, medical library management (administration, information, medical databases, collection development, first steps, additional resources).

Weblogs

Jane Dysart's InfoBuzzzz, http://www.dysartjones.com

Jenny Levine's Shifted Librarian, http://www.theshiftedlibrarian.com

Library Stuff (Steven M. Cohen), http://www.librarystuff.net

LIS News, http://www.lisnews.com

Marylaine Block's Neat New Stuff I Found on the Net This Week,
http://marylaine.com/neatnew.html

OPL Plus (Not Just for OPLs Anymore), http://opls.blogspot.com
   A blog by Judith Siess for librarians in smaller libraries—all kinds
of libraries, anywhere in the world—not just for one-person or solo
librarians. Management information, links, and marketing tips that you
can use right now.

ResearchBuzz (Tara Calishain), http://www.researchbuzz.com

ResourceShelf (Gary Price), http://www.resourceshelf.com

Stephen's Lighthouse, http://stephenslighthouse.sirsi.com
   Wit and—especially—wisdom from Stephen Abram, Vice President
of Innovation, Sirsi Dynix, Toronto, ON, Canada.

Walt Crawford's Cites and Insights ('zine), http://cites.boisestate.edu

Electronic Lists

Autocat, http://www.ublib.buffalo.edu/libraries/units/cts/autocat
   Very active and may discuss very advanced issues, but interesting.

CataList, http://www.lsoft.com/lists/listref.html
   The official catalogue of Listserv lists, 54,199 public lists. There are
315 with the word library in the list name.

Directory of Library Oriented Lists and Electronic Serials, http://www.
aladin.wrlc.org/gsdl/cgi-bin/library?p=about&c=liblists
   From the Washington Research Library Consortium, Washington,
DC, U.S.A.

Library and Computer Fields, JISCMAIL, http://www.jiscmail.ac.uk

465 lists using JISCMAIL, sponsored by the JISC, for the U.K. Higher and Further Education communities. Categories include: library projects, library staff in subject areas, electronic resources, general academic library, regional groups, library systems, metadata, official publications, library and information science, library committees, and public libraries.

LINC-L, Congregational Librarians Discussion List, http://members. shaw.ca/scbrouwer/linc%20List.htm

LINC stands for Libraries in Churches and is hosted by Trinity Western University, Langley, British Columbia, Canada. To join, send a blank e-mail to join-LINC-L@patience.twu.ca or visit the Web site where there are also links to sources and booksellers, library catalogues, and vendors.

OCLC-CAT, http://listserv.oclc.org/archives/oclc-cat.html

Discusses more than OCLC cataloging.

Here are some of the lists that I have joined. To subscribe to most, send an e-mail message to the address in parentheses with the message SUBSCRIBE listname yourfirstname yourlastname. For example, to subscribe to SOLOLIB-L—which you absolutely, positively must do—send an e-mail to listserv@silverplatter.org with the message SUBSCRIBE SOLOLIB-L Judith Siess (use your own name, please):

ACADEMICPR, publicity and marketing in academic libraries (listproc@ala.org)

AFLIB-L, African Libraries (AFLIB-L@nlsa.ac.za)

ALIAHEALTH, medical libraries in Australia (listporc@alianet.alia. org.au)

aliaNEWGRAD, Australian newly graduated librarians, http://lists. alia.org.au/mailman/opions/alianewgrad

ANZ-LAW-LIBRAIANS-ONE, librarians working in small law libraries in Australia and New Zealand (majordomo@uow.edu.au_)

ASIS-L, American Society for Information Science & Technology (listserv@asis.org)

BUSLIB-L, business librarians, mostly U.S.A. (listserv@listserv. boisestate.edu)

CLA, Canadian Library Association, http://lists.cla.ca/mailman/ options/cla

CORPORATELIBNS, Yahoo! Groups, http://finance.groups.yahoo.com/ group/corporatelibrns

"Most of us corporate Library & Information Professionals are single-person libraries. This is a forum to discuss our agonies, achievements, problems, creative solutions, tools and technologies, issues and literature with fellow professionals. Notifications about events and resources are also welcome."

EVIDENCE-BASED-LIBARIES, evidence-based practice in librarianship and information science, from the U.K. (listserv@jiscmail. ac.uk).

Free Pint, portal and various lists, based in the U.K. but worldwide coverage, lots of good stuff here, http://www.freepint.co.uk

IFLA-L, International Federation of Library Associations, http://info serv.inist.fr/wwsympa.fcgi/subrequest/ifla-l

LAW-LIB, law librarians, mostly in the U.S.A. (listproc@ucdavis.edu)

LAWLIBREF-L, reference issues in law libraries (listproc@ lawlib.wuacc.edu)

LIASA online, Library and Information Association of South Africa, http://www.liasa.org.za/liasa_online/liasa_online.php

LIS-UK, for U.K. academic librarians and support staff (jiscmail@ jiscmail.ac.uk)

MEDLIB-L, Medical Librarians, mostly in the U.S.A. (listserv@ listserv.acsu.buffalo.edu)

MEDREF-L, reference for medical librarians, http://www.kovacs.com/medref-l/medref-l.html

MRKTLIB, medical and special library marketing and promotion (listserv@listserv.louisville.edu)

NEWLIB-L, newly graduated librarians, mainly in the U.S.A. (listproc @usc.edu)

NZLLG, New Zealand Law Librarian's Group (majordomo@vuw.ac.nz)

PRIVATELAWLIB-L, librarians working for private law firms, mostly in the U.S.A. (listproc@lawlib.wuacc.edu)

REFCAN-L, reference and information services in Canadian libraries (listserv@infoserv.nlc-bnc.ca)

SLIS-NZ, special libraries in New Zealand (majordomo@vuw.ac.nz), archives at http://www.knowledge-basket.co.nz

Solo, Chartered Institute of Library and Information Professionals, U.K. (listproc@listproc.la-hq.org.uk). There are archives of all postings to Solo available at http://www.la-hq.org.uk/lists/solo/

Workplace, Chartered Institute of Library and Information Professionals, U.K. (listproc@listproc.la-hq.org.uk). There are archives of all postings to Solo available at http://www.la-hq.uk/lists/workplace/

Other Lists of Interest

ACQWEB, a portal for acquisitions and collection development, selection policies, etc., http://www.library.vanderbilt.edu/law/acqs/acqs.html

CHATTYLIBRARIANS, for just talking among ourselves, http://www.topica.com/lists/chattylibrarians

LM-NET, for teacher librarians (listserv@listserv.syr.edu)

CAREERS AND JOB HUNTING

Web Sites

101 Commonly Asked Interview Questions, http://www.indiana. edu/ ~libpers/interview.html

From the Indiana University Libraries, "tested" interview questions. Categories include: warm-up questions, work history, job performance, education, career goals, self-assessment, creativity, decisiveness, range of interests, motivation, work standards, leadership, oral presentation skills, written communication skills, flexibility, stress tolerance, stability and maturity, and interest in self-development.

Alternative Careers for Librarians, http://www.sla.org/chapter/ctor/ resources/career/casey.htm

A presentation by Vicky Casey to the SLA Toronto (Canada) Chapter, 1999.

Non-Traditional Jobs for Special Librarians, http://www.libsci.sc. edu/bob/class/clis724/SpecialLibrariesHandbook/non-traditional.htm

Written by Susanna Weaver, library student, University of South Carolina, U.S.A., for a class assignment.

Salary Information, http://www.salary.com/salary/layoutscripts/sall_ display.asp

Enter your job title and ZIP code and it will give an estimate of what your salary should be. From Salary.com, Needham, Massachusetts, U.S.A.

Sample Librarian Resumes, http://www.lisjobs.com/onlineresumes.htm

Resumes for 18 librarians (not necessary typical ones) who chose to post them online. From Rachel Singer Gordon and lisjobs.com.

Writing for Publication, http://www.freepint.com/issues/260804. htm#feature

An article by Rachel Singer Gordon. She also has a book on the subject, *The Librarian's Guide to Writing for Publication*, Lanham, Maryland: Scarecrow Press, 2004, ISBN 0-8108-4895-3.

Employment Agencies

Australia and U.K.

INFOmatch, http://www.cilip.org.uk/infomatch

The CILIP Recruitment Agency, 7 Ridgmount St., London WC1E 7AQ, U.K., phone: 44-0-20-7255-0570

The One Umbrella, http://www.oneumbrella.com.au

Also known as Knowledge People, Library Locums, Qualified Records People, ACT, NSW, QLD, Victoria, Australia

Sue Hill Recruitment, http://www.suehill.com

Borough House, 80 Borough High St., London SE1 1LL, U.K., phone: 020-7378-7068, fax: 020-7378-6838; 27 Hansell Drive, Solihull, West Midlands B93 8RQ, U.K., phone: 01564-773651, fax: 020-7378-6838

TFPL, Ltd., http://www.tfpl.com

17-18 Britton St., London EC1M 5NQ, U.K., phone: 44-207-251-5522, fax: 44-207-251-8318.

UniLinc Limited, http://www.unilinc.edu.au

Level 9, 210 Clarence St., Sydney 2000 Australia, phone: 02-9283-1488, fax: 02-9267-9247. "UNILINC is a not-for-profit organisation originally formed in 1978 to co-ordinate the cost-effective provision of sophisticated library technologies in the higher education sector with the aim of saving costs and facilitating resource-sharing. Since then the membership has expanded to include a number of other libraries within a variety of specialised organisations."

U.S.A.

Advanced Information Management (AIM), http://www.aimusa.com

P.O. Box 2600, Hollister, CA 95024-2600, phone: 1-831-630-1500, fax: 1-831-630-1501

C. Berger Group, Inc., http://cberger.com

P.O. Box 274, Wheaton, IL 60189, phone: 1-630-653-1115 or 1-800-382-4222, fax: 1-630-653-1691

Library Associates, http://www.libraryassociates.com

8383 Wilshire Blvd., Suite 355, Beverly Hills, CA 90211, phone: 1-323-852-1083 or 1-800-987-6794, fax: 1-323-852-1093

The Library Co-Op, Inc., http://www.thelibraryco-op.com

Birch Pointe Commons, 3840 Park Avenue, Suite 107, Edison, NJ 08820, phone:1-732-906-1777 or 1-800-654-6275

Pro Libra Associates, Inc., http://www.prolibra.com

6 Inwood Place, Maplewood, NJ 07040, phone: 1-800-262-0070 or 1-973-762-0070, New York–New Jersey area.

STG International, http://www.stginternational.com/html/home.html

Federal Government jobs only, offices in 32 states. 4900 Seminary Rd., Suite 1100, Alexandria, VA 22311-1811, phone: 1-703-578-6030, fax: 1-703-578-4474

Taylor & Associates, http://www.taylorlib.com

100 Bush Street, 25th Floor, San Francisco, CA 94104, phone: 1-415- 391-9170, fax: 1-415-217-5882

Wontawk, http://www.wontawk.com

Formerly Gossage Regan. 25 W. 43rd St., #814, New York, NY 10036, phone: 1-212-869-3348, fax: 1-212-997-1127; Boston, phone: 437-9311-617-867-9209, fax: 1-617-437-9317. Run by a librarian; the word Wontawk is New Guinea for "share your way of life."

Job Hunting

Advice on a public library interview, http://studentorg.cua.edu/agliss/libjobs.htm#advice

From Rory Litwin of *Library Juice*.

Everything's Gonna Be All Right, http://liscareer.com/peters_
interviews.htm

By Chrissie Anderson Peters, Northeast State Technical Community
College in Blountville, Tennessee, U.S.A.

Find a Library Job! http://www.lisjobs.com

From Rachel Singer Gordon.

First Impressions, Lasting Impressions: Tips for Job Interviews, http://
www.liscareer.com/klob_interviews.htm

By Priscilla Klob (now Priscilla K. Shontz), freelance writer and
former academic librarian, reprinted from *NMRT Footnotes* 26(2),
January 1997.

Frequently Asked Interview Questions, http://www.libsci.sc.edu/
career/invufaqs.htm

University of South Carolina School of Library Science, U.S.A.

HOWTO Apply for a Library Job, http://www.tk421.net/essays/
howto.html

From John Hubbard, a librarian at the University of Wisconsin-
Milwaukee, U.S.A.

The Info Pro's Survival Guide to Job Hunting, *Searcher*, http://www.
infotoday.com/searcher/jul02/mort.htm

Written a few years ago by Mary Ellen Mort, but most of the information is still pertinent. The author is director of a public library-
sponsored Web site providing job information for California and the
rest of the U.S.A. (http://jobstar.org).

International Librarianship: Getting There from Here, http://www.
liscareer.com/kear_international.htm

By Robin Kear, Nova Southeastern University, Fort Lauderdale,
Florida, U.S.A., who worked in Kenya.

Mount, Ellis, ed. *Expanding Technologies—Expanding Careers:
Librarianship in Transition*. Washington, DC: Special Libraries
Association, 1997, ISBN 0-87111-465-8.

Questions Asked by Employers, http://www.istweb.syr.edu/courses/ advising/careerplanning/empquestions.asp

Syracuse University School of Information, New York, U.S.A.

Sellen, Betty-Carol. *What Else Can You Do With a Library Degree: Career Options for the '90s and Beyond.* New York: Neal-Schuman, 1997, ISBN 1-55570-264-3.

LIBRARY SCHOOLS

Australia

ALIA-recognized courses in library and information studies, http:// alia.org.au/education/courses

New South Wales: Charles Sturt University, School of Information Studies, Locked Bag 675, Wagga Wagga 2678, phone: 02-6933-2584, fax: 02-6933-2733, http://www.csu.edu.au/courses/ug/sci/libinf

University of New South Wales, School of Information Systems, Technology, and Management, Faculty of Commerce and Economics, Sydney 2052, phone: 02-9385-7134, fax: 02-9662-4016, http://fce. unsw.edu.au

University of Technology, Sydney, Faculty of Humanities and Social Sciences, Faculty Student Centre, P.O. Box 123, Broadway 2007, phone: 02-9514-2729, fax: 02-9514-3722, http://www.hss.uts.edu.au

Northern Territory: Charles Darwin University, Faculty of Law, Business and Arts, Darwin 0909, 08-8946-7766, fax: 08-8946-6777, http://www.cdu.edu.au

Queensland: Queensland University of Technology, Gardens Point, School of Information Systems, Faculty of Information Technology, GPO 2434, Brisbane 4001, phone: 07-3864-2782, fax: 07-3864-2703, http://www.qut.edu.au; Kelvin Grove, School of Cultural and Language Studies, Victoria Park Rd., Kelvin Grove 4059, phone: 07-3864-3948, fax: 07-3864-3949

South Australia: University of South Australia, School of Communication, Information and New Media, St. Bernards Rd., Magill 5072, phone: 08-8302-4479, fax: 08-8302-4745, http://www.unisa.edu.au/itee/

Tasmania: University of Tasmania, School Information Systems, Private Bag 87, Hobart 7001, phone: 03-6226-6200, fax: 03-6226-6221, http://fcms.its.utas.edu.au/commerce/infosys/

Victoria: Monash University, School of Information Management and Systems, Level 7, 26 Sir John Monash Dr., P.O. Box 197, Caulfield East 3145, phone: 03-9903-2208, fax: 03-9903-2005, http://www.sims.monash.edu.au

Royal Melbourne Institute of Technology (RMIT), School of Business Information Technology, GPO Box 2476V, Melbourne 3001, phone: 03-9925-5969, fax: 03-9925-5850, http://www.mit.edu.au/dipcourses.html

Western Australia: Curtin University of Technology, School of Media and Information, GPO Box 7215, Perth 6845, phone: 08-9266-7215, fax: 08-9266-3152, http://smi.curtin.edu.au/infostudies/CourseInfo.cfm

Edith Cowan University, School of Computer and Information Science, 2 Bradford St., Mt. Lawley 6050, phone: 08-9370-6299, fax: 08-9370-6100, http://www.scis.ecu.edu.au

U.K.

Courses in library and information studies accredited by CILIP, http://www.cilip.org.uk/qualificationschartership/Wheretostudy

Aberdeen: School of Information and Media, The Robert Gordon University, Garthdee Road, Aberdeen AB10 7QE, phone: 01224 263900, fax: 01224 263939, http://www.rgu.ac.uk/~sim/sim.htm

Aberystwyth: Department of Information Studies, University of Wales, Llanbadarn Fawr, Aberystwyth, Ceredigion SY23 3AS, phone: 01970-622188, fax: 10970-622190, http://www.dil.aber.ac.uk/index. htm

Birmingham: School of Information Studies, University of Central England in Birmingham, Perry Barr, Birmingham B42 2SU, phone: 0121 331 5625, fax: 0121 331 5675, http://www.cie.uce.ac.uk

Brighton: School of Information Management, University of Brighton, Watts Building, Moulsecoomb, Lewes Road, Brighton BN2 4GJ, phone: 01273 642428, fax: 01273 642405, http://www.cmis. brighton.ac.uk

Bristol: Department of Continuing Education, University of Bristol, 8-10 Berkeley Square, Clifton, Bristol BS8 1HH, phone: 0117 928 7138 or 0117 928 7147, fax: 0117 925 4975, http://www.bristol.ac.uk/ education/ilm

Edinburgh: School of Computing, Napier University, 10 Colinton Road, Edinburgh, EH10 5DT, phone: 0131 455 2700, fax: 0131 455 2727, http://www.soc.napier.ac.uk

Department of Communication and Information Studies, Queen Margaret University College, Clerwood Terrace, Edinburgh EH12 8TS, phone: 0131 317 3502, fax: 0131 316 4165, http://www.qmced. ac.uk

Glasgow: Graduate School of Informatics, Department of Computer & Information Sciences, Livingstone Tower, 26 Richmond Street, Glasgow G1 1XH, phone: 0141 548 3700, fax: 0141 552 5330, http://www.gsi.strath.ac.uk

Leeds: School of Information Management, Leeds Metropolitan University, Priestley Hall, Becketts Park, Leeds, LS6 3QS, phone: 0113 283 2600 ext 7421, fax: 0113 283 7599, http://www.lmu.ac. uk/ies/im

Liverpool: Centre Information and Library Management Group, School of Business Information, Liverpool John Moores University, John Foster Building, 98 Mount Pleasant, Liverpool L3 5UZ, Contact: Janet Farrow, phone: 0151 231 3596, fax: 0151 7070423, http://cwis.livjm.ac.uk/bus/cilm/

London: Department of Information Science, The City University, Northampton Square, London EC1V 0HB, phone: 44 (0) 20 7040 0239 or 0248, fax: 20 7040 0233, http://www.soi.city.ac.uk

School of Library, Archive, and Information Studies, University College London, Gower Street, London WC1E 6BT, phone: 020 7679 7204, fax: 020 7383 0557, http://www.ucl.ac.uk/slais

Department of Applied Social Sciences, London Metropolitan University, Ladbroke House, 62-66 Highbury Grove, London N5 2AD, phone: 020 7133 4200, http://www.londonmet.ac.uk/depts/dass/subjectareas/informationmanagement/

Thames Valley University, St Mary's Road, Ealing, London W5 5RF, phone: 020 8579 5000, fax: 020 8566 1353, http://www.tvu.ac.uk

Loughborough: Department of Information Science, Loughborough University, Loughborough, Leics. LE11 3TU, phone: 01509 223051 or 223052, fax: 01509 223053, http://lboro.ac.uk/departments/ls/

Manchester: Department of Information and Communications, Manchester Metropolitan University, Geoffrey Manton Building, Rosamond Street West, off Oxford Road, Manchester M15 6LL, phone: 0161 247 6144, fax: 0161 247 6351, http://www.mmu.ac.uk/h-ss/dic/

Department of Information and Communications, Manchester Metropolitan University, Geoffrey Manton Building, Rosamond Street West, off Oxford Road, Manchester M15 6LL, phone: 0161 247 6144, fax: 0161 247 6351, http://www.mmu.ac.uk/h-ss/dic/

Newcastle: Division of Information and Communication Studies, Northumbria University, Lipman Building, Newcastle upon Tyne NE1

8ST, phone: 0191 227 4917, fax: 0191 227 3671, http://online.north
umbria.ac.uk/vaculties/art/information_studies/

Sheffield: Department of Information Studies, The University of
Sheffield, Western Bank, Sheffield S10 2TN, phone: 0114 222 2630,
fax: 0114 278 0300, http://www.shef.ac.uk/uni/academic/I-M/is/
home.html

U.S.A.

Alabama: University of Alabama, College of Communication and
Information Sciences, School of Library and Information Studies, Box
870252, 515 Gorgas Library, Capstone Drive, Tuscaloosa 35487-0252,
phone: 1-205-348-4610, fax: 1-205-348-3746, http://www.slis.ua.edu

Arizona: University of Arizona, College of Social and Behavioral
Sciences, School of Information Resources & Library Science, 1515
East First Street, Tucson 85719, phone: 1-520-621-3565, fax: 1-520-
621-3279, http://www.sir.arizona.edu

California: San Jose State University, School of Library and
Information Science, One Washington Square, San Jose 95192-0029,
phone: 1-408-924-2490, fax: 1-408-924-2476, http://slisweb.sjsu.edu

University of California, Los Angeles, Graduate School of Education
& Information Studies, Department of Information Studies, Graduate
School of Education & Information, Studies Building, Box 951520,
Los Angeles 90095-1520, phone: 1-310-825-8799, fax: 1-310-206-3076,
http://is.gseis.ucla.edu/

Colorado: University of Denver, College of Education, Library and
Information Science Program, Wesley Hall, 2135 East Wesley, Suite
103, Denver 80208, phone: 1-303-871-2747, fax: 1-303-871-3422,
http://www.du.edu/LIS

Connecticut: Southern Connecticut State University, School of
Communication, Information and Library Science, Department of
Information and Library Science, 501 Crescent Street, New Haven

06515, phone: 1-203-392-5781, fax: 1-203-392-5780, http://www.
southernct.edu/departments/ils/

District of Columbia: Catholic University of America, School of
Library and Information Science, 620 Michigan Avenue, NE,
Washington 20064, phone: 1-202-319-5085, fax: 1-202-319-5574,
http://slis.cua.edu

Florida: Florida State University, School of Information Studies,
Shores Building, Tallahassee 32306-2100, phone: 1-850-644-5772,
fax: 1-850-644-9763, http://www.lis.fsu.edu

University of South Florida, College of Arts and Sciences, School of
Library and Information Science, 4202 East Fowler Avenue, CIS 1040,
Tampa 33620, phone: 1-813-974-3520, fax: 1-813-974-6840,
http://www.cas.usf.edu/lis

Hawaii: University of Hawaii, College of Natural Sciences, Library
and Information Science Program, Information and Computer
Sciences, 2550 McCarthy Mall, Honolulu 96822, phone: 1-808-956-
7321, fax: 1-808-956-5835, http://www.hawaii.edu/slis

Illinois: Dominican University, Graduate School of Library and
Information Science, 7900 West Division Street, River Forest 60305,
phone: 1-708-524-6845, fax: 1-708-524-6657, http://www.gslis.dom.edu

University of Illinois at Urbana-Champaign, Graduate School of
Library and Information Science, 501 East Daniel Street, Champaign
61820-6211, phone: 1-217-333-3280, 1-217-244-3302, http://alexia.
lis.uiuc.edu/

Indiana: Indiana University, School of Library and Information
Science, 1320 E. 10th Street, LI 011, Bloomington 47405-3907,
phone: 1-812-855-2018, fax: 1-812-855-6166, http://www.slis.
indiana.edu

Iowa: University of Iowa, School of Library and Information Science,
3087 Main Library, Iowa City 52242-1420, phone: 1-319-335-5707,
fax: 1-319-335-5374, http://www.uiowa.edu/~libsci

Kansas: Emporia State University, School of Library and Information Management, 1200 Commercial, Campus Box 4025, Emporia 66801, phone: 1-620-341-5203, fax: 1-620-341-5233, http:// slim.emporia.edu

Kentucky: University of Kentucky, Communications and Information Studies, School of Library and Information Science, 502 King Library, Lexington 40506-0039, phone: 1-859-257-8876, fax: 1-859-257-4205, http://www.uky.edu/CIS/SLIS

Louisiana: Louisiana State University, School of Library & Information Science, 267 Coates Hall, Baton Rouge 70803, phone: 1-225-578-3158, fax: 1-225-578-4581, http://slis.lsu.edu

Maryland: University of Maryland, College of Information Studies, 4105 Hornbake Building, College Park 20742, phone: 1-301-405-2033, fax: 1-301-314-9145, http://www.clis.umd.edu

Massachusetts: Simmons College, Graduate School of Library and Information Science, 300 The Fenway, Boston 02115, phone: 1-617-521-2800, fax: 1-617-521-3192, http://www.simmons.edu/gslis

Michigan: University of Michigan, School of Information, 550 East University Avenue, 304 West Hall Building, Ann Arbor 48109-1092, phone: 1-734-764-9376, fax: 1-734-764-2475, http://www.si.umich.edu

Wayne State University, Library and Information Science Program, 106 Kresge Library, Detroit 48202, phone: 1-313-577-1825, fax: 1-313-577-7563, http://www.lisp.wayne.edu

Mississippi: University of Southern Mississippi, School of Library and Information Science, 118 College Drive #5146, Hattiesburg 39406-0001, phone: 1-601-266-4228, fax: 1-601-266-5774, http://www.usm.edu/slis

Missouri: University of Missouri, College of Education, Information Science and Learning, 303 Townsend Hall, Columbia 65211, phone: 1-573-882-4546, fax: 1-573-884-0122, http://sislt.missouri.edu

New Jersey: Rutgers, Communication, Information, Department of Library and Information, 4 Huntington Street, New Brunswick 08901-1071, phone: 1-732-932-7500 ext. 8955, fax: 1-732-932-2644, http://scils.rutgers.edu

New York: The State University of New York at Albany, School of Information Science and Policy, Draper 113, 135 Western Avenue, Albany 12222, phone: 1-518-442-5110, fax: 1-518-442-5367, http://www.albany.edu/sisp/

The State University of New York at Buffalo, School of Informatics, Library and Information Studies, 534 Baldy Hall, Buffalo 14260, phone: 1-716-645-2412, fax: 1-716-645-3775, http://informatics.buffalo.edu/lis/

Long Island University, College of Information and Computer Science, Palmer School of Library and Information Science, 720 Northern Boulevard, Brookville 11548, phone: 1-516-299-2866, fax: 1-516-299-4168, http://www.liu.edu/palmer

Pratt Institute, School of Information and Library Science, 144 West 14th Street, 6th Floor, New York City 10011, phone: 1-212-647-7682, fax: 1-212-367-2492, http://www.pratt.edu/sils

Queens College, Graduate School for Library & Information Studies, 65-30 Kissena Boulevard, Flushing 11367-1597, phone: 1-718-997-3790, fax: 1-718-997-3797, http://www.qc.edu/GSLIS

St. Johns University, St. John's College of Liberal Arts & Sciences, Division of Library and Information Science, 8000 Utopia Parkway, Jamaica 11439, phone: 1-718-990-6200, fax: 1-718-990-2071, http://www.stjohns.edu/libraryscience

Syracuse University, School of Information Studies, 4-206 Center for Science and Technology, Syracuse 13244, phone: 1-315-443-2911, fax: 1-315-443-5673, http://www.ist.syr.edu

North Carolina: North Carolina Central University, School of Library and Information Sciences, Durham 27705, phone: 1-919-530-6485, fax: 1-919-530-6002, http://www.nccu.edu

University of North Carolina-Chapel Hill, School of Information and Library Science, 100 Manning Hall, CB #3360, Chapel Hill 27599-3360, phone: 1-919-962-8366, fax: 1-919-962-8071, http://www.ils.unc.edu

University of North Carolina at Greensboro, School of Education, Department of Library and Information Studies, 349 Curry Building, Greensboro 27401-6170, phone: 1-336-334-3477, fax: 1-336-334-5060, http://lis.uncg.edu

Ohio: Kent State University, College of Communication and Information, School of Library and Information Science, P.O. Box 5190, Kent 44242-0001, phone: 1-330-672-2782, fax: 1-330-672-7965, http://www.slis.kent.edu

Oklahoma: University of Oklahoma, College of Arts and Sciences, School of Library and Information Studies, 401 West Brooks, Room 120, Norman 73019-6032, phone: 1-405-325-3921, fax: 1-405-325-7648, http://www.ou.edu/cas/slis

Pennsylvania: Clarion University of Pennsylvania, College of Education and Human Services, Department of Library Science, 210 Carlson Library Building, 840 Wood Street, Clarion 16214, phone: 1-814-393-2271, fax: 1-814-393-2150, http://www.clarion.edu/libsci

Drexel University, College of Information Science and Technology, 3141 Chestnut Street, Philadelphia 19104-2875, phone: 1-215-895-2474, fax: 1-215-895-2494, http://www.cis.drexel.edu

University of Pittsburgh, School of Information Sciences, Department of Library and Information Studies, 135 North Bellefield Avenue, Pittsburgh 15260, phone: 1-412-624-5142, fax: 1-412-624-5231, http://www.sis.pitt.edu

Puerto Rico: University of Puerto Rico, Information Sciences and Technologies, P.O. Box 21906, San Juan 00931-1906, phone: 1-787-763-6199, fax: 1-787-764-2311, http://egcti.upr.edu

Rhode Island: University of Rhode Island, Graduate School of Library and Information Studies, Rodman Hall, 94 West Alumni Avenue, Kingston 02881, phone: 1-401-874-2947, fax: 1-401-874-4964, http://www.uri.edu/artsci/lsc/

South Carolina: University of South Carolina, Mass Communications and Information Studies, School of Library and Information Science, Davis College, Columbia 29208, phone: 1-803-777-3858, fax: 1-803-777-7938, http://www.libsci.sc.edu/

Tennessee: University of Tennessee, College of Communication and Information, School of Information Sciences, 451 Communications Building, 1345 Circle Park Drive, Knoxville 37996-0341, phone: 1-865-974-2148, fax: 1-865-974-4967, http://www.sis. utk.edu

Texas: University of North Texas, School of Library and Information Sciences, P.O. Box 311068, Denton 76203-1068, phone: 1-940-565-2731, fax: 1-940-565-3101, http://www.unt.edu/slis

University of Texas at Austin, School of Information, 1 University Station D7000, Austin 78712-0390, phone: 1-512-471-3821, fax: 1-512-471-3971, http://www.ischool.utexas.edu

Texas Woman's University, School of Library and Information Studies, P.O. Box 425438, Denton 76204-5438, phone: 1-940-898-2602 or 2603, fax: 1-940-898-2611, http://www.twu.edu/cope/slis/

Washington State: University of Washington, The Information School, Mary Gates Hall, Suite 370, Box 352840, Seattle 98195-2840, phone: 1-206-685-9937, fax: 1-206-616-3152, http://www.ischool. washington.edu

Wisconsin: University of Wisconsin-Madison, College of Letters and Sciences, Library and Information Studies, 600 North Park Street,

Room 4217, H. C. White Hall, Madison 53706, phone: 1-608-263-2900, fax: 1-608-263-4849, http://www.slis.wisc.edu

University of Wisconsin-Milwaukee, School of Information Studies, P.O. Box 413, Milwaukee 53201, phone: 1-414-229-4707, fax: 1-414-229-6699, http://www.sois.uwm.edu

Canada

Alberta: University of Alberta, School of Library and Information Studies, 3-20 Rutherford South, Edmonton T6G2J4, phone: 1-780-492-4578, fax: 1-780-492-2430, http://www.slis.ualberta.ca

British Columbia: University of British Columbia, School of Library, Archival & Information Studies, Suite 301, 6190 Agronomy Road, Vancouver V6T 1Z3, phone: 1-604-822-2404, fax: 1-604-822-6006, http://www.slais.ubc.ca

Nova Scotia: Dalhousie University, School of Library and Information Studies, 3rd Floor, Killam Library, Halifax B3H 3J5, phone: 1-902-494-3656, fax: 1-902-494-2451, http://www.mgmt.dal. ca/slis

Ontario: University of Toronto, Faculty of Information Studies, 140 St. George Street, Room 211, Toronto M5S 3G6, phone: 1-416-978-3202, fax: 1-416-978-5762, http://www.fis.utoronto.ca

University of Western Ontario, Faculty of Information and Media Studies, Graduate Programs in Library and Inform. Science, North Campus Building, Room 240, London N6A 5B7, phone: 1-519-661-4017, fax: 1-519-661-3506, http://www.fims.uwo.ca

Quebec: McGill University, Graduate School of Library and Information Studies, 3459 McTavish Street, MS 57-F, Montreal H3A 1Y1, phone: 1-514- 398-4204, fax: 1-514-398-7193, http://www.gslis.mcgill.ca

Universite de Montreal, École de bibliothéconomie et des sciences, de l'information, CP 6128, succursale centre-ville, Montreal H3C 3J7, phone: 1-514-343-6400, 1-514-343-5753, http://www.ebsi.umontreal.ca/

LIBRARY SUPPLIERS

Books

ABE Books, http://www.abebooks.com

Addall, http://www.addall.com
   Compare prices from more than 40 suppliers.

Alibris, http://www.alibris.com/library
   For hard-to-find books.

American Overseas Book Company, http://www3.aobc.com

Best Book Buys, http://www.bestbookbuys.com
   Another comparison site.

Bibliofind, http://www.bibliofind.com
   More than 10 million used and rare books, periodicals, and ephemera, from Amazon.

Bibliomania, http://www.bibliomania.net/Search.html
   Searches for used books using many of the other comparison sites (U.K.).

Blackwell's Book Services, http://bookshop.blackwell.com/bobus/scripts/welcome.jsp

Bookfinder, http://www.bookfinder.com
   Multisearch engine site, can search in 4 languages (U.K.).

Bookpool.com Discount Computer Books, http://bookpool.com

Complete Book, http://www.completebook.com
   Aimed at the corporate market.

Co-op Bookstore, http://www.coop-bookshop.com.au
   For the academic market (Australia).

Fetchbook, http://www.fetchbook.info
   Compares more than 100 bookstores.

Ingram, http://www.ingrambookgroup.com

Leap, Steven and Nancy Sneed. Buy Books. *Journal of Hospital Librarianship* 3(3): 99+, 2003.

Majors', http://www.majors.com, medical books
  Now owned by Baker & Taylor.

Matthews Medical Books, http://www.matthewsbooks.com

Powell's Technical Books, http://www.powells.com

Opamp Technical Books, http://www.opamp.com

OrderPoint, http://www.orderpoint.com

Reiter's Scientific & Professional Books, http://www.reiters.com
  Technical, medical, and professional books.

Rittenhouse Book Distributors, http://www.rittenhouse.com
  Healthcare and medical books.

Total Information, http://www.totalinformation.com

U.K. Book World, http://www.ukbookworld.com
  Rare and out-of-print books.

United Techbook Co., http://www.utcbooks.com

Used Book Search, http://www.usedbooksearch.co.uk (U.K.)

Equipment and Services
Designing, Building, or Moving a Library

Appel, Linda. Moving A Library, Designing a New One, or Redesigning an Old One. *The One-Person Library* 19(4): 3–4, August 2002.

Brown, Carol R. *Interior Design for Libraries: Drawing on Function & Appeal*. Chicago: ALA Editions, 2002, ISBN 0-8383-0829-2.

Habich, Elizabeth Chamberlain. *Moving Library Collections: A Management Handbook*. Westport, CT: Greenwood Press, 1998, ISBN 0-31329330-9.

Lushington, Nolan. *Libraries Designed for Users: A 21st Century Guide*. New York: Neal Schuman, 2002, ISBN 1-55570419-0 (paper). Lushington is one of the most respected authorities on library design.

Margeton, Stephen G. Law Library Design Bookshelf: An Annotated Bibliography. *Law Library Journal* 97(1): 77-101, 2005. Not just for law librarians and source of many of the citations in this section.

Sannwald, William W. *Checklist of Library Building Design Considerations*, 4th ed. Chicago: American Library Association, 2001, ISBN 0-83893506-0 (paper).

Woodward, Jeannette. *Countdown to a New Library: Managing the Building Project*. ALA Editions, 2000, ISBN 0-8383-0767-9. This book is out-of-print, but you might be able to find it in a library.

Guides

Buyer's Guide and Web Site Directory, Annual special supplement to *Library Journal* and *School Library Journal*, December issue, 360 Park Ave. South, New York, NY 10010, phone: 1-646-746-6819, fax: 1-646-746-6734. Directory of library schools, associations (national, international, state, regional), architects specializing in libraries, companies (hardware, software, furniture, supplies, services—just about everything), indexes by product for products, services, and materials.

Cibbarelli, Pamela. *Directory of Library Automation Software, Systems, and Services*. Medford, NJ: Information Today, 2004–2005 edition, ISBN 1-57387-200-8.

Cohn, John M., Ann L. Kelsey, and Keith Michael Fiels. *Planning for Integrated Systems and Technologies: A How-To-Do-It Manual for Librarians*. New York: Neal-Schuman, 2001, ISBN 1-55570-421-2.

inCite Directory Issue (January-February), for Australia.

Librarian's Yellow Pages, http://librariansyellowpages.com

Library HQ, http://www.libraryhq.com

"Resources for the Wired Librarian," links to more than 6,000 Web sites (cataloged in MARC format and searchable), classified ads, news source, automation source, new titles in library technology.

Vendors

CAVAL Collaborative Solutions (Australia, New Zealand), 4 Park Drive, Bundoora 3083, phone: 61-3-9459-2722, fax: 61-3-9459-2733, http://www.caval.edu.au. Cataloging, acquisitions, document delivery, translations, information audits, training, and workshops.

Chess Moving (Australia), 48-50 Assembly Drive, Tullamarin 3043, phone: 03-9330-0750, fax: 03-0330-0480, http://www.chesmoving. com.au

CK Design International (Australia), Suite 13, 16-22 Australia St., Camperdown 2050, phone: 02-9557-9556, fax: 02-9557-9558, http://www.ckdesign.com.au

Harwell Drying and Restoration Services (U.K.), Harwell International Business Centre, B404.13, Harwell, Didcot, OX11 0RA, phone: 01235 432245, fax: 01235 432246, http://www.harwell-drying.co.uk. Salvage and restoration of fire and flood damage to paper.

John Stanley Associates, 142 Hummerston Road, Kalamunda, Western Australia, 6076, phone: 08-9293-4533, http://www.johnstanley.cc. Library design, team training, marketing strategies, merchandising, and lobbying.

JWA/Video (U.S.A.), 921 W. Van Buren St., Suite 220, Chicago Illinois 60607, phone: 1-800-327-5110 or 1-312-829-5100, fax: 1-312-829-9074, http://www.jwavideo.com

Library Associates (U.S.A.), 8845 W. Olympic Blvd., Suite 109, Beverly Hills California 90211, phone: 1-310-289-1067, fax: 1-310-289-9635, http://www.libraryassociates.com. Staffing, technical services, and recruiting internationally.

Librarycom (library automation) from Caspr (U.S.A.), 14395 Saratoga Ave, Suite 210, Saratoga, California 95070, phone: 1-800-852-2777 or 1-408-741-2322, fax: 1-408-741-2325, http://www.librarycom.com. You can get a 30-day free preview and the cost is based on the number of titles you will have. Most special and school libraries could choose the USD300 option. It seems very easy and complete. Catalog using MARC or LC records (or enter your own) and enter client records and circulation policies. You can even renew and hold items, print customized overdue notices and reports, link libraries to form virtual union collections, and allow customers to access the OPAC from any location on the Internet. One would think there's a catch, but I couldn't find one.

Plescon Security Products (U.K.), Unit 9, Sterling Complex, Sproughton Business Park, Farthing Road, Ipswich, Suffolk IP1 5AP, U.K., phone: 01473-747159, fax: 01473-747252, http://www.plescon. co.uk. For public, academic, school and business libraries.

Raeco (Furniture & Supplies, Australia, New Zealand), 75 Rushdale St., Scoresby 3179, phone: 1300-727-23, http://www.raeco.com.au

Resource Options, P.O. Box 6089, Buranda 4102, phone: 07-3391-3499, fax: 07-3391-3588, http://www.resource-options.com.au. Training, recruiting, database services, evaluation, and information management.

Softlink (Australia), 68 Commercial Drive, Shaller Park, QLD 4128, phone: 1-800-777-037 or 61-7-3801-4111, fax: 61-7-3801-4555. Library management, public, academic, corporate, legal, and medical libraries.

UniLinc (Australia and New Zealand), Level 9, 210 Clarence St., Sydney 2000, phone: 02-9283-1488, fax: 02-4929-7827. Cataloging and technical services, library systems, RFID, evaluation, and benchmarking

SUBSCRIPTION AGENCIES
Australia

DA Subscriptions, 648 Whitehorse Rd., Mitcham 3132, phone: 03-9210-7773, fax: 03-9210-7788, http://www.dadirect.com.au

EBSCO Australia, Level 7, 132 Arthur St., North Sydney 2060, phone: 02-9922-5600, 1-800-023-314, fax: 02-9922-6659, http://www.ebsco.com

Swets Information Services, 4 Bennetts Lane, Melbourne 3000, phone: 03-9655-3700, fax: 03-9639-8922, http://www. swets.nl

U.S.A.

Basch Subscriptions, 88 N. Main St., Concord, New Hampshire 03301, phone: 1-603-229-0662 or 1-800-226-5310, fax: 1-603-226-9443, http://www.basch.com

EBSCO Information Services, P.O. Box 1943, Birmingham, Alabama 35201-1943, phone: 1-205-991-6600, fax: 1-205-995-1518, http://www.ebsco.com

Swets Information Services, 160 Ninth Avenue, P.O. Box 1459, Runnemede, NJ 08078, phone: 1-856-312-2690 or 1-800-645-6595, fax: 1-856-312-2000, http://informationservices.swets.com.

Elsewhere

Caslini Libri, Via Benedetto Da Maiano, Fiesole 1-50014, Italy, phone: 39-055-5018-1, fax: 30-055-5018-201, http://www.caslini.it

DK Agencies Pty Ltd., A/15-17 Mohan Gardens, Najafgarh Rd., New Delhi 110 059, India, phone: 91-11-2535-7104, fax: 91-11-2525-7103, http://www.dkagencies.com

Prenax Ltd., 12 Oval Road, London, NW1 7DH, U.K., phone: 44-20-7428-6000, fax: 44-20-7428-6001, https://www.prenax.co.uk/start.asp

Swets Information Services, Heereweg 347 B, 2161 CA Lisse, P.O. Box 830, 2160 SZ Lisse, The Netherlands, phone: 31 (0) 252 435 111, fax: 31 (0) 252 415 888, http://informationservices.swets.com

PROFESSIONAL ASSOCIATIONS
Australia

Australian Government Libraries Information Network (AGLIN), GPO Box 1780, Canberra ACT 2601, http://www.nla.gov.au/flin

Australian Law Librarians Group (ALLG), http://www.allg.asn.au
Publishes *The Australian Law Librarian*.

Australian Library and Information Association (ALIA), P.O. Box 63335, Kingston, ACT 2604, phone: 02-625-8222, fax: 02-6282-2249, http://www.alia.org.au. Organized into groups, either geographic or subject, such as Agriculture & Environment Libraries, Academic & Research Libraries, Health Libraries, Public Libraries, Schools, Special Libraries, and One Person Australian Librarians (OPAL)—especially for OPLs.

Australian School Library Association (ASLA), P.O. Box 155, Zillmere Queensland 4034, phone: 61-7-3633-0510, fax: 61-7-3633-0570, http://www.asla.org.au

Council of Australian University Librarians (CAUL), LPO Box 8169, Australian National University, Canberra ACT 2601, phone: 61-2-6125-2990, fax: 61-2-6248-8571, http://www.caul.edu.au

Environmental Librarians Network (ELN), ELN Convenor: Kay L Winter, Library Director, Department of the Environment and Heritage, GPO Box 787, Canberra ACT 2601, http://www.deh.gov.au/about/library/eln

Health Leaders Network, Locked Bag 33, Australia Square 1215, phone: 02-8348-8612, fax: 02-9247-3688, http://www.hln.com.au

Library and Information Association of New Zealand Aotearoa (LIANZA), P.O. Box 12-212, Wellington, phone: 62-4-473-5834, fax: 63-4-449-1480, http://www.lianza.org.nz

Pacific Islands Association of Libraries and Archives (PIALA), P.O. Box 9, Koror, Palau 96940, http://www.uog.edu/rfk/piala/piala.html

SLA Australia and New Zealand Chapter (regular meetings in Sydney, Melbourne, and Auckland), http://www.sla.org/chapter/canz

U.S.A. and Canada

American Association of Law Libraries (AALL), 53 W. Jackson, Suite 940, Chicago, IL 60604, phone: 1-312-939-4764, fax: 1-312-431-1097, http://www.aallnet.org. The Private Law Libraries Special Interest Group has an OPL section, http://www.aallnet.org/sis/pllsis/Groups/oneperson.asp

American Association of Museums, 1575 Eye Street, NW, Suite 400, Washington, DC 20005, phone: 1-202-289-1818, fax: 1-202-289-6578, http://www.aam-us.org

American Library Association (ALA), 50 E. Huron St., Chicago, IL 60611, fax: 1-312-944-9374, http://www.ala.org. A *very* large organization, most members are active only in the divisions, such as American Association of School Librarians (AASL), Association of College and Research Libraries (ACRL), or Public Library Association (PLA).

American Society for Information Science and Technology (ASIS&T), 1320 Fenwick Lane, Suite 501, Silver Spring, MD 20910, phone: 1-301-495-0900, fax: 1-3101-495-0810, http://www.asis.org. Focuses on technology issues and research.

Association of Jewish Libraries (AJL), 15 East 26th St., 10th Floor, New York, NY 10010, phone: 1-212-725-5359, http://www.jewish libraries.org

Canadian Library Association (CLA), 328 Frank St., Ottawa, Ontario K2P OX8, phone: 1-613-232-9625, fax: 1-613-563-9895, http://www.cla.ca

Church and Synagogue Library Association (CSLA), P.O. Box 19357, Portland, OR 97280-0357, phone: 1-503-244-6919 or 1-800-542-2752, fax: 1-503-977-3734, http://www.csla.info

Medical Library Association (MLA), 65 East Wacker Place, Suite 1900, Chicago, IL 60601-7298, phone: 1-312-419-9094, fax: 1-312-

419-8950, http://www.mlanet.org. Most of the members of the Hospital Libraries Group are OPLs, http://hls.mlanet.org

Special Libraries Association (SLA), 331 South Patrick Street, Alexandria, VA 22314-3501, phone: 1-703-647-4900, fax 1-703-647-4901, http://www.sla.org. Organized by subject divisions (including the Solo Librarians Division, especially for OPLs) and geographic chapters in the U.S.A. and around the world. Non-U.S.A. chapters are in: Arabian Gulf, Asia, Australia and New Zealand, Europe, Eastern Canada, Caribbean (with Florida), Pacific (with Hawaii), Sub-Saharan Africa, Toronto, and Western Canada. Toronto Solos, subgroup of Toronto Chapter of SLA, http://www.sla.org/chapter/ctor. SLA has some outstanding resources. Perhaps the best are the information portals at http://www.sla.org/content/resources/infoportals/index.cfm. They are available only to members, but they are almost worth the cost of membership by themselves and are kept up-to-date by SLA librarian John Latham. They fall into nine categories: Careers, Intellectual Property, International, Internet/intranet, Knowledge Management/Communities of Practice, Competitive Intelligence, Management/Services, Marketing/Value, Technology/Software. Of special interest to OPLs are: career planning and competencies, salary surveys, copyright, electronic licensing, international library resources, digital libraries, Internet development, virtual library, Web design, knowledge management, benchmarking, disaster planning, information audit, instruction and end-user training, library advisory committee, costs and budgets, strategic plans, outsourcing, space planning, starting and managing a special library, marketing, value of the information center.

Visual Resources Association, P.O. Box 47, Bronx, NY 10464, http://wwwvraweb.org. A multidisciplinary community of image management professionals working in educational and cultural heritage environments. Covers documentation and access to images of visual culture, integration of technology-based instruction and research and intellectual property policy. Chapters in New England, Great Lakes, Northern California, and Greater New York.

U.K.

City Information Group, http://www.cityinformation.org.uk
  For those interested in business information.

Chartered Institute of Library and Information Professionals (CILIP), 7 Ridgmount Street, London WC1E 7AE, phone, 44-20-7255-0500, fax: 44-20-7255-0501, http://www.cilip.org.uk. *The* library organization in the U.K., many training courses, certifies library education programs and professional qualifications; organized into geographic branches and subject special interest groups, such as Colleges of Further & Higher Education, Education Libraries, Government Libraries, Industrial & Commercial Libraries, Prison Libraries, Public Libraries, School Libraries, and University, College and Research Libraries, and Youth Libraries.

Library Association of Ireland (LAI), 53 Upper Mount St., Dublin 2, phone: 353-1-612-2193, fax: 353-1-612-3093, http://www.library association.ie

Scottish Library and Information Council (SLIC), 1st Floor, Building C, Leechlee Rd., Hamilton ML3 6AU, phone: 44-0-1698-458-888, fax: 44-0-1698-283-170, http://www.slainte.org.uk/slic/

School Library Association (U.K.), Unit 2 Lotmead Business Village, Lotmead Farm, Wanborough, Swindon SN4 0UY, phone: 44 (0) 1793 791787, fax: 44 (0) 1793 791786, http://www.sla.org.uk

SLA Europe, http://www.sla-europe.org
  Most of the European Chapter meetings and officers are in England (primarily in London).

The Solo Professional Network, East Midlands Branch of CILIP, c/o Sue Robertson at SINTO (the Sheffield Information Service), Sheffield Hallam University, Collegiate Crescent, Sheffield S10 2BP, phone: 0-114-225-5740, fax: 0-114-225-22476

UKeIG (U.K. eInformation Group, formerly the Online Information Group), http://www.ukolug.org.uk; with two local user groups: AberOLUG (midWales) and EAOLUG (East Anglia)

U.K. Serials Group (UKSG), Bowman & Hillier Building, The Old Brewery, Priory Lane, Burford, Oxon OX18 4SG, http://www.uksg.org

Welsh Library Association (Cymdeithas Llyfrgelloedd Cymru), DIS, Llanbadarn Fawr, Aberystwyth SY23 3AS, phone: 01970 622 174, fax: 01970 622 190, http://www.dils.aber.ac.uk/holi/wla/wla.htm

Other Library Professional Organizations Serving Special Constituencies

For more organizations, see http://www.ala.org/ala/iro/intlassocorgconf/libraryassociations.htm

American Mental Health Information Management Association (AHIMA), 233 N. Michigan Ave., Suite 2150, Chicago, IL 60601-5800 U.S.A., phone: 1-312-233-1100, fax: 1-312-233-1090, e-mail: info@ahima.org, http://www.ahima.org/ Certifies specialists in medical coding and similar areas.

Art Libraries Society of North American (ARLIS/NA), 232-329 March Road, Box 11, Ottawa, ON K2K 2E1, Canada, phone: 1-800-817-0621 or 1-613-599-3074, fax: 1-613-599-7027, http://www. arlisna.org

Association for Health Information and Libraries in Africa (AHILA), http://www.ahila.org

Chapters in Burkina Faso, Cameroon, Guinea Bissau, Guinea Conakry, Ivory Coast, Kenya, Malawi, Mali, Nigeria, Senegal, South Africa, Swaziland, Uganda, Zambia, and Zimbabwe.

European Association for Health Information and Libraries (EAHIL), c/o Suzanne Bakker, Central Cancer Library, The Netherlands Cancer Institute, Plesmanlaan 121, NL-1066 CX Amsterdam, The Netherlands, phone: 31-20-512-2597, 31 20 512 25, http://www.eahil.net

European Bureau of Library, Information and Documentation Associations (EBLIDA), P.O. Box 16359, NL-2500 B J, The Hague, The Netherlands, phone: 31-70-309-0551, fax: 31-70-309-0558, http://www.eblida.org

Indian Association of Special Libraries and Information Centers, P-291, CIT Scheme No. 6M, Kankurgachi, Kolkata (Calcutta) phone: 700 054, 91-33-2352 9651, fax: 91-33-2354 9066, http://www.iaslic.org

International Association of Law Libraries (IALL), P.O. Box 5709, Washington, DC 20016-1309 U.S.A., http://www.iall.org

International Association of Music Libraries, in the U.S.A., c/o Mary Alice Fields, University of Alabama Libraries, Box 870266, Tuscaloosa, AL 35487-0266 U.S.A., phone: 1-205-348-6359, http://www. cilea.it/music/iamlhome.htm, Branches: Archives and Music Documentation Centres, Broadcasting and Orchestra Libraries, Libraries in Music Teaching Institutions, Public Libraries, and Research Libraries.

International Association of School Librarianship (IASL), The International Association of School Librarianship, PMB 292, 1903 W. 8th Street, Erie, PA 16505 U.S.A., http://www.iasl-slo.org

Israel Society of Libraries and Information Centres (ASMI), http://www.asmi.org.il/
Site is in Hebrew, formerly just for special libraries.

Japan Medical Library Association, http://www.soc.nii.ac.jp/jmla
Site only in Japanese.

Japan Special Library Association, c/o Japan Library Association Bldg. F6, 1-11-14 Shinkawa, Chuo-ku, Tokyo 104-0033, Japan, phone: 81-3-3537-8335, fax: 81-3-3537-8336, http://www.jsla.org.or.jp/eng/index.html

World List of Departments and Schools of Information Studies, Information Management, Information Systems, etc., http://informatonr.net/wl/wlist99.html.
From Prof. Tom Wilson, Professor Emeritus in Information Management, University of Sheffield, U.K. For 68 countries, searchable.

JUST FOR FUN AND MISCELLANEOUS

Citing Electronic Resources, http://www.cyberbee.com/citing.html
  Easy-to-use link to citation styles.

Library Cartoons: An annotated bibliography, http://pw1.netcom.
com/~dplourde/cartoons/index.html, alphabetical and chronological
  With original date published, source, and a description. Wonderful fun!

Library Conference Planner, http://www.fiu.edu/~hastyd/lcp.html
  Douglas Hasty of Florida International University has compiled a
list of library conferences around the world. He's probably missed a
few, but there are a lot there—and it is really international. For more
information, he also lists 16 Tips for a Successful Conference, the ALA
conference calendar, archives of past lists, and Librarian's Datebook,
2004–2013. He even has links to airlines, auto clubs, hotels, travel
agencies, currency converters, airport security rules, and the weather
so you can do all your planning in one place.

Library Songs, http://www.blisspix.net/library/songs.html

The Political Graveyard, http://politicalgraveyard.com/index.html
  "The Web Site That Tells Where the Dead Politicians are Buried,"
searchable by person, place, age, office, demographics, or cause of death.

UltraCondensed Books, http://rinkworks.com/bookaminute/classics.
shtml
  If you are a bit short of time, but still want to read the classic books,
check out this site. There are also sister sites with sci-fi books, children's bedtime stories, and movies. But seriously, it is just for fun—
great fun, that is.

Unshelved. This is a great comic strip, set in the Mallville Public
Library. The hero is Dewey, the young adult librarian. Not just for public librarians—everything is understandable to all of us. Comes by
e-mail *every* day (including weekends). Subscribe at Yahoo! Groups,
http://login.yahoo.com/

Virtual Reference, http://www.lis.uiuc.edu/~b-sloan/critbib.htm
  A wonderful critical bibliography by Bernie Sloan of the University
of Illinois at Urbana-Champaign (U.S.A.).

16

Medicine, Health, Nursing, and Medical Libraries

COMPLEMENTARY AND ALTERNATIVE MEDICINE

Books

Cherniack, P. and N. Cherniack, eds. *Alternative Medicine for the Elderly*. New York: Springer, 2003, ISBN 3-54044169-7.

Complementary and Alternative Cancer Methods Handbook. Atlanta: American Cancer Society, 2002, ISBN 0-944235-40-9. Order from http://www.cancer.org/docroot/PUB/content/PUB_1_1_American_Cancer_SocietysbrComplementary_and_AlternativebrCancer_Methods_Handbook.asp

Fetrow, C.H and J.R. Avila. *Professional's Handbook to Complementary and Alternative Medicines*, 3rd ed. Philadelphia: Lippincott, Williams, and Wilkins, 2003, ISBN 1-58255-243-6.

Freeman, Lyn W. and G. Frank Lawlis. *Mosby's Complementary and Alternative Medicine: A Research-based Approach*. St. Louis: Mosby, 2001, ISBN 0-32300697-3

Jonas, Wayne and Jeffrey S. Levin, eds. *Essentials of Complementary and Alternative Medicine*. Philadelphia: Lippincott, Williams, and Wilkins, 1999, ISBN 0-68330674-X.

Longe, Jacqueline. *Gale Encyclopedia of Alternative Medicine*. Farmington Hills, MI: Thomson Gale, 2004, ISBN 0-78767424-9.

Murray, Michael and Joseph Pizzomo. *Encyclopedia of Natural Medicine*, 2nd rev. ed., 2 volumes. New York: Three Rivers Press, 1997, ISBN 0-76151157-1.

Mills, Simon and Kerry Bone. *Principles and Practice of Phytotherapy: Modern Herbal Medicine*. London: Churchill Livingstone, 1999, ISBN 0-443306016-9.

Spencer, John and Spencer Jacobs. *Complementary/Alternative Medicine: An Evidence-based Approach*, 2nd ed. St. Louis: Elsevier Science, 2002, ISBN 0-32302028-3.

Also, check out other titles from publisher Churchill Livingstone on evidence-based alternative medicine.

Journals

Alternative Medicine Alert, http://www.altmednet.com
A 12-page monthly newsletter from American Health Consultants, USD299 per year.

Web Sites

Medical Library Association, http://colldev.mlanet.org/subject.html
Subject-based resource lists, both Web and print.

CONSUMER HEALTH INFORMATION WEB SITES

Cultural Issues and Multilanguage Information

Books

Andrews, Janice D. *Cultural, Ethnic, and Religious Reference Manual for Health Care Providers*, 2nd ed. Winston-Salem, NC: JAMARDA Resources, Inc., 1999, ISBN 0-96635521-0.

Culture and Nursing Care: A Pocket Guide. San Francisco: University of San Francisco Nursing Press, 1996, ISBN 0-94367115-9.

Pocket Guide to Cultural Health Assessment, 3rd ed. St. Louis: Mosby, 2002, ISBN 0-32301858-0.

Spector, Rachael E. *Cultural Diversity in Health & Illness*, 6th ed. New York: Prentice Hall Health, 2003, ISBN 0-13-049379-1 (paper).

Web Sites

Annotated Bibliography of Cultures & Cultural Medicine, http://www.geocities.com/SoHo/Study/8276/Bibliography.html

From Tanya Feddern, University of Miami Medical Center, Florida, U.S.A.

Cancer Resources in Languages Other than English, http://www.cancerindex.org/clinks13.htm

From Simon Cotterill, Senior Research Associate Faculty of Medical Sciences Computing, University of Newcastle, U.K.

Combined Health Information Database, http://chid.nih.gov/detail/detail.html

Foreign Language Health Information from the National Institutes of Health, U.S.A.

Cultural Medicine, http://www.geocities.com/nqiya/CulturalMed.html

Excellent set of links to resources on dealing with patients from diverse cultures, from Tanya Feddern, University of Miami Medical Center, Florida, U.S.A.

DiversityRX, http://www.diversityrx.org

Essentials, models and practices, policy, legal issues, and networking (links)—an excellent site. Sponsored by the National Conference of State Legislatures (NCSL), Resources for Cross Cultural Health Care (RCCHC), and the Henry J. Kaiser Family Foundation of Menlo Park, California, U.S.A.

Electronic Quality Information for Patients, http://www.equip.nhs.uk/

Quality checked sites for health and diseases information and support for patients; one page of non-English resources for ethnic groups, searchable. From the U.K. National Health Service.

Ethnomed, http://ethnomed.org

Ethnic medicine information from Harborview Medical Center from the University of Washington includes Amharic, Entrean, Oromo, Somali, Tigrean, Cambodian, and Vietnamese.

Medical Glossaries, http://xculture.org/resource/index.html

Each contains a word list of 1,000 to 2,600 and the expanded glossaries contain the term in English, the translation, and the definition of the term in English. Available in Cambodian, Chinese, Korean, Lao, Tigrignia, Amharic, Somali, and Bengali. Cost from USD10–25. Produced by the Cross Cultural Healthcare Program, Seattle, Washington, U.S.A.

Multilingual Glossary of Technical and Popular Medical Terms, http://allserv.rug.ac.be/~rvdstich/eugloss/welcome.html

In Danish, Dutch, English, French, German, Italian, Portuguese, Spanish. From the European Commission, the Heymans Institute of Pharmacology and Mercator School, Department of Applied Linguistics, Groningen, The Netherlands.

My Medicines, http://www.fda.gov/womens/taketimetocare/mymeds. html

Information on prescription medicines in Cambodian, Chinese, Hmong, Japanese, Korean, Laotian, Polish, Russian, Samoan, Tagalog, Thai, and Vietnamese, from the U.S. Food and Drug Administration.

Religious Traditions and Health Care Decisions Handbook Series, http://www.parkridgecenter.org/Page677.html

"Practical and easily accessible information on the beliefs and moral positions, rituals and practices, and theological doctrines of nineteen religious traditions on numerous healthcare decisions, such as: family, sexuality, procreation, death and dying, genetics, medical experimentation and research, mental health, and organ and tissue transplantation." From the Park Ridge Center for Health, Faith, and Ethics, Park Ridge, Illinois, U.S.A.

U.S. National Institutes of Health in Spanish, http://salud.nih.gov

"Provides access to high quality full-text consumer health information in English and Spanish." Searchable.

Databases

Health and Wellness Resource Center, http://www.galegroup.com/ HealthRC/02.htm

Web access to CareNotes, more than 400 journals, most full text, Gale Encyclopedia of Medicine, Clinical Reference Systems, PDR Family Guides, Mosby's dictionary, and many more resources. A module on complementary and alternative medicine is also available, as are other add-on modules. From the Gale Group.

Health Source: Consumer Edition, http://www.epnet.com/biomedical/

American Fitness, *Better Nutrition*, *Fit Pregnancy*, *Harvard Health Letter*, *HealthFacts*, *Men's Health*, *Muscle & Fitness*, *Prevention*, *Vegetarian Times*, and many others. Includes searchable full text for more than 1,000 health-related pamphlets and 135 health-reference books, including books published by the People's Medical Society.

Additionally, Health Source: Consumer Edition contains more than 4,500 Clinical Reference Systems reports (in English and Spanish); Clinical Pharmacology, which provides access to 1,100 drug monograph entries and 2,700 patient education fact sheets; and Stedman's Medical Dictionary. From Ebsco, available in CD-ROM and on the Web.

MDX Health Digest, http://www.ovid.com/site/products/fieldguide/ mdig/About_MDX_Health_Digest.jsp

A bibliographic database containing references and abstracts, from 1988 to the present, for medical articles from magazines and newsletters, general interest magazines and newspapers, medical school and hospital publications, and medical journals. Designed for use by both the general public and healthcare professionals for patient education. On the Ovid system, from Medical Data Exchange, available in CD-ROM and on the Web.

First Aid

Animal Bites, http://familydoctor.org/handouts/203.html

How to care for dog or cat bites at home or when to go to the doctor. From the American Academy of Family Physicians.

Captain Dave's Survival Center: Burns, http://survival-center.com/ firstaid/burns.htm

How to evaluate burns and treat each type. From a full-service Army/Navy store in Durham, North Carolina, U.S.A.

CPR & Choking, http://depts.washington.edu/learncpr

Step-by-step instructions, a video demo, and printable pocket card. Caution: not a substitute for taking a hands-on training course. From the University of Washington School of Medicine, U.S.A.

What is a Heart Attack? http://www.americanheart.org/presenter. jhtml?identifier=3007482

Warning signs and what to do, also links to warning signs of stroke, from the American Heart Association.

Health Literacy

Health Literacy Resources, http://www.chcs.org/publications3960/publications_show.htm?doc_id=213136

Health literacy fact sheets with background and tips, from the U.S. Center for Health Care Strategies.

Health & Literacy, http://www.worlded.org/us/health/lincs

For learners, teachers, and healthcare providers, searchable by subject and language. From the U.S. National Institute for Literacy Special Collection.

Help Your Patients Understand, http://www.ama-assn.org/ama/pub/category/8115.html

Links to U.S. state and local health literacy initiatives. You can order the Health Literacy Educational Kit here. From the American Medical Association Foundation.

Medicines and Lab Tests

Lab Tests Online, http://www.labtestsonline.org

When patients (or you) want to know more about the lab tests the doctor ordered, this is the site to use. It is easy to use and has clear, understandable explanations of the most common lab tests. Each entry includes: How is it used?; When is it ordered?; What does the test result mean?; and Is there anything else I should know? You can search by test name, condition or disease, or age (for screening tests usually prescribed). From the American Association for Clinical Chemistry.

Mental Health Medications, http://www.nimh.nih.gov/publicat/medicate.cfm

An online booklet discussing medications used for mental health problems and their implications for patients. "It is not a 'do-it-yourself' manual" but is very complete and helpful. From the National Institute of Mental Health, U.S.A.

Portals

The Cancer Survivors Network, http://www.acscsn.org

Great support for survivors and their families. Cancer treatment decision tools, sharing of personal experiences, a free monthly newsletter, member Web pages, news about cancer research and the American Cancer Society, and links to books and other resources.

Consumer Health Web Sites You Can Trust, http://caphis.mlanet.org/consumer/index.html

The Top 100 sites selected by the Consumer and Patient Health Information Section of the Medical Library Association. Divided into general health, women, kids and parenting, seniors, specific health problems, especially for health professionals, drug information, and other useful health sites.

Family Resource Library, http://www.mchfamilylibrary.ca/page.asp

Searchable and bilingual (English/French) from the Montreal Children's Hospital, this site provides information for parents on Medical Conditions, Parenting, and Pain Management. Lists of support groups, health search engines, and tests and procedures round out the offerings.

Neuro-Patient Resource Centre, http://www.mni.mcgill.ca/neuropatient/resource.html

Targeted at the neurological patents of Montreal (Canada) Neurological Hospital, you can find reading lists, subject files (journal articles, book reviews, etc.), diagnostic tests and procedures, and Patient Education Fact Sheets.

Patient Safety Network, http://psnet.ahrq.gov

From the Agency for Healthcare Research and Quality, University of California, San Francisco, U.S.A., includes journal articles, meetings and conferences. Resources are also broken out by error types, clinical area, setting, target audience, and approach.

Symptoms Web Sites

Clickable Person: Where Does It Hurt? http://tms.ecol.net/fitness/clickabl.htm

Poke the clickable person's sore spots to find out about the injuries that have the potential to interrupt your fitness program. From the Leader-Telegram newspaper, Eau Claire, Wisconsin, U.S.A.

EQUIP, Electronic Quality Information for Patients, http://www.equip.nhs.uk

Help with Treatment Decisions, http://www.lungusa.org/site/pp.asp?c=dvLUK9O0E&b=23042

Advice and links from the American Lung Association on athsma, chronic obstructive pulmonary disease, lung cancer, and hay fever.

Information for Families, http://www.gosh.nhs.uk/gosh_families/index.html

From the Great Ormond Street Children's Hospital, Institute for Child Health, London, U.K.

Integrative Medicine Conditions by Signs and Symptoms, http://www.healthandage.com/html/res/com/ConsLookups/Symptoms.html

From an alternative health organization.

NHS Direct Online (UK), http://www.nhsdirect.nhs.uk

Medical encyclopedia, plus excellent guide from symptoms to measures to be taken. From the U.K. National Health Service.

NOAH, New York Online Access to Health, http://www.noah-health.org

"Your link to quality-filtered consumer health information!" From the City University of New York Office of Library Services, the Metropolitan New York Library Council, the New York Academy of Medicine Library, the New York Public Library, the Queens Borough Public Library, and the Brooklyn Public Library, U.S.A.

Pain.com: A World of Information on Pain, http://www.pain.com

For both consumers and health professionals, includes categories of Pain, JCAHO pain standards, pain survey, pain inventory forms, interviews with experts, "ask the pain doctor," "ask the expert;" sponsored by the Dannemiller Memorial Education Foundation (San Antonio, Texas, U.S.A.) and several pharmaceutical firms.

Resources for Health Consumers, http://www.mlanet.org/resources/consumr_index.html

From the Medical Libraries Association (U.S.A.).

SPIRAL, Selected Patient Information Resources in Asian Languages, http://www.library.tufts.edu/hsl/spiral

Information in Chinese, Cambodian/Khmer, Hmong, Korean, Laotian, Thai, and Vietnamese. A joint initiative of the South Cove Community Health Center and Tufts University Health Sciences Library, Boston, Massachusetts, U.S.A., supported by a grant from the New England Region of the National Network of Libraries of Medicine.

Symptom Scout, http://www.intelihealth.com/IH/ihtIH/WSIHW000/24479/25417.html

From Harvard University Medical School, Cambridge, Massachusetts, U.S.A.

Wellness and Nutrition

Healthy Workforce 2010, http://www.prevent.org/publications/Healthy_Workforce_2010.pdf

Subtitle: An Essential Health Promotion Resource for Employers Large and Small, from the Partnership for Prevention, Washington, DC, U.S.A.

The Nutrition Source: Knowledge for Sound Eating, http://www.hsph.harvard.edu/nutritionsource/index.html

Nutrition news and interpretations from the Harvard School of Public Health. Topics include food pyramids, fats and cholesterol, carbohydrates, protein, fiber, fruit and vegetables, calcium and milk, alcohol, vitamins, healthy weight, exercise, and type 2 diabetes.

Wellness Councils of America, http://www.welcoa.org

Worksite wellness, from a national nonprofit membership organization in Omaha, Nebraska, U.S.A.

Other Web Sites

Accessible Travel, http://gatorsport.phhp.ufl.edu/travel_general.html

If you have clientele who are disabled, especially in wheelchairs, this site with links to eight Web sites with information or accessible travel. One site is a travel agency, one is an organization for disabled travelers, and the rest are guides to how and where to go and what you'll find when you get there.

CancerBACUP, http://www.cancerbacup.org.uk

"Europe's leading cancer information service," with over 4,500 pages of up-to-date cancer information, practical advice, and support for cancer patients, their families, and careers. Based in London, U.K.

Cancer Education.com, http://www.cancereducation.com

"Up-to-date and accurate educational programming and information for healthcare professionals, cancer patients, and their family members," patient and family and professional sections, from a private organization in New York, New York, U.S.A.

Cancercare Ontario, http://www.cancercare.on.ca

From the Ontario (Canada) provincial government's principal adviser on cancer issues.

Consumer Health Journal, http://www.consumerhealthjournal.com

The editor, Alison Stewart (CHJ Wire Service, Powell, Wyoming, USA), has developed this free electronic journal "to fill a gap I've observed in health reporting." Her goal is "to improve the quality of consumer health information by referencing everything (with links to source sites) and by improving depth, accuracy, and background." A recent issue has only four articles: Biology of Alcohol in the Body; New Moms Can Get More Sleep; Low-Carb Diets Work, Don't Hurt Cholesterol; and Risks of Not Feeding Infants Often Enough. There is an archive of past articles.

Golderman, Gail and Bruce Connolly. Taking the Pulse (e-reviews column). *netconnect* (Summer 2001): 44–50, (supplement to *Library Journal*), consumer health-information sites.

Guide to Working in Health Information, http://www.cilip.org/uk/groups/hlg/guide_workinghealth_information.pdf

This is an absolutely fabulous resource compiled by Tracey Hunter and Michelle Wake of the Health Libraries Group of CILIP in the U.K. It has four parts. Part 1 is an introduction to the health information profession, where they work, skills, pay, and job titles. Part 2 covers training and qualifications needed, including all U.K. universities offering accredited health information courses. Part 3 is a list of health information-related organizations, publications, and Web sites in the U.K. and elsewhere. The last part is the appendices with short articles on what it's like working in various types of NHS trust libraries and roles, plus one private-sector example. I am very impressed!

Health Care Information Resources, http://www-hsl.mcmaster.ca/tomflem/top.html

Compiled by Tom Flemming, McMaster University, Hamilton, Ontario, Canada.

Healthfinder, http://www.healthfinder.gov

Links to lots of resources, bilingual, section for children. From the Office of Disease Prevention and Health Promotion, U.S. Department of Health & Human Services.

HelpingPatients, http://www.helpingpatients.org

From a consortium of pharmaceutical manufacturers in the U.S.A., this site will help your clients find patient drug payment assistance programs for which they might qualify. Easy-to-use and completely confidential. There are separate interfaces for patients and medical professionals.

MEDLINEplus Informacion de Salud de la Biblioteca Nacional de Medicina, http://medlineplus.gov/esp/

Mental Health Resources on the Web for Families: http://www.rfmh. org/nki/mhguide.pdf

A quick reference guide, Nathan S. Kline Institute for Psychiatric Research, Orangeberg, New York, U.S.A., April 2002.

National Patient Safety Foundation, http://www.npsf.org/html/ patients.html

You can download safety tips or pamphlets on what patients or their families can do in the areas of preventing infections, moving from hospital to home, what to expect from the pharmacy, and role of the patient advocate. There's also an online version, Focus on Patient Safety, and a discussion list, patientsafety-L. NPSF is a nonprofit agency located in McLean, Virginia, U.S.A.

NIH Senior Health, http://nihseniorhealth.gov

"Makes aging-related health information easily accessible for adults 60 and older." Developed by the U.S. National Institute on Aging and National Library of Medicine.

People Living With Cancer, http://www.plwc.org/plwc/Home/1,1743,, 00.html

From the American Society of Clinical Oncology, this site contains medically approved information on over 50 types of cancer, including treatments, side effects, and clinical trials. Also includes coping techniques, message boards, links to patent support groups, live chats, and a drug database.

P.O.W.E.R. Surfers, http://www.windsorpubliclibrary.com/power/ home

Patients Online for Well-being, Education & Research, from Windsor Public Library, Hotel Dieu Hospital Windsor Regional

Cancer Centre, and Windsor Regional Hospital, Windsor, Ontario, Canada.

Sites for Communication Disorders and Sciences, http://www.mnsu.edu/comdis/kuster2/welcome.html

From Judith Kuster, a speech-language pathologist and associate professor at Minnesota State University, Mankato, U.S.A., this site has articles, links, electronic newsletters, and products for communications problems from stuttering to hearing disabilities. Very complete and probably one of the only sources for this information.

Surgery Door, http://www.surgerydoor.co.uk/so/detail1.asp

Information on over 125 of the most common surgical operations. These are listed alphabetically and also by specialty. From Intouch with Health Limited, Siddington, Cirencester U.K., the leading supplier of touch screen health information kiosks to the NHS. There is also a newsletter.

Sympatico Health MediResource, http://health.sympatico.ca

From Microsoft and Bell Canada.

Women's Health Matters, http://www.womenshealthmatters.ca

From Sunnybrook and Women's College Health Science Centre, Toronto, Ontario, Canada.

Want to Know More About Your Physician? http://www.healthgrades.com

For USD7.95, you can get a "Physician Quality Report" on any of over 600,000 MDs in the U.S.A. Much of the information is available elsewhere for free, but this site ties it all together, plus includes state and federal disciplinary actions, ratings of the hospitals in his or her geographic area, and a checklist of questions to ask about any physician. From Health Grades, Inc., a healthcare quality ratings and services company in Lakewood, Colorado, U.S.A.

Your Disease Risk, http://www.yourdiseaserisk.harvard.edu

Find out if you are at high risk for cancer, diabetes, osteoporosis, heart disease, or stroke. You just answer a few questions and are given your risk, why, and how you can improve your prognosis. Fascinating, if a bit scary. From the Harvard (University) Center for Cancer Prevention, Cambridge, Massachusetts, U.S.A.

CONTINUING MEDICAL EDUCATION SITES

Annotated List of Online Continuing Education Sites, http://www.cmelist.com/list.htm

Links to and descriptions of over 260 online CME sites with over 13,000 courses and 23,000 hours of credit (as of February 2005). From Bernard Sklar, MD, a psychiatrist and family physician for the Alameda County Behavioral Health Care Services in Oakland, California, U.S.A.

Geriatric Continuing Education, http://www.med.ufl.edu/med/gec/projects.html

From the University of Florida Geriatric Education Center, Gainesville, U.S.A.

Life-Long Learning for the Healthcare Professional, http://www.geocities.com/nqiya/EBMandCe.html

These tips and resources are applicable to all types of medical professionals, but were written for occupational therapists by Tanya Feddern of the University of Miami (Florida, U.S.A.) School of Medicine Library. Also has a good list of evidence-based practice links.

Supercourse, http://www.bibalex.org/SuperCourse/

Supercourse: Epidemiology, the Internet and Global Health is a project to create a free lecture library of PowerPoint slides, from the Graduate School of Public Health, University of Pittsburgh, Pennsylvania, U.S.A.. 2,045 lectures from 10,300 faculty members from 151 countries online as of February 2005. Some with lectures in other languages.

DICTIONARIES AND LEXICONS

Acronyms and Initialisms for Health Information Resources, http://www.geocities.com/~mlshams/acronym/acr.html

Compiled by Marie-Lise Shams, MSLS, RN, University of Detroit Mercy, Detroit, Michigan, U.S.A., available in English and French.

ARGH Biomedical Acronym Resolver, http://invention.swmed.edu/argh/

The University of Texas Southwestern Medical Center in Dallas, U.S.A. processed over 12 million Medline records and 7 million Medline abstracts, identified over 5 million acronyms and abbreviations, and created a database of over 220,000 unique acronyms and over 800,000 unique definitions (as of December 2004). You can search by acronym or definition. I found 28 different definitions for "ebm," with most being "evidence-based medicine," the one I expected. There's also a link to a context example, and the date it first appeared in Medline. This could be very useful.

Directory of Health Organizations Online, http://dirline.nlm.nih.gov

You can find an organization by name, acronym, or MeSH subject heading. Records have the organization's address and phones, e-mail, Web site, and a short description of what the group does. There is also a searchable directory of health hotlines.

Medi Lexicon, http://www.medilexicon.com

Formerly titled Pharma-Lexicon, this site has a dictionary of over 70,000 medical, pharmaceutical, biomedical, and healthcare acronyms and abbreviations, plus medical news and resources for medical professionals and patients. You can search by abbreviation, definition, company, drugs, conferences, clinical trials, and medical books.

MedTerms.com Medical Dictionary, http://www.medterms.com
    100 percent doctor-produced, by MedicineNet, Inc., Sam Clemente, California, U.S.A.

EVIDENCE-BASED MEDICINE

Articles

Chan, Kitty S., Sally C. Morton, and Paul G. Shekelle. Systematic Reviews for Evidence-based Management: How to Find Them and What to Do With Them. *The American Journal of Managed Care* 10, Part I: 806-812, November 2004.

McKibbon, A. Evidence-based practice. *Bulletin of the MLA* 96:396–401, July 1998.

Morely, S.K. and H.S. Buchanan. Clinical Medical Librarians: Extending Library Resources to the Clinical Setting. *Journal of Hospital Librarianship* 1(2):15–30, 2001.

Netting the Evidence, http://www.shef.ac.uk/~scharr/ir/netting.html
    Introduction to Evidence Based Practice on the Internet, from University of Sheffield, U.K., School of Health and Related Research (ScHAAR).

Perry, G. Evidence-based Health Care on a Budget: Free (and Easy) Internet Resources. *Journal of Hospital Librarianship* 1(2):89–92, 2001.

Schardt, C. Evidence-based Medicine and the Hospital Librarian. *Journal of Hospital Librarianship* 1(2):1–14, 2001.

Scherer, C.S. and J.L. Dorsch. The Evolving Role of the Librarian in Evidence-based Medicine. *Bulletin of the MLA* 87(3): 322–328, July 1999.

Books

Sackett, et al. *Evidence-Based Medicine: How to Practice and Teach EBM*, 2nd ed. London: Churchill Livingstone, 1999, ISBN 0-44306240-4. Written by the original developers of EBM, comes with a CD-ROM.

Clinical Trials and Systematic Reviews

CenterWatch, http://www.centerwatch.com/patient/trials.html

Searchable database of clinical trials sponsored by industry that are looking for patients. From Thomson CenterWatch, Boston, Massachusetts, U.S.A.

ClinicalTrials.gov, http://clinicaltrials.gov

Searchable database of over 7,000 trials, most from the U.S. National Institutes of Health.

James Lind Library, http://www.jameslindlibrary.org

Created by the Library and Information Services Department of the Royal College of Physicians of Edinburgh, Scotland to mark the 250th anniversary of the publication of James Lind's Treatise of the Scurvy, the first systematic review. Contains examples from over a 100 books and journal articles, illustrated by images of the key passages of text.

National Research Register (U.K.), http://www.update-software.com/National/

Database of over 70,000 ongoing and recently completed trials funded by the National Health Service.

NHS Health Technology Assessment Programme, http://www.hta.nhs Web.nhs.uk/

Trials Central, http://www.trialscentral.org

Access to lists of ongoing and past clinical trials, and links to support groups, healthcare information, and other EBM sites.

Databases

Bandolier: Evidence Based Thinking about Health Care, http://www.jr2.ox.ac.uk/bandolier/index.html
  Online version of *Bandolier*, an independent journal about evidence-based healthcare, written by scientists at Oxford University, U.K.

CASP: Critical Appraisal Skills Programme, http://www.phru.nhs.uk/casp/casp.htm
  From the Public Health Resource Unit, Oxford, U.K.

Evidence-Based Decision Making, http://www.nelh.nhs.uk/ebdm/
  Resources and methods for researchers, skills for individuals, critical appraisal checklists, and user guides. From the U.K. National Electronic Library for Health.

Evidence-Based Medicine Reviews, http://www.ovid.com/site/catalog/ DataBase/904.jsp?top=2&mid=3&bottom=7&subsection=10
  From the American College of Physicians, available on Ovid Technologies.

PEDro, http://www.pedro.fhs.usyd.edu.au
  A physiotherapy Evidence database from the Centre for Evidence-Based Physiotherapy, University of Sydney, Australia.

PsychDirect: Evidence-Based Mental Health Education, http://www.psychdirect.com/
  A public education and information program of the Department of Psychiatry and Behavioral Neurosciences at McMaster University in Hamilton, Ontario, Canada.

Electronic Discussion Lists

EBHC, Evidence-Based Health Care Discussion List, http://www. mlanet.org/education/telecom/ebhc/ebhcdiscuss.html

Go to Web site or send an e-mail to majordomo@mlahq.org with the message subscribe mla-ebhc, from the Medical Library Association.

EBHCLIB-L, Clincal Librarianship, Evidence-based healthcare, and the informationist concept. To join, go to http://list.umassmed.edu, select library science, follow instructions.

Evidence-Based Health (U.K.), http://www.jiscmail.ac.uk/lists/ evidence-based-health.html

Journals

Evidence-Based Mental Health, peer-reviewed, published by the BMJ Group, the Royal College of Psychiatrists, and the British Psychological Society, ISSN 1362-0347, USD210 for institutions, USD104 for individuals.

Inpharma Weekly, pharmaceutical industry and conference news, studies, and research and development.

Organizations

Australia Centre for Evidence Based Clinical Practice, http://www. acebcp.org.au/acebcp.htm

This Adelaide-based organization has three core service groups: Health Care Research Facilitation Service, Clinical Practice Improvement Service, and the Education Service. The last group has developed a flexible delivery Web-based course in Evidence Based Practice for health professionals and holds workshops on the same subject. Available for free are links to some wonderful EBCP resources, located at http://www.acebcp.org.au/intro.htm

Centre for Evidence-Based Dentistry, Institute of Health Sciences, Old Road Campus, Headington, Oxford, OX3 7LF U.K., phone: 44-1865-226991, fax: 44-1865-226845, http://www.cebd,.org

Centre for Evidence-Based Mental Health (U.K.), http://www.cebmh.com

Centre for Health Evidence, http://www.cche.net/che/home.asp

Health Information Research Unit, McMaster University (Canada), http://hiru.mcmaster.ca

NHS R&D Centre for Evidence-Based Medicine at Oxford (U.K.), http://cebm.jr2.ox.ac.uk

Portals and Lists of Resources

Australian Centre for Evidence Based Clinical Practice, http://www.acebcp.org.au/acebcp.htm,

Workshops, online courses, a clinical audit tool, but most importantly links to EBP sources such as a glossary of EBP terms, What is ...? Series on EBM, definition of EBP, ScHARR's introduction to EBP on the Net, and others.

Bringing Effective Skills & Technology Together (EBM), http://www.allconet.org/ahec/bestt/

Information, links, and bibliography on critical thinking, best practices; from the Institute of Museum & Library Services, University of South Carolina School of Medicine Library, West Virginia Library Association, and Western Maryland Area Health Education Center.

Evidence-Based Health Care Resources on the Internet, http://www.mlanet.org/education/telecon/ebhc/resource.html

Master lists of Web resources, tutorials and how-to sites, search filters, practice guidelines and systematic reviews, organizations, and journals. From the Medical Library Association.

Navigating the Maze: Obtaining Evidence-Based Medical Information, http://healthsystem.virginia.edu/internet/library/collections/ebm/index.cfm

Tutorials on the major resources for EBM, from the University of Virginia Health Sciences Library, U.S.A.

TRIP (Turning Research into Practice), http://www.tripdatabase.com

"Direct, hyperlinked access to the largest collection of 'evidence-based' material on the Web as well as articles from premier on-line journals ..." Created in 1997, it now has nearly 30,000 links from 70 sources that you can search by title or keyword. Includes cites from the Cochrane Database of Systematic Reviews, general and specialist peer-reviewed journals, e-textbooks, etc. It seems pretty comprehensive to me. This resource, hosted by the Centre for Research Support in Wales, aims to support those working in primary care. The database has 8,000 links covering resources at 28 different centres and allows both Boolean searching (AND, OR, NOT) and truncation.

University of York, NHS Centre for Reviews and Dissemination, http:// www.york.ac.uk/inst/crd/

Includes links to Effective Health Care and Effectiveness Matters.

Surgery Web Sites

Continuous Quality Improvement, http://www.facs.org/cqi/index.html

Links to advocacy and health policy, cancer programs, education, research and optimal patient care, and trauma programs. From the American College of Surgeons, Chicago, Illinois, U.S.A.

Evidence Based Practice, http://www.rcseng.ac.uk/services/library/hi_resources/ebs_html

Links to organizations and guides, guidelines and protocols, clinical trials, research registers, reports, critical appraisal and literature searching, and statistics and data. From the Royal College of Surgeons of England, London, U.K.

Resources for Evidence-Based Surgery, http://www-hsl.mcmaster.ca/ebsurgery

Databases, online journals, clinical practice guidelines, critically appraised topics, metasearches, tutorials, directories, clinical skills, and other resources from the Health Sciences Library, McMaster University, Hamilton, Ontario, Canada.

Other EBM Web Sites

EB On-call (UK), http://www.eboncall.co.uk

Based on the book *Evidence-based Acute Medicine*, from the Oxford Centre for Evidence-based Medicine.

EBM Librarian: Bibliographies, http://www.geocities.com/nqiya/EBMbib.html

English-language articles of possible readings for an EBM Syllabus from Tanya Feddern (University of Miami Medical Center, Florida, U.S.A.), under construction as of January 2005.

Evidence-Based Health Care Web, http://www.uic.edu/depts/lib/lhsp/resources/ebm.shtml,

Annotated directory of organizations, databases, journals, e-journals, Internet resources, and guide to searching the literature on EBM, from the University of Illinois-Chicago, Peoria Library of the Health Sciences (U.S.A.) and HealthWeb.

EvidenceNetwork, http://www.evidencenetwork.org/home.asp

Open to users in the research community, the voluntary sector, local and central government, public agencies and commercial organizations, providing search tools and a referral framework to enable users to pursue their enquiries, and a forum for debate and discussion of issues and problems in relation to evidence-based policy, with sections for the public and for associates of the network only. From the Centre for Evidence Based Policy & Practice, University of London, U.K.

Glossary of EBP terms, http://www.cebm.utoronto.ca/glossary/

Interactive with hyperlinks to example calculations of statistical terms. From Mount Sinai Hospital, University of Toronto, Canada.

OTseeker, http://www.otseeker.com

Occupational Therapy Systematic Evaluation of Evidence, abstracts and quality ratings of randomized control trials from the Department of Occupational Therapy, University of Queensland, Brisbane, Australia.

Resources for Practicing Evidence-Based Medicine, http://pedsccm. wustl.edu/EBJ/EB_Resources.html

Critical appraisal of the literature, statistics and trial design, systematic reviews, EBM in critical care, EBM groups on the Web, EBM databases, MEDLINE search strategies, pediatric and general online journal clubs, teaching resources and tutorials. From Pediatric Critical Care Medicine Web site and IntensiveCare.com and the American Academy of Pediatrics, Elk Grove Village, Illinois, U.S.A.

Scottish Intercollegiate Guidelines Network, http://www.sign.ac.uk

79 evidence-based clinical guidelines—published, in development, or under review—covering a wide range of topics. Many of the SIGN guidelines relate to the NHS priority areas of cancer, cardiovascular disease, and mental health. Based in Edinburgh, U.K.

What is ...? Series, http://www.evidence-based-medicine.co.uk/ What_is_series.html

These short, practical bulletins provide a fresh slant on evidence-based medicine and the ideas behind it. All the publications in the series have been written by respected figures from various NHS backgrounds. From Hayward Medical Communications, Newmarket, U.K.

World Wide Web-Based EBM Hedges, http://www.mssm.edu/library/ ebm/ebmhedges.htm

A collection of links to evidence-based medicine hedges from the Mount Sinai School of Medicine, New York, New York, U.S.A.

EBM Nursing

Journals

Advances in Nursing Science, not online.

Annual Review of Nursing Research, from Springer, not online.

Biological Journal of Nursing Research, http://brn.sagepub.com/
Searchable archives and current issues.

Canadian Journal of Nursing Research, http://www.cjnr.nursing.mcgill.ca/
Searchable archives and current issues.

Clinical Evidence, http://www.clinicalevidence.com/ceweb/conditions/index.jsp
From BMJ, Web and paper based, updated every six months.

Evidence Based Nursing, http://www.evidencebasednursing.com
An abstract journal similar to ACP Journal Club and EBM.

Evidence Based Nursing Online, http://ebn.bmjjournals.com

Journal of Nursing Management, http://www.ingentaconnect.com/content/bsc/jnm;jsessionid=29qif0lhtosbk.victoria?
52 issues are available electronically.

Journal of Nursing Scholarship, http://www.journalofnursingscholarship.org
The official journal of Sigma Theta Tau International, nursing honor society.

Journal of Transcultural Nursing, http://tcn.sagepub.com
Searchable archives and current issues.

Nursing Research, http://www.nursingresearchonline.com
Searchable archives and current issues.

Nursing Science Quarterly, http://nsq.sagepub.com
Searchable archives and current issues.

Oncology Nursing Forum, http://www.ons.org/publications/journals/ONF/index.shtml

Online for members only.

Online Journal of Clinical Innovations, http://www.cinahl.com/cexpress/ojcionline3/

Includes integrative reviews with practice recommendations.

Research in Nursing and Health, http://www3.interscience.wiley.com/cgi-bin/jhome/33706

Searchable archives and current issues.

Scholarly Inquiry for Nursing Practice, not online

Western Journal of Nursing Research, http://wjn.sagepub.com/

Searchable archives and current issues.

Worldviews on Evidence Based Nursing, http://www.blackwellpublishing.com/wvn

Resources

Cullum, Nicky, *Users' Guides to the Nursing Literature: An Introduction, Evidence-Based Nursing* 2000, 3:71–72, http://ebn.bmjjournals.com/cgi/content/extract/3/3/71

DiCenso, Alba, Gordon Guyatt, and Donna Ciliska, eds. *Evidence-Based Nursing: A Guide to Clinical Practice*, C.V. St. Louis: Mosby, 2004, ISBN 0-32302591-9.

Evaluated Resources in Nursing, Midwifery and Allied Health, http://nmap.ac.uk

The NMAP gateway provides free access to "evaluated, quality Internet resources aimed at students, researchers, academics, and practitioners." It is part of the BIOME service from various health agencies in England, including the University of Nottingham, U.K. There are more than 3,000 records in the database, which can be searched or browsed. There are also two free tutorials: Internet for Allied Health and Internet for Nursing, Midwifery, and Health Visiting.

Evidence-based Nursing Practice: Needs, Tools, Solutions, http://nahrs.library.kent.edu/resource/symposium/.#fulltext

Nurses' knowledge-based information needs, tools for evidence-based nursing practice, and what works: new directions for facilitating evidence-based nursing practice. Proceedings of an Evidence-Based Nursing Practice symposium, Medical Libraries Association 2003 Annual Conference, San Diego, California, U.S.A.

Nursing Resources, http://www.library.vcu.edu/tml/bibs/nursing.html#evidence

By Jodi Koste of Virginia Commonwealth University, Richmond, Virginia, U.S.A., with an EBN section.

Teaching & Learning Resources for Evidence Based Practice, http://www.mdx.ac.uk/www/rctsh/ebp/main.htm

From the Research Centre for Transcultural Health, Middlesex University, London, U.K.

Web Sites

Center for Nursing Research, http://www.jgh.ca/resarch/nursing/ikndex.html

From the Sir Mortimer B. Davis Jewish General Hospital, Montreal, Canada, here is background information on evidence-based practice, carefully selected Web sites by clinical specialty, and links to nursing and research resources.

Centre for Evidence-Based Nursing, http://www.cebm.utoronto.ca/syllabi/nur/

Introduction, resources, sample scenarios, search strategies, completed worksheets, and CATs. By Alba DiCenso from the University of Toronto (Canada) Health Network.

Cochrane Wounds Review Group, http://www.update-software.com/Abstracts/WOUNDSAbstractIndex.htm

Abstracts of Cochrane reviews, from Update Software, Ltd, Oxford, U.K.

Evidence-Based Practice Web site, http://www.ahrq.gov/clinic/epcix.htm

Links divided into clinical categories, healthcare services, and technical. From the Agency for Healthcare Research and Quality Rockville, Maryland, U.S.A.

Joanna Briggs Institute for Evidence Based Nursing, Adelaide, Australia, http://www.joannabriggs.edu.au/about/home.php

An initiative of Royal Adelaide Hospital and the University of Adelaide, the Institute provides for a collaborative approach to the evaluation of evidence derived from a diverse range of sources, including experience, expertise, and all forms of rigorous research and the translation, transfer, and utilization of the "best available" evidence into healthcare practice. The collaboration now includes state collaborating centres within Australia, as well as Hong Kong, New Zealand, U.S.A., Scotland, China, South Africa, Spain, Canada, Thailand, and England.

McGill University Health Centre Research Resources for Evidence Based Nursing, http://www.muhc-ebn.mcgill.ca

Similar to Joanna Briggs Institute Web site, but with the addition of systematic reviews, clinical practice guidelines and tools organized by country and specialty, a virtual reference desk, and health statistics sites.

New Zealand Resources, http://www.nzgg.org.nz

From the New Zealand Guidelines Group, Inc., Wellington.

Nursing Guidelines, http://www.rnao.org/bestpractices/index.asp

Best Practice Guidelines from the Registered Nurses Association of Ontario, Canada.

Research & Clinical Resources for Evidence Based Nursing, http://www.muhc-ebn.mcgill.ca/index.html

Evidence-Based Practice in Cancer Nursing from McGill University, Montreal, Canada.

HANDHELD COMPUTER RESOURCES

Embi, P.J. Information at Hand: Using Handheld Computers in Medicine. *Cleveland Clinic Journal of Medicine* 68(10): 840–842, 945–846, 949–848, 853, October 2001.

Harris, C.M. Handheld Computers in Medicine: The Future Is Not Here Yet. *Cleveland Clinic Journal of Medicine* 68(10): 854, 856, October 2001.

PalmSource, http://www.palmsource.com/interests/education_medical/
Here you can find 14 pages of programs available for Palm-powered devices for medical students, arranged as free, cheap, and "not cheap, but worth it." There are also testimonials, and Web links. There are similar lists for anesthesiology, dentistry, and medicine. This is a fantastic resource if you have one of these devices. From the developer of the Palm operating system.

LABORATORY TESTING

Note: Hospital laboratory personnel are often non-users of libraries. Perhaps if you publicize these resources you can gain them as customers.

Consumer Laboratory Testing Information Page, http://www.ascls.org/labtesting
Frequently Asked Questions about most common laboratory tests. From the American Society for Clinical Laboratory Science, Bethesda, Maryland, U.S.A.

Guide to Clinical Laboratory Testing, http://www.aruplab.com/testing/lab_testing.jsp
Collection of over 2,000 lab tests and test combinations, with description and significance. From Arup Laboratories, an independent reference laboratory owned by the University of Utah, Salt Lake City, U.S.A.

Interpretation of Lab Test Profiles, http://Web2.iadfw.net/uthman/lab_test.html

Definitions and normal ranges. From Ed Uthman, a forensic pathologist in Houston, Texas, U.S.A.

KidsHealth for Parents: Medical Tests & Exams, http://kidshealth.org/parent/system

Good information for children and parents, in English and Spanish. Sponsored by Nemours Center for Children's Health Media, Nemours Foundation, Wilmington, Delaware, U.S.A.

Lab Tests Online, http://www.labtestsonline.org

Supposed to be one of the best collections of resources on lab tests, including the latest news. The site is the product of a collaboration of 15 professional societies representing the lab community.

MEDICAL STATISTICS

Canadian Institute of Health Information, http://secure.cihi.ca/indicators/en/tables2004.shtml

Epidemiology Statistics (Public Health, Biosciences, Medicine), http://www.epibiostat.ucsf.edu/epidem/epidem.html

From the Department of Epidemiology and Biostatistics at the University of California–San Francisco, U.S.A.

Health Statistics: Finding and Using Them, http://www.nlm.nih.gov/nichsr/usestats/sld001.htm

A Web-based tutorial from the U.S. National Library of Medicine.

HealthWeb: Health Statistics, http://healthWeb.org/browse.cfm?categoryid=1505

Links to national and international sites, from Public Health Information Services & Access, University of Michigan, Ann Arbor, U.S.A.

National Institutes of Health Related Health Services Research, http://www.nlm.nih.gov/nichsr/hsrsites.html

Epidemiology and health statistics links, from the U.S. National Library of Medicine.

State Health Facts Online, http://www.statehealthfacts.org

This resource contains the latest state-level data on demographics, health, and health policy, including health coverage, access, financing, and state legislation. From the Kaiser Family Foundation, Menlo Park, California, U.S.A., it has individual state comparisons and individual state profiles. There is a wealth of very detailed information here.

Statistical Resources in Medicine & Healthcare: Recommended Web Sites, Books, and Serials, http://bagel.aecom.yu.edu/resources/statsource.htm

From the Albert Einstein School of Medicine, Yeshiva University, New York, New York, U.S.A.

Statistics and Resources, http://depts.washington.edu/hsic/resource/

Links divided into Behavior and Risk Factors, Diseases and Conditions, Economics, Policy and Programs, Family and Reproduction, Health Care, Mortality/Death, Populations and Demographics, and Research Resources. From the University of Washington School of Public Health and Community Medicine Health Services Library Information Center, Seattle, U.S.A.

Web Sites for Health Statistics, http://www.unmc.edu/library/reference/stats.html

From the McGoogan Library of Medicine, University of Nebraska, U.S.A.

World Health Organization Links to National Health-Related Web sites, http://www3.who.int/whosis/national_sites/

Also, most organizations such as the Cancer Society, etc. have statistics on their Web sites.

MENTAL HEALTH

American Psychological Association Help Center, http://helping.
apa.org/
   Good information on anger management, workplace stress, etc.

Auseinet, http://www.auseinet.com
   From the Australian Network for Promotion, Prevention, and Early
Intervention for Mental Health.

Emental Health, http://www.emental-health.com
   Information on Alzheimer's, bipolar and other depressions, and
schizophrenia, plus other links and discussion. From the Psychmed
Group, a company under the stewardship of Professor Tonmoy
Sharma, Clinical Neuroscience Research Centre at Dartford, Kent,
U.K.

Mental Health Care, http://www.mentalhealthcare.org.uk
   For those providing support to someone experiencing mental illness. Research findings from the Institute of Psychiatry and South
London, U.K., and Maudsley Trust. Includes personal stories written
about autism, bipolar disorder, eating disorders, psychosis and schizophrenia, and young people and mental health.

National Electronic Library for Mental Health, http://nelmh.org
   Divided into background topics (core clinical skills, health policy,
mental health promotion, and therapeutic approaches), mental health
conditions, and populations (child and adolescent, later life, primary
care, and prison). The NeLMH project is led by the Centre for
Evidence-Based Medicine in Oxford, U.K.

Royal College of Psychiatrists, http://www.rcpsych.ac.uk/info/
index.htm
   Informational pamphlets.

For more on mental illness, try:

> Barber, Graeme. Internet Sites of Interest: Mental Health Service Users. *CILIP Health Libraries Group Newsletter* 21(4): 10, 12–13, June 2004 and Mental Health and Psychology, *CILIP Health Libraries Group Newsletter* 20(3): 9–12, September 2003.

> Mental Health & Psychology Web Site Links, http://www.ex.ac.uk/stloyes/netlinks/lnk4ment.htm

NURSING

Continuing Education, http://www.nurseceu.com/free.htm

The Free Directory of Online Continuing Education for Nurses, Occupational Therapists, and Physical Therapists, sponsored by some of the providers.

LfN: Libraries for Nursing, Special Interest Group of CILIP, http://www.cilip.org.uk/ groups/hlg/lfn/index.html

PASTORAL CARE

The Association of Christian Counselors, P.O. Box 739, Forest, VA 24551 U.S.A., phone: 1-800-526-8673 or 1-434-525-9470, fax: 1-434-525-9480, e-mail: contactmemberservices@AACC.net, http://www.aacc.net

American Association of Pastoral Counselors,** 9504 A Lee Highway, Fairfax, VA 22031 U.S.A., phone: 1-703-385-6967.

An international organization of ministers, priests, rabbis, and religious oriented professionals. Provides certification for competent practice and training.

American Protestant Correctional Chaplains Association,** 5235 Greenpoint Drive, Stone Mountain, GA 30088 U.S.A., phone: 1-404-469-8294 or 1-404-469-8703.

Certifies chaplains for ministry in correctional institutions.

Association for Clinical Pastoral Education, Inc.,** 1549 Clairmont Rd, Suite 103, Decatur, GA 30034 U.S.A., phone: 1-404-320-1472, fax: 1-404-320-0849, e-mail: acpe@acpe.edu, http://www.acpe.edu

An interfaith organization that fosters training in pastoral care and counseling through clinical pastoral education (CPE). Accredits CPE centers and certifies CPE supervisors.

Association of Professional Chaplains,** 1701 E. Woodfield Road, Suite 760, Schaumburg, IL 60173 U.S.A., phone: 1-847-240-1014, fax: 847-240-1015, e-mail: info@professionalchaplains.org, http://www.professionalchaplains.org

An interfaith organization of Jewish, Protestant, and Roman Catholic clergy. AMHC is engaged in ministry to the emotionally troubled and people with mental illnesses. Membership is open to parish clergy as well as chaplains.

Chaplaincy Commission, New York Board of Rabbis, 10 E. 73rd St., New York, NY 10021 U.S.A., phone: 1-212-879-8415, http://www. nybr.org

Endorses and certifies Jewish chaplains for correctional and health-related facilities.

Council on Ministries in Specialized Settings, c/o Human Care Ministries, Lutheran Church-Missouri Synod, 1333 South Kirkwood Rd., St. Louis, MO 63122-7295 U.S.A., phone: 1-314-965-9917, ext. 1384.

Composed of representatives from faith groups and professional pastoral care associations.

International Conference of Police Chaplains (ICPC), Route 5, Box 310, Livingston, TX 77351 U.S.A., phone: 1-409-327-2332.

An interfaith organization of chaplains who serve law enforcement agencies.

National Association of Catholic Chaplains, PO Box 070473, Milwaukee, WI 53207-0473 U.S.A., phone: 1-414-483-4898, fax: 1-414-483-6712, e-mail: info@nacc.org, http://www.nacc.org

A professional association for certified chaplains and clinical pastoral educators. Provides standards, certification, education, advocacy, and professional development for its members, certifies chaplains in the name of the U. S. Conference of Catholic Bishops.

National Institute of Business and Industrial Chaplaincy,** Institute of Worklife Ministry, 9449 Briar Forest Dr., Houston, TX 97063-1034 U.S.A., phone: 1-713-266-2456.

An interfaith organization to serve employees and their families in business and industrial settings through pastoral care and counseling ministry.

** Joint sponsor of *The Journal of Pastoral Care & Counseling*, http://www.jpcp.org/about.html

PHARMACY

A Pharmacist's Guide to Prescription Fraud, http://www.deadiversion. usdoj.gov/pubs/brochures/pharmguide.htm

Abbreviations for Disease States and Physiologic States Relevant to Dosing, http://pharmsci.buffalo.edu/courses/phc311.latin.html (very complete).

Abbreviations to Avoid in Prescriptions, http://snipurl.com/blk6

Adis Online, Pharmaceutical Portal, http://www.adisonline.info

Wolters Kluwer has announced two new free services. One provides free access to abstracts from 33 of Adis's drug reviews, journals, and newsletters, with searching; the full articles can be purchased. The other is an electronic table of contents. Check them out—the price is certainly right.

Advisory Statement, Prevention of Medication Errors, American Academy of Orthopaedic Surgeons, http://www.aaos.org/wordhtml/ papers/advistmt/1026.htm

All Info about Alternative and Complementary Medicine Prescription and Pharmaceutical Abbreviations, http://altmedicine.allinfo-about. com/features/pharm.html

Australian Drug Information Network, http://www.adin.com.au

Search over 1,000 reviewed Web sites or use the search engine. There are also links for alcohol and drug services, information for young people, and information in indigenous (Australian) languages. The site is presented by the Australian Drug Foundation and the Department of Health and Ageing.

BIAM: Banque de Donées Autmatisee sur les Médicaments (France), http://www.biam2.org

In French only. Free, but you have to register.

British National Formulary, http://www.bnf.org/bnf/

Authoritative and practical information on the selection and clinical use of medicines.

Common Abbreviations Used in Prescriptions, and other Latin Triva Ad Nauseum, http://www.sendemissary.com/compass.nsf/key/abbreviations.htm

ConsumerLab.com Online, http://www.consumerlab.com

Independent testing of health and nutrition products, recalls and warnings, test results for brand-name products, encyclopedia of natural products, with drug interactions. Produced by a private company in White Plains, New York, U.S.A.

Dictionary of Prescription and Medication Abbreviations, http://www.drugintel.com/physiccians/abbreviations.htm

DrugInfoZone, http://www.druginfozone.org

Providing medicines information to the NHS. This is the Web site for London, South East and Eastern Medicines Information Services.

European Agency for the Evaluation of Medicinal Products, http://www.emea.eu.int

Information on human and veterinary medicines and drug inspections from a decentralized body of the European Union with headquarters in London, U.K.

Guidelines for Writing Prescriptions, http://www.fammed.wisc.edu/
medic/policies/prescriptions.html

Headaches and Migraine Medical Abbreviations, http://headaches.
about.com/od/abbreviations

InPharm.com, http://www.inpharm.com
 Providing executives in the biopharmaceutical and healthcare industries with relevant information services such as news, articles, jobs, directories, and Internet links. Now owned by U.S. publisher John Wiley.

Legal Requirements and Practical Tips in Writing Prescriptions,
http://www.dhep.astate.edu/pharm/pharmlegalreq.htm

Lilley, L. L. and R. Guanci. Look-alike Abbreviations: Prescriptions
for Confusion. *American Journal of Nursing* 97(11):12, November
1997, http://snipurl.com/bljv

*Massachusetts College of Pharmacy & Health Sciences Sites (Boston,
U.S.A.) Recommended Web sites in Pharmacy/Pharmacology:*

 Drug Education, http://www.mcphs.edu/MCPHSWeb/library/
 subjectGuides/druged.html

 Pharmacoepidemiology, http://www.mcphs.edu/MCPHSWeb/
 library/subjectGuides/pharmacoepidemiology.html

 Pharmacy Law, http://www.mcphs.edu/MCPHSWeb/library/
 subjectGuides/pharmlaw.htm

NetDoktor, http://www.netdoktor.de/medikamente/index.shtml
 Information in German only.

Patient U.K., http://www.patient.co.uk/showdoc/11/
 Information on medicines, drugs, and supplements. Primary links
are to Electronic Medicines Compendium, Medicine Chest, Health
Supplements Information Service, and British National Formulary, but
there are many other links. A joint venture of two MDs in Tyne and
Wear, England and Egton Medical Information Systems, an automation vendor.

Pharmacy Related Electronic Lists, http://www.pharmacy.org/lists.html

From David Bourne, University of Oklahoma, U.S.A. Bourne also produces Virtual Library for Pharmacy, http://www.pharmacy.org

PharmWeb, http://www.pharmweb.net

"Serving the Patient and Health Professional." Conferences and meetings, pharmacy colleges and schools, discussion lists and forums, jobs, information for patients on drugs and diseases, companies and hospitals, government and regulatory bodies around the world, pharmaceutical and medical societies around the world, newsgroups, continuing education, pharmaceutical publications and applications of the Internet to pharmacy. From the School of Pharmacy and Pharmaceutical Sciences, University of Manchester, U.K.

Prescription Abbreviations, http://www.medterms.com

From MedicineNet., Inc., San Clemente, California, U.S.A.

Preventing Medication Errors, http://www.ismp.org

Medication safety reports and error reporting. From the Institute for Safe Medicine Practices, a nonprofit organization, Huntingdon Valley, Pennsylvania, U.S.A.

RxList, http://www.rxlist.com

Drug equivalents for many countries, side effects, drug interactions, drug names, medical terminology, patient information, top 200 drugs by prescriptions dispensed, top 200 by U.S. sales, and an archive of RxLaughs, a great cartoon. From RxList LLC, Rancho Santa Fe, California, U.S.A.

Thériaque: http://www.theriaque.org

Information in drugs available in France, in French.

Vidal, http://www.vidalpro.net

Information in drugs available in France, in French for medical professionals only.

PHYSICAL THERAPY

HealthWeb, http://healthWeb.org/browse.cfm?subjectid=74

Physical Medicine and Rehabilitation section. A collaborative project of the health sciences libraries of the Greater Midwest Region (GMR) of the National Network of Libraries of Medicine (NN/LM) and those of the Committee for Institutional Cooperation. Currently there are over 20 actively participating member libraries.

University of South Alabama (U.S.A.), http://southmed.usouthal.edu/library/specialt/pt.htm

Associations, organizations, suggested sites, and electronic publications.

PORTALS AND SEARCH ENGINES

Asian American Health, http://asianamericanhealth.nlm.nih.gov

A portal from the U.S. National Library of Medicine.

Knowledge Path: Children and Adolescents with Special Health Care Needs, http://www.mchlibrary.info/KNowledgePaths/kp_CSHCN.html

This site provides lots of links to "recent, high-quality resource for health professionals and families about caring for children and adolescents with special health care needs." It is divided into General Resources, including Web sites, electronic publications, print publications, databases, electronic newsletters and online discussion groups, journal articles, and Resources on Specific Aspects of Care and Development. The second section covers Adolescent Transition, Advocacy, Child Care, Community Interactions (Community-Based Care and Service Coordination), Data (Prevalence of Special Health Care Needs Among Children and Adolescents), Education, Environment, Financing Services and Insurance, General Health and Safety Resources, Genetic Services, Hospice, Hospitals and Patient Travel and Lodging, Medical Home, Mental Health, Parenting and Family Supports, Rehabilitation, Screening, and Sports Recreation and the Arts. Obviously very comprehensive, this site is a product of the

Maternal and Child Health Library of Georgetown University, Washington, DC, U.S.A.

MedExplorer, http://www.medexplorer.com
Health & Medical Information: Online Pharmacy, Health, Medical Directory, from Calgary, Alberta, Canada.

MedHunt, http://www.hon.ch/MedHunt
Labels hits in this hierarchy: sites subscribing to the HON code, sites visited and described by HON, and other sites retrieved by their search robot. Also news, conferences, and images. Available in English, French, German, Spanish, and Portuguese. From Health on the Net Foundation, Geneva, Switzerland.

Medic8, http://www.medic8.com/index.htm
U.K. Medical Information Portal for Healthcare Professionals. Includes medical resources by subject, clinical tools, medical news, a free newsletter, quick links, non-medical sites, discussion forum. More than 480 health-related articles written by qualified medical professionals. All content reviewed by a qualified U.K. doctor prior to listing.

Medifocus, http://www.medifocus.com
Current Medical Guides on Major Diseases and Conditions, free preview of for-fee guides (c. USD12 each). From Medifocus, Inc., Silver Spring, Maryland, U.S.A.

Medizin-online, http://www.multimedica.de/public/fachportal/home/index.html
From Germany. For the professional community, in German.

Medizin-index, http://www.medizinindex.de
From Germany. A database of medical servers, in German.

MedWebPlus, http://medWebplus.com
Free access to nearly 25,000 links and offline sources, by subject (diseases and conditions, specialties, institutions, publishing and publications, alternative and complementary medicine, geography and geographical) or location (North America—19,000+ entries, Europe—

6,000+, Asia—1,000+, Australia and Oceania—700+, South American—400+, and Africa—200+). From Flexis, Inc., a knowledge management company in Palo Alto, California and Lexington, Kentucky, U.S.A.

OMNI: Organising Medical Networked Information, http://www.omni.ac.uk

"Free access to a searchable catalogue of hand-selected and evaluated, quality Internet resources in Health and Medicine." From BIOME, University of Nottingham, U.K.

Reproductive Health Gateway, http://www.rhgateway.org

A project of the Health Information and Publications Network and managed by the Information and Knowledge for Optimal Health Project at Johns Hopkins University, Baltimore, Maryland, U.S.A.

Researching Medical Literature on the Web, http://www.llrx.com/features/medical2003.htm

A wonderful pathfinder, from Gloria Miccioli and llrx.com.

Search 22, http://www.search-22.com/health.html

Choose from 22 search engines for health (and other) information.

University of Buffalo (New York, U.S.A.) Health Sciences Library has two wonderful resources:

Biomedical Databases, http://ublib.buffalo.edu/libraries/units//hsl/resources/biomed.html

Biosciences, communicative disorders, dentistry, epidemiology, medicine, nursing, public health, pharmacy, and toxicology.

Reference Tools, http://ublib.buffalo.edu/libraries/units//hsl/resources/reftools.htm

Clinical reference tools, clinical trials information, dictionaries, abbreviations, and encyclopedias, directories, drug and pharmacy, government and regulatory sites, meta sites, statistics, and resources for authors.

MISCELLANEOUS SITES

AMEDEO: The Medical Literature Guide, http://amedeo.com/index. htm

A free current awareness service. You can get weekly updates (by e-mail and on a personalized Web site) based on your choice of 22 specialties and journals plus monthly overviews. Paid for by unrestricted grants from several pharmaceutical manufacturers, based in Paris, France.

Cardiovascular Diseases Specialist Library, http://rms.nelh.nhs.uk/ cardiovascular

Information to assist clinical decision making and to advise patients on risks. Guidelines, systematic reviews, bibliographies, clinical database, reviewed Internet sites, and new papers (with hyperlinks). Part of the National Electronic Library for Health, U.K.

ClusterMed, http://www.vivisimo.com/clustermed

This URL is Vivisimo's demonstration page for its new ClusterMed service. It is a tool that clusters your results by author, MeSH headings, and date. You can sign up for a free 30-day trial with up to 500 results per query. Unregistered users can try it, but only get 100 results per question. It looks really good, but I couldn't find any information on cost. Started by Carnegie Mellon University, Pittsburgh, Pennsylvania, U.S.A.

Dermatological Internet Service, http://www.dermis.net/index_d.htm

Includes DERMIS: Dermatology Online Information Atlas, "the real future of medical internet," combined text and images arranged by diagnosis and linked to PubMed. In German, a cooperative venture of the Universities of Heidelberg and Nürnberg, Germany.

End of Life Care, http://www.eperc.mcw.edu/index.htm

The Medical College of Wisconsin, U.S.A., has provided a wonderful resource called EPERC: Advancing End of Life Care Through an Online Community of Educational Scholars. Included are study guides, course syllabi, self-study guidebooks, slide presentations, standardized patient materials, and evaluation forms. There are links to EPERC's complete database of peer-reviewed educational materials, annual conferences, research centers, evidence-based medicine information, and resources for personal digital assistants.

For Health Policy Students, http://www.kaiseredu.org

Developed by the Kaiser Family Foundation, Menlo Park, California, U.S.A., kaiserEDU "gives health policy students and faculty easy access to data, literature, news and developments regarding major health policy topics and debates." Contains information on specific issues as well as broad health policy topics. E-mail updates available.

KoreaMed, http://www.koreamed.org/SearchBasic.php

Provided by the Korean Association of Medical Journal Editors (KAMJE), here you can find articles published in Korean medical journals. A nice tool to know about—just in case you need it.

The Medicaid Resource Book, http://www.kff.org/medicaid/2236-index.cfm

If you need information about Medicaid rules and benefits, you'll find it at this site from the Kaiser Family Foundation, Menlo Park, California, U.S.A.

Public Health Image Library, http://phil.cdc.gov/Phil/about.asp

PHIL offers an organized, universal electronic gateway to CDC's (the U.S. Centers for Disease Control and Prevention) pictures. Designed for public health professionals, the media, laboratory scientists, educators, and the worldwide public for reference, teaching, presentation, and public health messages. Organized into hierarchical categories of people, places, and science, and is presented as single images, image sets, and multimedia files. Searchable.

Registry of Australian Drug and Alcohol Research, http://www.alcoholinfo.nsw.gov.au/research_data

A project of the Alcohol and other Drugs Council of Australia, "the register contains up-to-date records of current and recently completed research projects with details of published research. There is also information about researchers, their organizations and research funding bodies." Searchable.

Virtual Naval Hospital, http://www.vnh.org
A service of the U.S. Navy Bureau of Medicine and Surgery and the Electric Differential Multimedia Laboratory, University of Iowa (U.S.A.) College of Medicine, this site has information for patients and providers or many regular medical topics, but also has Navy Medical Department administrative information, information on biological, chemical and nuclear warfare, and information for authorized U.S. Navy medical personnel only.

ESPECIALLY FOR LIBRARIANS

Advocacy and Marketing

Communications Toolkit, http://www.mlanet.org/publications/tool_kit/index.html
From Medical Library Association (U.S.A.).

Hay Group/Medical Library Association (U.S.A.) 2001 Compensation and Benefits Survey, http://www.mlanet.org/publications/hay_mla_02ss.html

Hospital Library Advocacy Blog, http://hosplib.blogspot.com
This blog is maintained by Jeannine Gluck, Director of the Medical Library of the Eastern Connecticut (U.S.A.) Health Network and chair of the Medical Library Association Hospital Library Standards Committee. If it's by Jeannine, it has to be worth reading.

Job Description Project, Medical Library Association (U.S.A.), http://lbrary.uvm.edu/dana and http://www.lib.mcw.edu

LibQual+, http://www.libqual.org
A suite of services that libraries use to solicit, track, understand, and act upon users' opinions of service quality. These services are offered

to the library community by the Association of Research Libraries (U.S.A.).

Medical Library Association (U.S.A.) Benchmarking Network, http://www.mlanet.org/members/benchmark/index.html (members only)

The Value of Medical Librarians: Hot Quotes, http://www.mcmla.org/libnvalue.htm

Thirteen wonderful quotes about the value medical librarians bring, with full citations, collected by the Midcontinental Chapter of the Medical Library Associations.

Books and Articles

Anderson, P. F. and Nancy J. Allee, eds. *The Medical Library Association Encyclopedic Guide to Searching and Finding Health Information on the Web.* New York: Neal Schuman, 2004, 3 vol., ISBN 1-55570-496-4, with CD-ROM, USD495.

Boorkman, Jo Anne, Jeffrey Huber and Fred Roper, eds. *Introduction to Reference Sources in the Health Sciences,* 4th ed. New York: Neal-Schuman, 2004, ISBN 1-55570-418-6, USD75.

Cadogan, Mary P., Cheryl Franzi, and Dan Osterweil. Barriers to Effective Communication in Skilled Nursing Facilities: Differences in Perception Between Nurses and Physicians. *Journal of the American Geriatrics Society* 47(1): 71–75, January 1999.

Dale, P. *Guide to Libraries and Information Sources in Medicine and Healthcare,* 3rd ed. London: British Library, 2000, ISBN 0-712308-56-3.

Homan, J. Michael. *Medical Evidence and Knowledge-Based Resources in Reducing Medical Errors: The Role of the Medical Librarian,* http://www.mlanet.org/pdf/resources/homan_med_errors.pdf

Hulsman, R. L., et al. Teaching Clinically Experienced Physicians Communication Skills: A Review of Evaluation Studies. *Medical Education* 33(9): 655, September 1999.

Kiley, R., ed. *A Guide to Healthcare Resources on the Internet.* London: Royal Society of Medicine, 2001, ISBN 1-85315473-3.

King, D. N. The Contribution of Hospital Library Services to Patient Care. *Bulletin of the Medical Library Association* 75: 291–301, 1987. A classic.

Madge, B. *How to Find Information: Complementary and Alternative Care.* London: British Library, 2001, ISBN 0-712308-85-7.

Madge, B. *How to Find Information: Health Care.* London: British Library, 2001, ISBN 0-712308-73-73.

Marshall, Joanne Gard. The Impact of the Hospital Library on Clinical Decision Making: The Rochester Study. *Bulletin of the Medical Library Association* 80: 196+, 1992. Another classic.

Ryder, J., ed. *Directory of Health Library and Information Services in the United Kingdom and the Republic of Ireland 2002-3*, 11th ed. London: Facet, 2003. ISBN 1-85604-491-2.

Scura, G. and F. Davidoff. Case-Related Use of the Medical Literature. *Journal of the American Medical Association* 245(1): 52, 1981.

Thirion, Benoit. Current Journals for Health Sciences Librarians, *EAHIL Newsletter to European Health Librarians* (67): 41–44, May 2004. Journals from the U.S.A., U.K., Europe, Japan, Canada, Germany, and the Netherlands.

Urquhart, C. J. and J. B. Hepworth. The Value of Information Supplied to Clinicians by Health Libraries: Devising an Outcomes-Based Assessment of the Contribution of Libraries to Clinical Decision-Making. *Health Libraries Review* 12: 201–313, 1995.

Urquhart, C. J. and J. B. Hepworth. Comparing and Using Assessments of the Value of Information to Clinical Decision-Making. *Bulletin of the Medical Library Association* 84: 482–489, 1996.

Walton, G. and A. Booth, eds. *Exploiting Knowledge in Health Services*. London: Facet, 2004, ISBN 1-85604479-3.

Welsh, S., B. Anagnostelis, and A. Cooke. *Finding and Using Health and Medical Information on the Internet*. London: Aslib-IMI, 2001, ISBN 0-85142384-1.

Electronic Discussion Lists

Evidence-Based Healthcare Discussion Lists, http://www.shef.ac.uk/scharr/ir/e-mail.html
From the University of Sheffield, U.K.

Evidence-Based Medicine Resource Center listservs, http://www.ebmny.org/lists.html
From the New York Academy of Medicine Library and American College of Physicians, New York (U.S.A.) Chapter.

Listservs for Medical Librarians, http://www.chu-rouen.fr/documed/lis.html#medlist
From Benoit Therion, Medical Library, University of Rouen, France.

Useful Links, http://www.umslg.ac.uk/links.html
University Medical School Librarians Group, U.K.

AGELIS-L, Special Interest Group on Gerontology and Geriatrics, Medical Library Association (agelis-l@usc.edu).

AHILA-NET: Association for Health Information and Libraries in Africa, http://list.who.int/wa.exe?SUBED1=ahila-net&A=1

aliaHEALTH, Health Libraries Australia, http://www.alia.org.au/groups/healthnat

BackMed, http://lists.swetsblackwell.com/mailman/listinfo/backmed
Informal exchange of medical serial back issues and books.

BIB-MED (Spain), http://www.rediris.es/list/info/bib-med.es.html
In Spanish only.

BiblioSante (France), http://listes.crihan.fr/wws/arc/bibliosante
For French-speaking medical librarians.

BIOMEDBIB (The Netherlands), http://listserv.surfnet.nl/archives/
biomedbib.html

CANMEDLIB-L (Canada) (listserv@morgan.ucs.mun.ca)
For Canadian medical librarians.

CLIN-LIB, Clinical Librarians Electronic List (listserv@www.
harthosp.org).

CLUG Cochrane Library Users Group, http://www.york.ac.uk/inst/
crd/clug.htm

EAHIL-L, European Association of Health Information Libraries
(listserv@listserv.kib.ki.se).

HEALTH-INFO, New Zealand Health Librarians (health-info-
subscribe@vuw.ac.nz).

Irish Health Sciences Librarians Group, http://www.topica.com/lists/
ihslg

LIS-MEDICAL, for all members of the medical library community
from the University Medical School Librarians Group, U.K.
(jiscmail@jiscmail.ac.uk).

MEDBIBL (Scandinavia), http://www.kib.ki.se/tools/base/medbibl_
se.html, Scandinavian medical librarians.

MEDINFO (Germany), see their blog at http://medinfo.netlib.de,
mostly in German, but there are some posts in English.

MEDLIB-L, medical librarians in the U.S.A. and elsewhere (listserv@
listserv.acsu.buffalo.edu).

MEDLIBS, IFLA's Health and Biosciences Libraris Group, http://infoserv.inist.fr/wwsympa.fcgi/subrequest/medlibs

VETLIB-L, http://groups.yahoo.com/group/vetlib-l
Veterinary medicine library issues.

Organizations

Arbeitgemeinschaft fuer medizinisches Bibliothekswesen (Germany), http://www.agmb.de

Associação Portuguesa de Documentação e Informação de Saúde (Portugal), http://www.apdis.org

Association for Health Information and Libraries in Africa, http://www.ahila.org

Chapters in Burkina Faso, Cameroon, Guinea Bissau, Guinea Conakry, Ivory Coast, Kenya, Malawi, Mali, Nigeria, Senegal, South Africa, Swaziland, Uganda, Zambia, and Zimbabwe.

Association of Information Officers in the Pharmaceutical Industry (UK), http://www.aiopi.org.uk

Represents over 800 professionals in the U.K.

Bibliotecari Documentalist della Sanita (Health Librarians—Italy), http://biblio.area.cs.cnr.it/bibliotecario/bibliossn/

Bibliotekkarforbundet—Faggruppen for Medicinsk Information (Denmark), http://grupper.bf.dk/medicin/

Bibliothecarii Medicinae Fenniae (Finland), http://www.terkko.helsinki.fi/bmf

Consortium of Health Independent Information Libraries in London (CHILL), http://www.chill-london.org.uk

Three meetings per year, plus training opportunities, a serials group, and discussion list.

Directory of Health Organizations Online, http://dirline.nlm.nih.gov

You can find an organization by name, acronym, or MeSH subject heading. Records have the organization's address and phone numbers, e-mail, Web site, and a short description of what the group does. There is also a searchable directory of health hotlines.

European Association for Health Information and Libraries (EAHIL), http://www.eahil.net

About 400 members from 25 European countries, sponsors and annual conference, continuing education opportunities, and a newsletter to European Health Librarians. Two subgroups: Pharmaceutical Information Group and European Veterinary Libraries Group. Headquarters in Utrecht, The Netherlands. Librarians in the U.S.A. can join EAHIL through the Medical Library Association.

Grupo de trabajo de Bibliotecas de Ciencias de la Salud (Spain), http://www.sedic.es/gt_cienciassalud.htm

Gruppo Italiano Documentalisti dell'Industria Farmaceutica de degli Istituti di Recerca Biomedica (Pharmaceutical and Biomedical Research Librarians), http://www.gidif-rbm.it

Health Libraries Group (HLG), Chartered Institute of Library and Information Professionals (CILIP), UK, http://www.cilip.org.uk/hlg

IFLA Health and Biosciences Section, http://www.ifla.org/VII/s28/index.htm

Information for the Management of Healthcare (IFMH), http://www.ifmh.org.uk

A partnership of CILIP groups Libraries for Nursing and Health Libraries Group to improve provision of information to health professional managers. Sponsors study days, a newsletter (INFORM), and discussion list. Headquarters in York, U.K.

Irish Health Sciences Libraries Group, special interest group of the Library Association of Ireland, contact Bernard Barrett (bbarrett@

mwhb.ie), reports in *CILIP Health Libraries Group Newsletter,* electronic list is at http://www.freelists.org/list/ihslg

Libraries for Nursing (LfN), http://www.cilip.org.uk/groups/hlg/lfn/
Reports in *CILIP Health Libraries Group Newsletter.*

Medical Library Association, http://www.mlanet.org
Founded in 1898, MLA is a nonprofit, educational organization of more than 1,100 institutions and 3,600 individual members in the health sciences information field, committed to educating health information professionals, supporting health information research, promoting access to the world's health sciences information, and working to ensure that the best health information is available to all. Headquartered in Chicago, Illinois, U.S.A.

MOKSZ Hungarian Medical Library Assocation, http://www.clib.dote. hu/moksz

National Library of Medicine, http://www.zbmed.de
Deutschen Zentralbibliothek für Medizin, Web site in English and German, located in Cologne.

The Netherlands: BioMedical Information section of Netherlands Association for Library, Information and Knowledge Professionals, http://www.nvbonline.nl

Nordic Association for Medical and Health Information NAMHI, http://www.namhi.org
The Association consists of the following associations: Bibliotekarforbundet, Faggruppen for Medicinsk Information, Denmark; Norsk Bibliotekforening, Spesialgruppen for Medisin og Helsefag, Norway; Svensk Biblioteksförening, Specialgruppen för vårdbibliotek, Sweden; Samtarfshópur Laeknisfraedibókavarda, Iceland and Bibliothecarii Medicinae Fenniae, Finland.

Norsk Bibliotekforening Tidsskriftformidlingen: Spesialgruppe for Medisin og Helsefag (Norway), http://www.norskbibliotekforening. no/smh/

Professionels de l'Information et de la documentation, http://www.adbs.fr/site/qui/secteurs/18.php

Sciences Libraries Section of the Library Association of Ireland, http://www.libraryassociation.ie/sections/healthlibs/

Scottish Health Information network, http://www.shinelib.org.uk

U.K. Council for Health Informatics Professionals (UKCHIP), http://www.ukchip.org

Formed in 2002 to promote professionalism in Health Informatics (HI). It operates a voluntary register of HI professionals who agree to work to clearly defined standards.

U.K. Health Informatics Society (UKHiS), http://www.bmis.org

University Health Science Librarians (U.K.), http://www.uhsl.ac.uk

For academic health sciences librarians in the U.K., sponsors study days.

University Medical School Librarians Group (UMSLG), http://www.umslg.ac.uk

UMSLG is the representative group for the librarians of undergraduate and postgraduate medical schools in the United Kingdom and the Republic of Ireland. The Web site has continuing professional development presentations back to 2001 available for download and a union list of serials (some available to the public). Headquarters in Hamilton, Scotland.

World Health Organization, http://www.who.int/en/

The World Health Organization is the United Nations specialized agency for health. Governed by 192 Member States through the World Health Assembly, composed of representatives from WHO's Member States. Headquartered in Geneva, Switzerland.

Healthcare Journals

David Crawford's List of free full-text journals medical journals, http://www.internatlibs.mcgill.ca/freeim.htm

Journals in English that are also indexed in Index Medicus and/or in PubmedCentral and offer free access to full text. As of April 2004 this list was no longer being updated. There are links to other lists that are being updated.

Directory of Open Access Journals, http://www.doaj.org

List of free, full-text, quality controlled scientific and scholarly journals. Covers all subjects and languages. As of February 2005 there were 1,463 journals in the directory, 364 searchable at article level, and 64,304 articles. From Lund University Libraries, Sweden.

E-journals and Open Access, Health Sciences, http://nnlm.gov/libinfo/ejournals/

From the U.S. National Library of Medicine.

Free LinkOut Journals by title, http://www.ncbi.nlm.nih.gov/entrez/journals/free_noprov/free_full_noprov.html

A list of PubMed Journals that provide some freely available full-text articles. As of February 24, 2005, a total of 131 providers supply free full text for 593 journals. From the National Center for Biotechnology Information, National Library of Medicine, Bethesda, Maryland, U.S.A.

Free Medical Journals.com, http://freemedicaljournals.com/htm/index.htm

From Flying Publisher, Paris, France, no advertising.

Online Periodicals and Newsletters for Librarians, http://nnlm.gov/libinfo/mgmt/online.html

From the U.S. National Library of Medicine.

Professional Journals

BMA Library Bulletin, http://www.bmalibrarybulletin.com

From the library of the British Medical Association, all issues online (only started in 2004).

BMC-Biomedical Digital Libraries, http://www.bio-diglib.com

Health Inform (Australia), print only, Health Libraries Inc.

Health Information and Libraries Journal, peer reviewed, Health Libraries Group, CILIP.

He@lth Information on the Internet (U.K.), http://www.rsmpress. co.uk/hii.htm

A compact bimonthly newsletter, for the U.K.-based physician, sponsored by the WellcomeTrust and published by the Royal Society of Medicine Press. Back issues available free on the Net in .pdf format.

Health Libraries Group Newsletter, ISSN 0266-853X, http://www. blackwellpublishing.com/hlr/newsletter

Online for free.

Health on the Internet: The Newsletter of Health Information Sources, ISSN 1367-0393 (print), ISSN 1360-2258 (e-mail).

Covers only sources in English, also available as a searchable database with monthly updates.

Internet Medicine: A Critical Guide, ISSN 1086-5691, http://www. internetmedicine.com

"Top medical school resources on the net." Monthly, from Lippincott Williams & Wilkins.

Journal of the Canadian Health Libraries Association/Journal de l'Association des bibliotheques de al sant du Canada, http://www. chla-absc.ca/journal/

New name for *Bibliotheca Medica Canadiana*, electronic only.

Journal of Consumer Health on the Internet, http://www.haworthpress. com/Web/JCHI/

Peer-reviewed journal devoted to locating consumer health information via the Internet. Formerly Health Care on the Internet, From Haworth Press, abstracts free, full text by subscription only.

Journal of Electronic Resources in Medical Libraries, http://www. haworthpressinc.com/Web/JERML/

Peer-reviewed professional journal devoted to the access, evaluation, and management of electronic resources in the medical library environment. Will complement articles published in *Medical Reference Services Quarterly*—both from Haworth Press.

Journal of Hospital Librarianship, https://www.haworthpress.com/Web/JHSPL/

Focuses on the technical and administrative issues that most concern you. From Haworth Press, not online.

Journal of the Medical Library Association, http://www.mlanet.org/publications/jmla/index.html

International, peer-reviewed journal published quarterly that aims to advance the practice and research knowledgebase of health sciences librarianship. Free with membership, current issue and all back issues available online.

Medical Reference Services Quarterly, http://www.haworthpress.com/store/product.asp?sku=J115

Peer reviewed, from Haworth Press, tables of contents online.

Medicine on the Net, ISSN 1085-3502, http://www.corhealth.com/MOTN/Default.asp

Monthly, from COR Healthcare Resources.

Medizin Online, Beilage für Arzte, Free supplement with Springer medical journals.

Newsletter to European Health Librarians, from EAHIL (European Association for Health Information and Libraries), published quarterly since June 1987.

NLM Technical Bulletin, http://www.nlm.nih.gov/pubs/techbull/tb.html

A free newsletter for online searchers that use NLM Web sites. It gives updates to new features used in their Web sites and also news about changes. Published bimonthly and online by MEDLARS Management Section, National Library of Medicine, Bethesda, Maryland, U.S.A.

Portals and Lists of Medical Web Sites

Barber, Graeme. Internet Sites of Interest, Cancer. *CILIP Health Libraries Group Newsletter* 21(1):11–12, March 2004.

BioMed Central, http://www.biomedcentral.com/default.asp

Over 100 Open Access journals covering all areas of biology and medicine.

Consumer Health Web Sites You Can Trust, http://caphis.mlanet. org/consumer/index.html

The top 100 sites selected by the Consumer and Patient Health Information Section of the Medical Library Association. Divided into general health, women, kids and parenting, seniors, specific health problems, especially for health professionals, drug information, and other useful health sites.

Directory of Open Access Journals, http://www.doaj.org

Free, full-text, quality controlled scientific and scholarly journals. As of May 2005, nearly 73,000 articles in over 1,550 journals, 390 of which are searchable at the article level. From the University of Lund, Sweden.

Free Medical Journals, http://freemedicaljournals.com

From Flying Publisher. 1,410 journals, sorted by specialty, title, or language (English, French, German, Spanish, Portuguese, and others).

Health Care Information, http://www.bl.uk/collections/health/health. html

HighWire Press, http://highwire.stanford.edu/lists/freeart.dtl

An archive of free full-text science, as of May 2005 there were nearly 900,000 full-text and 2.2 million total articles.

Librarians' Tips: Exhaustive Literature Searching in Health, (Australia), http://www.salus.sa.gov.au/Portals/c7ea0d2d-1004-4039-aea8-f4c703c045ce/litsearchtips.html

This is the third edition of this valuable resource from Ruth Sladek, Repatriation General Hospital, Daw Park, South Australia. It includes strategies and links.

medIND, http://medind.nic.in

Indian Medlars Centre, one point resource of peer-reviewed Indian biomedical literature covering full text of IndMED journals.

Medical Reference for Non-Medical Librarians, http://Denison.uchsc. edu/outreach/medbib3.htm

Extremely complete list of links, not for non-librarians only. Compiled by Jean C. Blackwell, Health Sciences Library, University of North Carolina-Chapel Hill (U.S.A.); updated and additional material by Lynne M. Fox, University of Colorado Health Sciences Center, Denver, U.S.A.

Med Web Sites, http://www.geocities.com/nqiya/MedWeb sites.html

From Tanya Feddern of the University of Miami (Florida, U.S.A.) School of Medicine Library, this is a list of sites that you might not have seen before.

National Electronic Library for Health portal, http://www.nelh.nhs. uk/librarian

From the U.K. National Health Service. Portal to resources from the British Library, including medicine, complementary and alternative medicine, allied health professions including: physiotherapy, occupational therapy, speech and language therapies, and podiatry, nursing, healthcare management, pharmaceuticals, healthcare services and products, and history of medicine.

Online Full-text (Medical) Journal Articles: Journals and other publications, http://library.uthct.edu/jrnlpage.htm

From Watson W. Wise Medical Research Library, University of Texas Health Center at Tyler (U.S.A.), lists both free and paid, available at UTHC and outside.

PLoS, the Public Library of Science, http://www.plos.org

A San Francisco, California, U.S.A., nonprofit organization of scientists and physicians committed to making the world's scientific and medical literature a freely available public resource. Divided into PLoSBiology and PLoSMedicine.

PubMedCentral, http://www.pubmedcentral.nih.gov
U.S. National Institutes of Health's free digital archive of biomedical and life sciences journal literature.

Smith, Mary. Internet Sites of Interest, Mental Health Service Users. *CILIP Health Libraries Group Newsletter* 21(4):10, 12-13, June 2004. An excellent list.

Wake, Michelle. Spotlight on … Pharmacy. *EAHIL Newsletter to European Health Libraries* (66):34–35, February 2004. Portals and gateways, organizations, pharmaceutical companies, books, free journals, and electronic lists.

Professional Resources

Basic Medical Library Management, http://www.nnlm.nlm.nih.gov/libinfo/mgmt
"For both professional and non-professional librarians new to health or hospital libraries." Covers administration, sources, databases, collection development and interlibrary loan, and "first steps for new medical librarians," from the U.S. National Library of Medicine.

CAPHIS, Consumer and Patient Health Information Section, Medical Library Association (U.S.A.) http://www.caphis.mlanet.org

The Informationist: Background Reading, http://www.mlanet.org/research/informationist/reading.html
Prepared by the Medical Library Association (U.S.A.) for the Informationist Invited Conference, April 2002.

Professional Resources for Librarians, http://colldev.mlanet.org/additional-res.html
A fantastic list of all kinds of resources, including discussion lists, books, databases, journals, Web sites, directories, associations, review sources, and special collection, from the Medical Library Association (U.S.A.).

Subject-Based Resource Lists, Print and Web-based, http://colldev.m lanet.org/subject.html

35 categories cover allied health to veterinary medicine, from the Medical Library Association (U.S.A.).

Other Web Sites

Antiquarian Medical Book Trade: A Survey and Directory of Dealers and a List of Internet Resources, http://www.alhhs.org (under the Watermark link).

From the Archivists and Librarians in the History of Health Sciences (ALHHS), Louse Darling Biomedical Library, University of California at Los Angeles, U.S.A.

Guide to Using PubMed, http://nnlm.gov/psr/training/tutorials.html

An updated tri-fold user guide, suitable for passing out to your customers.

Guide to Working in Health Information, http://www.cilip.org.uk/ groups/hlg/guide.html

From the Health Information Group, Chartered Institute of Library and Information Professionals, London, U.K.

Information Rx Store, http://www.informationrx.org

The National Library of Medicine (U.S.A.) created information prescription pads that physicians can use to refer patients to the MedlinePlus.gov Web site. Why not create some of your own to refer the patients to you?

Librarian's Guide to a JCAHO Accreditation Survey, http://www. pubmedcentral/gov/articlerender.fcgi?artid-128964

"The purpose of this guide is to provide answers to questions that librarians might have about the Joint Commission on Accreditation of Healthcare Organizations (JCAHO) accreditation process as it relates to libraries and information services."

Librarians' Rx, http://www.library.ualberta.ca/mt/blog/librariansrx/

A blog "with postings on a wide variety of topics of interest to Canadian [and other] health sciences librarians." From Denise Koufogiannakis, University of Alberta, Edmonton, Canada.

Medicine in Quotations, http://www.acponline.org/medquotes

Over 3,000 entries, searchable by author or subject, from the American College of Physicians.

NLM-Announces, http://www.nlm.nih.gov

Weekly announcement-only list of new and updated files on the National Library of Medicine (U.S.A.) Web site.

When to OVID and When to Use PubMed, http://www.lib.umich.edu/taubman/ovidvspm.html

The librarians at Taubman Medical Library, University of Michigan, have created a table comparing the two major medical resources, OVID and PubMed.

Who Named It? http://www.whonamedit.com

A biographical dictionary of over 6,000 medical eponyms, from Oslo, Norway.

World Health Organization Research Tools, http://www.who.int/research/en/

WHOLIS, the WHO library database on the Web, indexes all WHO publications from 1948 and articles from 1985. Also available, a guide to WHO's epidemiological and statistical information.

17

Science, Engineering, and Technology

GENERAL SCIENCE

BBC Science and Nature Hot Topics, http://www.bbc.co.uk/science/hottopics

Billed as "the science behind the news," this site has short articles on topics in the news. Included are alcohol, animal experiments, biochemical weapons, cannabis, chocolate, climate change, computer viruses, cooking, extreme cosmetics, football (soccer), intelligence, James Bond, love, marathons, mobile phones, natural disasters, obesity, sunshine, superheroes, tennis, and transport. There is also a message board for further discussions. The British Broadcasting Service also has similar sites on animals, prehistoric life, the human body and mind, genes, and space.

Building Websites for Science Literacy, http://www.library.ucsb.edu/istl/00-winter/article2.html

This is a great article on creating a Webliography and evaluating and organizing Web sites on science topics. It includes a discussion of science literacy, a sample Webliography, and a good bibliography. An article by Victoria Welborn and Bryn Kanar of the Science Library at

University of California, Santa Cruz, U.S.A. from *Issues in Science and Technology Librarianship*.

Dictionaries of Units of Measurement, http://www.unc.edu/~rowlett/units

Definitions of many kinds of measuring units, including where and how they are used, all types of tables and scales (from drought severity to paper sheet sizes), and links to related sites. From Russ Rowlett, Director, Center for Mathematics and Science Education, University of North Carolina at Chapel Hill, U.S.A.

A Dictionary of Units, http://www.ex.ac.uk/cimt/dictunit/dictunit.htm

"This provides a summary of most of the units of measurement to be found in use around the world today (and a few of historical interest), together with the appropriate conversion factors needed to change them into a 'standard' unit of the SI [Systeme International]." Just about everything you need to know about measurement. From the University of Exeter, Devon, England.

Discover Information, http://www.vascoda.de

A partnership of 37 German libraries brings you this interdisciplinary portal to scientific information. Most of the information is free, but some fee-based information is available as pay-per-view.

eNature, http://www.enature.com

Includes online field guides to birds, butterflies, native plants, seashells, and more. Also provides regional wildlife guides by ZIP code, "bird of the day," and "ask an expert." From eNature, San Francisco, California, U.S.A.

E-STREAMS, Electronic review of Science & Technology References, http://www.e-streams.com

Thirty or more reviews every month covering new titles in engineering, agriculture, medicine, and science. Free in electronic form. A collaboration of H. Robert Malinowsky of the University of Illinois at Chicago, U.S.A., and YBP Library Services.

Great Science Site from Australia, http://www.abc.net.au/science/

Programs from the Australian Broadcasting Corporation and original items, daily news, and forums. Not searchable, but chock-full of interesting and education information.

Knovel, http://www.knovel.com

Online scientific and engineering handbooks, references, and databases from CRC Press, McGraw-Hill, Reed Elsevier, Kluwer Academic, Noyes, Industrial Press, Society of Plastics Engineers, John Wiley and others. As of February 2005, there are more than 500 titles. From a commercial vendor, the service is not free, but a two-week free trial is available.

Ology, http://ology.amnh.org

Honored by Scientific American as the best children's science site, this site has interactive educational games and presentations. Very well done.

Pathfinder Science Network for Student and Citizen Science, http://pathfinderscience.net

"Creating student scientists, not just science students." Includes science projects, discussions, and discussion list, and mentors from the science and business community. Pathfinder Science is an open, international community made up of researchers, teachers, citizens, and students interested in conducting collaborative research. The research community building process began in October 1997 supported by a U.S. Department of Education, Technology Innovation Challenge grant, and the Kansas Collaborative Research Network.

Science News for Kids, http://www.sciencenewsforkids.org

Don't let the name of this site fool you—there's a lot more here than news. Aimed at children ages 9–13, there are articles and news on subjects from agriculture to weather and a newsletter. But there are also six "zones." My favorite is GameZone, but you might like PuzzleZone, SciFiZone, or LabZone better. And there's a TeacherZone, too. SciFairZone's project ideas will make parents and kids happy when science fair time comes around. From the nonprofit publisher of Science News, Washington, DC, U.S.A.

Scientific World, http://www.thescientificworld.com

Databases include scienceWAREHOUSE (online scientific equipment, chemicals, and biological resources, including Fisher Scientific), worldMEET (searchable database of more than 3,500 scientific conferences, symposia, and workshops), sciBASE (free access to more than 19 million documents including MEDLINE, PASCAL, CAB ABSTRACTS and BIOSIS, plus access to journals from Blackwell Science, Mary Ann Liebert and Taylor & Francis), and *TheScientificWorldJOURNAL*. From TheScientificWorld Limited, Newbury, Berkshire, U.K.

Technical Information Superstore, http://www.techstreet.com

Books, standards, training, software from more than 10,000 publishers. More than 93,000 downloadable documents (not all free, however). Browse standards catalogs from some of the major publishers, including ANSI, ASTM, IEEE, ISO, and NFPA. Headquartered in Ann Arbor, Michigan, U.S.A.

Very "Ingenious" Site, http://www.ingenious.org.uk

This British site certainly fits its tagline, "seeing things differently." For each featured subject you can read (articles), debate (respond), see (images), create (you need to register for this—I didn't try it), or search. There is also a "Dig down deeper!" section with audio clips and links to related sites. I especially liked the topic on "Dumbing down science." From the U.K. National Museum of Science and Industry. Major contributors to the site are the Science Museum, the National Museum of Photography, Film & Television, the National Railway Museum, the Science & Society Picture Library and the Science Museum Library.

ENGINEERING

Architecture and Building Resources, http://library.nevada.edu/arch/rsrce/webrsrce/

From the University of Nevada–Las Vegas (U.S.A.) Library, includes reference tools and resources by topic. Covers architecture, building and construction, design, housing, planning, preservation, facility management, energy and the environment, and landscape architecture.

E4: The 24-hour Service for Engineers and Industry, http://www.e4engineering.com

Weekly news, analysis, product notes, and features from *The Engineer* magazine, London, U.K.

EEVL: The Internet guide to engineering, mathematics, and computing, http://www.eevl.ac.uk

An engineering portal with links to more than 5,000 sites including search engines, databases, engineering guides, other portals, employment agencies, events, industry news sources, teaching and learning resources, literature searching sites, list of the top 25 engineering sites, contact directory for university science and technology librarians. The EEVL lead site is Heriot Watt University, with Cranfield University, University of Birmingham, and University of Ulster (U.K.) as strategic partners.

EngineerSupply.Com, http://www.engineersupply.com

Designed by engineers for engineers, here is a bookstore, links to directories, consultants, professional organizations, education and regulatory agencies, and careers. You may have to register for parts of the site. Based in Evington, Virginia, U.S.A.

Guide to Greener Living, http://www.nrdc.org/cities/living/gover.asp

Make your world greener by implementing some of the ideas offered by the Natural Resources Defense Council, New York, New York, U.S.A. Topics include save energy on the road, save energy at home, save resources at home, save resources at work, conserve water, support organic and sustainable farming, invest responsibly, and act for the environment. There are also links to many other environment-friendly sites.

Pocket Guide to Transportation 2004, http://www.bts.gov/publications/ pocket_guide_to_transportation/2004/

"Everything" you might need to know about the U.S. transportation system. For example: accidents, security, oil imports, number of vehicles, top 20 airports, freight shipments, automobile sales. From the Bureau of Transportation Statistics, Department of Transportation, Washington DC, U.S.A.

Statistical Agencies, Geological Surveys, Meteorological Services, etc., http://www.library.uu.nl/geosource/cat7.html

Gateways to statistical agencies and sources and links to international statistical agencies, national and regional statistical offices (by country), statistical resources outside the above agencies, geological, geophysical, volcanological and geographical surveys by country, and meteorological services by country. From Geosource, University of Utrecht, the Netherlands.

TRIS Online, http://trisonline.bts.gov/search.cfm

Online version of the U.S. Transportation Research Board, with more than 400,000 bibliographic records dating from the 1960s. Searchable, many records have online links.

The Virtual Technical Reports Center, http://www.lib.umd.edu/ENGIN/TechReports/Virtual-TechReports.html

"EPrints, Preprints, & Technical Reports on the Web." Welcome to the Virtual Technical Reports Center! Links to technical reports, preprints, reprints, dissertations, theses, and research reports of all kinds, by institution. Some metasites are listed by subject categories, as well as by institution. Updated monthly. From the University of Maryland, College Park, U.S.A.

TECHNOLOGY

Built in America, http://memory.loc.gov/ammem/collections/habs_ haer/index.html

More than 350,000 digital images of measured drawings, black-and-white photographs, color transparencies, written histories, and more from the U.S. Library of Congress and National Park Service's Historic American Buildings Survey and Historic American Engineering Record. Search by geographic area to see if any of the 35,000 historic structures and sites are near you.

Home Depot's Calculator, http://www.homedepot.com, then search for the calculator

Calculate the amount of material you need for a project, also air-conditioning, grass seed, wallpaper, etc. From the large U.S.A. home products chain.

How Everyday Things are Made, http://manufacturing.stanford.edu

Ever want to know how Jelly Bellies are made? You can see a video on this site from the Alliance for Innovative Manufacturing at Stanford University, U.S.A. Requires Flashmedia, and a fast connection helps a lot. Really interesting.

Mrs. Fixit, http://www.mrsfixit.com

If you've ever needed to know how to repair a scratch in your dining room table (I did), this is the Web site for you. In addition to the FIXITs (searchable tips), there are archives of the questions asked of Mrs. Fixit (of whom you ask specific questions by e-mail), products you can buy, and a free newsletter. All seems very useful. From Terri McGraw, Syracuse, New York, U.S.A.

Readymade: Instructions for Everyday Life, http://www.readymade mag.com

Online version of a print magazine "for people who like to make stuff." This site has articles with instructions on building practical and impractical things out of almost everything. Published in Berkeley, California, U.S.A.

This is Broken, http://broken.typepad.com

See what others have contributed about bad designs or experiences in advertising, current affairs, food and drink, places, product design, signs, and the Web. You can add your complaints, too. Lots of duplication, but still interesting; check out Harvard's Book Drop sign. From Mark Hurst, founder of Creative Good, a customer experience consulting firm in New York City, U.S.A. There is also a free e-newsletter.

AERONAUTICS

Airchive: The Museum of Commercial Aviation, http://www.airchive. com/

This cool site has great graphics, even if it is a bit slow to load. It includes the history of airlines around the world (both living and dead), told through timetables and route maps, a visual guide to airplanes and airports, and lots more. From Chris Sloan, a television producer and aviation fan in Miami Beach, U.S.A.

Direct from the Space Station, http://spaceflight.nasa.gov/station/ crew/exp7/luletters

NASA Science Officer Ed Lu's descriptions of his experiments and experiences in the International Space Station are fascinating. There are also pictures. A really cool site.

AGRICULTURE

AGORA: Access to Global Online Research in Agriculture, http://www.aginternetwork.org/en

Here you can find articles from more than 500 journals in agriculture and related disciplines. Abstracts are free, articles cost USD25. I'd check AGRICOLA from the U.S. Department of Agriculture first, but this is a good additional source.

I Never Promised You a Rose Garden, http://www.urbanext.uiuc.edu/roses

The University of Illinois at Urbana-Champaign, U.S.A. provides you with almost everything you need to know about roses: history, selection, planting, pruning, rose societies, mail-order sources, and articles. And it has some very nice pictures, too.

BIOSCIENCES

Image Bank, http://www.bioscience.heacademy.ac.uk/imagebank/

More than 1,000 copyright-cleared downloadable images from the biosciences. All are searchable and have accompanying text. You can even contribute your own images to the file or post a request for ones not found. From the Centre for Bioscience, University of Leeds, U.K.

CHEMISTRY

ChemDex, http://www.chemdex.org

A meta-index of chemistry sites, with more than 7,000 links. From the Chemistry Department of the University of Sheffield, U.K.

Chemfinder, http://chemfinder.cambridgesoft.com

Search about 3,800 compounds from various free and fee-based databases. From "a world chemistry community" based in Cambridge, Massachusetts, U.S.A. They also produce Chemhumor, http://chemclub.cambridgesoft.com/chemhumor, which features many funny chemical structures in their Comical Compounds Gallery—really cute—look for Mercedes Benzene.

Chemical Backgrounders, http://www.nsc.org/library/chemical/chemical.htm

Here is information on nearly 100 commonly found chemicals from the (U.S.) National Safety Council. Very informative.

Chemindustry.com, http://chemindustry.com/index.asp

Links to business resources, millions of full-text pages. Produced in Monrovia, California, U.S.A.

Hazardous Chemical Database, http://ull.chemistry.uakron.edu/erd/

Information on 23,000-plus chemicals, from the University of Akron, Ohio, U.S.A.

Household Products Database, http://householdproducts.nlm.nih.gov

This database from the National Library of Medicine (U.S.) has detailed information on the manufacturer, ingredients, and health effects of most household products. You can search by brand, category, or ingredients. Material Safety Data Sheets are also available.

Links for Chemists, http://www.liv.ac.uk/Chemistry/Links/links.html

Chemistry section of the WWW Virtual Library. Links to about 8,000 resources on the Web, from the U.K. From the Chemistry Department of the University of Liverpool, U.K.

Molecule of the Month, http://www.chm.bris.ac.uk/motm/motm.htm

Each month the Chemistry Department at the University of Bristol, U.K., chooses a molecule to feature. The department even accepts your own molecule of the month. The page either comes from the department itself or is a link to another site. Included are sources, the chemical structure, uses, and articles related to the molecule. There are also links to other molecule-of-the-month sites at Imperial College, London and Oxford University, U.K., Virginia Commonwealth University (U.S.A.), and Prous (Spain).

This Week in the History of Chemistry, http://web.lemoyne.edu/~giunta/week.html

Did you know that John Calvin Giddings, pioneer in high-pressure liquid chromatography, was born 26 September 1930? If this is of interest to your users, you can find information like this at this site. There are also links to more information on many of the events. While you're in the vicinity, check out the Classic Chemistry page also compiled by Carmen Giunta (Dept. of Chemistry, LeMoyne College,

Syracuse, New York). It has the texts of classic papers from the history of chemistry and classic calculations, quantitative exercises based on the papers.

MATERIALS SCIENCE

Note: Taken from Hook, David, Web Reviews, SciTech News 59(1):29–31, February 2005.

The American Society of Metals, http://www.asm-intl.org

Lists of standards that you can order online, materials information, heat treating resources, discussion forums on heat treating, atmospheres, failure analysis and testing and surface engineering, industry news, classic papers, newsletter archives, tables of contents of current issues of magazines, and many resources available to members only. The Society is in Materials Park, Ohio, U.S.A.

Ceramics Properties Databases, http://www.ceramics.org/cic/proper tiesdb.asp

Links to nine free databases, seven fee-based ones, and selected books that contain ceramic property data. From the American Ceramic Society, Westerville, Ohio, U.S.A.

CINDAS, https://cindasdata.com

CINDAS LLC provides critically evaluated materials properties databases for thermal, mechanical, electrical, physical and other properties of various materials. We provide CD-ROM and Web-based applications for searching and comparing continually updated data. There are more than 5,000 materials and 50,000 data curves in the Thermophysical Properties of Matter Database (TPMD), and more than 750 materials and 15,000 data curves in the Microelectronics Packaging Materials Database (MPMD). Free demonstrations, but the databases are very expensive. From Purdue University, West Lafayette, Indiana, U.S.A.

Data and Properties Calculation Sites on the Web, http://tigger.uic.
edu/~mansoori/Thermodynamic.Data.and.Property_html

Links to nano, quantum and statistical mechanics and thermodynamics data and properties calculation and download sites, organizations involved with data compilation and property calculation, and
bibliographic data. From the Thermodynamics Research Laboratory,
University of Illinois-Chicago, U.S.A.

The Materials Gateway, http://www.mrs.org

You can sign up for a free monthly e-newsletter with materials
research news and society information and access Materials
Connections, their online newsletter (http://www.mrs.org/connection/
index.html), but most of the resources are for members only. From the
Materials Research Society, Warrendale, Pennsylvania, U.S.A., an
international society of about 12,000 members.

MatWeb, http://www.matweb.com/index.asp

A searchable database of nearly 50,000 material data sheets, including property information on thermoplastic and thermoset polymers.
Basic searching is free, but registered and premium users have access
to more features. MatWeb is a division of Automation Creations, Inc.,
Blacksburg, Virginia, U.S.A.

Plastics.com, http://www.plastics.com

Blogs, industry news, free classifieds, and forums; search for materials, information, people, suppliers, trade names, companies, or sales
leads; links to trade magazines, definitions, acronyms, and trade
names. From plastics.com, Fitchburg, Massachusetts, U.S.A.

Polymer Search on the Internet, http://www.polymer-search.com/
home/default.asp

A free Internet search engine dedicated to the polymer industries.
Only sites that offer considerable content directly related to rubber,
plastics, or adhesives are indexed. By using a selection criteria, we
now provide a focused alternative to the major Internet search engines,
resulting in quick, relevant answers to your queries. From Rapra

Technology (formerly the Rubber and Plastics Research Association), Shrewsbury, Shropshire, U.K.

Steel Works, http://www.steel.org

News, statistics, policy, publications, and links to Steel Related Trade Associations, Technology & Research, Member Companies, Government and Policy, Consumer Organizations, Steel News & Publications, Steel Marketplace (for buyers and sellers), and other resources (http://www.steel.org/hotlinks/). From the American Iron and Steel Institute, Washington DC, U.S.A.

ThermoDex, http://thermodex.lib.utexas.edu/about.html

A finding aid to compilations of thermodynamic and physical property data for chemical compounds and other substances. No data, but annotated records that describe. Most of the compilations included are printed books; some are freely available Web-based databases. Enter both a type of compound and a property to get a list of handbooks that might contain these data. From the Chemistry Library, University of Texas at Austin, U.S.A.

World Metals Information Network, http://www.amm.com/index2.htm

Industrial metals news, and the Metals Marketplace with information on more than 750 vendors in the metals market. You can narrow down your search results by specifying the metal category, the metal type, and geographic area you are interested in or search for a company by name. From American Metal Market LLC, a member of the Metal Bulletin Plc Group, New York, New York, U.S.A.

PHYSICS

Fear of Physics, http://www.fearofphysics.com

Divided into virtual physics, homework help (including auto-graded assignments to help teachers), and a physics dictionary. Find out the physics behind everything from roller coasters to basketball to Einstein's Theory of Relativity. Even I could understand this. From Mark Kaufman, Cambridge, Massachusetts, U.S.A.

The Laws List, http://alcyone.com/max/physics/laws/

Glossary of terms, laws, rules, principles, effects, paradoxes, limits, constants, experiments, and thought-experiments in physics, including astronomy. From Eric Max Francis, San Jose, California, U.S.A.

NIST Physical Reference Data, http://physics.nist.gov/PhysRefData/

Searchable database of physical constants and other physics-related data. From the U.S. National Institute of Standards and Technology.

PhysLink Online, http://www.physlink.com

Online articles and links to reference sites, list of university physics departments worldwide, and an "ask the experts" feature. From a Long Beach, California, U.S.A. organization.

PhysNet, http://physnet.uni-oldenburg.de/PhysNet/

Lists of links to worldwide physics institutions, such as institutes and departments at universities, ordered by continent, country, and town; links to document sources, such as preprints, research reports, annual reports, and lists of publications or worldwide physics institutions and individual physicists; lists of physics-related journals, which are freely available full-text on the Net; online educational resources for physics, for which you can choose the resource by the type of information required (for example, Lecture Notes, Seminars Talks, Visualization and Demonstration Applets); and lists of conferences and job listings. Produced under the auspices of the European Physical Society and several national societies and hosted by the Department of Physics, Carol von Ossietzky University of Oldenburg, Germany.

Physics Preprints, Abstracts, Reports, http://www.csc.fi/physics/Preprints.html

From Center for Scientific Computing, Espoo, the Finnish IT center for science.

Physics.org, http://www.physics.org

Set up by the Institute of Physics, London, U.K., this site uses natural language querying to recommend Web sites from its database of refereed resources to answer questions. Free registration required.

BLOGS FOR SCIENCE LIBRARIANS

Confessions of a Science Librarian, http://jdupuis.blogspot.com
From John Dupuis, York University, U.K.

Englib for the Scitech Librarian, http://englib.info
From Catherine Lavallee-Welch, University of Louisville, Kentucky, U.S.A.

Karlsruhe Virtual Katalogue (KVK), http://www.ubka.uni-karlsruhe.de/hylib/en/kvk.html
Search many European university and union catalogs and national union catalogs worldwide.

Need to Decipher a Journal Abbreviation? http://www.library.ubc.ca/scieng/coden.html
Thanks to the University of British Columbia (Canada) for this site to help you interpret the abbreviations for scientific journal titles.

The SciTech Library Question, http://stlq.info
From Randy Reichardt and Geoff Harder, University of Alberta, Canada.

Ten or So Things That Every Chemistry Librarian Absolutely, Positively Has to Have to Keep From Being an Absolute Plonk, by F. Barton Culp, *SciTech News* 58(1): 10, February 2004, publication of the Science-Technology Division, Special Libraries Association:

1. Aldrich catalog
2. Chemical Information Sources discussion list, http://listserv.indiana. edu/archives/chminf-1.html
3. *CRC Handbook of Chemistry & Physics*
4. Google
5. *Hawley's Condensed Chemical Dictionary*
6. *Merck Index*
7. NIST Chemistry WebBook, http://webbook.nist.gov/chemistry

8. Spectral Database for Organic Compounds,
   http://www.aist.go.jp/RIODB/ SDBS/menu-e.html
   From the National Institute of Advanced Industrial Science
   and Technology, Japan.

9. WebElements Periodic Table,
   http://www.webelements.com/webelements/ scholar/index.html
   Click on an element and find out all about it.

18

Social Sciences

ANTHROPOLOGY

Anthrosource, http://www.anthrosource.net

Although there is a great deal of anthropological material here, it is not all-inclusive. In addition, most of the content is available only to members of the American Anthropological Association. That said, this site has a complete electronic archive of all journals of the AAA from its beginning in 1888 to the present. Nonmembers can view the table of contents and abstracts, but full text is available only through JSTOR and for members only. There are also current issues of 11 of the AAA's peer-reviewed journals, including *American Anthropologist, American Ethnologist, Anthropology and Education Quarterly, Anthropology and Humanism, Archeaological Publications of the American Anthropological Association, Cultural Anthropology, Ethos, Journal of Linguistic Anthropology, Medical Anthropology Quarterly, NAPA Bulletin,* and *PoLAR: The Political and Legal Anthropology Review.* You can sign up to be notified when new content is available from your chosen journals.

ArchNet: WWW Virtual Library, Archaelogy, http://archnet.asu.edu

From the University of Arizona, Tucson, U.S.A., this is a very comprehensive guide to museums (physical and virtual), sources, societies, organizations, academic departments (with curricula and courses), and news. Coverage is international. You can approach it by region, type of resource, or subject. The site is still under construction and some of the more intriguing sections are not yet functional, but it is very promising.

EDUCATION

BBC Schools, http://www.bbc.co.uk/schools/

From the British Broadcasting Corporation, this site is keyed to the educational standards of the U.K., but its resources can be used by all children, parents, and teachers. There are games, worksheets, teaching techniques, and more, divided into preschool, ages 4–11, 11–16, and 16 and up.

Britkid, http://www.britkid.org

A wonderful Web site about race, racism, and growing up in Britain. It features nine British youngsters from varying backgrounds (White, Caribbean, Chins, Jewish, Indian, etc.). Clicking on their images lets you find out about their family, religion, ethnic group, food, and friends. Another approach is by visiting their hangouts or homes in "Brichester." There are also fact sheets on "serious issues" such as immigration law, housing, crime, refugees, plus maps. A project of University College Chichester, Comic Relief, ChildLine, and the Runnymede Trust, U.K.

Dictionary of Cultural Literacy, 3rd ed., http://www.bartleby.com/59/

Online version of the book by E. D. Hirsch, Jr., Joseph F. Kett, and James Trefil. "The 6,900 entries … form the touchstone of what it means to be not only just a literate American but an active citizen in our multicultural democracy."

DonorsChoose, http://www.donorschoose.org

An intriguing site where public school teachers propose projects that individuals can choose to fund through the site. As of February 2005, 3,729 teachers from 1,620 schools have submitted 8,559 proposals that were screened and posted by DonorsChoose; residents of 49 states have funded 5,826 teacher proposals to give students the resources they need to learn, and 2,335 classrooms have received $2,867,756 worth of student resources. There is even a link to help you create a DonorsChoose for your own school—or library! Founded by Charles Best at Wings Academy, an alternative public high school in the Bronx, New York, U.S.A.

Games Kids Play, http://www.gameskidsplay.net
   "Rules for playground games, verses for jump-rope rhymes, and much more." Created by Geof Niebeor, U.S.A.

Homeschooling Information from the National Home Education Network for Librarians, http://www.nhen.org/librarian/default.asp? id=193
   Tells librarians what kind of support home schooling parents want from libraries. NHEN is based in Hobe Sound, Florida, U.S.A.

KidsClick!: Web Search for Kids by Librarians, http://sunsite.berkeley. edu/KidsClick!/
   A good master directory of kids' sites; the search engine searches just the chosen sites. From the Ramapo Catskill Library System, Middletown, New York, U.S.A.

Links to Statistics Education Resources, http://www.math.ccsu.edu/ larose/stat%20ed.htm
   From Central Connecticut State University, New Britain, U.S.A.

Statistical resources in education and psychology, http://www.lib. berkeley.edu/EDP/statistics.html
   From the Education and Psychology Library at the University of California at Berkeley (U.S.A.).

What Can I Do With This Major?, http://career.utk.edu/students/ majors.asp.
   From Career Services, University of Tennessee, Knoxville, U.S.A.

Learning Disabilities

American Association on Mental Retardation, 444 North Capitol St., NW Suite 846, Washington DC 20001-1512 U.S.A., phone: 1-202-387-1968 or 1-800-424-3688, fax: 1-202-387-2193, http://www.aamr.org

British Institute of Learning Disabilities, Campion House, Green St, Kidderminster, Worcs, U.K., DY10 1JL, phone: 44(0)1562 723010, fax: 44(0)1562 723029, http://www.bild.org.uk

Downs Syndrome Association (U.K.), Langdon Down Centre, 2a Langdon Park, Teddington, U.K., TW11 9PS, phone: 44(0)845 230 0372, fax: 44(0)845 230 0373, http://www.downs-syndrome.org.uk

Downs Syndrome Medical Interest Group (U.K.), http://www.dsmig.org.uk
Information on "best practices," aimed at medical professionals. Based at City Hospital Centre, Nottingham, U.K.

English Sports Association for People with Learning Disability (U.K.), Unit 9, Milner Way, Ossett, West Yorkshire, U.K., WF5 9JN, phone: 44(0)8451 298992, fax: 44(0)1924 267666, http://www.esapld.co.uk
Governing body for the U.K. for sports for the learning disabled.

Foundation for People with Learning Disabilities (U.K.), Sea Containers House, 20 Upper Ground, London, U.K., SE1 9QB, phone: 44(0)20 7802 0300, fax: 44(0)20 7802 0301, http://www.learning disabilities.org.uk
Biggest, most comprehensive Web site for LD in the U.K.

Learning Disabilities U.K., http://www.learningdisabilitiesuk.org.uk

Learning Disability, http://www.learningdisability.co.uk
A new and developing site that appears to be independent of any agency or organization.

Mencap (U.K.), 123 Golden Lane, London EC1Y 0RT, phone: 44(0)20 7454 0454, fax: 44(0)20 7696 5540, http://www.mencap.org.uk

The National Autistic Society (Autism and Asperger Syndrome) (U.K.), 393 City Road, London, U.K., EC1V 1NG, phone: 44(0)20 7833 2299, fax: 44(0)20 7833 9666, http://www.nas.org.uk

National Electronic Library for Learning Disabilities (U.K.), http://libraries.nelh.nhs.uk/learningdisabilities/

U.K. Government, http://www.dh.gov.uk/PolicyAndGuidance/ HealthAndSocialCareTopics/LearningDisabilities/fs/en

HISTORY

Best of History, http://www.besthistorysites.net

Divided into eras, provides rates lists of links, lesson plans, maps, and art history. Created by Thomas Daccord, academic technology specialist and history teacher at the Noble & Greenough School in Dedham, Massachusetts, U.S.A., and President of the Center for Teaching History With Technology.

British History, http://www.history.uk.com

More than 28,000 listings of history-related organizations and experts in the U.K. Also has news, contests, and a neat searchable timeline of British history from 10,000 BC to the present. There are even recipes! From the University of Sussex, U.K.

Canadian Broadcasting Corporation Archives, http://archives.cbc.ca

If you are interested in Canadian history, this is the site to bookmark. It has everything from radio and video clips to today in history. Coverage includes people, conflict and war, arts and entertainment, politics and economy, life and society, disasters and tragedies, science and technology, and sport.

Collect Britain: Putting History in Its Place, http://www.collect britain.co.uk

This "panorama of images from the British Library's famous collections" is their biggest digitization project. There are collections, virtual exhibits, themed tours, a pick of the week, and a newspaper search feature. Included are maps, prints, drawings, photos, documents, and early sound recordings.

A Common Place, an Uncommon Voice, http://www.common-place.org

Sponsored by the American Antiquarian Society, Worcester, Massachusetts, U.S.A., and the Florida State University Department of History, Tallahassee, U.S.A., this online magazine has articles and columns to "take you on a tour of what's best in early American scholarship, teaching, and curatorship." There's even the "Common-Place Coffeeshop," an electronic discussion list and searchable archives. I was fascinated by one of the articles in the July 2004 issue: "Samson Occom at the Mohegan Sun: Finding history at a New England Indian casino." Now you historians have a good excuse to go to the casino— research.

Digital History, http://www.digitalhistory.uh.edu

I can't remember when I was so excited about a Web site. If you have any interest in American history at all, you will be fascinated with all the material on the site from the University of Houston (Texas), Chicago Historical Society (Illinois), Gilder Lehrman Institute of American History (New York, New York), Project for the Active Teaching of American History (Houston, Texas), Museum of Fine Arts of Houston, and the National Park Service. The site is divided into an online textbook, primary sources (such as court cases, historic newspapers, and other documents), ethnic voices (slaves and Mexican-, Asian-, and Native-Americans), materials especially for teachers (including lesson plans and handouts), active learning (create your own exhibits), multimedia (e-lectures, film trailers, games, and music), an interactive timeline, visual history, virtual exhibitions, special topics (ethnic American, science and technology, among others), and a history reference room. You can even "Ask the Hyperhistorian," Prof. Steven Mintz of the University of Houston. Set aside a lot of time to explore this site.

Early Americas Digital Archive, http://www.mith2.umd.edu:8080/eada/index.jsp

Electronic texts dating from 1492 to 1820 by and about early settlers, explorers, and political and religious leaders. Searchable links by author. From the Maryland Institute for Technology in the Humanities, University of Maryland, College Park, U.S.A.

Edgar Governo, Historian of Things That Never Were, http://www.mts.net/~arphaxad/history.html

This neat site has links to timelines for television shows (*Buffy the Vampire Slayer, Star Trek, Alias, West Wing*), movies (*Indiana Jones, Star Wars*), comics and video games. From Edgar Governo, Winnipeg, Manitoba, Canada.

Got a History Question? http://chnm.gmu.edu/tools/h-bot/

A work in progress, H-bot, is a tool for answering history reference questions. For instance, ask it "who was Lincoln?" and you may or may not get the right answer, but ask, "Who was Abraham Lincoln?" gives the correct information—you need to be rather specific. Answers are rather short, but useful. From the Center for History and New Media, George Mason University, Fairfax, Virginia, U.S.A.

Historical Timelines, http://www.worldhistory.com/populartimelines.htm

Need to compare when various events happened? This neat site will help. There are timelines for science, people, the Great Wall of China, and the World Trade Center bombings. Also at the main site is information on various wars, U.S.A. and world history, famous people, top 10 lists, etc.

On This Day, http://www.nytimes.com/learning/general/onthisday

Has a long list of events on this date, with some of the more important described in one paragraph, plus current and historic birthdays. Part of the New York Times Learning Network, which also links to resources for students (news summaries, daily news quiz, word of the day), teachers (lesson plans, issues in depth, crossword puzzles), and parents (conversation starters, movie guide, discussion topics).

Open Video Project, http://www.open-video.org

Video clips include historical figures and events, lectures, documentaries, and lots of material from NASA (National Aeronautics and Space Administration; hurricanes, wetlands, earthquakes). Searchable and browsable and brought to you by the University of Chapel Hill, North Carolina, U.S.A.

The Story of Africa, http://www.bbc.co.uk/worldservice/africa/features/storyofafrica

This is a beautiful site with text, photos, and audio files. The producer, the British Broadcasting Company, "tells the history of the continent from an African perspective." It is well worth spending an hour or two here.

Today in History, http://lcweb2.loc.gov/ammem/today/today.html

An absolutely fascinating site that provides a page from the American Memory collection at the U.S. Library of Congress every day, plus appropriate links.

PSYCHOLOGY

PsycARTICLES, http://www.apa.org/psycarticles/

The American Psychological Association, the Canadian Psychological Association, and Hogrefe & Huber provide full-text articles from their journals. Searching and browsing abstracts are free, but full-text costs USD11.95.

RELIGION

Adherents.com, http://www.adherents.com

"A growing collection of over 41,000 adherent statistics and religious geography citations, references to published membership/adherent statistics and congregation statistics for over 4,200 religions, denominations, religious bodies, faith groups, tribes, cultures, movements, ultimate concerns, etc."

BeliefNet, http://www.beliefnet.com

"A multi-faith e-community." But what I like best is that you can sign up for the Religious Joke of the Day—they're really good.

Congregational Resource Guide, http://www.congregationalresources. org/

News and resources for all congregations on issues like building programs, administration, leadership, congregational vitality, and more. From the Alban Institute, Herndon, Virginia and Indianapolis (Indiana) Center for Congregations, U.S.A.

Internet Sacred Text Archive, http://www.sacred-texts.com

Sacred texts, poetry, and myths of the world's religions, not just the major ones, but those of the ancient near east, Native Americans, neo-paganism, the tarot, Greek, Roman, and Norse mythology, Baha'I, Nostradomus, and more. Another useful feature is the hyperlinked timeline of sacred texts. Based in Santa Cruz, California, U.S.A.

Papal Encylicals Online, http://www.papalencyclicals.net

Searchable by papacy (beginning with Honorius III in 1216) or keywords. Only includes encyclicals or other official documents that are available online. Has definition of various papal documents and pictures of some Medieval church documents. From Catholic source.

URBAN PLANNING AND GEOGRAPHY

All the World's Maps, http://www.embassyworld.com/maps/maps.html

National maps, maps of major cities, links to city maps, directories of embassy and consulate locations, information on visas, etc. From various sources.

American Planning Association, http://www.planning.org

Searchable index of articles, legislation tracking, guides to policy statements, and links to many planning sites.

Blank and Outline Maps, http://geography.about.com/cs/blankoutline maps

Printable outline maps of the world, continents, regions, countries, U.S.A. states, and Canadian provinces. Free for educational or personal use. From Scott Kurnit and About.Com (now part of PRIMEDIA Inc., which is now a part of the New York Times empire).

Cyburbia: The Urban Planning Portal, http://www.cyburbia.org/directory

Everything from bulletin boards and electronic lists to classes to professional organizations dealing with urban planning, community and economic development, housing, history and preservation, land use and zoning, and transportation. As of February 2005 they had 1,858 links in 473 categories. Maintained by its founder, Dan Tasman, Painesville, Ohio, U.S.A.

GEsource Geography and Environment Gateway, http://www.gesource. ac.uk/home.html

Aimed at the higher-education sector, this U.K. portal "includes a core database of high-quality Internet resources for Geography and the Environment catalogued by subject specialists." There are also links to databases, reference sources, timelines, career and job information, and training materials. As of February 2005 there were 6,652 resources. From the Library at the University of Manchester, England.

KnowledgePlex, http://www.knowledgeplex.org

This site will be of interest to most local government officials (in the U.S.A. at least). Provided by the Fannie Mae Foundation, Washington, DC, U.S.A., the information comes from the various partners, including the American Planning Association, the Enterprise Foundation, National Conference of Black Mayors, U.S. Conference of Mayors, and the Urban Institute, to name just a few. Sections include a calendar, discussion boards, expert chats, multimedia, top news stories (from LexisNexis—more than 1,500 as of February 2005), the week in review, and a free weekly newsletter. Documents include case studies, best practices, and scholarly articles, all searchable. Topics covered are: affordable housing, development and finance, economic revitalization, fair housing, homelessness, home ownership, mortgage markets, land use, housing, planning, organizational development, personal finance and asset creation, and public housing. Registration is requested and free, but not required.

Map History: History of Cartography, http://www.maphistory.info

Find information about old maps, both on the Web and in collections. Also information on cartography conferences, discussion lists, exhibitions, research, map collecting and collections, thefts, journals, and Web articles. There are no pictures of maps on this site, but links to image sites. From Tony Campbell, Institute of Historical Research, University of London, U.K.

Official City Sites, http://www.officialcitysites.org

Links to Web sites for cities in Australia, Canada, France, Germany, Japan, The Netherlands, New Zealand, the U.K., and the U.S.A.

Search for a Town—Any Town, http://www.epodunk.com

This site has profiles of about 25,000 communities in the U.S.A. It also has information on counties, airports, cemeteries, colleges, museums, and newspapers. You can search by town or use already set-up reports or rankings, such as "best places if you're 50 and gay," Single men and women, by county," or "walkable small towns." Once you find a community, you get everything from latitude and longitude to population, to attractions, census detail, economy, events, restaurants, doctors and dentists, history, obituaries, aerial photos, ZIP codes, and weather. Based in the not-so-small town of Ithaca, New York, U.S.A.

U.S. Environmental Protection Agency Violations, http://www.epa.gov/echo

Put in a ZIP code or city and find what companies have been inspected and which have environmental violations. Very interesting.

Vital Communities: Community Revitalization and Reinvention, http://www.vitalcommunities.com

From the Davenport (Iowa, U.S.A.) Public Library, this site has loads of links on community planning and cooperation. It is divided into Creating Community, Smart Growth, The New Urbanism, Sustainable Communities, Planning and Funding, and Resources. Seems quite comprehensive.

Water Resources of the United States, http://water.usgs.gov

If you need to know anything about water in the U.S.A., this is where to look. It has data, maps, software, publications, glossaries, and—in WaterWatch—information on floods, drought, streamflow, groundwater, and water projects. Very complete and easy to use. From the U.S. Geological Survey, Washington, DC.

OTHER WEB SITES

Anthropological Index Online, http://aio.anthropology.org.uk/aio/AIO.html

This is the searchable index of the current periodicals held by the Anthropology Library at the British Museum. The site is owned by the Royal Anthropological Institute.

Center for Spatially Integrated Social Science, http://www.csiss.org/resources/litsearch.html

A user-searchable database of more than 17,000 bibliographical references that feature aspects of Spatial Analysis techniques in the social sciences. The Center is at the University of California, Santa Barbara, U.S.A.

CRInfo2000: The Conflict Resolution Information Source, http://www.crinfo.org

Produced by the Conflict Research Consortium, University of Colorado, U.S.A., here you can find resources for adversaries, bystanders, students, educators, practitioners, and researches, including FAQs. Links, grant news, daily tips, books, and networking.

HEARTH (Home Economics Archive: Research, Tradition, History), http://hearth.library.cornell.edu

A core electronic collection of books and journals in Home Economics and related disciplines published between 1850 and 1925.

The full text of these materials, as well as bibliographies and essays, are available. Subjects covered are: applied arts and design; child care, human development, and family studies; clothing and textiles; food and nutrition; home management; housekeeping and etiquette; housing, furnishing, and home equipment; hygiene; institutional management (the hospitality industry); retail and consumer studies; and teaching and communication. Courtesy of the Cornell University Library, Ithaca, New York, U.S.A.

Selected Web Resources for Statistics in the Social Sciences, http://www.library.uiuc.edu/edx/webstats.htm

From the University of Illinois at Urbana-Champaign (U.S.A.) Library.

Social Science Research Network, http://www.ssrn.com

An abstract database of more than 87,600 scholarly working papers and forthcoming papers and an electronic paper collection with about 62,000 downloadable full-text documents in Adobe Acrobat PDF format (numbers as of February 2005). The eLibrary also includes the research papers of a number of fee-based partners. Divided into accounting, economics, financial economics, information systems, legal scholarship, management research, marketing research, negotiations research, and social insurance research networks. Based in Rochester, New York, U.S.A.

Social Work Statistical Sources, http://infodome.sdsu.edu/research/guides/socialwork/swstats.shtml

From the library at San Diego State University, California, U.S.A.

SOSIG, http://www.sosig.ac.uk

The Social Science Information Gateway provides annotated links to a wide variety of trusted resources (Web sites, databases, journal contents pages, full-text resources, etc.) in the social sciences, business and law. It is part of the U.K. Resource Discovery Network.

Tourism and Leisure Statistical Sources, http://www.uwe.ac.uk/ library/resources/tour/tourstat.htm

Links to U.K. tourism statistics from the Civil Aviation Authority, Department of Transport, Economist Intelligence Unit, National Statistics Office, U.K. Research Liaison Group (national tourist boards), Visit Britain, and international tourism statistics from Euromonitor, Eurostat, the International Air Transport Association, the International Civil Aviation Organisation, and the World Tourism Organisation. From the University of West England, Bristol, U.K.

19

Miscellaneous

CALCULATORS OF ALL KINDS

Convert-me.com, http://www.convert-me.com

The standards (weight, mass, length, volume, area, etc.) plus computer storage units, relative temperatures, and links to other conversion sites. Produced by a husband and wife team, Sergey and Anna Gershteins.

Dictionary of Measures, Units and Conversions, http://www.ex.ac.uk/cimt/dictunit/dictunit.htm

Descriptions of units of measurement, with conversion factors and a conversion calculator. From the Centre for Innovation in Mathematics Teaching, University of Exeter, Devon, U.K. For obscure or historical measures, try the Dictionary of Units of Measurement, http://www.unc.edu/~rowlett/units/ from the University of North Carolina at Chapel Hill, U.S.A.

Institute of Chemistry's Conversion of Units, http://www.chemie.fu-berlin.de/chemistry/general/units_en.html

From the Freie Universitat Berlin, Germany, conversion factors for many, many units (no conversions done, however).

Salary Calculator, http://www.homefair.com/homefair/calc/salcalc.
html

Compare the cost of living between two cities, mostly U.S.A., but
also Canada and other countries. From the National Association of
Realtors, Chicago, Illinois, U.S.A.

The Universal Currency Converter, http://www.xe.com/ucc/

Easy to use, uses up-to-the-minute conversion rates. This is the one
I use. From XE.com Currency Services, Canada.

Web Pages that Perform Statistical Calculations!, http://members.
aol.com/johnp71/javastat.html

From John C. Pezzullo, Retired Associate Professor in the
Departments of Pharmacology and Biostatistics at Georgetown
University, in Washington, DC, U.S.A.

FUN STUFF

Board Game Central, http://boardgamecentral.com

"This site is a central resource for board game information, rules,
software and links." It has a few too many "order this game here" links
for my taste, but there is good stuff on everything from backgammon
to How to Host a Teen Mystery (party), to Candyland. By Randy Rasa
of Olathe, Kansas, U.S.A.

Cool Quiz, http://www.coolquiz.com/trivia/

Need your daily fix of trivia? Here's the site for you. It also provides
a daily quote, word of the day, a cartoon, Today in History, a trivia
directory, a quote directory, various quizzes and puzzles, bad predictions (see below), "The Name's Familiar," and country-specific trivia
for the U.S.A., Canada, and Great Britain. What more could you ask of
a site? From a husband-wife team in Jamison, Pennsylvania, U.S.A. A
sample bad prediction: "The modern gasoline-powered car will disappear ... Around the turn of the century, we will indeed run out of a few
key things, like fuel. Hence, in 1984 or 2000 we will still be running

around in cars—but not the type we now use." Richard Farmer, *The Real World of 1984*, 1973.

Europeans: Who Are the Sexiest? Rudest? Funniest?, http://www.readersdigest.co.uk/magazine/europeans04.htm

Readers' Digest magazine (Pleasantville, New York, U.S.A.) surveyed nearly 4,000 people in 19 European countries in to see how they felt about each other. The results are sometimes predictable—Germans are the most efficient—and sometimes surprising—the most-liked are the Italians. The complete results are available along with the summary article.

The Left Hand, http://www.thelefthand.com

For products for the left-handers among us, this site sells items such as scissors, notebooks, knives, measuring cups, etc. From a company in Fort Myers, Florida, U.S.A.

Measure 4 Measure, http://www.wolinskyweb.net/measure.htm

"A collection of interactive sites on the Web that estimate, calculate, evaluate, translate, etc. In other words, they do the work for you." Divided into Science and Math, Health, Finances, All 'Round the House, and "A Measure of Everything Else." Check out Judi Wolinsky's (Homewood [Illinois, U.S.A.] Public Library) other sites: Word Play (http://www.wolinskyweb.net/word.htm) and Serendipitous Sites—sites found while looking for something else—http://www.homewoodlibrary.org/serendip.htm

The Phobia List, http://www.phobialist.com

All about phobias, including an indexed list, how phobias are named, categories, treatment, and quotes. From Fredd Culbertson, who also has a neat page explaining the relationships of cousins (what second cousin twice removed means) at http://www.sonic.net/~fredd/cousins.html.

Solitaire Central, http://www.solitairecentral.com

Everything you ever wanted to know about solitaire and many other online card games. You can download more ways to "waste" your time and keep your carpal tunnel syndrome active. By Randy Rasa of Olathe, Kansas, U.S.A.

TRAVEL

Seat Guru, http://www.seatguru.com

Do you want to find the most comfortable seat on the plane for your next trip? This site will help you identify good, marginal, and bad seats on most planes on most U.S. airlines (and some non-U.S. as well). It also shows you where the power outlets are and what audio or video you can expect. By Matthew Daimler, Seattle, Washington, U.S.A., a frequent flier and avid traveler.

Werner's "Not Disney" Theme Parks, Fairs, and Amusement Parks, http://www.yesterland.com/parklinks.html

This site has links to sites covering theme park history, directories, world's fairs, attraction design, and engineering, and theme parks other than Disney properties. There are also links to his pages on just Disney theme parks and Yesterland, "featuring discontinued Disneyland attractions."

World Electric Guide: Electricity Around the World, http://kropla.com/ electric.htm

Check out voltage, type of plugs, etc. From Steve Kropla, who also has other good resources at http://www.kropla.com

OTHER USEFUL SITES

America's Most Literate Cities, http://www.uww.edu/npa/cities

Rankings of U.S. cities with population of 200,000 or more based on education, publications, newspapers, libraries, and booksellers. The top five? Minneapolis, Seattle, Pittsburgh, Madison, and Cincinnati. The top five in library support, holdings, and use: Akron (Ohio), Kansas City (Missouri), St. Louis, Pittsburgh, and Columbus (Ohio).

Jack Miller, chancellor of the University of Wisconsin-Whitewater, U.S.A., is author of the study

Calendars of Holidays and Observances, http://www.butlerwebs.com/holidays/calendar.htm

This site has a grid with U.S. federal and other holidays for 2003–2005. Although billed as "bizarre, crazy, silly, unknown holidays and observances," this is really a good site with observances by month. There is also a page of links to other sites with holiday information and holidays by months, http://www.brownielocks.com. Produced by ButlerWebs.com, Chicora, Pennsylvania, U.S.A. A similar site is found at http://www.religioustolerance.org/main_day.htm. It has the main holy days for Christianity, Judaism, Islam, Hinduism, Buddhism, Sikhism, Baha'i World Faith, and Wicca. The site also has links to various articles and sites dealing with religious tolerance. This one is from the Ontario (Canada) Consultants on Religious Tolerance.

Classical Cooking Glossary, http://www.masterfoods.com.au/cookbook/glossary.asp

Translations and explanations of many food terms, news, a virtual recipe book, information on herbs and spices, and recipes—from food vendor Masterfoods, a division of Mars, Inc., West Chester, Pennsylvania, U.S.A.

Horse Sense, http://www.equineinfo.com

Sponsored by Flying Rose Ranch (Waco, Texas, U.S.A.) thoroughbreds, this searchable site has information about breeds and breeding, basic horsemanship, events, racing, bloodlines, equipment, training, and horse-related projects.

20

Bibliography and Sources Cited

This is a list of sources with comments on particular books or articles of interest. To help you to find or order these sources, ISBN numbers are sometimes included.

Abram, Stephen. 1997. Post Information Age Positioning for Special librarians: Is Knowledge Management the Answer? In SLA, *Knowledge Management: A New Competitive Asset*. Washington, DC: Special Libraries Association.

Alencar, Maria Cleofas F. 1996. Personal communication, Professor of Library Science, Pontificia Universidade, Catolica de Campenas, Sao Paolo, Brazil.

Allen, Sydney K., and Heather S. Miller. 2000. Libraries on the Book Buying Merry-go-round: Internet Bookseller vs. Library Book Vendor. *Against the Grain* 12(2):1, 1618, 1620, 1622.

Alsop, Stewart. 1995. If You Think Information Is Free, You Must Have Stolen this Column from Someone (Column: Distributed Thinking). *InfoWorld* 17(49):126.

Anderson, M. Elaine, and Patricia T. Pawl. 1979. When You Are the Staff: Tips for Managing a Small Library/media/learning Center. *Wisconsin Library Bulletin* 75:271–274.

Appel, L. 1996. Personal communication.

Arist, Suzanne. 2004. Non-Traditional Library Careers: Interview with Solo Military History Librarian Jill Postma. *Membrain*, 17 March, http://www.slaillinois.org/membrain/modules.php?name=News&file =article&sid=19 (retrieved 1 January 2005)

Austin, Rhea. 1996. Personal communication, 1996–1997 Chair of the SOLO Librarians Division.

Australian Institute of Criminology. Existence and Purpose of Prison Libraries. *Australian Prison Libraries: Minimum Standard Guidelines,* http://www.aic.gov.au/research/corrections/standards/ PrisonLibraries/existence.html (retrieved 5 February 2005).

Baker, Brian L. 1995. Librarians Online Might Get Entangled in the Web. *National Law Journal* 2:B13–14.

Bates, Mary Ellen. 1997. Avoiding the Ax: How to Keep From Being Downsized or Outsourced. *Information Outlook* 1(10):18–21.

Bauwens, Michel. 1993. The Emergence of the 'Cybrarian': A New Organizational Model for Corporate Libraries. *Business Information Review* 9(4):65–67.

Beckwith, Harry. 1997. *Selling the Invisible: A Field Guide to Modern Marketing*. New York: Warner Books, ISBN 0-46-52094-2.

Bender, David R. 1994. A Study of the Continuing Education Needs of SLA Members and Education Activities at SLA Conferences. Washington, DC: Special Libraries Association Board Memorandum.

Bierbaum, Esther G. 1986. Professional Education Doesn't Stop with your MLS. *The One-Person Library* 2(12):2. A *must-read* for all librarians.

Bluhdorn, Frances. 1996. OPALs. *Specialties* (ALIA [Australian Library and Information Association] Special Libraries Section, NSW Group) (18):6–8.

Bonaventura, Mike. 1997. The Benefits of a Knowledge Culture. *Aslib Proceedings* 49(4): 82–89, April and in SLA.

Bott, Ed. 1996. Internet Lies. *PC Computing*, October. (Quoted in *Library Journal* 122(20):39.)

Brandt, D. Scott. 1996. Evaluating Information on the Internet. *Computers in Libraries* 16(5):44–46.

Brinkman, Rick, and Rick Kirschner. 1994. *Dealing With People You Can't Stand: How to Bring Out the Best in People at their Worst*. New York: McGraw-Hill, ISBN 0-07-007838-6.

Broadbent, Marianne. 1997. The Emerging Phenomenon of Knowledge Management. *Australia Library Journal* 46(1):6–24.

—————. 1998. The Phenomenon of Knowledge Management: What Does It Mean to the Information Professional? *Information Outlook* 2(5):23–36.

Bryant, Sue Lacey. 1995. *Personal Professional Development and the SOLO Librarian* (Library Training Guides). London: Library Association Publishing, ISBN 1-85604-141-7.

—————. 1999. Interesting Times for Solos in the U.K. *The One-Person Library* 16(7):4–5.

Buchanan, Leigh. 1999. The Smartest Little Company in the World. *Inc.* 21(1):42–54. (Cover story on the Highsmith Company and its librarian's close working relationship with the President.)

Caldwell, Bruce. 1996. The New Outsourcing Partnership. *Information Week* (585):50.

Callea, Donna. 2004. Romance Novels, Legal References Best Sellers Behind Bars. *Tallahasse.com*, http://www.tallahassee.com/mld/Tallahassee/news/local/8681506.html (retrieved 5 January 2005).

Coccia, Cynthia. 1998. Avoiding a 'Toxic' Organization. *Nursing Management* 29(5):32–33, May.

Collins, William. Inmate Rights and Privileges: Access to the Courts. *Association of State Correctional Administrators Contracting Manual*, pp. 61–62, http://www.asca.net/public/contract.pdf (retrieved 5 January 2005).

Corcoran, Mary, Lynn Dagar, and Anthea Stratigos. 2000. The Changing Roles of Information Professionals: Excerpts from an Outsell, Inc. Study. *Online* 24(2):28–34.

Corrall, Sheila M. 1995. Strategic Management of Information Resources: Planning for a Better Future. *The Law Librarian* 26(3):399–403.

Costanzo, Emauela. "ABC" and the Italian Prison Libraries. *World Library and Information Congress: 69th IFLA General Conference and Council, August 2003, Berlin, Germany*, http://wotan.liu.edu/dois/data/Papers/juljuljin5086.html (retrieved 5 January 2005).

Cram, Jennifer. 1995. Moving from Cost Centre to Profitable Investment: Managing the Perception of a Library's Worth. *Australasian Public Libraries and Information Services* 8(3):107–113.

Crawford, Walt. 2000. Principled Libraries: Finding Stability in Changing Times. *Online* 24(2):48–53.

Crawford, Walt, and Michael Gorman. 1995. *Future Libraries: Dreams, Madness, and Reality*. Chicago: American Library Association Editions, ISBN 0-8389-0647-8.

Cronin, Blaise, and Joan Williamson. 1988. One Person Libraries and Information Units: Their Education and Training Needs. *Library Management* 9(5):1–72.

Davenport, Thomas H., David W. DeLong, and Michael C. Beers. 1998. Successful Knowledge Management Projects. *Sloan Management Review* 39(2):43–57, Winter 1998. (Studies of 31 knowledge management projects in 24 companies.)

DiMattia, Susan. 1995. When the 'Dumb' Increases, Increase the Smarts, Sci-tech News. *Corporate Library Update* 4(15):4.

Drake, David. 1990. When Your Boss Isn't a Librarian. *American Libraries*, February 1990:152–153. (From an academic librarian but relevant to all.)

Duranceau, Ellen Finnie. 1997. Beyond Print: Revisioning Serials Acquisitions for the Digital Age, http://web.mit.edu/waynej/www/duranceau.htm (retrieved 11 September 2000).

Eiblum, Paula. 1995. The Coming of Age of Document Delivery. *Bulletin of the American Society for Information Science* 21(3):21–22.

Eide-Jensen, Inger. 1977. The One-man Library. *Scandinavian Public Library Quarterly* 10(1):15–17.

Ferguson, Elizabeth, and Emily R. Mobley. 1984. *Special Libraries at Work*. Hamden, CT: Library Professional Publications, ISBN 0-208-01939-1.

Ferguson, Tony. 1996. The "L" Word. *Against the Grain* 8(2):80, 89.

Ferner, Jack D. 1995. Successful Time Management: A Self-Teaching Guide, 2nd Edition. New York: Wiley.

Field, Judith J. 1997. Information+Technology+You Equals Knowledge Management. In SLA.

Fletcher, Lloyd Alan. 1996. The New Economics of Online. *Searcher* 4(5):30–44.

Flynn, Louise. 2000. Personal communication.

Foy, Patricia S. 1997. Lessons from the Field—Part I. In SLA.

Garman, Nancy. 1996. Be a Savvy Online Consumer. *Online User*, July–August:5.

Gervino, Joan. 1995. Establishing Fees for Service. *Marketing Treasures* 8(3):4–6.

Gilder, George. 1996. Feasting on the Giant Peach. *Forbes ASAP*, August 26:85–96.

Gillies, Malcolm. 2000. Cybraries Will Gather No Dust. *The Australian*, http://news.com.au (retrieved 2 August 2000).

Gorman, Michael. 1995. The Corruption of Cataloging. *Library Journal* (120):34.

—————. 1996. Dreams, Madness and Reality: The Complicated World of Human Recorded Communication. *Against the Grain* 8(1):1,16–18.

Griffiths, Jose-Marie. 1996. Presentation at Betty Burrows Memorial Seminar, Cleveland Ohio, USA, 19 April.

Griffiths, Jose-Marie, and Donald W. King. 1993. *Special Libraries: Increasing the Information Edge.* Washington, DC: Special Libraries Association, ISBN 0-87111-414-3.

Hadden, R. Lee, 1991. *An Appeal to Heavenly Library Patrons.* Reston, VA: U.S. Geological Society Library.

Hammerly, Hernan D. 1999. The Success and Education of Professional Librarians: A Study of Correlations Between Occupational Success and Some Educational Factors as Perceived by a Group of Argentine Librarians. Ph.D. Dissertation, Ann Arbor, MI: The University of Michigan.

Hane, Paula J. 2005. Wrapping Up 2004; Looking Forward. *Information Today Newsbreaks*, http://www.infotoday.com/newsbreaks/nb050103-1.shtml (retrieved 3 January 2005).

Harrison, Paige M. and Allen J. Beck. 2004. *Prisoners in 2003, Bureau of Justice Statistics Bulletin.* Washington, DC: U.S. Department of Justice, Office of Justice Programs, November, http://www.ojp.usdoj.gov/bjs/pub/pdf/p03.pdf (retrieved 6 March 2005).

Hart, Clare. 2000. There's a New Librarian in Town ... [guest editorial]. *The Electronic Library* 18(3):169–170. (President and CEO, Factiva.)

Healy, Leigh Watson and David Curle. 2004. Outlook 2005: Power Play In the Information Industry. *InfoAboutInfo* No. 7, from Outsell, Inc., 17 December.

Kanter, Rosabeth Moss, 1997. *Rosabeth Moss Kanter on the Frontiers of Management.* Cambridge, MA: Harvard Business School Press, ISBN 0-87584-802-8.

Kearns, Kevin. 1997. Managing Upward. *Information Outlook* 1(10):23–28.

Kennedy, Toni. 2000. Personal communication.

Koenig, Michael E.D. 1997. Intellectual Capital and How to Leverage It. In SLA.

Knapp, Ellen. 1998. Keynote Speech, European Business Information Conference. In Lettis, Lucy. Be Proactive—Communicate Your Worth to Management. *Information Outlook* 3(1):25–29.

Knudsen, Mark. How My Library Affected My Life in Prison. *Education Libraries* 24(1):20, 2000. By an inmate.

Knusen, Kurt. 1985. The Norwegian Library Service: The Advantages and Disadvantages of Small Units. *Scandinavian Public Library Quarterly* 18(3):71–73.

Kurtz, Patricia L. 1994. *The Global Speaker: An English Speaker's Guide to Making Presentations Around the World.* New York: Amacom/American Management Association, ISBN 0-8144-7878-6.

Ladner, Sharyn. 1996. Personal communication, 27 January.

LaForte, Susan R. 1982. Information Brokers: Friend and/or Foe? *Public Library Quarterly* 3:83–91.

Lehmann, Vibeke. 2003. The Right to Read. In Schneider.

Leibovich, Lori. 2000. Choosing Quick Hits Over the Card Catalog. *New York Times* 10 August, http://www.nytimes.com/library/tech/00/08/circuits/articls/10thin.html (retrieved 10 August 2000).

Lemon, Marjorie. 1997. Prison Libraries Change Lives. *Information Outlook* 1(11), November.

Library Association. *The Code of Ethics.* London: The Library Association.

Liebowitz, Jay. 1995. A Look Towards Valuating Knowledge. In Line.

Line, Maurice B. 1995. Is Strategic Planning Outmoded? *Alexandria* 77(3):135–139.

LITA (Library and Information Technology Association, of the American Library Association). 2000. Top Technology Trends, http://www.lita.org/committee/toptech/mw2000.htm (retrieved 15 May 2000).

Local School Libraries Struggle While Prison Libraries Get Millions. WFTV.com, http://www.wftv.com/print/3302191/detail.html (retrieved 5 January 2005).

Macintosh, A. 1998. Organisational Knowledge Management, Position Paper on Knowledge Asset Management, http://www.aiai.ed.ac.uk/~alm/kam.htm (retrieved 3 January 2005).

Mackenzie, Alec. 1990. *The Time Trap*. New York: American Management Association, ISBN 0-8144-5969-2.

Martin, Mary C. 2000. Managing Your Library's Computer Nerds. *Computers in Libraries* 19(2):8, 10.

Matarazzo, James M., and Miriam A. Drake. 1994. *Information for Management: A Handbook*. Washington, DC: Special Libraries Association, ISBN 0-87111-427-5.

Merry, Susan A. 1994. How to Talk to Senior Management. In James M. Matarazzo and Miriam A. Drake, eds. *Information for Management: A Handbook*, Washington, DC: Special Libraries Association.

Metcalfe, Bob. 1995. Predicting the Internet's Catastrophic Collapse and Ghost Sites Galore in 1996. *InfoWorld* 17(49):61.

Mickey, Bill. 2000. Thrive or Survive. *Online* 24(2):6–7.

Morgan, Eric Lease. 1999. Libraries of the Future: Springboards for Strategic Planning. *Computers in Libraries* 19(1):32–33.

Morgenstern, Evelin. 1999. From 'Excuse Me Please, I Am Only ...' To on Everyone's Lips: One-person Librarians and One-person Libraries in Germany. *The One-Person Library* 15(11):6–8.

—————. 2000. Personal communication, July and August.

Muir, Robert F. 1993. Marketing Your Library or Information Service to Business. *Online* 17(4):41–46.

Nicolson, Marion. 1998. The Remaking of Librarians in the Knowledge Era: Skills to Meet Future Requirements. *Education for Library and Information Services: Australia (ELIS:A)*, 15(1):33–35, May.

O'Donnell, William S. 1976. The Vulnerable Corporate Special Library/information Center: Minimizing the Risks. *Special Libraries* 67:179–187.

O'Leary, Mick. 1987. The Information Broker: A Modern Profile. *Online* 11:24–30. Eleven interviews.

————. 2000. New Roles Come of Age. *Online* 24(2):20–25.

Oxbrow, Nigel, and Angela Abell. 1997. *Putting Knowledge to Work: What Skills and Competencies are Required?* Washington, DC: Special Libraries Association.

————. 1998. The Role Of Information Management In Knowledge Management: Stimulating Creativity And Innovation Through Information, Continuing Education course. American Society for Information Science, Pittsburgh, Pennsylvania, 25 Oct 1998.

Paris, Marion, and Herbert S. White. 1986. Mixed Signals and Painful Choices: The Education of Special Librarians. *Special Libraries* 77(4):207–212.

Paul, Meg, and Sandra Crabtree. 1995. *Strategies for Special Libraries*. *SMR Special Report 1*. New York: SMR International.

Penniman, W. David. 1999. Strategic Planning to Avoid Bottlenecks in the Age of the Internet. *Computer in Libraries* 19(1):50–53.

Perelman, Lewis J. 1997. DYNAMIC Ignorance. In SLA.

Peters, Tom. 1998. Interview. In Diane Cyr. The guru game. *Attache* (U.S. Airways Magazine), September:34–37.

Pitts, Roberta L. 1994. A Generalist in the Age of Specialists: A Profile of the One-person Library Director. *Library Trends* 43(1):121–135.

Pollar, Odette. 1996. *365 Ways to Simplify Your Work Life*. Chicago: Dearborn, ISBN 0-7931-2281-3.

Prison Library, *LiveJournal* list, http://www.livejournal.com/community/libraries/360441.html (retrieved 5 January 2005).

Prusak, Laurence (Larry). 1993. Blow Up the Corporate Library. *International Journal of Information Management* 13:405–412.

————. 1994. Corporate Libraries: A Soft Analysis, a Warning, and Some Generic Advice. In James M. Matarazzo and Miriam A. Drake, eds. *Information for Management: A Handbook*, Washington, DC: Special Libraries Association.

Prusak, Laurence, and James M. Matarazzo. 1990. Tactics for Corporate Library Success. *Library Journal* 115(15):45–46. (A survey of 164 larger U.S. companies.)

————. 1995. The Value of Corporate Libraries: The 1995 Survey. *SpeciaList*, November:9, 15.

Purifoy, Randy. 2000. You Are Here: A Guided Tour of the Oshkosh Correctional Institution Prison Library. *Education Libraries* 24(1):18–29 (by an inmate, with map)

Quint, Barbara. 1991. Connect Time. *Wilson Library Bulletin*, November:59.

————. 1995. Competition. *Searcher* 3(10):1.

————. 1996a. Disintermediation. *Searcher* 4(1):4, 6.

————. 1996b. Professional associations react to the challenge. *Searcher* 4(5):8–18.

Raitt, D. 1994. The Future of Libraries in the Face of the Internet. *Electronic Library* 12(5):275–276.

Ravitch, Diane. Quoted in Leibovich, Lori. 2000. Choosing Quick Hits Over the Card Catalog. *New York Times* 10 August, http://www.nytimes.com/library/tech/00/08/circuits/articls/10thin.

html (retrieved10 August 2000). (Ravitch is a historian of education, New York University.)

Reprieve for Prison Libraries Following Protests by Librarians. *CILIP Library and Information Update*, December 2003, http://www. literacytrust.org.uk/Database/prisonlibs.html (retrieved 5 January 2005).

Riggs, Donald E., and Gordon A. Sabine. 1988. *Libraries in the '90s: What the Leaders Expect*. Phoenix, AZ: Oryx Press, ISBN 0-897-74532-9.

Rothstein, Samuel. 1985. Why People Really Hate Library Schools. *Library Journal* 110(1):41–48.

St. Clair, Guy. 1976. The One-Person Library: An Essay on Essentials. *Special Libraries* 67(3):233–238.

————. 1987. The One-Person Library: An Essay on Essentials Re-visited. *Special Libraries* 78(4):263–270.

————. 1989. Interpersonal Networking: It is Who You Know. *Special Libraries* 80(2):107–112.

————. 1993. To Memo or Not to Memo? *The One-Person Library* 10(1):6.

————. 1994. A Tale of Two Corporate Libraries. *InfoManage* 1(3):6–7.

————. 1995a. When You Downsize: Focus, Connect and Network. *InfoManage* 2(6):8.

————. 1995b. Trish Foy: Matching Corporate Information Services to Corporate Information Needs. *InfoManage* 2(11):1–5.

————. 1995c. *Finances and Value: How the One-Person Library is Paid For*. *SMR Special Report 5*. New York: SMR International.

————. 1995d. How Well Do You Know Your Boss? *The One-Person Library* 11(12):3.

————. 1996a. The OPL Profile: Joan Williamson. *The One-Person Library* 12(9):1–5.

————. 1996b. Real Estate Management: When It's Part of Your Job. *InfoManage* 3(2):6–7.

————. 1996c. *Dealing with Downsizing: A Guide for the Information Services Practitioner. SMR Special Report 6.* New York: SMR International.

————. 1996d. To Partner or Not to Partner? *The One-Person Library* 13(1):1–3.

————. 1996e. Not Waiting for it to Happen—Outsourcing. *The One-Person Library* 12(2):6–8.

————. 1997. *25 Years of One-Person Librarianship: Identity, Trends, and Effects.* New York: SMR International.

St. Clair, Guy, and Andrew Berner 1996. Insourcing: The Evolution of Information Delivery. *The One-Person Library* 13(4):1.

St. Clair, Guy, and Joan Williamson. 1992. *Managing the New One-Person Library.* New York: Bowker-Saur, ISBN 0-86291-630-5.

Saunders, Rebecca M. 2000. Asserting Yourself: How to Say 'No' and Mean It. *Harvard Communication Letter* 3(7):9–11.

Schement, Jorge Reina. 1996. A 21st Century Strategy for Librarians. *Library Journal* 121(8):34–36.

Schneider, Julia. 2003. Three Experts Describe How to be a Successful Prison Librarian: Preparation for a Foreign Land. *Interface* 25(3), 2003. (Web Companion Newsletter of the Association for Specialized and Cooperative Agencies, a Division of the ALA) http://www.ala.org/ala/ascla/asclapubs/interface/archives/contentlistingby/volume25/successprisonlib/howsuccessful.htm (retreived 5 January 2005). (From ALA conference in Toronto, articles by Viebeke Lehmann, "The Right to Read;" Naomi Angier, "YA Training Made to Order, Juvenile detention facility, Multnomah County, OR;" and Ann Curry, "Intellectual Freedom for Canadian Prisoners.")

Schneiderman, R.A. 1996. Why Librarians Should Rule the Net. *e-node* 1(4).

Shaffer, Roberta. 1996. The Future of the Law Library and Law Librarian. *LEXIS-NEXIS Information Professional Update* (3):37.

Shirley, Glennor L. 2003. Correctional Libraries, Library Standards, and Diversity. *Journal of Correctional Education* 54(2):70–74, June. (Shirley is the Library Coordinator, Maryland State Department of Education.)

Shuter, J. 1984. *The Information Worker in Isolation*. Bradford, UK: MCB University Press.

Siess, Judith A. 1997. *The SOLO Librarian's Sourcebook*. Medford, NJ: Information Today.

—————. 2003. *The Visible Librarian: Asserting Your Value With Marketing and Advocacy*. Chicago: ALA Editions, ISBN 0-8389-0848-9.

Singer, Glen 2000. Prison Libraries. *Bulletin of the Eastern Canada Chapter, SLA*, 66(1):8–14, Fall, http://www.sla.org/chapter/cecn/Archive/bulletin/Nov_2000 (retrieved 5 January 2005). (An excellent article, good description of a prison library.)

SLA (Special Libraries Association). 1992. *Presidential Study Commission on Professional Recruitment, Ethics and Professional Standards*. Washington, DC: Special Libraries Association.

SLA (Special Libraries Association). 1997. *Knowledge Management: A New Competitive Asset* (1997 SLA State-of-the-Art Institute). Washington, DC: Special Libraries Association, ISBN 0-87111-480-1.

Smock, Raymond W. 1995. What Promise Does the Internet Hold for Scholars? *The Chronicle of Higher Education* September 22: B1–2.

Spiller, David, Claire Creaser, and Alison Murphy. 1998. *Libraries in the Workplace. Library and Information Statistics Unit* (Occasional Paper 20, Department of Information and Library Studies). Loughborough, UK: Loughborough University, ISBN 1-901786-13-7.

Stathis, Andrew L. 1995. Technology Offers Incentive to Downsize Law Libraries. *The National Law Journal* 18(5):B9, B11. (President of architectural design firm specializing in law offices, not a librarian.)

Stear, Edward B. 1997. Outsourcing: Competitive Threat or Technology Trend? *Online* January/February 80. (Gartner Group Sr. Research Analyst.)

Svoboda, Olga. 1991. The Special Library as a Competitive Intelligence Center. *Electronic Library* 9(4/5):239–244.

Talley, Mary and Joan Axelroth. 2001. Talking About Customer Service. *Information Today* 5(12):6–13.

Taylor, R.M. 1996. Knowledge Management, http://ourworld. compuserve.com/homepages/roberttaylor/km.htm (retrieved 5 January 2005).

Tees, Miriam. 1986. Graduate Education for Special Librarians: What Special Libraries Are Looking for in Graduates. *Special Libraries* 77(4):190–197.

Tennant, Roy. 1999. Letter to the editor. *Library Journal* 124(17):8.

—————. 2001. The Convenience Catastrophe. *Library Journal* 126(20):39–30.

Tenopir, Carol. 2000. I Never Learned about that in Library School. *Online* 24(2):42–46.

Tillman, Hope. 1995. Personal communication.

Tomlin, Anne. 2000. The OPL Column. *National Network* 24(2):10. (Librarian, Auburn Memorial Hospital, Auburn, New York.)

Trefethen, Dan. 1996. Personal communication.

Vavrek, Bernard. 1987. Libraries Alone: The American Experience. In James Henri and Roy Sanders, eds. *Libraries Alone: Proceedings of the Rural and Isolated Librarians Conference*. Wagga Wagga, New South Wales, Australia: Libraries Alone, pp. 5–13.

Walsh, Virginia. 1998. ALIA Explores the Value of Libraries. *InCite* 19(4):6–7, 20–21. (Executive director, Australian Library and Information Association [ALIA].)

Weingand, Darlene E. 1994. Competence and the New Paradigm: Continuing Education of the Reference Staff. *The Reference Librarian* (43):173–182.

White, Herbert S. 1984. *Managing the Special Library: Strategies for Success Within the Larger Organization*. White Plains, NY: G.K. Hall, ISBN 0-86729-088-9.

————. 1988. Basic Competencies and the Pursuit of Equal Opportunity. *Library Journal* 113(12):56–57.

————. 1995. *At the Crossroads: Libraries on the Information Superhighway*. Englewood, CO: Libraries Unlimited, ISBN: 1-56308-165-2. (A collection of his writings from 1980 to 1994.)

————. 1997a. Planning and Evaluation. *Library Journal* 122(9):38–39.

————. 1997b. Getting the Word Out: Marketing Your Library's Information Services, Federal Library and Information Center Committee, Symposium on the Library Professional, December 1966. *FEDLINK Technical Notes* 15(1), January 1997.

White, Herbert S., and Sarah L. Mort. 1995. The Accredited Library Education Program as Preparation for Professional Library Work. In Herbert S. White, ed. *At the Crossroads: Libraries on the Information Superhighway*. Englewood, CO: Libraries Unlimited, ISBN: 1-56308-165-2, pp. 211–236.

Williamson, Joan. 1984. How to be an OMB. *Information and Library Manager* 4(2).

Wilson, Marsha, and Ellis Mount. 1997. Survival of the Fittest. *Sci-Tech News* November:19–23.

Working Woman. 1995. July:40, http://www.loc.gov/flicc/tn/97/01/tn9701.html (retrieved 26 October 2004).

Young, Ron. 1998. Cutting the Key to the Future (Interview). *Information World Review* (144):21, February.

Zamparelli, Roberto. 1999. Copyright and Global Libraries: Going with the Flow of Technology. First Monday (peer-reviewed Internet journal), http://www.firstmonday.org/issues/issue2_11/zamparelli/ (retrieved 5 July 2005).

About the Authors

Judith Siess was the publisher and editor of *The One-Person Library: A Newsletter for Librarians and Management*, which had an international circulation, from 1998 to 2006. She now writes the blog, OPL Plus (Not Just for OPLs Anymore), which can be read at http://opls.blogspot.com. She spent 16 years as a working librarian, most of the time as an OPL. She was the first chair of the Solo Librarians Division of the Special Library Association. She has visited and presented workshops to librarians all over the U.S.A. and in South Africa, Canada, Germany, England, Spain, Australia, and New Zealand. She is a member of the American Association of Law Libraries, Australian Library and Information Association, Canadian Library Association, Chartered Institute of Library and Information Professionals (U.K.), Church and Synagogue Library Association, Library and Information of New Zealand Aotearoa, Library and Information Association of South Africa, Medical Library Association, and Special Libraries Association. She received her MSLIS from the University of Illinois at Urbana-Champaign in 1982. Judith lives in Richmond Heights, Ohio (a suburb of Cleveland) with her husband, Steve Bremseth, and two cats, Harry Potter and Hermione Granger.

Judy is the author of five other books: *The SOLO Librarian's Sourcebook* (1997), *The OPL Sourcebook* (2001), *The Visible Librarian: Asserting Your Value with Marketing and Advocacy* (2003), and *The Essential OPL, 1998–2004: The Best of Seven Years of The One-Person*

Library: A Newsletter for Librarians and Management (2005). She has also written articles for several professional publications.

A product of the former College of Librarianship Wales, Aberystwyth, the editor of Part 2, **John Welford**, spent the first half of his career as a librarian in institutes of higher and further education in the U.K. In 1987 he returned to Aberystwyth to take a master's degree in computer applications for libraries and then changed direction toward the high-tech industrial sector, working as a solo librarian for H-P Labs and Marconi before being made redundant (laid off) in 2002. He now works as a freelance proofreader and indexer with a portfolio of customers that includes international students, a translator in Kazakhstan, the Dickens Fellowship, and *The One-Person Library*. He lives in central England with wife Sue, son David, and cat Edwy.

Index

417

More Great Books
from Information Today, Inc.

The Successful Academic Librarian
Winning Strategies from Library Leaders

Edited by Gwen Meyer Gregory

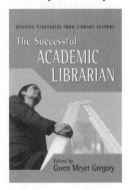

While every academic librarian works to meet the research needs of faculty and students, many are expected to assume other obligations as part of a faculty or tenure system—including publication, research, service, and professional activities. If this were not enough to test a librarian's mettle, the widely varying academic focuses and cultures of college and university libraries almost certainly will. This book, expertly edited by academic librarian, writer, and speaker Gwen Meyer Gregory, is an antidote to the stress and burnout that almost every academic librarian experiences at one time or another. Gregory and nearly 20 of her peers and mentors take a practical approach to a full range of critical topics facing the profession.

2005/256 pp/hardbound • ISBN 1-57387-232-6 • $39.50

The Librarian's Internet Survival Guide, 2nd Edition
Strategies for the High-Tech Reference Desk

By Irene E. McDermott
Edited by Barbara Quint; Foreword by Joseph Janes

In this updated and expanded second edition of her popular guidebook, Searcher columnist Irene McDermott once again exhorts her fellow reference librarians to don their pith helmets and follow her fearlessly into the Web jungle. She presents new and improved troubleshooting tips and advice, Web resources for answering reference questions, and strategies for managing information and keeping current. In addition to helping librarians make the most of Web tools and resources, the book offers practical advice on privacy and child safety, assisting patrons with special needs, Internet training, building library Web pages, and much more.

2006/328 pp/softbound • ISBN 0-57387-235-0 • $29.50

The Accidental Library Manager

By Rachel Singer Gordon

In *The Accidental Library Manager*, Rachel Singer Gordon provides support for new managers, aspiring managers, and those who find themselves in unexpected management roles. Gordon fills in the gaps left by brief and overly theoretical library school coursework, showing library managers how to be more effective in their positions and how to think about their work in terms of the goals of their larger institutions. Included are insights from working library managers at different levels and in various types of libraries addressing a wide range of management issues and situations. This readable and reassuring guide is a must for any librarian who wishes to succeed in a management position.

2005/384 pp/softbound • ISBN 1-57387-210-5 • $29.50

The NextGen Librarian's Survival Guide

By Rachel Singer Gordon

Here is a unique resource for next generation librarians, addressing the specific needs of GenXers and Millenials as they work to define themselves as information professionals. The book focuses on how NextGens can move their careers forward and positively impact the profession. Library career guru Rachel Singer Gordon—herself a NextGen librarian—provides timely advice along with tips and insights from dozens of librarians on issues ranging from image and stereotypes, to surviving library school and entry-level positions, to working with older colleagues. A special section for current library administrators and managers makes this a must-read not only for NextGen librarians, but for those who recruit, work with, and mentor them.

2006/240 pp/softbound • ISBN 1-57387-256-3 • $29.50

Net Effects
How Librarians Can Manage the Unintended Consequences of the Internet

Edited by Marylaine Block

> *"A lifeline for librarians. Outstanding!"*
> *—Gary Price*

The Internet is a mixed blessing for libraries and librarians. On the one hand, it provides opportunities to add services and expand collections; on the other, it increases user expectations and contributes to techno-stress. In *Net Effects*, nearly 50 articles by dozens of librarians—expertly selected by the editor—suggest practical and creative ways to deal with the range of Internet "side effects," regain control of the library, and avoid being blindsided by technology again.

2003/380 pp/hardbound • ISBN 1-57387-171-0 • $39.50

The Web Library
Building a World Class Personal Library with Free Web Resources

By Nicholas G. Tomaiuolo
Edited by Barbara Quint; Foreword by Steve Coffman

With this remarkable, eye-opening book and its companion Web site, Nicholas G. (Nick) Tomaiuolo shows how anyone can create a comprehensive personal library using no-cost Web resources. And when Nick says "library," he's not talking about a dictionary and thesaurus on your desktop: He means a vast, rich collection of data, documents, and images that—if you follow his instructions to the letter—can rival the holding of many traditional libraries. This is an easy-to-use guide, with chapters organized into sections corresponding to departments in a physical library. *The Web Library* provides a wealth of URLs and examples of free material you can start using right away, but best of all, it offers techniques for collecting new content as the Web evolves. Start building your personal Web library today!

2004/440 pp/softbound • ISBN 0-910965-67-6 • $29.95

Super Searchers Make It on Their Own
Top Independent Information Professionals Share Their Secrets for Starting and Running a Research Business

By Suzanne Sabroski; Edited by Reva Basch

If you want to start and run a successful Information Age business, read this book. Here, 11 of the world's top research entrepreneurs share their strategies for starting a business, developing a niche, finding clients, doing the research, networking with peers, and staying up-to-date with Web resources and technologies. You'll learn how these super searchers use the Internet to find, organize, analyze, and package information for their clients. Most importantly, you'll discover their secrets for building a profitable research business.

2002/336 pp/softbound • ISBN 0-910965-59-5 • $24.95

Building and Running a Successful Research Business
A Guide for the Independent Information Professional

By Mary Ellen Bates
Edited and with a foreword by Reva Basch

This is the handbook every aspiring independent information professional needs in order to launch, manage, and build a research business. Organized into four sections, "Getting Started," "Running the Business," "Marketing," and "Researching," the book walks you through every step of the process. Author Mary Ellen Bates covers everything from "Is the right for you?" to closing the sale, managing clients, promoting your business on the Web, and tapping into powerful information sources beyond the Web. Bates, a popular author and speaker and a long-time successful independent info pro, reveals all the tips, tricks, and techniques for setting up, running, and growing your own information business.

2003/488 pp/softbound • ISBN 0-910965-62-5 • $29.95
